AF594121

THE POLITICS OF IMPERIAL MEMORY IN FRANCE, 1850–1900

THE POLITICS OF IMPERIAL MEMORY IN FRANCE, 1850–1900

CHRISTINA B. CARROLL

CORNELL UNIVERSITY PRESS
Ithaca and London

First published 2022 by Cornell University Press

Library of Congress Cataloging-in-Publication Data
Names: Carroll, Christina B., 1984– author.
Title: The politics of imperial memory in France, 1850–1900 / Christina B. Carroll.
Description: Ithaca [New York] : Cornell University Press, 2022. | Includes bibliographical references and index.
Identifiers: LCCN 2021054747 (print) | LCCN 2021054748 (ebook) | ISBN 9781501763083 (hardcover) | ISBN 9781501763120 (pdf) | ISBN 9781501763137 (epub)
Subjects: LCSH: Imperialism—History—19th century. | Imperialism—Public opinion—History—19th century. | Collective memory—Political aspects—France. | France—History—19th century.
Classification: LCC DC252 .C375 2022 (print) | LCC DC252 (ebook) | DDC 944.06—dc23/eng/20211123
LC record available at https://lccn.loc.gov/2021054747
LC ebook record available at https://lccn.loc.gov/2021054748

To Anna

Contents

Acknowledgments

This book would not exist without the support of many individuals and organizations. Lloyd Kramer's guidance at the University of North Carolina at Chapel Hill shaped this project from the beginning; our conversations about intellectual and cultural history helped me formulate my early research questions, and he has supported this project through its many stages. I am deeply grateful for his detailed feedback on my numerous drafts. Dan Sherman, who sparked my interest in memory and colonialism, has also offered very helpful advice on my work. Emily Burrill, Don Reid, and Jay Smith suggested new analytical frameworks, pointed me toward new sources, and asked important questions that helped me reconceptualize the material. Christopher Browning, Konrad Jarausch, Lisa Lindsay, and Steven Vincent also helped shape the project at different stages.

I have presented on different aspects of this book at numerous conferences, including those of the Western Society for French History, the Society for French Historical Studies, and the Society for the Study of French History, as well as the Nineteenth-Century French Studies Association. I am grateful for the questions and comments offered by fellow panelists, commentators, and audience members. Members of the Triangle French History and Culture Seminar also provided thoughtful and formative feedback on my first chapter. Finally, the Breisach Colloquium at Western Michigan University and the Faculty Study at Kalamazoo College generously invited me to present on sections of later chapters.

I have also benefited from the support of my colleagues and friends, who have spent more years than I'd like to count listening to me talk about this book. Nancy Bisaha at Vassar College supported my interest in history and encouraged me to pursue it. Zach Smith, Alison Boyd, and Brittany Lehman all read drafts of the project and helped me sharpen my ideas. At various stages, conversations and meals with Tiffany Ball, Maeve Doyle, Emily Fishbaine, Nicole Giannella, Lesley Graybeal, Mike Hardin, Margaret Hazel, Derek Holmgren, Sarah Lowry, Aman Luthra, Firth MacMillan, Brad Proctor, Danielle Purifoy, Ben Reed, and Matthew Thomann have kept me sane.

My fellow French historians at UNC—Joseph Bryan, Bethany Keenan, Greg Mole, Anndal Narayanan, and Laura Sims—formed an intellectual community that sustained me both in Chapel Hill and France. Finally, my colleagues at Kalamazoo College have also served as an ongoing source of support. The members of the history department welcomed me warmly, and they have offered advice that has helped steer me through the publication process. The members of my writing group—Justin Berry, Beau Bothwell, Anne Marie Butler, Ivett Lopez Malagamba, Shanna Salinas, and Francisco Villegas—offered invaluable feedback on drafts and proposals.

Research support from the Belle Skinner Fellowship at Vassar College, the George Mowry Fund at the University of North Carolina–Chapel Hill, the Société des professeurs français et francophones d'Amérique, the Society for French Historical Studies, and the Doris G. Quinn Foundation made this project possible. Colgate University and the Marlene Crandell Francis Endowment at Kalamazoo College funded additional research trips critical to the book's development. I am also grateful to the librarians and archivists at the Archives nationales d'outre-mer, the Bibliothèque nationale de France, the Archives nationales, the Service historique de la défense, and the Archives diplomatiques for offering essential guidance and finding aid.

I also want to express my gratitude for the team at Cornell University Press. Emily Andrew was an incredibly supportive editor; she and her editorial assistant, Allegra Martschenko, played an indispensable role in bringing this project to fruition. Bethany Wasik stepped in at a critical moment to shepherd the book through its final stages. Thanks, too, to Don McKeon for his excellent copyediting and to Jennifer Savran Kelly for overseeing the production process. The insights and feedback of the two anonymous reviewers have made the book much stronger than it otherwise would be. An earlier version of chapter 1 appeared as "Imperial Ideologies in the Second Empire: The Mexican Expedition and the 'Royaume Arabe'" in *French Historical Studies* 42, no. 1 (February 2019). Carol Harrison's feedback and support were essential in helping me rethink the way that I was structuring my arguments in that chapter. An excerpt of chapter 4 first appeared in "Defining 'Empire' under Napoleon III: Lucien-Anatole Prévost-Paradol and Paul Leroy-Beaulieu," in *Journal of the Western Society for French History* 41 (2013). Finally, an excerpt from the introduction first appeared in "Republican Imperialisms: Narrating the History of 'Empire' in France, 1885–1900," in *French Politics, Culture, and Society* 36, no. 3 (December 2018).

I want to end by thanking my family, without whose support this project would never have been possible. My grandmother, Cynthia Bowen, who did not live to see the book between covers, sparked my interest in history long ago. My parents have consistently encouraged my work and cheered on my successes. My brother's insightful questions have always kept me on my toes. My cats, Ari and Oliver, have made life more interesting by knocking over my books and sleeping on my drafts. My greatest thanks goes to Anna Gutman, who has provided me with a seemingly endless fount of practical, intellectual, and emotional support. Without her, none of this would have been possible.

Note on Translation and Transliteration

For consistency, this book makes use of the French spellings of Arabic, Wolof, Vietnamese, and Merina names, places, and institutions, except in cases where there is a more common spelling that appears in English-language literature. I have placed alternatives in parentheses when these names, places, and institutions are first mentioned. All translations from French are my own unless otherwise indicated.

THE POLITICS OF IMPERIAL MEMORY IN FRANCE, 1850–1900

Introduction

Empires, Republics, and French Political Culture in the Long Nineteenth Century

In 1892 Émile Zola published *La débâcle*, a fictional account of the Franco-Prussian War written, he claimed, as a "scientific" investigation of the reasons behind the French defeat and civil war that had occurred some twenty years earlier. Advertised as the penultimate book in his famous and controversial Rougon-Macquart series, which traced the fortunes of two branches of one family tree through the Second Empire, it attracted immediate attention. But the book outstripped even the fame of the series. It sold one hundred thousand copies in the first four weeks and half as many again in the next four months. It went on to become Zola's most popular novel during his lifetime: there were eight French editions before the First World War.[1]

The novel placed the blame for France's loss in the Franco-Prussian War squarely at the feet of the Second Empire of Napoleon III, which Zola described as "acclaimed by plebiscites, but rotten at the base, having weakened the idea of the nation by destroying liberty . . . ready to collapse the moment it could no longer satisfy the appetite for pleasure it had itself unleashed."[2] The empire, he maintained, was marked by decline and excess; Napoleon III's despotic rule caused the people to lose all self-respect. They turned instead to "decadence," particularly in Paris—to alcohol, cafés, and illegitimate sexual relationships. This rotten political and social culture weakened the military and led directly to French defeat by creating a class of nervous, effeminate men who were too disorderly and emotional to deal with the hardships of war. Worse still, Napoleon III had cultivated a romanticized myth of Napoleonic invincibility by staging commemorations of his uncle's victories and trying to convince the population that he had revivified his uncle's empire. This Napoleonic aura fed into a jingoistic patriotism that led the country into a war it was too weak to win. The more recent legacy of French colonial wars in North Africa compounded the problem, as it fueled this sense of false self-assurance, leaving the army command "too confident of victory to attempt the great effort of trying the new military science."[3] When the Germans invaded, the French army was therefore unprepared.

Zola's novel was sharply critical of Second Empire politics and society. But it nevertheless held out hope for the French nation because Zola described defeat and civil war as a process of purification that had eliminated French "decadence." During the war, he maintained, the French had turned against the empire, which had enabled an uncertain but healthy republican order to emerge in its place. Zola described this new republican order as the direct antithesis of the Second Empire—sensible, masculine, democratic, and hardworking—and implied that it might be able to redeem the country.

Zola was far from the only writer in Third Republic France who was interested in the relationship between "empire," "republic," overseas colonial expansion, and French national identity. But at least some writers imagined those relationships in very different terms. In 1912, for example, Georges Saint-Paul, an army doctor who had served in both Algeria and Tunisia, argued that the Third Republic in fact needed to adopt what he called a *politique impérialiste* and embrace empire.[4] Empire, he contended, did not refer to Napoleon or Bonapartist politics at all; instead, it was a republican enterprise that sought to cultivate "democratic practices" in France's conquered territories. Empire was thus not equivalent to despotism, fruitless colonial warfare, and national degeneration, as Zola had implied, but instead a tool that republicans could use to spread republican values around the world.

What is an empire? How do empires relate to nations? How were the British colonial empires in Asia and Africa similar to or different from the continental Austro-Hungarian Empire or the Napoleonic empire? Are empires always exploitative and authoritarian, or can they coexist with republican institutions, democratic principles, and human rights? European and global historians often discuss such questions, but they were also asked by writers, intellectuals, and politicians in late nineteenth-century France. And the conclusions that these individuals developed helped structure both the colonial empire and the domestic political systems that France built during that period.

Throughout the second half of the nineteenth century, "empire" in all its configurations served as a source of debate in French political and intellectual circles. Disagreements about empire stemmed partly from divergent strategies for promoting national prestige. But these disagreements also resulted from the fact that empire had an ambiguous history that was itself bound up in political divisions and turmoil. As Zola and Saint-Paul's different usages make clear, French writers, intellectuals, and politicians could use the concept to equally refer to a political system within continental France, to a vision of French dominance across Europe, or to the state structure used to rule conquered territories overseas. The term could also invoke the memory of the monarchy's expansion into North America or the Bonapartist expansion across the continent—as well as the specter of German unification or British overseas conquest.[5] The nature of the empire's relationship to republicanism, Bonapartism, French national identity, and colonial expansion was thus both shifting and fraught. The multiple valences of empire during this period, moreover, had both political and intellectual consequences: they played an important role in shaping the ways that intellectuals, writers, and politicians articulated their ideas about France's political organization, its national identity, and its colonial ambitions.

The memory of both Napoleonic empires lay at the center of these tangled understandings of "empire" in the early Third Republic. The vividness of these memories owed much to Napoleon III, who, throughout his reign, sought to provide substance to his imperial regime by associating himself with his uncle and by popularizing sometimes contradictory "theories of empire." In the early years of his rule, Napoleon III usually described empire as an internal form of political organization that drew on the legacy of the French Revolution but tempered that legacy with "order" and "security."[6] He thus treated "the French Empire" as functionally equivalent to "the French nation." But in the 1860s Napoleon III began to focus more on France's overseas territories. He extended France's investment in Indochina, tried to expand France's foothold in North America by creating an allied "Latin" empire in Mexico, and sought to reimagine Algeria as a *royaume arabe*, or Arab kingdom. In Mexico and in Algeria especially, Napoleon III paired this renewed overseas investment with a more comprehensive vision of empire. This understanding operated differently in Mexico and in Algeria, but in both cases he posited empire as not only a specific political system within France but also as a way of organizing overseas territory. This model—which proved deeply unpopular in Mexico, Algeria, and France—thus merged "continental" or "domestic" empire with "colonial empire," if not necessarily in an equal way.

The legacy of Napoleon III's understandings of empire was problematic for republicans in the early years of the Third Republic. France's defeat in the Franco-Prussian War tarnished Bonapartism generally and Napoleon III in particular in the eyes of much of the population.[7] Despite its brief duration, the conflict left France territorially dismembered and in debt to Germany, and it also brought about a political revolution and civil war that left deep internal divisions. In the wake of this destruction, numerous popular publications came to associate the very word "empire" with weakness, decadence, internal strife, and defeat. Indeed, the republican government that came to power in the wake of 1870–71 defended its legitimacy by defining itself against the imperial government that preceded it.[8] As the republicans embarked on their own overseas empire-building project in the years that followed, the ambiguity of "empire" and its referents therefore became increasingly troubling—especially since republicans' political opponents often made use of the ambiguities inherent in republicanism's relationship to empire when they criticized republican-driven colonial expansion. Questions about the relationship between continental and colonial empire thus intersected with and complicated republicans' attempts to solidify their political platforms. Over the next thirty years, they struggled to redefine empire, free it from its Napoleonic legacy, and justify their colonial ambitions. This project was, overall, successful: by the early decades of the twentieth century, the colonial empire became widely accepted across most levels of French society.

The question of how to understand the relationship between colonial projects overseas on one hand and social, cultural, economic, and political programs in the metropole on the other has been a longstanding focus of the scholarship on European imperialism. But for much of the twentieth century, scholars tended to treat the histories of European overseas empires separately from the history of European continental empires. There were nevertheless key exceptions to this pattern, especially in the years following the Second World War, when anticolonial activists and scholars grappled with the intersections between European overseas empires, Nazi Germany, and sometimes the Soviet Union.[9] Aimé Césaire's 1950 *Discourse on Colonialism* and Raphael Lemkin, the lawyer who developed the term "genocide" in 1944, thus both argued that the Nazi genocide had colonial origins.[10] Hannah Arendt's 1951 *Origins of Totalitarianism* took an even more expansive approach, comparing Roman empire building, European overseas imperialism, European continental imperialism, and fascism. Her work distinguished between ancient empires and modern imperial structures; she argued that the rise of the modern nation-state had made true empire building, such as the kind undertaken by the Roman Republic, impossible.[11] But she also placed what she called "continental" and "overseas" imperialism within the same analytical framework. She used "continental imperialism" to refer to the nineteenth-century pan-German and pan-Slavic movements; she maintained that racism, expansionism, the preference for rule by bureaucratic decree over rule by law, and the commitment to violence as a strategy for consolidating power characterized both these movements and overseas imperialism.[12] The Nazis, she argued, built on both overseas and continental imperial traditions to construct their totalitarian empire.

Arendt's arguments about the relationship between European overseas imperialism and Nazism were largely dismissed by political scientists and ignored by historians for much of the twentieth century. It was mostly in the 1990s that scholars interested in thinking through empire as a political category returned to her work, and Arendt's "boomerang thesis," as it came to be called, became a point of discussion and disagreement.[13] If anticolonial movements and reactions to the Holocaust had sparked interest in the relationship between empires inside and outside of Europe during the 1950s, the end of the Cold War, transformations in the global economic order, and the American invasions of Afghanistan and Iraq helped trigger this new wave of scholarship.[14] These dynamics made empire seem like a relevant framework through which to describe contemporary American foreign policy and the global distribution of power, even if neither completely resembled the overseas empires of the nineteenth and twentieth centuries.[15]

This recent scholarship has revisited some of the questions Arendt's work raised about the relationship between empires and nations, empires and domestic politics, and different kinds of imperial structures. And perhaps partly because of its interest in thinking through what empire might mean in our contemporary era, recent scholarship has become more explicitly interested than Arendt in integrating the history of European overseas empires into a more global account of empire's pasts, and it has sought to develop frameworks through which different kinds of imperial structures might be understood and compared.[16] These frameworks tend to be somewhat more capacious than those suggested by scholars earlier in the twentieth century who were seeking to describe the operations of European overseas imperialism, which, following John Hobson and Vladimir Lenin, they often tied to a particular capitalist model.[17] In their influential history of global empires, Jane Burbank and Frederick Cooper thus suggest that we should imagine empires as "large political units, expansionist or with the memory of power expanded over space, polities that maintain distinction and hierarchy as they incorporate new people. The nation-state, in contrast, is based on the idea of a single people in a single territory constituting itself as a unique political community."[18] But, as they go on to note, even this differentiation is complicated by the fact that empires and nations coexisted and overlapped with one another.[19] Scholars have thus emphasized the importance of thinking about empire flexibly, especially since, in Ann Laura Stoler and Carole McGranahan's words, imperial spaces are inevitably characterized by "blurred genres of rule and partial sovereignties" and they "operate as states of exception that vigilantly produce exceptions to their principles and exceptions to their laws."[20]

Some scholars have also focused more specifically on understanding the relationship between Europe's overseas colonial empires and its continental imperial structures. They have noted that part of the reason that overseas empires such as Britain's and France's were treated as unique for so long was because they described themselves as "modern" while positioning their contemporary continental counterparts, such as the Russian, Austro-Hungarian, and Ottoman Empires, as antiquated and doomed to decay. But, in fact, scholars have suggested nineteenth-century Europeans themselves often imagined their imperial projects in broader terms than such propaganda would suggest. Stoler and McGranahan highlight the multiple referents of "colony" in nineteenth-century European thought, which they show could apply to settlements overseas or to domestic institutions for paupers, children, and criminals. These different "colonies" were not simply homonyms: Europeans saw—and treated—them as interrelated, suggesting that overseas colonial projects were not consistently perceived as distinct from metropolitan ones in the nineteenth century.[21] Moreover, it was not just European understandings of "colony" that echoed both in the metropole and overseas. Europe's nineteenth-century continental empires also had much in common with its colonial empires; they often engaged with and borrowed from one another.[22]

Nineteenth-century France is a particularly rich field in which to investigate these convergences because different groups of French politicians and intellectuals self-consciously defined the country as both a continental European empire and as an overseas colonial one during the era. And yet there are few political and intellectual histories of the French Empire that consider French imperial projects overseas and on the continent in conjunction with one another. This is in part because most of the extant scholarship focuses on the Third Republic and beyond. It thus looks primarily at the decades in which French continental imperial models were receding, as republican control over the government was increasingly assured. The focus on later periods is understandable: it reflects the growth in size and popularity of the new colonial empire itself. But just as recent scholarship has shown that many of the political and social transformations traditionally located in the Third Republic had their origins in the Napoleonic Second Empire, new interest has emerged in the Second Empire's colonial policies and the ways in which they affected the Third Republic's later imperial projects.[23] After all, the construction of France's "new" colonial empire began to accelerate under Napoleon III. The Second Empire laid the foundations for what would later become French Indochina, and it also established policies in Algeria that would form the basis for French administration of the territory well into the twentieth century.[24] And during these formative years, the relationship between colonial and continental models of empire remained an open, complicated question.

As in our contemporary moment, the slipperiness of the term "empire" in Second Empire and early Third Republic France had much to do with competing collective memories—of earlier empires, of revolution, and of war. But one of the consequences of the scholarly focus on the late nineteenth and early twentieth centuries is that little attention has been paid to the role played by memory in shaping popular understandings of the new colonial empire as it was being constructed. While a number of historians have noted that an interest in historical models is characteristic of modern imperialism, most scholarship on memory and colonialism has focused on postcolonial eras.[25] Most extant work on earlier periods has tended to look specifically at the role played by visions of ancient Rome in French and British debates about empire.[26] The vibrant historiography on the memory of Napoleon and the Napoleonic empire in nineteenth-century France has remained largely detached from work on French colonialism—with the exception of studies on the legacies of Napoleon I's Egypt expedition.[27] But looking at the roles played by both the memory of older empires and competing contemporary imperial models in shaping nineteenth-century French understandings of empire is critical to understanding the intellectual world in which French writers, journalists, and politicians were operating.

Examining the transition between the Second Empire and the Third Republic can also provide new insights into the relationship between republicanism, liberalism, and empire, which has been the focus of most existing scholarship on French understandings of empire. This scholarship—echoing broader debates in postcolonial theory—has been divided over an argument about whether liberalism and republicanism are inherently imperialistic and oppressive. While some historians have described colonialism as a failure to apply republican universalist principles to overseas territories, others have claimed that the origin of republican colonialism lies in those universalist principles themselves and in the republic's inability to accommodate difference.[28] These arguments have not only taken place between scholars; they have also reverberated—albeit in different ways—in French politics and marked contemporary debates about immigration and the value of diversity.[29] In recent years, scholars studying French and British liberal thinkers have pushed back against such totalizing accounts of liberalism's relationship to empire, emphasizing instead that liberalism and republicanism have always been evolving ideologies understood distinctly by different people at particular historical moments. The relationship between republicanism, liberalism, and empire, moreover, did not unfold in an ideological vacuum. Other developments such as the abolition of slavery, new ideas about racial hierarchy, and growing competition between European powers to acquire territory around the world helped shape it.[30]

Looking at debates over empire in the Second Empire and the early Third Republic demonstrates that when France's second colonial empire was first being constructed, the shifting relationship between empire, liberalism, and republicanism was not only structured by republicans' conflicting interpretations of liberal universalist principles and their mixed experiences trying to apply those principles to colonial contexts. It was also affected by conflicts with other political groups whose antecedents had largely been responsible for constructing France's earlier empires. These competing political groups—Bonapartists and monarchists alike—had their own complex relationship with the liberal political tradition, and they drew on that and other traditions to articulate their own models of empire. Republican understandings of empire developed in dialogue with and in opposition to these alternative models. These arguments over empire, moreover, were deeply tied into ongoing conflicts over France's political organization and the legacy of the Revolution.

This book thus contends that throughout much of the nineteenth century "empire" served as a contested category in French public discourse, which individuals of different political and ideological persuasions defined against one another by appealing to an array of historical memories and political values. I focus on the relationship between continental and colonial understandings of empire and consider how the memory of Bonapartist empire influenced and challenged beliefs about overseas empire in Third Republic France. Geographically the book therefore bridges the metropole and the colonies to show that shifts in the conversation about empire were driven by developments in both places. Each chapter focuses on an event or development that excited discussion about empire within the public sphere. It uses those events as windows into the changes that occurred in understandings of empire over time. The earliest chapters focus especially on Algeria, the colony that commanded the most metropolitan attention during the Second Empire and the early Third Republic. But I also consider how war and political revolution in metropolitan France and attempted colonial expansion in Mexico, West Africa, Indochina, and Madagascar—beginning in the 1860s but especially in the 1880s and the 1890s—intersected with these debates over the meaning of empire.

If events in the colonies partly shaped these arguments over empire, the arguments themselves did not have direct effects on colonial operations. As other scholars have shown, colonial officials, indigenous notables, and local negotiation, not armchair colonial theorists back in France or even the metropolitan government, primarily shaped the dynamics of French colonial rule.[31] Metropolitan political leaders and colonial theorists' ideas about empire were often only hazily based on local conditions, and the effects of their ideas were usually limited and contradictory. But if these conversations often did not have direct practical implications, they nevertheless had important effects on French political ideologies and on imperial imaginaries. They also became entangled in politicized debates about national identity that had become especially pressing after the military disaster and subsequent civil war of 1870–71. As socialists, radicals, republicans, Legitimists, and Orleanists searched for ways to define France in the wake of defeat, empire—because of its semantic, historical, and political ambiguity—came to operate as a shared discursive field that all groups attempted to appropriate for their respective visions of what it meant to be French. As a result, defining "empire" and interpreting its meaning in specific colonial contexts became an important component of the debates about the nation and national identity.

The public sphere that these debates over empire emerged in was expanding in the late nineteenth century, but it remained exclusive, contested, and fractured by both geography and political orientation. Although Jürgen Habermas imagined the public sphere as a realm in which citizens could come together as equals to rationally debate questions of general interest, this model never reflected the reality of eighteenth- or nineteenth-century Europe.[32] The public sphere was not as unified as Habermas's model implied. Even though railroads, steamships, and telegrams allowed for wider distribution of books and other kinds of publications, many still circulated primarily within local markets. Geographic divides played a still larger role outside of metropolitan France; even in Algeria, which was just across the

Mediterranean, many publications did not circulate between metropole and colony. Much of the correspondence from more distant colonies such as Indochina and Senegal moved through the auspices of the colonial administration and usually only indirectly found its way into public circulation. In fact, outside of large colonial scandals, which were extensively covered in the French press, journalists and writers often struggled to gather basic data about what was happening in the French colonies even well into the 1890s, thanks to the colonial ministry's efforts to control information.[33] Aside from these logistical issues, most people also tended to read only newspapers and political pamphlets that matched their political affiliation.[34] And while some of the books written about empire in the nineteenth century were written with general audiences in mind, many also circulated within narrow groups of experts. In an age of increasing literacy and relatively inexpensive print, a growing number of people had access to books, pamphlets, and newspapers, but a range of factors—including location, ideology, class, gender, language, education, citizenship status, religion, and race—affected the kinds of texts any individual might consume.[35] It would thus be misleading to see the conversation about empire that transpired in late nineteenth-century France as one unified "debate." Instead, there were a multiplicity of shifting conversations that included distinct but often overlapping groups at different moments.

Similar factors also affected whose ideas about empire could enter wide circulation in the first place; the content of these conversations was intertwined with the social hierarchies that structured the nineteenth-century French Empire. Elites mostly dominated debates about empire. As scholars have shown, empire only became a subject that consistently commanded popular attention in the early twentieth century.[36] Even elite communities, however, entered these debates from different positions of power and influence; French politicians, intellectuals, journalists, novelists, colonial administrators, settler communities, and colonial subjects all had different abilities to command audiences. As the levels of influence of different groups shifted, so too could the conversation around empire. The transformations in the debates that occurred during the early Third Republic, for example, partly reflected the fact that settler communities in Algeria were able to command a larger audience in the metropole than they had been able to beneath the Second Empire, thanks to their ties with republican politicians, while indigenous elites were more thoroughly excluded. For most of the second half of the nineteenth century, the conversation about empire was in fact usually dominated by French voices; relatively few members of colonized communities were able to participate in it as direct interlocutors, thanks to both colonial hierarchies and linguistic divisions. Ongoing censorship also played a role. Even though Napoleon III reduced censorship in the 1860s and in 1881 the Third Republic lifted censorship on the political press, censorship practices remained in place for longer in the colonies, and they targeted publications not written in French and by those without French citizenship.[37] That said, the French elites who dominated the conversation were responding to a much wider array of groups, including working-class communities in the metropole and colonized communities overseas, whose actions and resistance both influenced and challenged the visions of empire in circulation.

To analyze these debates over empire, the book draws on a mixture of official political speeches, government correspondence, colonial administrative documents, newspaper and journal articles, theoretical treatises, academic histories, political propaganda, and novels. It considers the content of these different texts and reflects on their circulation and their impact, highlighting who could—and could not—directly participate in these conversations about empire. Its analysis is in dialogue with the insights of the new intellectual history, which, as Elizabeth Clark explains, "explores the material embeddedness of ideas and their relation to power . . . [and] appeals to climates of opinion, literary movements, ideologies and their diffusion, and to an anthropologically infused notion of culture."[38] I also draw on the body of collective memory scholarship that has developed across academic disciplines in the past twenty years. Specifically, I employ Jan and Aleida Assmann's notion of "cultural memory": a particular form of collective memory they define as "oligarchic" and "institutionalized." In other words, it is formulated by elites, cultivated by specialists, and manifested in objects and texts. But it also affects the way that a wider array of individuals understand the past and their own identity.[39]

Overall, the book's analysis of these debates over empire shows that "continental empire" and "colonial empire" were far from clearly defined concepts in late nineteenth-century France. French writers, intellectuals, and politicians disagreed just as fervently about their individual content and significance as they did about the nature of their similarities and differences. Indeed, especially under Napoleon III and in subsequent years, not everyone even agreed that they were distinct ideas. The book thus does not treat "continental" and "colonial" visions of empire as two inherently separate models. Instead, it analyzes how these visions *became* separate models during the late nineteenth century and traces the way that colonial empire gained increasing support even as continental empire lost its appeal in response to changes within both France and its overseas territories. By analyzing the relationship between France's internal and external imperial systems, I demonstrate that

French representations of empire were ensconced in longstanding internal political conflicts because discourses of European racial superiority over colonial others intersected with older arguments about the ideal organization of the French state. I also explain how French republicans eventually succeeded in differentiating transoceanic empire from continental empire to create a new model of republican colonial empire. This new model of colonial empire, I argue, was itself shaped by a complicated set of influences, including the memory of both Napoleons, republican ideological values, political conflict within France, concerns about the French nation, international competition, racial science, and specific events in the colonies. Finally, the book also suggests how the history of ideas about empires continues to shape both French political ideologies and the meaning of French national identity—even in the "postcolonial" era of the twenty-first century.

Defining the Nation: French Revolutionary Republicanism and Napoleonic Imperialism

In the early years of the Third Republic, the legacy of Napoleon III and his vision of empire was problematic for republicans partly because of its associations with the memory of French defeat during the Franco-Prussian War. More generally, however, this legacy also intersected with ongoing debates over the nature of the French nation, the Second Empire's relationship to French republicanism and later French imperialism, and the implications of this relationship for colonized people who lived under French imperial rule. These debates were embedded in the long history of French continental and overseas empire, which stretched back at least to the seventeenth century, when the monarchy conquered what would later come to be known as France's first colonial empire. France lost much of this empire in the late eighteenth century, but during the French Revolution the remaining colonies came under scrutiny as republicans sought to redefine the French state by describing it as a united republican nation.

Although the French Revolution's project of nationalization had a limited reach, revolutionaries saw unified nationhood as the basis for the new political order that they were establishing. Instead of locating political authority in a monarch or a set of elites, republicans grounded sovereignty theoretically in what they referred to as the "French people" who collectively made up the "French nation."[40] So, while from our own historical perspective it is clear that nationalism and democratic traditions have not always been linked (and have often been in tension), revolutionaries saw the French nation and the republic as inextricably bound together. To speak of the nation after 1792 was to invoke republican values of political participation and political equality. As a result, many republicans positioned the republic as the natural political expression of the nation itself.

This interweaving of "republic" and "nation" was complicated by the universalist implications of the ideals that defined French revolutionary republicanism. The Declaration of the Rights of Man and of the Citizen did not set forth rights for French men but for all men, and it was grounded in an Enlightenment belief that "human nature . . . was a universal impervious to cultural and historical difference."[41] And, as a result, in the earliest years of the revolution some revolutionaries imagined French citizenship as potentially universally accessible to all republicans, wherever they came from. This was always the minority view, however, and it sat uneasily with the idea of France as a united and discrete nation.[42] Instead, most revolutionaries contended that human history consisted of slow progress toward global recognition of human equality and that the political reorganization of the world into nation-states would guarantee citizens the "natural" rights they had been born with. They saw republican France as the "model nation" or torchbearer in this global march toward equality and claimed that it would help lead other nations toward enlightenment.[43]

From the beginning, questions emerged about the boundaries of the republican nation and about the ability of France's different inhabitants to exercise the rights of citizenship. The earliest iterations of the constitution included women and poor men in the nation while denying them political rights by designating them "passive citizens."[44] Those perceived as outsiders, including immigrants and religious minorities, also occupied an ambiguous place in the new republic. Their ability to exercise political rights or lay claim to republican citizenship remained an ongoing subject of debate, even though many such groups were able to claim some rights during the First Republic.[45]

The success of revolutionary armies in Europe sharpened these tensions over the boundaries of the nation, raising questions about whether a republic could rule over other peoples or whether such an arrangement was a violation of revolutionary principles. Revolutionaries developed two different strategies for dealing with this problem. In 1793 the republican government declared that France's "natural frontiers" stretched to the Rhine; as a result, the inhabitants of borderland territories could be assimilated into the French nation. When French armies moved beyond these boundaries, they set up conquered territory as "sister republics"—states that they had "liberated" from the tyranny of the ancien régime. These states were ostensibly independent, but they remained under French hegemony. Within Europe, revolutionaries thus drew clear boundaries around the nation, annexing only territory that they believed they could describe as "French." And although other European powers viewed French policies as imperial, the revolutionary government refused to describe its actions that way.[46]

The ambiguities that attended the interweaving of "nation" with "republic" were even clearer in France's overseas colonies, as white colonists, free people of color, and enslaved peoples began to challenge the place of France's colonial holdings in the new political order. These groups—and the conflicts between them in the colonies—raised questions about the relationship of those living overseas to the French nation. Were those living abroad French and therefore entitled to the same political rights granted to men in France? Would such statuses and rights apply to all the inhabitants of overseas colonies, including those who were currently enslaved? If some or all the inhabitants of French colonies were not French, what was their relationship to the nation? Could the republic rule over them, or should inhabitants of overseas colonies form their own nations instead? Revolutionaries asked these questions but had no clear answers to them: they debated about whether they should leave the colonies alone, integrate them into the French nation, or grant them autonomy. Even those who embraced the idea that France should integrate the colonies into the nation disagreed about the meaning and consequences of this decision. Some argued that different inhabitants of integrated overseas territories should enjoy the rights of citizenship, but others maintained that France should assimilate some inhabitants while leaving others—especially enslaved people and free people of color—on the outside.[47]

These debates over what to do with France's colonies hinged partly on the question of how to understand the relationship between Frenchness and universalism. Because of their tendency to locate enlightenment, human rights, and human progress in the French nation-state, many revolutionaries came to believe that to exclude the inhabitants in overseas colonies from French citizenship would be to deny them access to liberation. But, at the same time, they also worried that enslaved people and free people of color were insufficiently French to belong to the political and cultural life of the nation. To participate in the revolutionary political project, revolutionaries expected those living in overseas territories to assimilate into French culture. This friction between France as the bearer of "universal" rights and France as a particular nation-state composed of a "people" who embodied specific cultural practices and assumptions would haunt both French republicanism and imperialism throughout the nineteenth and twentieth centuries.[48]

In 1794 and 1795 the Convention temporarily resolved this ongoing argument about what to do with the colonies by decreeing that all enslaved people in French colonies were free and that all residents of French overseas holdings could exercise citizenship rights. France's colonies were thus now part of the French nation rather than associated with or subordinated to it. But the Convention did not pass these decrees because it was concerned about squaring republican ideals with colonial realities. Instead, it was responding to conflicts between free communities of color and whites as well as the slave uprising in Saint Domingue, British and Spanish threats to French overseas colonies, and ongoing political disputes within France.[49] The revolutionaries were thus trying to resolve political and military crises—although, as Laurent Dubois in particular has argued, they were also influenced by "the concrete and radical universalism" that enslaved peoples had invoked when they claimed freedom for themselves.[50] The promise of revolutionary citizenship was never realized in France's colonies during this period—tellingly, it came closest to realization when Haiti declared its independence from France.[51] But despite these limitations, the revolutionaries' decision to declare overseas subjects French citizens set an important precedent in France's administration of overseas territories: the revolutionaries had reconciled the colonies with the republican nation by at least technically folding overseas territory into the nation.

These conversations about colonies, the French nation, and the assimilation of other peoples did not end with the rise of Napoleon. If anything, Napoleon's expansive European conquests magnified the problems faced by revolutionaries trying to define their relationship to a relatively small number of overseas colonies and a handful of "sister republics." After all, even though Napoleon broke away from the ideals of political participation and individual rights defended by revolutionaries, he propounded the republican vision of the nation-state—even as he modified its political implications. Under the Napoleonic empire, "nation" lost its association with "republic." Instead, "nation" became a term not necessarily associated with any specific political organization: indeed, the French nation was subject to authoritarian political rule, which claimed to embody national sovereignty.[52] Napoleon, moreover, also broke away from republican usage to place "empire" and "nation" into a direct relationship with one another—like many other empires in the modern world. France became a privileged nation surrounded by affiliated territories that had access to different rights and operated under French administrative systems to various degrees. Napoleon himself was the emperor of the French but was equally emperor over Western and Central Europe. He was thus able to overcome the republican dilemma about how to deal with "outsiders" or those who were not clearly French because he could transform conquered peoples into subjects of the Napoleonic empire without integrating them into the French republic as citizens.

In recent years, the relationship between Napoleon's European empire and overseas colonial empire has become the subject of scholarly debate. These arguments stem in part from the question about the degree to which Napoleon himself differentiated between territories that he conquered in Europe and territories overseas. But they are also connected to a disagreement over whether Napoleon's empire had a central ideology or project—as most colonial empires at least claimed to—or whether it was simply "pragmatic."[53] These debates are in turn part of a larger conversation about the nature of the Napoleonic empire's relationship to the French Revolution and French republicanism more broadly.[54]

Most of the extant scholarship on Napoleon's overseas empire has focused on the Egyptian campaign, which, starting with Edward Said, scholars have described as foundational to a shift in French understandings of their relationship with non-European people.[55] Napoleon's campaign was in many respects distinct from his later European campaigns. He brought with him a host of orientalists, archaeologists, and painters, and in addition to fighting battles against Egyptian troops, he visited cultural landmarks so these experts could acquire information about Egypt.[56] The specialists approached Egypt with profound self-confidence about their ability to label and categorize this non-European culture. Moreover, both they and their critical audience described the invasion as an encounter between "civilization and barbarism": they emphasized France's technical dominance and posited France as the true heir to ancient Egypt.[57] Some even suggested that France, coming into Egypt, might be able to "restore" the "decadent race" and return Egypt to its former glory better than the Egyptians themselves. As a result of these claims, many scholars link the emergence of the "civilizing mission"—which would later become central to republican colonial ideology—to Napoleon's Egyptian campaign.[58]

The Egyptian campaign is difficult to classify politically, as it was led by Napoleon but organized by the Directory—a technically republican government. And despite its distinctive characteristics, it also intersected with France's other occupations overseas and in Europe. On one hand, many of the legislators, savants, and soldiers described Egypt as a potential French "colony." Some even explicitly proposed it as an alternative to the overseas empire in North America that France had lost during the Seven Years War. But at the same time, many also described it as a "satellite republic" like the ones that Napoleon had already established in Italy. Napoleon's policies in Egypt have also been interpreted different ways. Napoleon clearly made more concessions to local traditions in Egypt than he had in Italy. He attempted to ally with Muslim religious leaders and local elites, whereas in Italy he had tried to curtail the power of the Catholic Church. But he also used the language of republican liberation in his public pronouncements and tried to rally the population around republican symbols—much as he had in European "sister republics." His alliances with Muslim religious leaders also foreshadowed his future policies toward the church.[59]

Even the idea of a French duty to "civilize" Egypt was not entirely distinct from Napoleon's policies in Europe. Imperial officials also portrayed European states and territories as technologically, politically, or culturally "backward" and claimed that France was spreading "universal principles" to them. French officials acted with greater condescension toward Egyptians than toward Italians or Eastern Europeans, but the belief that the French were spreading the ideals of a more "advanced civilization" characterized both encounters.[60] After all, the Napoleonic empire exported many of the ideals of the French revolutionary government across Europe and restructured the administrative systems of some conquered countries along "enlightened" lines—abolishing seignorial privileges, streamlining hierarchies, establishing a universal law code, and creating a unified imperial nobility.[61]

Napoleon's relationship with France's Caribbean colonies was more distinct from his policies in Europe than his policies in Egypt had been, however. Napoleon rejected the revolutionary legacy more dramatically there; even as Napoleon abolished privileges in Europe, he reinstituted slavery and legalized racial inequality in the Caribbean. While it is true that Napoleon did little in Eastern Europe to liberate the peasantry from serfdom, nowhere else did he deliberately reinstitute unfree labor systems or inequality before the law. These decisions stemmed partly from Napoleon's alliance with the white planter classes and his conflicts with Toussaint Louverture, the governor of Saint-Domingue. But Napoleon justified these policies by declaring that France's colonies in the Caribbean were not part of France at all; instead, they were separate territories governed by distinctive laws and regulations. He thus separated the colonies from the French nation-state and proposed to rule them beneath a separate regime. These policies resulted in a widespread uprising in the Caribbean that ended with the loss of France's most important remaining colony, Saint-Domingue, to a powerful independence movement.[62] The loss of Saint-Domingue then led Napoleon to surrender Louisiana to the United States and to focus his attention on Europe and the Mediterranean.[63]

Even if Napoleon's policies in the Caribbean broke with republican decision-making in 1794, his vision of the empire as an internally differentiated space had clear republican antecedents; many white revolutionaries in both France and the colonies had successfully argued for exactly this imperial model throughout the first years of the Revolution in order to defend slavery and the colonial racial order.[64] These policies also did not completely diverge from Napoleon's treatment of the territory he conquered in Europe. His decision to separate the colonies from France and create distinct constitutions for them—while clearly a cover for the reinstitution of slavery—was in line with his constitutional policy in European satellite states.[65] Moreover, Napoleon's European empire was itself not internally homogeneous; in fact, the empire governed people differently according to various criteria, including when their particular state was conquered, where it was located, and the types of resources that Napoleon hoped to extract from it.[66] And while the empire applied the same law codes and roughly similar administrative systems to each territory, no one state occupied a place that was equal to the others. Each was subject to a distinct set of military obligations and tariffs and given different levels of latitude in selecting its own administration.[67] At the head of some, Napoleon placed tributary rulers who were often his own family members. Other states kept their traditional elites and even to some degree their traditional privileges.[68] What bound them together was that they were all beneath France in the political hierarchy. Napoleon's policies thus included multiple models of imperial domination, both in Europe and overseas, and they raised further questions about the relationship between empire and nation and their relationship with revolutionary values.

Memories of the different strategies for dealing with conquered territories and colonies embraced during the Revolution and the Napoleonic empire continued to inflect conversations about French colonialism for much of the nineteenth century, partly because later French governments invoked idealized versions of these strategies (which never reflected the way that either revolutionary or Napoleonic rule had actually worked) to describe and justify their colonial policies. When the July Monarchy established French rule in Algeria in the 1830s, it pointed to the rudimentary government established during the Napoleonic Egyptian campaign as a precedent for the structure of its administration.[69] In 1848, on the other hand, when the revolutionary government decided to change French "colonies" into "territories" and give them representation in the National Assembly, they explicitly described the model of assimilation as a legacy of the French Revolution.[70] When Napoleon III declared himself emperor of France in 1852, questions about whether France should assimilate its subjugated territories or treat them as separate dependent states thus had a political charge in the metropole. Insisting that overseas territories should be integrated politically or even culturally into the French nation could invoke memories of the Revolution. Contending, on the other hand, that these territories should remain distinct or separate from France could invoke memories of the empire of Napoleon I—although administrative assimilation was certainly remembered as part of the Bonapartist legacy as well. Napoleon III's attempt to transform the Napoleonic imperial model would only further complicate these long-standing debates over the relationship between the administration of overseas territories and the political organization of France.

Chapter 1

The Second Empire's Imperial Ideologies in Mexico and Algeria

On April 29, 1865, Emperor Napoleon III left Paris for a highly publicized trip to Algeria. He landed on May 3 in Algiers, where he gave a speech to a crowd composed largely of French colonists. He began by noting that he had traveled to Algeria to learn more about his subjects' needs, as well as to assure them that they had the protection of the metropole behind them. He encouraged them to "have faith in the future; attach yourselves to the soil that you cultivate as a new fatherland." The colonists, he implied, would come to "belong" to Algeria as they worked its soil, and, in collaboration with the metropole, they would bring new prosperity to the territory. He then introduced a different note, asking colonists to "treat the Arabs in your midst as compatriots. We are necessarily the masters, because we are the most civilized; we should be generous, because we are the strongest." He finished by urging the colonists to "justify" France's conquest of Algeria by cultivating an attitude toward the indigenous population based on "peace" and "charity."[1] The speech thus praised the colonists and implied that Algeria would eventually become their homeland. But at the same time, it highlighted the centrality of the indigenous population to the French imperial project and implied that French claims to Algeria rested on France's guarantee of their happiness. The speech therefore sought to balance settler interests with indigenous rights, depicting the settlers as allies in the government's attempt to secure the prosperity of conquered indigenous peoples.

Napoleon III's attempt to define the respective roles of colonists and indigenous peoples in Algeria was part of a broader project to rethink the territory and its relationship with France. This project emerged partly out of ongoing conflicts between the French administration, the settler population, and indigenous Algerians over their social positions in the territory, their respective legal rights, and the nature of the institutions that should administer them.[2] But it was also driven by Napoleon III's desire to redefine the image of the Second Empire. Throughout the 1850s, Napoleon III had promoted the empire as a political program that could integrate revolutionary principles with the need for security and stability within France while spreading what he called "the politics of nationality" to its European neighbors.[3] But in the face of growing popular frustration with France's domestic and foreign policies at the end of the decade, he began to search for opportunities to recast the Second Empire, affirm its importance, and secure its popularity in a new way.[4] One of the strategies he adopted was to associate his regime with the memory of ancient Rome and Napoleon I's legacy of expansion. Napoleon III had always made use of both Roman symbolism and the Napoleonic myth, but in his early years he at least publicly rejected his uncle's legacy of military conquest—even if he did not avoid war itself.[5] It was only in the 1860s that he began to use the language of expansionary politics.[6]

The embrace of expansionism was not simply rhetorical. In the 1860s Napoleon III also began to look for ways to increase the size of the empire he ruled. In Mexico he sought to create a "Latin" empire under Archduke Ferdinand Maximilian of Austria that would serve as France's ally in the Americas. In Southeast Asia he worked to establish French control over Cochinchina and increase French access to East Asian commerce. And, at the same time, he also began to eye the weakening Ottoman Empire on the other side of the Mediterranean and dream of expanding his imperial reach into North African territories that had once belonged to Rome. He hoped to recast the Second Empire as both a particular political program within France and as an expansive, multinational "Mediterranean empire"—much like ancient Rome.[7] Napoleon III made a series of efforts to increase French influence in these Ottoman territories, although he never attempted to seize them.[8] Instead, he sought to redefine France's relationship with Algeria in order to use it as a model for this still unconquered Mediterranean empire by transforming the territory into a royaume arabe.

Both the Third Republic's construction of an extensive overseas empire and the diverse attempts of politicians, administrators, and writers to justify that empire by developing an imperialist ideology have attracted extensive scholarly attention over the past twenty years. Recently scholars have also begun to look more closely at the Second Empire's specific policies in Algeria and have highlighted some of the ways that debates over these policies influenced the Third Republic's colonial practices.[9] Gavin Murray-Miller's work, for example, has shown how arguments over the Second Empire's colonial strategies informed French conversations about national identity, unity, and difference into the Third Republic and beyond.[10] But this scholarship has not explained how the Second Empire's colonial practices intersected with contemporary French understandings of empire. In fact, despite growing attention to the multiple referents of terms such as "colony" in nineteenth-century European thought—and the important consequences of that semantic flexibility—few scholars have investigated the complex intellectual history of the meanings of "empire" during this period.[11] Even the growing body of scholarship that has begun to reflect critically on "empires" and their relationship to "nations" has not examined how that relationship was understood within nineteenth-century French thought.[12] Moreover, most existing scholarship has treated European overseas empires separately from the history of European continental empires. As a result, there has been little investigation of how ideas about overseas empires and continental empires interacted—especially in France.

During the last years of the Second Empire, the contradictions between domestic and overseas visions of empire would emerge in a series of arguments about the French invasion of Mexico and the ideal organization of Algeria. These arguments were primarily waged by a relatively narrow group of French politicians, colonial administrators, colonists, intellectuals, and pamphlet writers whose critiques of government policy expressed different understandings of empire and its purpose. But the arguments were also influenced by petitions and publications written by conservative Mexican émigrés living in Europe and to a lesser extent by a wider array of Mexican politicians. Elite indigenous Algerians—and Napoleon III's perceived relationship with them—also played an indirect role in shaping these conversations.

The public sphere that these arguments over empire emerged in was enlarging during the 1860s. Throughout the early years of his reign, Napoleon III had taken extensive measures to censor newspapers and books and to limit their circulation, especially in Paris. But he loosened press laws in 1860 as a sign of his commitment to a new "liberal" empire, which meant that newspapers and other publications not only were more likely to publish a wider set of opinions, but they could also circulate more freely.[13] Increasing literacy rates and the emergence, by the mid-1860s, of inexpensive daily newspapers such as *Le petit journal*, which were aimed at nonelite audiences, also widened the reading public.[14] In Algeria, too, the number of newspapers and the scope of their circulation increased at the same moment.[15] As a result, a wider array of readers would have been aware of these debates than might have been even a decade before.

That said, the scope of the audience for these debates over empire should not be overstated; it remained fractured, uneven, and exclusive. Newspapers and editors claimed to represent "public opinion," but liberal elites continued to dominate the publishing industry.[16] The ostensibly nonpolitical identity of the new mass dailies, which had the widest audience, made them less likely to cover arguments over empire.[17] The press in Algeria in particular remained more tightly controlled than in France, and all of the newspapers and presses were run by settlers—they certainly did not reflect the perspectives of Algeria's different indigenous communities.[18] The French army and Maximilian's regime also closely censored the press in occupied Mexico, and few Mexican publications circulated back to France.[19] But if the audience for the publications that these arguments about empire appeared in remained predominantly elite, both the government and the political opposition nevertheless saw them as capable of shaping popular opinion and, in turn, electoral results.[20] And perhaps partly because of the resulting sense that the arguments about empire that appeared in these publications had political consequences, these arguments would influence the wider conversation about colonial expansion during the early years of the Third Republic.

This chapter examines Napoleon III's attempts to redefine the Second Empire in the last years of his reign, when the foundation for these later debates began to develop. I connect his attempts to found a new empire in Mexico with his redefinition of Algeria as a royaume arabe and consider what the conflicts over both territories reveal about the tensions that characterized the discourses of empire during the last years of his reign. This approach follows Frederick Cooper and Ann Laura Stoler's suggestion that focusing on tensions can be "a way of exploring how imperial projects were made possible and vulnerable at the same time."[21] I also look at the ways in which various intellectual legacies—from Napoleonic imperialism and revolutionary nationalism to Saint-Simonian ideas about race—shaped the new understanding of empire that Napoleon III proposed. And, finally, I reflect on the legacy of Napoleon III's imperial visions in the early Third Republic. The chapter thus provides insight into the different intellectual frameworks through which French writers, politicians, and theorists understood colonial expansion during this period. It also highlights the interconnections between continental and colonial understandings of empire and shows how they evolved over time.

Napoleon III's Imperial Vision: Defining the French Empire

From the beginning of his rule, Napoleon III sought to provide a theoretical backbone to the Second Empire that would legitimize it politically. Even in the early years of his political career, he developed a theory of empire in dialogue with his uncle's rule, whose legacy he both drew on and distanced himself from. During his presidential campaign in 1848, Louis Napoleon made explicit reference to his connection to Napoleon I as evidence of his fitness to lead the country—even as he promised that he would, unlike his uncle, uphold the values of the republican constitution and preserve the republican state.[22] In a speech to the National Assembly in the early part of his presidency, he went even further, allying himself with what he identified as his uncle's politics, maintaining, "The name Napoleon is itself a program. It says: in the interior, order, authority, religion, the well-being of the people: on the exterior, national dignity. This is the politics that I have enacted with the support of the assembly since my election."[23] Of course, this assessment of Napoleon I's political program failed to mention the authoritarian nature of the former emperor's rule and made only oblique reference to the extensive military campaigns that had characterized it. But the quote shows how, from the beginning, Louis Napoleon drew on aspects of Napoleon I's imperial legacy to create his own vision of empire, centered on a commitment to order, the suppression of political radicalism, and the guarantee of economic and social security for all classes of society.

After the coup d'état in 1851, Napoleon III's references to his uncle became more frequent and direct. In the new constitution, he based the government's organization on Napoleon I's administrative, military, judicial, financial, and religious institutions—even though he still claimed that he was not restoring the empire.[24] But although he relied on his uncle's prestige, he worked to redefine Napoleon I's legacy. He was particularly interested in refuting the republican claim that "the empire means war." In a speech in 1852, he assured his listeners that Napoleon I's importance lay not in his external wars but in the "internal peace" he established. Only under the First Empire, Napoleon III maintained, had the French people set aside their ideological differences and worked together for their common interest.[25]

According to Napoleon III, the new empire would follow the Bonapartist legacy of creating domestic peace by outlawing fractious political parties, even as it extended suffrage. Without these parties, elections would no longer cause division; instead, the population would come together to vote on the emperor's plebiscites. Like the first Napoleonic empire, the second Napoleonic empire would thus maintain the appearance of democratic principles and practices while depoliticizing the population and ending social strife.[26] This depoliticization, Napoleon III claimed, would enable a return to stability and prosperity for rich and poor alike. He thus defined the "Napoleonic empire" as the combination of the "best" aspects of the Revolution—its belief in democratic principles, political expression, and human progress—with the guarantee of order and security.[27]

If Napoleon III drew on Napoleon I to define the Second Empire domestically, his attempt to articulate the empire's position, identity, and purpose on the international stage was more complicated. In the early years, two interrelated goals drove this process of articulation: he wanted to restore France's position in Europe and to secure his empire's international prestige.[28] He accomplished these objectives in two contradictory ways. On one hand, he reassured both his subjects and his neighbors that he would not attempt to dominate Europe. On the other, however, he strove to restore the myth of French imperial grandeur—a myth based on Napoleon I's military prowess.[29] He resolved the contradictions between these strategies by positioning the French Empire as the defender of nationalities in Europe. Drawing on romantic nationalism, Napoleon III insisted that Europe would only see peace when each "people" had its own state. The French Empire would help bring about this era of harmony by supporting nationalist movements across Europe as they sought independence from larger empires. This, he argued, was the real legacy of the first Napoleonic empire, which had striven to found "a solid European association resting on complete nationalities and general interests."[30]

In the early years of his reign, Napoleon III thus pursued what he described as the "politics of nationality" or "the liberation of peoples" in conflicts across Europe. In Italy in particular, he deployed troops to support the independence movement led by Victor Emmanuel II against the Austro-Hungarian Empire.[31] He had long criticized European empires such as Austria-Hungary as outdated and claimed that their incorporation of diverse peoples—combined with their failure to rule these peoples in a systematic way—both impeded historical progress and oppressed the "national minorities" who lived beneath their yoke.[32] By casting the French Empire as the defender of these minorities, bound to "prepare [them] for a common nationality," Napoleon III defined it as a "progressive force" in European politics, helping to spread freedom and construct future peace in Europe.[33] He thus borrowed directly from the revolutionary conviction that France was a vanguard nation meant to lead other nations in the path of human progress. But, at the same time, he distanced France from democratic politics: while he supported Victor Emmanuel's attempt to reconfigure Italy into an independent monarchical state, he suppressed the Italian republican movement. Napoleon III thus made it clear that he sought to spread not a set of political ideas but a model of state organization. A Europe composed of nation-states, he maintained, would both "found a solid system of European association" and "satisfy the general interests" of the different European peoples. By contending that the French Empire intended to bring about this future, Napoleon III defined his empire as a force bent not on conquest or inciting revolution but on liberating peoples and enforcing international justice.[34]

Throughout the 1850s, Napoleon III thus sought to define the French Second Empire as a unique kind of state. Internally, it integrated revolutionary principles with stability and security. Externally, it spread its progressive ideology to its European neighbors without threatening their sovereignty or promoting radical democratic movements. In this vision, "empire" came to signify a mixture of liberal and repressive policies within metropolitan France and a foreign policy agenda based on a messianic understanding of France's place in the world. However, Napoleon III did not define the French Empire as a grouping of multiple states—in part because he was positioning it against multiethnic empires such as Russia and Austria-Hungary. In fact, during the first decade of Napoleon III's reign, the emperor usually treated the "French Empire" as functionally equivalent to the "French nation." This was distinct from Napoleon I's vision of a French Empire. Like Napoleon III, he had used "empire" in opposition to the "republic" or the "monarchy"—to refer to a specific kind of political organization within France. But, at the same time, the term also signified strategies for dealing with conquered territory. For Napoleon I, the French "nation" was thus part of the French Empire but not equivalent to it.[35]

During the early 1860s, the Second Empire moved into a period of political transition. Economic prosperity, successful European wars, and authoritarian control had marked the first decade of Napoleon III's reign.[36] But, by the end of that decade, several developments incited Napoleon III to modify the empire's structure and political identity. The most important of these shifts was the growing cost and unpopularity of France's wars supporting the nationalist movement in Italy. By the end of the 1850s, Napoleon III's inconsistent attempts to secure Italian independence had met with frustration: the nationalist movement had taken on republican overtones that he opposed, his armies were expensive, and he had alienated the revolutionaries, the pope, and French Catholics alike.[37] When ongoing military spending weakened the French economy, Napoleon III's claim that the empire had ended partisan politics and created political consensus began to openly fall apart. Increasingly vocal opposition groups on the left and the right began to attack him and his empire.

Out of this frustration, Napoleon III began to envision different identities for the French Empire. He began to seek new ways to secure French glory abroad and appease dissenters at home, while challenging expanding international competition from Britain and Prussia. On one hand, he passed a series of measures to "liberalize" the empire's domestic institutions. In addition to relaxing censorship, he allowed Senate debates to be published and fostered the creation of some political parties.[38] At the same time, Napoleon III decided that he would extend the international influence of the French Empire—not in Europe but overseas.

Latinité and Empire in Mexico

The most notorious example of Napoleon III's attempts to extend French influence overseas was his failed attempt to establish Archduke Ferdinand Maximilian, a younger brother of Austrian emperor Franz Joseph, as the emperor of Mexico. In 1862 France invaded Mexico as part of a coalition that included Britain and Spain. Officially the powers were reacting both to President Benito Juárez's decision to suspend payments on foreign debts for two years and to security threats to their citizens. Even at the time, however, the powers' real motivations were a subject of extensive debate.[39]

The argument over the powers' motivations partly stemmed from the way that political conflict in Mexico intersected with the invasion. Starting in 1857, a civil war waged between conservative and liberal forces known as the War of Reform had divided Mexico. The conflict centered on the position of the Catholic Church and to a lesser extent the military in Mexican society and politics, but it was also bound up in arguments over the structure of Mexico's government and the political rights of its different communities. The liberal and conservative positions in this conflict are difficult to summarize because of the divisions within each camp. But, in general, the liberals wanted to transform the Mexican nation into a community of equal and autonomous individuals held together by a constitution that would protect their rights against the national government. In this vision, a federated system granting the country's constituent states substantial independence would also limit the national government's authority. Conservatives, on the other hand, tended to defend the traditional privileges of communal structures such as the church, the military, and Indian tribes; they also embraced a more hierarchical vision of Mexican society and endorsed a powerful central government—perhaps headed by a monarch.[40] In 1860 the liberal forces under Juárez won out, and several conservative leaders fled into exile in

Europe, where they petitioned European governments to intervene in Mexico on their behalf.[41]

These exiled Mexican conservatives clearly hoped that the invasion would function as a continuation of the civil war by other means. The three invading powers disagreed about the aims of the expedition, however.[42] In early 1861 they had signed an agreement stating that they were invading the country to restore order and force the Mexican government to pay its debts, but that they had no intention of forcing a regime change. Napoleon III nevertheless suggested early on that he would be interested in "supporting a change [in government] . . . that would be in the interest of civilization as a whole."[43] Conflicts between the French, Spanish, and British commanders on the ground compounded this difference in intention, eventually leading the Spanish and the British to withdraw from the expedition.[44]

The venture thus met with trouble from the beginning. The subsequent military conflict did not proceed smoothly either. The French army encountered more resistance than expected, losing an early battle against a small Mexican republican army at Puebla on May 5, 1862, which led to a popular backlash in France.[45] Eventually French troops gained control of the capital and created a provisional government dominated by Mexican monarchists. The provisional government offered Archduke Ferdinand Maximilian—whom Napoleon III had recommended—the position of hereditary emperor of Mexico.[46] Maximilian agreed to accept the position only if most Mexican people approved, so the provisional government worked with the French army to stage a plebiscite modeled on the ones that Napoleon III used in France. The plebiscite only included the votes of the notables, but the provisional government used its results to claim that the Mexican people themselves had chosen Maximilian.[47] Once Maximilian arrived in Mexico in 1864, however, it became clear that he had little support from the Mexican people; he was too liberal for the conservatives and too monarchical for the liberals.[48] His government also inherited the financial problems of the republican regime, and it struggled to decisively defeat Juárez's republican army.[49] At the same time, popular opposition to the Mexican expedition in France continued to mount. In response to this opposition in France, Maximilian's inability to decisively establish his authority across Mexico, and pressure from the United States that began to grow after the end of the American Civil War, Napoleon III withdrew French troops.[50] Without French support, the regime collapsed, and Juárez's republican forces executed Maximilian.

Napoleon III's expedition to Mexico, on its surface, had little in common with the wars of imperial expansion waged by Napoleon I. In fact, the Mexican intervention shared many commonalities with the Second Empire's earlier conflicts in Crimea and Italy: France invaded in concert with other European powers and did not lay claim to the territory that it conquered. Napoleon III's public pronouncements on Mexico also echoed those made during these earlier conflicts. He continued to draw on the language of nationality, claiming that he was interested in creating a Mexico "founded on the will of the people" and able to "conserve its independence and maintain its territorial integrity" in the face of US territorial ambitions that had become clear during the Mexican-American War.[51] He thus positioned France as the defender of the Mexican nation, protecting the Mexican people against their republican government and the predations of their northern neighbor. Even his interest in reconstituting Mexico beneath a monarch echoed his support for Victor Emmanuel II in Italy. In multiple ways, the invasion of Mexico thus followed the model of foreign policy that Napoleon III had pursued throughout the 1850s, especially in the stated support for national self-determination and antirepublican politics.

At the same time, however, the Mexican expedition also differed from these previous expeditions. Napoleon III had sent French troops to Italy with the claim that he was supporting an independence movement against the Austrian Empire. Mexico, on the other hand, was already an independent state, and the territorial ambitions of the United States were no longer an immediate threat. Instead of "liberating" the Mexican people from foreign rule, the Second Empire had invaded a sovereign republican nation and instituted a new ruler and form of government that resembled France's own imperial system.[52] Even if Mexico was not joining the French Empire, the invasion brought it within France's sphere of influence.[53]

The Mexican expedition was not only structurally different from Napoleon III's earlier military expeditions; both Napoleon III and his ministers also described the Second Empire's role there in new ways. In fact, they used France's intervention in Mexico to recast the purpose and practice of empire—both in Mexico and in France. This evolving understanding of empire became a point of public controversy in France, partly because Mexico was the first foreign invasion undertaken after Napoleon III loosened press laws.[54] In political pamphlets and newspapers, critics attacked the French government's policies in Mexico, leading to a series of public debates about the invasion and its consequences that serve as a window into broader shifts in views of empire during the 1860s.

The controversies over Napoleon III's imperial project in Mexico extended beyond Second Empire France. Much of the early scholarship on the expedition in both France and Mexico drew on accounts written by the Mexican Empire's contemporary critics. These accounts treated the expedition as a tragically farcical event that was driven by a handful of delusional Mexican émigrés as well as by self-interested, scheming, and incompetent ministers in the French legation to Mexico. More recent scholarship, however, has pushed back against the idea that the venture was doomed from the start. It has also highlighted the role played by a wider array of Mexican politicians and intellectuals in shaping the French government's vision of the expedition.[55] This chapter is not directly concerned with the question of how to interpret the expedition, but its account of how arguments over empire in Mexico affected ideas about empire in France is grounded in this more recent scholarship's interactive understanding of the Second Mexican Empire. It centers its analysis on French debates about empire, but it also considers where—and how—Mexican arguments influenced those debates.[56]

French debates about Mexican empire emerged in dialogue with nineteenth-century racial thinking, which structured French understandings of Mexico. Most French commentators embraced the belief dating at least to the Enlightenment that Europe stood at the pinnacle of civilization and that all other peoples—including Mexicans—fell beneath it.[57] But "race" itself was often used in contradictory ways in these debates, reflecting the term's semantic instability. As scholars have shown, "race" in eighteenth-century France had been used in several different ways: to refer to the *limpieza de sangre*, or "purity of blood" laws in Spain and Portugal, which discriminated against Jewish families who had converted to Christianity, to differentiate between the aristocracy and ordinary people within metropolitan France, and to enforce legal hierarchies in France's colonies in the Caribbean that defended the privileges of white Europeans over those with African ancestry. "Race" also could be used more broadly to describe lineage and descent.[58]

Even though by the 1850s, the study of race was becoming institutionalized and increasingly described as a science, arguments about how to classify races and explain the consequences of those classifications continued. Anthropologists created elaborate racial hierarchies that they claimed were grounded in measurable bodily difference—often in skull shape, although they invoked other physical criteria as well.[59] They disagreed, however, about the structure and content of their racial hierarchies and where different groups of people belonged within them. They also remained divided between monogenism, which held that all humans had a common origin, and polygenism, which contended that humans descended from different sources, and partly as a result they disagreed about whether racial differences were permanent and hereditary, or temporary and caused by environment.[60]

Napoleon III's regime had fostered the institutionalization of anthropology as a scholarly discipline in France, but neither he nor his critics drew directly on the ideas about race formulated within anthropological circles.[61] And outside of anthropology, "race" had even looser meanings: it had both biological and cultural overtones and worked interchangeably with "nation" or even "class."[62] Contemporary observers also did not agree about how any type of racial theory applied to Mexico, as its population comprised a diverse mix of creole, mixed-race or mestizo, and indigenous peoples. Some French commentators treated all Mexicans as belonging to one "Mexican" race—equating race with nation—while others contended that different groups fell into distinct racial categories.[63] These disagreements also echoed among Mexican politicians and intellectuals. While a growing number of thinkers, especially in liberal circles, had begun to define Mexican national identity as specifically mestizo, the conservatives who were more closely in touch with the French government more often imagined Mexico as a country divided into distinct races structured hierarchically.[64]

Despite these disagreements, nineteenth-century French representations of Mexico—which were numerous, thanks to the large French colony there—were relatively consistent.[65] As Guy-Alain Dugast has highlighted, these representations portrayed Mexican land as wealthy by invoking myths of El Dorado. They then contrasted Mexico's immense natural resources with depictions of impoverished Mexican people, creating a narrative that positioned Mexico as "less advanced" than Europe.[66] Portrayals of Mexican society varied more widely, but most contended that the experience of oppression under the despotic Spanish monarchy had created deep disorder. They also argued that a series of incompetent postindependence governments had encouraged criminality and political division.[67] This political division was then compounded by racial division between Mexico's European and indigenous populations.[68] French commentators held this political division and weakness responsible for Mexico's defeat in the Mexican-American War of 1846–48, which had resulted in the loss of a third of the country's territory.[69] These portrayals did not only echo across popular and scholarly works; they were also repeated by France's minister in Mexico, Count Jean Alexis de Gabriac, who warned that Mexico was in danger of becoming a "nineteenth-century Poland," as well as by his successor, Alphonse Dubois de Saligny.[70]

These descriptions of Mexico were also influenced by the accounts of some conservative Mexican politicians and intellectuals, who appealed to Napoleon III and other imperial government officials, contending that the country was both too divided and insufficiently educated to be governed by a democratic system.[71] José María Gutiérrez de Estrada was one of the most visible of these politicians; he had written a pamphlet in 1840 arguing that monarchy by a foreign prince alone could create stability in Mexico and bring political peace to the country.[72] The pamphlet had led to his exile, and he spent the following decades in European courts, petitioning European monarchs to intervene in Mexico.[73] Estrada was detached from Mexican politics, but in the years following the Mexican-American War a growing number of conservatives came to share his concerns about Mexico's political instability, which they saw as particularly problematic in the face of US expansionary ambitions.[74] Some were also inspired by the way that Napoleon III's regime combined authoritarian politics with the appearance of popular suffrage, and they argued that a close connection with a Catholic European country would help Mexico counterbalance American influence.[75]

Napoleon III and his supporters drew on these understandings of Mexico to position empire as the solution to the country's problems. In an 1861 letter to Count Flahaut, the French ambassador in London, Napoleon III contended that empire alone could save Mexico from "anarchy" and "approaching ruin." Such a government would be able to develop Mexico's misused natural resources and "establish order in a country torn apart by factions."[76] He repeated these sentiments in two published letters to General Élie Frédéric Forey, the commander in chief of the French army in Mexico, in which he argued that empire—if chosen freely by the Mexican people—would stabilize, strengthen, and "regenerate" the country by combining "order" with "progress."[77] These explanations of empire's political role in Mexico were nearly identical to Napoleon III's vision of its role in France.

In Mexico, though, Napoleon III and his supporters imagined that empire would produce an even more powerful transformation: it would heal not only political division but also the racial division that they believed lay beneath it. Napoleon III contended that empire would have a "civilizing" effect on Mexico—an idea informed by Saint-Simonian racial theory, which played an important role in Napoleon III's thought during the 1860s.[78] Saint-Simonians contended that humans progressed at different rates through stages of social organization in response to historical circumstances. All races could reach the same advanced level of civilization, but some would be ahead of others. The Saint-Simonians believed that Europeans were more advanced than other peoples and argued that imperial relationships could bring "backwards" peoples into the historical present.[79] According to this logic, an empire in Mexico, headed by a European prince, would do more than end internal division; it would also "civilize" Mexico and bring it even closer to the country that it already resembled—France. Empire was thus both a political salve and a driver of civilization itself.[80]

These themes also appeared in French propaganda in Mexico, including in the army's official statements to the Mexican people. Forey's proclamations contended that Mexico was in "ruin," exploited by a small group of ambitious men whose "fratricidal struggles" had threatened the country's independence and returned it to a state of "barbarism." France, Forey maintained, would remake Mexico as a "rich, strong, and free nation" by protecting "real liberty, which can only be defended by order." He promised that, as a result, Mexico would become a nation that "everyone could recognize as civilized."[81] General Juan Almonte, a Mexican monarchist who led the Mexican auxiliary forces before the French army made him a regent in the provisional government, echoed these sentiments, describing the French intervention as "just" and "civilizing," promising that it would restore order and prosperity to Mexico—again combining the language of order, political peace, and civilization.[82]

More informal propaganda also promulgated Napoleon III's vision of empire's role in Mexico. In 1864 Charles de Montholon, who had been named France's foreign minister to the new provisional Mexican government, hired Émile Masseras, a journalist with strong Bonapartist sympathies who had run a French-language journal in New York, to edit a new journal called *L'ere nouvelle de Mexico*, which was intended to promote Mexican and French unity.[83] Shortly after arriving in Mexico—a country that he had never visited—Masseras published a pamphlet in both French and Spanish titled *The Program of the Empire* that promoted empire to the Mexican people.[84] Maximilian's empire, he promised, would bring true liberty to Mexico by creating a clear legal code, reorganizing the government, and eliminating divisive political parties. Empire, he contended, signified above all "the intimate alliance between the democratic and progressive principle . . . and the conservative principle of governmental stability."[85] It would give Mexicans the opportunity to participate in political life while preventing political differences from dividing them. At the same time, the imperial structure would enable both French and Mexican leaders to educate ordinary Mexicans so that they would learn to vote "for their own best interests."[86]

If Napoleon III and his supporters envisioned empire as a powerful political solution for Mexico, they also used the Mexican expedition to propose a new identity for the Second Empire itself. This new identity drew on a discourse of Latin unity, or *latinité*. An imagined association with Rome was neither new nor unique to France; for much of the eighteenth and nineteenth centuries, both the British and French positioned themselves as Rome's heirs, although the British were more ambivalent about Rome's legacy. But latinité went beyond association—it positioned the French and other Latin peoples as actual descendants of the Romans.[87] Napoleon III's use of pan-Latin discourses did not begin with the Mexican expedition. As historian Käthe Panick has shown, Napoleon III had borrowed the idea of Latin unity from liberal thinkers to justify military involvement in Italy several years earlier, transforming it in the process. He had argued that France, Italy, and Spain were natural allies, united by a common culture and Roman heritage that gave France a vested interest in ensuring that all members of the "Latin race" could prosper. In the late 1850s Napoleon III primarily deployed latinité to show a French public increasingly hostile to the government's expenditures in Italy that those expenditures were necessary.[88]

As historians Guy Martinière and Maike Thier have demonstrated, however, latinité was never understood solely in a European context; even in the 1850s, a number of French intellectuals argued that South Americans were also "Latins."[89] After the Mexican-American War, some thinkers in Latin America also invoked the concept, primarily to protest against US expansion into the Southern Hemisphere and to argue for unity among countries in South and Central America.[90] But several conservative Mexican politicians in the 1850s and early 1860s also invoked pan-Latinist language to call for a French or Spanish intervention in Mexico.[91] Pan-Latinist ideas thus emerged out of a transnational conversation in the mid-nineteenth century, and they were driven by a combination of French expansionary ambition and by concerns about the growing power of Britain and the United States.[92]

One of the most prominent advocates of latinité was Michel Chevalier, a former Saint-Simonian, a prominent political economist, and Napoleon III's economic adviser.[93] Chevalier had spent a significant amount of time traveling in the United States and in Mexico and had personal ties with Gutiérrez de Estrada.[94] And while he wrote in French, his ideas about latinité were translated into Spanish and commanded an audience among Mexican conservatives.[95] Chevalier centered his 1862 pamphlet, written to justify the French invasion of Mexico, around the idea of latinité. He argued that France would only be able to preserve its position in Europe if it could "maintain and develop the strength" of other Latin peoples around the world.[96] He warned that Mexico's weakness was threatening the very existence of Latin peoples in both the Americas and Europe. By invading and "regenerating" Mexico, he promised, the Second Empire would secure the support of other nations on two continents and build an "influence that would [otherwise] escape it."[97] Latin unity was thus not only a humanitarian ideal; it was also a strategy that would enable the Second Empire to compete with its Anglo-Saxon and Germanic neighbors in the Americas and Europe alike.[98]

Over the course of the Mexican expedition, Napoleon III and his supporters would draw on the discourse of latinité—despite the fact that this vision of Mexico as "Latin" rested uneasily with the contention that Mexico was made up of numerous races.[99] But advocates of latinité did not necessarily see these visions as at odds.[100] They tended to use "Latin race" and "Latin civilization" synonymously and invoked a mix of language, history, culture, and Catholicism to describe both.[101] They usually assumed that the Spanish had destroyed Indian civilization and, as a result, either treated the indigenous population as irrelevant to latinité or assumed that indigenous peoples would integrate into it. At the same time, they either ignored or discursively circumscribed Mexico's Afro-Mexican communities.[102] The idea that Mexico was a "Latin" race thus did not necessarily contradict the contention that it was also inhabited by multiple races, because the word was used differently in both cases. Napoleon III and his supporters could use "latinité"—however loosely defined—to position the conflict in Mexico as part of a larger struggle between "Latins" and other races competing for global dominance.[103] In his writing, Napoleon III argued that a French invasion of Mexico would benefit the entire "Latin race" because it would preserve Latin influence in the Americas against the Anglo-Saxons in the United States to the north, whose territorial ambitions French commentators—and Mexican conservatives—had been concerned about ever since the Mexican-American War.[104] At the same time, he and his supporters also used "latinité" to defend France's imperial project in Mexico by maintaining that all "Latin races" needed to be governed by a monarchy.[105]

Notably, Napoleon III and his supporters did not envision Latin unity as an equal confederation of nations. Like Chevalier, most writers assumed that the French Second Empire would be the leading power of Latin peoples in Europe and the Americas. Even Masseras, who was writing at least partly for a Mexican audience, echoed this perspective. He described Napoleon III as a "clairvoyant" and "energetic" leader who had "rejoined the fragmented Latin race in Europe" and wanted to "complete this work by bringing the same race in the New World to the rank that it belongs to."[106] Works aimed at French audiences were even more hyperbolic. Auguste-Saint-Hilaire Mercier de Lacombe, the editor of the progovernment French newspaper *Le correspondent*, went so far as to argue that Napoleon III had been "called" to this position by way of his Bonapartist heritage.[107] These writers did not just highlight Napoleon III's personal qualities as the reason behind France's leadership position; they also argued that France should serve as a model because it alone among Latin countries had been able to stave off decadence and decay.[108] If "Latins" were thus one race, they were nevertheless unequal. Commentators tended to put Mexico in a particularly inferior position; one anonymous pamphlet, for example, described it as a "child" of the Latin race that needed protection.[109] The discourse of latinité thus symbolically extended France's influence over both Europe and the Americas because it positioned Napoleon III as the head of a group of stratified nations.[110] It also placed Mexico within France's sphere of influence without turning it into a conquest.

During the early 1860s Napoleon III and his supporters thus used the idea of latinité to justify the Mexican invasion and to claim a new and larger role for the Second Empire itself. According to this evolving vision, the Second Empire was a global power destined to lead all "Latin peoples" because its political system was ready for universal export. The Second Empire, in this theoretical framework, would not exercise direct control over Latin countries or undermine their national sovereignty; in fact, France would continue to act as the defender of Latin nations, much as it had throughout the 1850s. Implicitly, however, the claim of a shared Latin identity gave the Second Empire a reason to interfere with other Latin countries' governments if Napoleon III decided that those governments were not acting in the best interests of their nations. This vision of the Second Empire drew on both the legacy of Rome and on the expansive vision of Napoleon I. On one hand, this description of the Second Empire imagined that "Latin nations"—Rome's heirs—would come together in a new federative or neoimperial system, directed by France, that would restore the Latin peoples to greatness. At the same time, it positioned the Second Empire as a model government that could inspire and peacefully unify many of the countries that the first Napoleonic empire had tried to conquer.

The argument that the Second Empire should lead a federation of Latin nations, bound together by heritage, culture, and political values, provoked controversy in both Mexico and France. The republican government in Mexico vehemently rejected the idea—partly by maintaining that this imperial vision did not describe either French ambitions or Mexican wishes. In 1863 Mexico's Congress released an official statement that accused France of undermining "the laws of nations" by attempting to "subjugate" Mexico.[111] The statement implied that the French intervention was not defending the independence of a nation with a shared Latin identity from its Anglo-Saxon neighbor; instead, it was attempting to undermine Mexico's sovereignty. At the same time, Juárez made a series of proclamations that described the

French intervention as an "unjust invasion of our soil" and contended that Napoleon III's real goal was to "humiliate and destroy a free and democratic republic." The Mexican people, he implied, did not share France's political values and had no interest in being tied to a broader imperial system.[112] These accounts of the French intervention attacked Napoleon III's attempt to portray himself and the French Empire as a defender of nations and described France instead as a power bent on conquest and on the destruction of democratic systems of government.

At the same time, Mexican liberals also attacked the model of empire that the French purported to bring to Mexico. Some explicitly rejected the idea that empire would promote order and unity; instead, they maintained, the intervention had continued the disorder and violence of the civil war. Members of the liberal government also attacked the idea that empire would "civilize" Mexico, contending that it was the French, not the Mexicans, who acted "barbarically."[113] Others rejected the idea that empire would transform Mexico into an "analogue" of Napoleonic empire and maintained that empire would instead transform Mexico into a French colony—substituting Napoleon III's federative if unequal vision of empire for one based explicitly on domination.[114]

Even some Mexican conservatives came to criticize elements of Napoleon III's vision for empire in Mexico. These criticisms focused primarily on the role of the Catholic Church in the new imperial system, but they also disagreed with Bonapartist interpretations of latinité. Napoleon III had instructed General Forey to declare that the new imperial government would maintain key aspects of the reform laws passed by its liberal predecessor, including the sale of clerical property and the proclamation of religious tolerance.[115] He then integrated Forey's declaration as a secret provision into the Treaty of Miramar, which named Maximilian the emperor of Mexico.[116] Even as Napoleon III partly rested the legitimacy of his imagined imperial system on Mexico and France's shared Catholicism, he thus clearly envisioned religious tolerance and a weaker church as a constitutive component of the "civilization" that France proposed to promote in Mexico.[117] This vision was disappointing for some Mexican conservatives, who were more likely to contend that the new empire should focus on defending the position of the Catholic Church in Mexican society and politics.[118] These conservatives—led by the archbishop of Mexico City, Pelagio Antonio de Labastida y Dávalos, who was originally one of the three figures leading the regency—pushed back against French policy using the language of latinité, which they cast in primarily Catholic terms. In their eyes, what tied the Mexican and French people together was their devotion to the church, which should become an integral part of the new political system built in Mexico.[119] These conservatives thus suggested that a different model of empire—rooted in a different understanding of latinité—should take shape in the country.

Mexican criticisms of Napoleon III's imperial vision did not circulate widely in France. Even the Juárez's government's official proclamations did not appear in most French newspapers. As a result, the educated French reading public would not have had direct access to these Mexican complaints. Members of the metropolitan government, however, would have been familiar with Mexicans' protests, as officials in the French legation and in the army were concerned enough about them to translate them and send them back to France. The metropolitan government in fact often produced propaganda that explicitly addressed Mexican criticisms—by emphasizing, for example, that French officials intended to defend, not undermine, the sovereignty of the Mexican nation and that the French government only wanted to help the Mexican people choose their own government.[120] But these assurances did not quell Mexican concerns about this new imperial system. Arguments over the nature and meaning of empire in fact only intensified when the French handed political authority over to Maximilian.

In France, too, Napoleon III's vision was greeted with skepticism—even among supporters of the principle of latinité and the invasion. Some commentators, like their Mexican counterparts, argued that France's actual strategies did not reflect the language used to justify the invasion; they questioned why Napoleon III had chosen to support Maximilian as the candidate to the Mexican throne when he did not even belong to the "Latin race." Instead of supporting an Austrian, they argued, France should choose a "Latin" candidate.[121] Others—primarily republicans—implied that Napoleon III's support for Maximilian had not strengthened Mexico but violated its sovereignty, as the Mexican people had never been consulted about their nation's new political structure.[122]

Although some authors questioned the French government's commitment to this new understanding of the Second Empire, others took issue with the model of empire proposed. An anonymous pamphleteer, for example, insisted that instead of trying to replicate the Second Empire within Mexico and bringing that country into a Latin union, Napoleon III should adopt the model of colonial settlement that both Britain and ancien régime France had used.[123] Sending French settlers to Mexico and transforming it into a colony, he argued, would "civilize" and "regenerate" Mexico while providing France with influence in the New World.[124] This pamphleteer thus proposed to replace Napoleon III's empire with one based on colonial settlement.

Other critics—from across the political spectrum—argued against the attempt to extend France's influence into the New World altogether. Adolphe de Belleyme, a Bonapartist member of the Corps législatif, contended that creating an empire in Mexico would "chain" France to a country that was poor and ungovernable.[125] Agénor de Gasparin, a republican living in exile in Geneva, claimed that the Second Empire's attempt to exert its influence over the Americas was misguided because the Americas would resist all European influence. He even argued that Latin unity did not apply in Mexico, as most Mexicans felt little allegiance to other Latin peoples due to their hatred of the Spanish.[126] Henry Moreau, a liberal lawyer and economist who wrote extensively about the Americas, took the argument against latinité a step further by maintaining that the very idea that France had a connection with Mexico because both belonged to the "Latin race" was specious; most Mexicans, he claimed, were not even of European descent.[127] These authors not only opposed the Second Empire's invasion and occupation of Mexico; they also questioned Napoleon III's attempt to recast the Second Empire as a leader of latinité and as a model political organization that could be exported.

As these writers' criticisms make clear, the debates over the invasion of Mexico quickly spread into broader arguments over the purpose and practice of empire in Europe and Mexico alike. Critics took issue both with the imperial model that Napoleon III proposed and with the interpretation of latinité on which it was based. Similar disagreements over the meaning of empire also characterized Napoleon III's attempt to restructure Algeria in the early 1860s. In Algeria, too, Napoleon III appealed to both the legacy of Rome and the memory of Napoleonic grandeur in an attempt to recast the Second Empire as larger than it was—and his ideas met with a similar lack of enthusiasm, at least among the settler population.

Empire and Algeria: *Le Royaume Arabe*

Napoleon III's interest in Algeria stemmed from his growing desire to supplant the Ottoman Empire's position in the western Mediterranean by extending French influence in its territories.[128] If France came to control the Mediterranean Sea, Napoleon III believed, it could entrench itself against the expanding British colonial empire and the ambitions of Prussia.[129] The same sense of international competition thus drove both the Mexican expedition and the restructuring of Algeria. Yet Napoleon III envisioned empire in the Mediterranean and empire in Mexico in different terms. His model for empire in Mexico was based on a sense of racial or civilizational unity and the establishment of a similar imperial political system—not political control. In the Mediterranean, on the other hand, his imagined empire would directly incorporate many diverse peoples. This distinction sharpened the tensions and contradictions in the conceptions of empire and nation that beset Napoleon III in Mexico. How could an emperor ostensibly devoted to liberating peoples and guiding them on the path to national self-determination justify ruling—let alone conquering—non-French peoples? How would such an empire remain distinct from the multinational Russian, Austro-Hungarian, and Ottoman Empires that Napoleon III criticized as oppressive? Napoleon III engaged with these questions as he sought to transform Algeria into a model Arab state for the new Mediterranean empire he dreamed of constructing. But his attempt to restructure Algeria was not just shaped by his geopolitical ambitions and theoretical concerns about empire. Ongoing French debates about Algeria that dated back to the conquest of the city of Algiers in 1830 also affected his ideas.

Starting as early as the 1830s, many French politicians, military officers, and intellectuals had envisioned Algeria as a territory with especially close ties to France. This perception partly reflected Algeria's relative proximity to the metropole in comparison with France's other overseas territories, which facilitated the flow of individuals and information. But it also stemmed from the fact that intellectuals and politicians from across the political spectrum had described Algeria as a promising site for French settler colonialism, which they imagined would transform the territory into a "new France" across the Mediterranean.[130]

As scholars Jennifer Sessions and Jennifer Pitts in particular have shown, the embrace of settler colonialism as an imperial model in the nineteenth century emerged partly out of Enlightenment-era criticisms of both overseas colonialism and Napoleonic empire. In the late eighteenth and early nineteenth centuries, liberal thinkers in both Britain and in France had criticized early modern imperial systems as tyrannical and exploitative, contending that their reliance on monopoly trade, enslaved labor, and the political dominance of the metropole over overseas territories undermined liberty both overseas and at home.[131] Benjamin Constant, a prominent liberal thinker, had in fact explicitly connected the exploitative policies used by overseas empires to Napoleon I's "fantasy of global hegemony," which had ended so destructively for France.[132] Many of these thinkers nevertheless were unwilling to abandon overseas conquest altogether because they saw it as critical to France's economic prosperity, global political standing, and social stability. They thus came to embrace settler colonialism—which they tied to ancient Greece and Rome as well as to Britain's colonies in North America—as both a morally preferable and more sustainable model, since it depended on free agricultural labor.[133]

The vision of Algeria as a site for settler colonialism nevertheless rested uneasily with the Convention of Capitulation signed between General Louis Bourmont, the commander of the French troops, and Husayn Dey, the governor of Algiers. The convention deliberately echoed the proclamations used by Napoleon in Egypt. It contended that the French were liberating the Algerians (like the Egyptians before them) from despotic Turkish rule, and it promised to protect the liberty, property, industry, and religious practices of Algeria's inhabitants while respecting Algerian women.[134] The convention's promises reflected French preconceptions about Algerian society and Muslim values, but they were rooted in an agreement to preserve Algeria's existing social and legal structures such as the French understood them.[135] This agreement contradicted the vision of Algeria as a "new France" made up of settler farming families from the metropole, which was based, like all settler colonialisms, on the imagined elimination of at least Algeria's existing society and culture—and perhaps its population as well.[136]

The French army violated the convention from the beginning, embarking on a campaign of looting and violence that alienated even the Algerian notables who had proposed initially to work with the French.[137] But as historian Judith Surkis has made clear, by 1833 the expedition's disorganization and brutality led the French parliament to create a commission of inquiry to impose order on the occupation. The commission denounced the "barbarism" that had characterized French rule so far and contended that French sovereignty over Algeria would only be secure if it were rooted in law. The French government would thus have to at least appear to take the stipulations in the convention seriously, which meant that it needed to set up an administrative structure that ruled indigenous communities according to existing legal systems. The French state would thus become responsible for enforcing Muslim, Mosaic, and customary law—a proposition that would prove quite fraught. At the same time, the commission also recommended that the colonial government encourage European agricultural settlement. These recommendations stood in tension with one another, most obviously because local law upheld the usage or ownership rights of Algerian communities to nearly all the land in Algeria, but also because they raised questions about the legal and administrative systems through which the colonial state would rule both indigenous populations and European settlers.[138]

In the years that followed, French policy unsurprisingly remained confused and contradictory. As the military conquered more of the Algerian countryside, however, the colonial administration became increasingly committed to settler colonialism as an institution that would secure French rule.[139] The administration thus sought to find ways to undermine Algerians' property rights and used a variety of methods—including sequestration, expropriation, and cantonment—to secure land for French settlers. These measures led to conflicts in the territory between Algerians, settlers, and the colonial administration that persisted even after the French defeated the bey of Constantine in 1837 and Abd el-Kader (Abd al-Qadir) in 1848, the two Algerian leaders who had resisted the extension of French rule most effectively.[140]

This unrest, combined with the military occupation's expense and the contradictions in French policy, all contributed to arguments within the metropolitan government and colonial administration over Algeria's future. These arguments centered on French policies toward Algerian land, the position of settler and Algerian communities within the colony, and the structure of the colony's administrative and legal systems. They were influenced by the actions of different Algerian groups, but they did not usually directly include the voices of Algerian people, due to a combination of linguistic divisions and French discrimination. Instead, competing groups of French military officers, civilian officials, members of the metropolitan government, and settlers dominated the debates. These groups drew on contradictory French understandings of race, "the Orient," and Islam and invoked the language of "assimilation" and "association" to defend their respective positions.[141]

Assimilation had multiple meanings in nineteenth-century France. As we have seen, free people of color, enslaved communities, and some white republicans had used the term during the Revolution of 1789 to argue that all inhabitants of French colonies should have the same rights, be ruled by the same laws, governed by the same political institutions, and subject to the same tariffs as the metropole.[142] In general, settlers and their metropolitan allies invoked this language—with its revolutionary associations—to demand that the French government "assimilate" Algeria into the metropole. From the beginning, however, it was clear that most settlers did not want this political assimilation to include Algerians, who made up most of the population. Granting Algerians political rights, they feared, would render the settlers a political minority and threaten their ability to take Algerians' land. Settlers and their allies justified this position by invoking orientalist traditions and racist thinking to condemn the religious, political, social, and gendered practices of most Algerians and locate them outside the French political community. As historian Patricia Lorcin and others have shown, these condemnations hinged on a highly negative vision of Islam, which claimed that fanaticism, blind hierarchy, and violence characterized the religion and that its practitioners necessarily fell into social decay and effeminacy. Some commentators suggested that a minority of the population (the Kabyles, or Berbers) was less committed to Islam, more democratically oriented, and more "European" and that they thus might be able to assimilate into the settler population and exercise some political rights. But most maintained that such a day was far in the future, if it would ever come to pass, for the majority Arab population.[143] Instead of including Algerians in the colony's political assimilation, they maintained, the administration should instead culturally and legally assimilate indigenous communities by undermining local leadership, banning polygamy and sharia, subjecting Algerians to the French justice system, abolishing Algerian communal property, and making that property available for settlers. These measures would prepare indigenous communities to potentially enjoy limited political rights at some always unspecified future moment, and in the meantime they would enable the settlers to remake Algeria in their own image.[144] Settlers thus modified the principles behind the revolutionary "assimilationist" model—which had been partly based on the idea that it was problematic for a republican state to rule over a subject population that did not have political rights—even as they made use of its discourses. But this exclusionary interpretation of "assimilation" also had older roots: white plantation owners had invoked a version of it early in the 1789 revolution to demand economic and political rights for themselves while maintaining slavery and colonial racial hierarchies.[145]

A cadre of military officers and administrative officials, whom their critics often grouped together as "Arabophiles," countered these calls for assimilation. Many of these officers had connections to the Saint-Simonian movement as well as to the *bureaux arabes*, a system of colonial outposts staffed by army officers that had been formalized in 1844 to mediate between the French government and Algerian leaders in the countryside.[146] In a variety of publications—from journals such as *La revue de l'Orient et de l'Algérie*, *La revue de Paris*, and *La revue orientale et algérienne* to brochures and scholarly treatises—they contended that France should not directly integrate Algeria or its peoples but instead preserve the structure of Algerian societies while slowly pushing them to "progress." They thus articulated a colonial vision of "association" in which the administration would "modernize" Algerians without forcing them to accept French laws or customs.

This vision of "association" in Algeria was to some extent grounded in the same Saint-Simonian hierarchical understanding of universalized civilizational progress that inspired Napoleon III's vision of empire in Mexico. Saint-Simonian understandings functioned differently in Mexico and Algeria, however. In Mexico, Napoleon III and his supporters contended that the Mexicans and the French belonged to a shared Latin "race" or "civilization"—terms that they often used interchangeably—but that the Mexican people had fallen behind the French. In Algeria, advocates of association similarly contended that Algerians were behind the French, but they usually also distinguished Algerians not only from "Latin" peoples but also from Europeans more broadly. They based this distinction on a commixture of religious and racial grounds; by the early nineteenth century, French thinkers had begun to treat Islam as a sign of racial difference in Algeria, much as Catholicism could serve as a signifier of a shared Latin racial identity in Mexico.[147] These divergent understandings of Mexico and Algeria's respective relationships to France led, in turn, to distinct visions of France's role in both places. Napoleon III's imperial policy proposed to help Mexico become more like France, while advocates of association in Algeria tended to argue that the French should help Algerians achieve a more "modern" stage of their own civilization or alternatively fuse elements of "French civilization" with "Algerian civilization."[148]

The differences between advocates of assimilation and association are nevertheless important not to overstate. As historian Osama Abi-Mershed has made clear, advocates of association also aimed "to legitimize colonial hegemony" and "secure the colonial dominion and state."[149] Their understandings of Algeria were equally rooted in orientalist discourses and in beliefs about racial or civilizational hierarchy, although they imagined "the Orient," Islam, and Algerian social structures in more positive terms than advocates of assimilation did. Arabophiles often even argued, following Michel Chevalier (the former Saint-Simonian thinker who had defended the Mexican expedition) and Saint-Simonian leader Prosper Enfantin, that merging aspects of "Oriental" Algerian culture into "Western" French society would resolve the spiritual and social problems besetting industrial France and lead to a more advanced civilizational synthesis.[150] But if they implied that the French might learn something from the Algerians, they nevertheless described Algerian society and culture as "behind" or "inferior to" France's. France would always serve as the senior—or, depending on the writer, male—partner in the relationship.[151]

The respective political orientations of advocates of assimilation and association also should not be oversimplified. Tellingly, Saint-Simonians also numbered among defenders of the colonists' position, reflecting the complexity of the movement and the divisions that had emerged within it. Procolonist Saint-Simonians tended to envision Algeria not as a place where "East" and "West" might converge but instead as a blank slate, which could be used to create ideal European communities that would resolve the inequality and conflicts besetting contemporary European society.[152] The skepticism that some Arabophiles expressed toward the assimilation demanded by colonists and their allies, on the other hand, did not always stem from their sympathy for indigenous communities but from their authoritarian political beliefs and skepticism of republican political practices.[153]

If advocates of "assimilation" and "association" thus had much in common, they nevertheless articulated divergent visions of Algeria's future. Advocates of association usually envisioned themselves as defenders of indigenous interests; they particularly worked to protect indigenous property rights, maintaining that it was unjust and impractical to strip Algerians of their land to benefit a handful of Europeans. They also tended to be skeptical of calls to expand Algeria's civil administration and increase political rights for the settler community. Instead, they usually defended military rule. This set of attitudes put them in conflict with ambitious settlers searching for more land and those who remained invested in the republican principles of representative government and assimilation.[154] Advocates of association were not able to structure the Algerian colony according to their ideals, but they came to shape the "dissenting voice" of the colonial administration during the 1850s.[155]

Napoleon III had devoted little attention to Algeria in the early years of his rule; as historian Annie Rey-Goldzeiguer has argued, he used it to solve domestic problems and reward allies.[156] His early decisions to revoke much of the legislation passed by the Second Republic when he became emperor had nevertheless alienated much of the settler population. The Second Republic declared Algeria an "integral" part of France, divided it into three *départements*, introduced a civil administration, invested colonists with the right to elect representatives to the National Assembly, and granted colonists who lived in European towns in "civil" or "pacified" territory the right to choose their own local officials.[157] The republic also proposed a large-scale official program of colonization that would move working-class families from French cities and settle them in agricultural communities in Algeria.[158] It simultaneously sought to weaken the authority of the much-hated bureaux arabes and even proposed to incorporate "mixed" and "Arab" territories beneath a centralized civil administration.[159] In 1851 Napoleon III undid some of this legislation: he restored the authority of the governor-general over "civil" territory, rescinded colonists' electoral rights, and promulgated a land law that sought to protect indigenous property.[160] Many colonists linked these measures—which they saw as oppressive—to the fact that the Algerian settlers had failed to endorse the plebiscite that made him emperor. Napoleon III, they felt, was prejudiced against them because of their opposition to his rule.[161]

It is unclear whether Napoleon III resented French colonists for their lukewarm support of his bid for imperial power. Throughout the early part of his reign, he mostly ignored Algeria. And despite settler complaints, his administration undertook several measures that further transformed the territory into a settler colony. Jacques Louis Randon, Algeria's governor-general, continued to expropriate land to make it available to European settlers.[162] The administration also turned over large tracts of territory to European corporations.[163] In 1858, moreover, Napoleon III even experimented once again with a civil administration headed by his cousin, Prince Napoléon-Jérôme , in response to the subjugation of Kabylie in 1857 and a scandal involving an officer of the bureaux arabes.[164] Napoléon-Jérôme, who governed the territory from Paris, sympathized with the settlers and sought to dismantle the traditional leadership systems in Algeria while sequestering additional Algerian property for European use. Unsurprisingly, these years of civil administration led to rising discontent among Algeria's military administration and indigenous populations.[165]

If Napoleon III devoted little attention to Algeria in the first decade of his reign, he nevertheless sought to make use of the territory as a political and military symbol, as his publicly cultivated relationship with Abd el-Kader demonstrates. Abd el-Kader was a *sharif*, or learned and devout man, whose prominent family belonged to a powerful tribe and ran a *zawiya*, or learning center, that served as the headquarters of the influential Qadiriyya Sufi brotherhood. He had come to rule much of western Algeria in the wake of the Ottoman state's collapse and then organized the primary resistance to the extension of French rule from 1839 to 1847.[166] He surrendered to the French army in 1847 and was imprisoned in the Château d'Amboise until 1852, when Napoleon III freed him in a highly publicized ceremony.[167] Napoleon III then organized a publicized tour across France for Abd el-Kader and his entourage, which included a military review, meetings with the director of the National Press and National Library, a performance of an orientalist symphony at the Academy of Music, and visits to Saint-Cloud and Versailles. The tour culminated with Abd el-Kader's decision to publicly vote in favor of the plebiscite that endorsed Napoleon III's decision to dismantle the Second Republic and establish the Second Empire.[168] Even after he went into exile in the Ottoman Empire, Abd el-Kader remained in public correspondence with Napoleon III's administration, which supplied him with a pension.[169]

The publicity around these ceremonies positioned Abd el-Kader as the noble, honorable, and learned representative of a "brave and barbaric"

FIGURE 1. Jean-Baptiste-Ange Tissier, *The Prince-President Frees Abd-el-Kader at the Chateau d'Amboise on October 16, 1852*. 1861. Oil on canvas, 350 x 465 cm. Inv. MV5030. Photo: Franck Raux. RMN-Grand Palais/ Art Resource, NY.

people who had fought against insurmountable odds and whose surrender had consolidated French control over Algeria. It thus used Napoleon III's decision to free Abd el-Kader to highlight the power of the French army and to portray French rule over Algeria as secure—but also as both just and merciful. Progovernment writers also used the occasion to compare Napoleon III to Charlemagne or to the Roman emperors and Abd el-Kader to Widukind or to the residents of ancient Spain, thereby positioning both figures in familiar stories that associated them with ancient imperial greatness.[170] This publicity was partly intended to enable the Second Empire to appropriate the July Monarchy's victory over Abd el-Kader; many of the news articles emphasized that Abd el-Kader's friendship with Napoleon III had led him to accept French sovereignty over Algeria and even describe himself as a French citizen who wanted to vote for the "sultan."[171] But because these publications effectively positioned Abd el-Kader as the symbol of the Arab people or even an "Arab nation," they also sat somewhat uneasily with the vision of Algeria as a settler colony.

Napoleon III's relationship with Abd el-Kader became, if anything, a greater source of prestige for his regime in 1860, after a series of religious conflicts between the Druze and Maronite Christian communities in the Mount Lebanon emirate, which was part of Ottoman Syria. Economic dislocations and shifting political and social structures, which had led to tensions between Maronite peasants and Druze landlords, drove these conflicts.[172] By May 1860 the conflict had transformed into open warfare, and it culminated in a massacre of five thousand to ten thousand Christians in Damascus—an event that prompted an international outcry. Abd el-Kader, who was living in Damascus at the time, used his prestige and personal army to protect thousands of Maronites and members of European consulates by guarding them at his house and guiding them out of the city.[173]

By July 1860 French newspapers filled with dramatized accounts of the massacres that positioned Maronites as the helpless victims of their violent Druze neighbors (often incorrectly describing them as "Muslims"). But they also focused on Abd el-Kader's heroism, often positioning him and his Algerian followers as the lone force that had defended the Christian community, even though other Muslim notables had also protected Christians.[174] Journalists emphasized Abd el-Kader's bravery and calm competence, contending that both had enabled him to navigate the crisis.[175] Many writers described his behavior as not merely an expression of Abd el-Kader's personal qualities, however, but as symptomatic of his "loyalty" or "gratitude" to France.[176] F. Camus, writing for the prestigious *Le journal des débats*, even suggested that it demonstrated that Abd el-Kader had "become convinced of our moral superiority."[177]

Some newspapers went beyond celebrating Abd el-Kader's defense of Christians in Syria and suggested that his actions had demonstrated that he was uniquely qualified to play a key role in Syria's future. As early reports of the conflicts in Syria came to France, Rochaïd Dahdah, a Maronite who edited *Birgys Barys*, an Arabic-language journal in Paris, suggested that European powers should restructure Syria as an "Arab empire" with Abd el-Kader at its head. This idea echoed through a number of publications in late 1860, thanks partly to an anonymous publication titled *Abd-el-Kader: Empereur d'Arabie*, which was reviewed in a number of prominent newspapers.[178] The publication contended that an Arab empire would "free the Arab race from Turkish domination" and "reconstruct Arab nationality," which would lead to progress and peace in the Muslim world.[179] As historian Charles-Robert Ageron has shown, this publication's vision of Syria's future sought to appeal to Napoleon III by invoking the language of nationality that the emperor had long used to describe France's foreign policy.[180] Many of the writers who advocated for the construction of an Arab empire under Abd el-Kader also saw the conflicts in Syria as an opportunity to extend French influence into

Syria. They contended that Abd el-Kader would serve as "an auxiliary to our civilization" and rule beneath French tutelage.[181]

It is not clear how seriously Napoleon III or the French administration was considering creating an Arab empire in Syria beneath Abd el-Kader's control in 1860.[182] But Napoleon III certainly used the crisis to tie his regime to Abd el-Kader even more tightly. *Le moniteur*, the official mouthpiece of the regime, published Abd el-Kader's letters about the crisis in Syria in translation, and in August 1860 Napoleon III granted him the Grand Cross of the Legion of Honor.[183] This celebration of Abd el-Kader was again at least partly calculating. Napoleon III saw the massacres as an opportunity to increase French influence in the Ottoman Empire by claiming that France was the historic protector of Syrian Maronites, who were in full communion with the Catholic Church.[184] He thus sent Édouard Thouvenel, the minister of foreign affairs, to convince Britain, Austria, Russia, and Prussia to coordinate a general European response to the massacres. These countries agreed to send a European force headed by Charles-Marie-Napoléon de Beaufort d'Hautpoul, a French general with military experience in Algeria, which would remain in Syria for six months and coordinate with the Ottoman government to restore order. Describing Abd el-Kader as a French auxiliary clearly contributed to this broader project of positioning France as the European power with privileged ties to Syria.

In practice, the Syrian expedition had limited effects. If Napoleon III also envisioned this multinational force as an opportunity to instigate a regime change—as he later would in Mexico—it was not particularly effective. The Ottoman government, which was concerned about European interference, worked quickly to independently impose order in Syria, punish the perpetrators, and minimize the influence of French officials. At the same time, other European powers were suspicious of France's ambitions and insisted that the force withdraw after six months instead of extending its mandate.[185] Abd el-Kader proved reluctant to work in tandem with Beaufort d'Hautpoul, and he also made it clear that he had no interest in serving as a French auxiliary in Syria.[186] But despite these failures, Napoleon III would return to this vision of an Arab empire under French tutelage in Algeria.

In the midst of these conversations about France's role in Syria, Napoleon III planned his first trip to Algeria in September 1860, marking the first time any head of state had visited Algeria since its conquest.[187] The trip occurred at a fraught moment. Discontent was rising among the Algerians under a civil administration that clearly represented settler interests, and at the same time the conflicts in Syria had reinvigorated discourses in both Algeria and the metropole that described Islam as an inherently problematic religion and as the cause of France's problems in the colony.[188] The trip was also a small affair because the death of the empress's elder sister cut it short after three days. Napoleon III and his wife stayed in Algiers, visited key landmarks, including the city cathedral and the casbah, met with important colonial officials, inspected Christian orphanages, and watched an Arab *fantasie*.[189] The military administration had additionally arranged for key Algerian notables and indigenous army squadrons to travel to Algiers to welcome the emperor.[190]

Despite the trip's short duration, Napoleon III was impressed by the Algerian notables that he had he met. When he returned to Paris, he again eliminated Algeria's civil administration—which he decided aligned too closely with settler interests—and reinstated the governor-general.[191] Against the advice of that new governor-general, he also invited several of the most prominent Algerian leaders to visit his palace at Compiègne in 1862. Like Abd el-Kader's visit a decade earlier, the meeting was highly ceremonial, but Napoleon III also consulted the visiting Algerian notables on property rights and administrative issues.[192] In the wake of their visit, Napoleon III began to develop his vision of the royaume arabe, which was influenced by his broader imperial ambitions in the Mediterranean and the ongoing conflicts over Algeria's land and administration.

As he formulated his vision of Algeria's future, Napoleon III again drew on the advice of Michel Chevalier, whose writing had formed the foundation of Saint-Simonian visions of the "Orient" in the 1830s and driven the Mexican intervention. He also borrowed from Arabophile writers and colonial administrators such as General Émile Fleury and Frédéric Lacroix, the former director of civilian affairs and prefect of Algiers who had helped organize an Arabophile circle in Paris.[193] But he was especially influenced by the ideas of Ismaël Urbain.[194] Urbain was born in French Guyana to a merchant from Marseille and a free woman of color. Educated in Marseille, he joined the Saint-Simonians and accompanied them when they went to Egypt. There he learned Arabic and converted to Islam. In 1840 he applied for the position of military interpreter in Algeria, where he married an Algerian woman.[195] During the 1840s and 1850s he took increasingly visible and prestigious positions in the colonial administration, becoming first the personal translator of the duc d'Aumale before being promoted to the Directorate of Algerian Affairs at the Ministry of War in Paris. Over this period, he also became a vocal advocate for indigenous rights in Algeria, publishing articles in metropolitan journals that were critical of French colonial policy.[196] He also began an active correspondence with Abd el-Kader.[197] After Napoleon III's visit to Algeria in 1860 and his pronouncement that France's primary obligation in

Algeria was to see to the needs of the Arab population, Urbain began to believe that the French government might listen to his ideas.[198] As a result, in the early 1860s, Urbain published a series of pamphlets about Algeria that came to Napoleon III's attention. These pamphlets argued that indigenous Algerians were capable of progress and that they deserved the protection of the state.[199] They also tried to create a path for Algerians toward political enfranchisement by defending their rights to their own civilization and implying that they would gradually assimilate into French culture.[200]

Napoleon III recorded his lengthiest reflections on his vision of Algeria in two much-noted letters to Aimable Pélissier, the governor-general of Algeria, which were published in *Le moniteur universel* and in pamphlets in 1863 and 1865. While most historians have usually read these two letters together, there are important differences between them, reflecting the shifts in Napoleon III's vision for Algeria over time. As other scholars have shown, Urbain's ideas echoed throughout both letters—an intellectual debt that Napoleon III acknowledged in his private correspondence.[201] The vocabulary that some French journalists had used to imagine France's role in Syria appeared as well.

The first letter began with an exposition on the current Algerian administration's flaws. It noted that despite complaints that the land available to settlers was insufficient, European colonists were cultivating only a small percentage of the available territory. Napoleon III argued that colonists' inability to make Algeria prosperous thus resulted not from restrictions on property, as some prosettler advocates had suggested, but from the fact that the colonial project was doomed. To make the territory viable, the French needed to invest not in settlers but in the Arab population. With encouragement, the nomadic groups that roamed the countryside would settle down and farm. Europeans, on the other hand, should work as technicians while facilitating the imperial project of "improving" Arabs and reconciling them to French rule.[202] The indigenous and colonist populations would thus complement rather than compete with one another.

After laying out the roles of both colonists and indigenous peoples (whom he grouped together as "Arabs"), Napoleon III's letter went on to redefine Algeria itself by declaring that it was "not a colony" but a royaume arabe.[203] His insistence that Algeria was not a colony was based on the belief that the term "colony" did not just signify a state's overseas territory; it also referred to a territory that a state intended to populate with its own citizens.[204] Because Napoleon III thought that indigenous peoples would remain the primary population of Algeria, he believed that calling it a colony would be misleading. His contention that the territory should instead be understood as a royaume arabe emerged from his commitment to the "politics of nationality."[205] Especially in light of his promise to a group of Arabs in 1865 that France did not invade Algeria "to destroy the nationality of a people," it seems clear that Napoleon III saw Algeria as a country of Arabs who had a cohesive sense of shared identity.[206] By calling Algeria a royaume arabe, Napoleon III was not only emphasizing the importance of the Arab population in the territory but also describing Algeria as an Arab nation. In his conclusion, he reaffirmed both the centrality of indigenous people to Algeria and his vision of the territory as an Arab nation. "The natives have the same right to my protection as the colonists do," he explained, "and I am as much the Emperor of the Arabs as I am the Emperor of the French."[207] This statement, when deployed with the description of Algeria as a royaume arabe, had wide-reaching implications. If, as the letter contended, Napoleon III was equally the emperor of both the French and the Arab peoples, it followed that he was also the emperor of both the French and Algerian or Arab nations. This formulation proposed to reorient understandings of the North African territory, its relationship to the French nation, and the position of both France and Algeria in the French Empire.

Napoleon III's contention that Algeria was an "Arab nation" distinct from the "French nation" deviated from the vision of the French Second Empire that he had long promoted. Early in his reign, Napoleon III had treated the "French nation" and the "French Empire" as functional equivalents: he had used the term "empire" to designate a specific kind of political program in France, mobilizing it in opposition to "republic" or "kingdom." But according to this new model, the French Empire was a multinational entity, composed of distinct nations ruled by the same central administration. Beneath this new regime, "empire" would refer both to a form of domestic political organization and to a way of ordering different peoples beyond the metropole beneath one governing body.[208] The model thus collapsed domestic policies and France's relationship to overseas territories together into one overarching imperial entity. It also extended the reach of Napoleon III's faltering empire, casting it as larger than the French nation itself. The French nation would continue to occupy the privileged position in this constellation of nations, but it would stand beneath a wider imperial structure.

This vision of empire also reflected Napoleon III's desire to reconcile the "politics of nationality" with an imperial structure—an inherently contradictory undertaking. Napoleon III had long criticized the Russian, Austrian, and Ottoman Empires because they failed to respect the rights of different peoples to rule themselves, and he called, at least privately, for their dissolution into nations.[209] In his letters and speeches, Napoleon III argued that the French Empire could respect the rights of nationalities in a way that other empires could not since it was both "civilizing" and "progressive."[210] By indicating that the empire would help the Arab people "regenerate" just as the Romans under Julius Caesar enabled the Gauls to "develop" into a great people, Napoleon III portrayed the French Empire as a catalyst that would enable Arab nationality to emerge.[211] The French Empire's control over Algeria (and, presumably, the other parts of the Ottoman Empire that Napoleon III hoped to annex) would therefore not oppress Arab nationality but "liberate" it.

This view of the Second Empire and its relationship to Algeria echoed Napoleon III's vision of the Second Empire's relationship to Mexico. Both latinité and Napoleon III's plans for a multinational Mediterranean empire cast the influence of the Second Empire beyond the borders of the French nation. Both also sought to imagine more indirect ways of projecting that influence that invoked neither the discredited colonialism of the ancien régime, based on slavery, trade monopolies, and political subjugation nor the settler colonialism that had proven so fraught in Algeria. These visions of indirect empire were designed to avoid the charges of political despotism and aggressive militarism that were still sometimes associated with the colonialism of the ancien régime and Napoleonic empire, even as they remained based on military force. They claimed to be liberatory, as they were ostensibly grounded in a defense of nationality and a progressive vision of history, but at the same time both reified Bonapartist principles of populist and authoritarian politics. And, finally, both drew on the legacy of Rome and the memory of Napoleon I, albeit in different ways: latinité brought nations with a Roman heritage together and united them beneath the leadership of Napoleon III, whereas Napoleon III's Mediterranean empire would place territory that had once belonged to Rome into a new iteration of the ancient multiethnic empire. These programs thus configured the relationship between "nation" and "empire" differently. In Mexico, Napoleon III positioned empire as both a national and global project; it involved a set of domestic policies that could strengthen different branches of one "Latin" race while informally uniting them. In Algeria, he positioned empire as a multinational political formation that could incorporate different peoples or races—much as some commentators had suggested that he might in Syria.

The differences between these programs stemmed partly from circumstance: Napoleon III did not plan to conquer Mexico, and Algeria was already a French possession. But they also emerged from different understandings of Mexico and Algeria. Napoleon III treated Mexico as part of a "Latin" civilization or race shared with France, while he saw Algeria as "Arab" in character.

Although Napoleon III and his supporters described Mexico as "less civilized" than France and held it up as an example of the Latin race's decay, they still treated it as connected to Europe—which was, according to Saint-Simonian logic, the pinnacle of nineteenth-century civilization.[212] Algeria, as a non-European nation, was "less civilized" still and could thus be incorporated into a multinational French Empire because it required direct tutelage.

These divergent visions of Mexico and Algeria were, in some sense, arbitrary. Both Mexico and Algeria included a mixture of Europeans and indigenous peoples. But in Mexico, Napoleon III and his supporters ignored the indigenous population and classified the country as "Latin." In Algeria, on the other hand, Napoleon III swept aside European settlers and non-Arab indigenous groups to describe the territory as "Arab."[213] The apparent contradiction in these approaches may have stemmed partly from demographics; there were more people of European descent in Mexico than there were in Algeria.[214] Napoleon III also had an especially contentious relationship with Algerian settlers, and he had developed a personal interest in his Arab subjects.[215] These differences between Napoleon III's visions for Mexico and Algeria thus demonstrate how local circumstances and domestic politics helped shape metropolitan conceptions of empire in the mid-nineteenth century. Notably, even though the Mexican expedition and the reorganization of Algeria occurred at approximately the same time, Napoleon III used them to articulate distinct if overlapping visions of a French Empire—both of which would prove to be equally controversial.

Opposition to the Royaume Arabe

Napoleon III's new description of the Second Empire's relationship to Algeria was unpopular among the colonists who had settled there during the thirty-odd years since its conquest—at least in part because it was accompanied by the *sénatus-consulte* of April 22, 1863, which sought (but failed) to make it more difficult for settlers to expropriate tribal lands.[216] Colonists wrote petitions, protested in journals, posted placards on buildings, and gathered in squares to protest.[217] Napoleon III's claim that Algeria was "not a colony" but a "royaume arabe" especially attracted anger. A petition in the Algerian city of Bône—published in a local newspaper with four hundred signatures—condemned the royaume arabe as "a nation without nationality, an agglomeration of *hordes sauvage*, all enemies of one another."[218] It thus insisted that Algeria could not be a nation because none of its inhabitants were united; they were, depending on the signatories' meaning of *sauvage*, either too "wild" or too "savage" to identify with one another. *Le courrier d'Algérie* also condemned the proposal in a scathing critique. "It is no longer the Arabs who will become French," the editors complained, "but the French who will become Arabs."[219] By categorizing Algeria as a royaume arabe, the emperor was collapsing the differences between colonists and the colonized and subsuming the Europeans into the indigenous population. From these reactions, it is clear that many colonists saw Napoleon III's reimagining of Algeria's relationship with France as tantamount to abandoning the nation's civilizing project and dooming the territory to "barbarism."

Settlers extended their discontent from the colonial press into Parisian pamphlets that were less inflammatory in tone. Because they were seeking a wide audience and wanted to escape censorship laws, many did not criticize the emperor but instead blamed Ismaël Urbain for misleading him—much as the press under the ancien régime tended to blame the king's behavior on poor advisers.[220] These pamphleteers tried to demonstrate to Napoleon III and the metropole that, contrary to Arabophile claims, European colonization alone could make Algeria prosperous. Many colonists argued that Napoleon III's royaume arabe was based on a misunderstanding of Algeria and the Arab population. Auguste-Hubert Warnier, a Saint-Simonian and physician who had worked closely with Urbain in the 1840s but who became, over the 1850s, one of the most prominent lobbyists for colonists' interests, claimed that it made no sense to transform Algeria into a "royaume arabe" because many of the indigenous Algerians were not Arabs.[221] The indigenous population was multiethnic, which meant that it had no unity—or a sense of national identity. Warnier thus condemned not only the emperor's plan to restructure French rule in Algeria; he also attacked the intellectual structure behind that plan. He maintained that France should incorporate Algeria instead of treating it as a separate "nation" only connected through an overarching imperial system.[222]

Pamphlets by colonist writers found an audience in the metropole, especially among republican groups. Republican newspapers were sympathetic to the colonist position partly because they were ready to endorse anything that cast Napoleon III in a bad light. But the affinity between the groups was also due to the fact that many colonists seeking publication in the metropole were republicans who had been deported to Algeria in 1851 and 1852; the heads of *Le courrier de l'Algérie*, *L'indépendant*, and *L'écho d'Oran*—three of the major Algerian newspapers—were deportees.[223] These writers thus drew on republican language to reject Napoleon III's vision of the French Empire and to propose a different model for Algeria's future. Pamphleteers mobilized assimilation's republican associations to portray the colonists as underdogs in a fight against imperial despotism. The colonists, they maintained, were clamoring for assimilation to secure civil rights from a repressive administration. Assimilation, they insisted, would also liberate the Algerians by freeing them from their despotic chiefs and religion.[224] If Napoleon III made the territory into a royaume arabe, on the other hand, all its inhabitants would continue to live under an oppressive political system.

Most republican newspapers in France did not intervene in this debate about Algeria's future, but they offered their publications as a platform for colonists. By the end of 1863, the opposition to the royaume arabe was becoming a component of metropolitan republican thought.[225] The colonists' decision to send a delegation to the Senate's debates over Arab property led by Warnier and Jules Duval, a liberal economist with Fourierist ties and another vocal advocate for colonists' interests, brought further attention to the colonist cause in the metropole, even outside of republican circles.[226] Debates about Algeria's future—and its implications for the wider French Empire—were not front-page news in Paris, but Napoleon III's Algerian policies became a target of the emerging political opposition.

These critiques attracted enough attention that the leader of the Arabophile circle in Paris and an ally of Urbain, Frédéric Lacroix, decided that it was necessary to condemn them.[227] Lacroix approached the debates surrounding Napoleon III's royaume arabe cautiously. In fact, he only used the term once in the ninety-two-page pamphlet—to note that Algeria was a "royaume arabe . . . as India is a *royaume indien*."[228] By comparing Napoleon III's conception of Algeria as a royaume arabe to the British system in India, Lacroix defended his use of the term, discredited colonist interpretations of it, and domesticated its implications. If both Algeria and India could be called royaumes, as Lacroix contended, then the term just signified a territory where indigenous peoples were the most important part of the population. It did not imply, as some colonists had argued, that Napoleon III would eliminate the colonist population or force it to "become Arab." According to Lacroix's pamphlet, the decision to call Algeria a royaume arabe simply reflected the territory's demographic composition.

Lacroix's defense of the term "royaume arabe" diverged from Napoleon III's vision of an empire that would span across nations. First, by placing Algeria alongside a set of territories that the British did not describe as a nation and claiming they were both "royaumes," Lacroix undermined Napoleon III's association of "nation" with "royaume arabe." According to Lacroix, a royaume arabe was just a type of overseas possession and not tied to any conception of "nation." Indeed, Lacroix made it clear that he thought that Algeria would only temporarily remain a royaume arabe. He implied that Algeria would slowly assimilate into France—even if he disagreed with the colonizers about the pace and methods of the process.

As Lacroix's treatment of the term "royaume arabe" makes clear, even he (one of the Arabophiles who had helped shape Napoleon III's thinking about Algeria) had hesitations about the emperor's vision of Algeria as an Arab nation ruled by a multinational French Empire. This hesitation stemmed partly from the belief of Lacroix—and most other Arabophiles, including Urbain—that the goal of association was to reconcile the Algerians to French rule, however slowly. Napoleon III's conception of empire did not seem to envision this kind of future assimilation, which left Arabophiles like Lacroix and Urbain concerned about how Arabs would ever become equal in the eyes of the state.[229]

Napoleon III's vision of colonization, Algeria, and the French Empire thus attracted minimal support in France and among the settlers. There is evidence that at least some Algerian notables welcomed elements of his promises, however. Si Hassan, a writer for *Le Mobacher*, the official bilingual newspaper founded by Ismaël Urbain and produced by the colonial administration, sought to publish a translation of Napoleon III's letter in Arabic—a request that Governor-General Pélissier, who disapproved of the royaume arabe, denied. But Si Hassan distributed the translation to mosques and stores in major Algerian cities. And even in the countryside, most Algerian communities contained at least one person who could translate the proclamation from French. In response to the letter, key Algerian leaders, including Si Mohamed Saïd ben Ali Chérif, who had visited Compiègne in 1862, sent tokens of appreciation to Napoleon III—or, alternatively, penned letters asking him to rectify long-standing wrongs committed by the colonial administration.[230] Several Algerian notables even tried to organize prayers in mosques across Algeria in Napoleon III's honor.[231] The official reports from the military administration also emphasized the general "immense favorable response" among Algeria's different indigenous populations to both Napoleon's letter and to the 1863 sénatus-consulte.[232]

Even among initially sympathetic Algerian communities, however, enthusiasm for Napoleon III's proposals faded quickly in response to the violence of the settler opposition and the colonial administration's clear ongoing commitment to cantonment.[233] In early 1864 the Ouled Sidi Cheikh (also known as the Awlad Sidi al-Shaykh), a powerful tribal confederation in southern Oran, rose in revolt against colonial policies that continued to undermine the structure of tribal life and impoverish indigenous Algerians. The military responded to the uprising with a violent and terrible repression that lasted two years. The revolt also undermined Arabophile military officers' enthusiasm for Napoleon III's proposed policies.[234]

In response to the entrenched opposition of the colonists and many members of the colonial administration, along with the decline in support among military officers, Napoleon III modified his vision of Algeria's relationship to France and empire in his second 1865 letter. Written after a longer trip to Algeria earlier that same year, it backed away from many of the positions laid out in the first letter. Napoleon III now contended that compromise was essential to Algeria's success because it had three identities at once: it was "at the same time a royaume arabe, a European colony, and a French military camp."[235] To secure Algeria's future, these elements should work together because they depended on one another.

To some degree, the letter's description of the respective positions of indigenous Algerians and European colonists echoed the 1863 letter. The differences lay in the emphasis. In 1865 Napoleon III treated the colonists as more important to Algeria's future than he had two years earlier. Even though he continued to insist that the territory was a royaume arabe, he transformed the implications of the term by claiming that Algeria was also a colony and a camp. Within the context of this trifecta, "royaume arabe" no longer implied that Arabs in Algeria constituted their own nation. Instead, the term simply referred to the parts of Algeria mostly inhabited by Arabs. Napoleon III did not withdraw his earlier contention that Arabs had their own nationality.[236] But instead of promising to preserve that nationality, he indicated that the French could suppress it as long as they tried to "civilize and improve" the Arab people.[237] He thus proposed active steps to assimilate the indigenous population into the French nation, claiming that for the sake of future peace in Algeria "the Algerians [must be] declared French, because Algeria is a French territory." This did not mean, he noted, that Algerians would have to accept French law or traditions. They could continue to follow their own customs unless they asked to become citizens. At the same time, however, Napoleon III tried to attach all indigenous Algerians more firmly to the French state. Even as he allowed the Algerians to live within their traditional social structures and according to their own laws, he ensured that they would find contact with French institutions inescapable.[238]

In 1863 Napoleon III had sought to increase his empire's prestige and redefine its meaning by expanding its reach beyond France. He had begun to describe "empire" not only as a form of political organization in the metropole but also as a way of ordering different peoples beneath one governing structure. By incorporating Algeria (and perhaps other North African nations) into the empire while preserving Algeria's identity, he had hoped to associate his rule with that of his uncle while preserving his reputation as a "champion of nationalities." But under the 1865 model, indigenous Algerians would not retain a separate identity. Instead, they would slowly assimilate into the French nation. Napoleon III's second letter expressed the hope that over time, more Arabs would see the benefit of French liberties and law and therefore choose to adopt French citizenship for themselves. As a result, the royaume arabe would start to disappear as Algeria merged with France. This vision of Algeria's future thus collapsed Napoleon III's earlier distinction between "nation" and "empire." The French Empire again became coterminous with the French nation—it only signified a particular way of ruling France. Algeria became a temporary anomaly on the nation's borders, eventually destined to merge with it.

Even though Napoleon III's second letter backed away from the claims of his first in several important ways, most colonists found Napoleon III's new ideas similar to his old ones. Joseph Guérin, the editor of *L'akhbar*, claimed, for example, that the emperor's letter—especially his description of Algeria as a "royaume arabe"—was dangerous because it would lead "inevitably to the declaration of Arab nationality." The very idea of the royaume arabe was for Guérin incompatible with Algeria's status as a French territory.[239]

The second letter also generated a new wave of criticism aimed at metropolitan audiences.[240] The level of negative metropolitan newspaper coverage of Napoleon III's policies in Algeria was in fact higher in 1865 than it had been in 1863, partly reflecting the ongoing revolt in the south. But it also stemmed from the convergence of Napoleon III's second trip to Algeria with Abd el-Kader's first visit to Paris after the massacres in Syria. The visit itself was highly ceremonial and received largely positive press coverage that echoed many of the themes that had appeared in French papers in 1860; journalists continued to emphasize Abd el-Kader's heroic role in Syria and position him as an auxiliary of France. Several once again suggested that Abd el-Kader should serve as the head of a French-affiliated Arab empire in Syria, although this opinion seems to have been less widely expressed, probably partly as a result of the problems facing the Mexican expedition at the time.[241] The controversy thus stemmed not directly from the activities of either Abd el-Kader or Napoleon III's government but from an article published by Émile de Girardin, an influential journalist and the editor of the widely circulating penny press *La presse*.[242] He suggested that instead of constituting an Arab empire beneath Abd el-Kader in Syria, the French government should consider asking Abd el-Kader to serve as the "Vice Roy" of an Algerian nation that would function as a vassal state to France and "abandon" all attempts to colonize the territory.[243] This article created a sensation in both France and among the settlers in Algeria, partly because it echoed rumors that had already been circulating about Napoleon III's plans for the territory during his second trip to Algeria.[244]

There is no evidence that these rumors were true. Napoleon III was still trying to convince Abd el-Kader to serve as a French auxiliary in Syria during the 1865 trip, and he had no intention of asking him to govern Algeria.[245] Girardin also had a complicated relationship with Napoleon III's administration and certainly was not a mouthpiece for the regime. But he had been involved in planning Abd el-Kader's trip, and a number of commentators in both France and Algeria interpreted the article as an expression of Napoleon III's plans for the territory—even after an article in *Le moniteur* denied it.[246] For some commentators in France and Algeria, Abd el-Kader's visit and Girardin's coverage revealed Napoleon

FIGURE 2. Colonist opponents to the royaume arabe also objected to the press coverage of Napoleon III's second visit to Algeria, which they argued overrepresented indigenous Algerians and obfuscated settlers' accomplishments. This sketch, which appeared in the popular journal *L'illustration*, exemplifies the type of image they objected to. It places figures marked as indigenous Algerians in the foreground. *Visite de l'empereur à Sidi-Bel-Abbès*, *L'illustration* (June 3, 1865), 360.

III's ongoing commitment to a vision of Algeria as an Arab nation and to authoritarian—even ancien régime—politics. Instead of encouraging the development of representative government in Algeria, these writers implied, Napoleon III remained invested in his relationships with "feudal chiefs."[247]

The relatively high level of critical coverage of the royaume arabe in the metropolitan press was also a result of the colonists' publicity strategy—especially the work of Jules Duval, the Fourierist who had defended the interests of colonists before the Senate in 1863. He used his relatively prominent position as the editor of *L'économiste française* to try to convince metropolitan audiences that Napoleon III's policies were problematic not just for Algerian settlers but for metropolitan France as well.[248] Like others before him, he condemned the emperor's administrative policies and maintained that the term "royaume arabe" was technically inaccurate and potentially dangerous.[249] But he took his criticism of the emperor a step further after 1865 by contending that Napoleon III's misguided attempt to redefine the territory reflected the incompatibility of colonies and empires. Napoleon III's Algerian policies, he argued, suffered from "colonial Caesarism."[250] "Colonial Caesarism," Duval maintained, was not unique to Napoleon III; it prevented all absolutist governments—whether monarchies or empires—from understanding or operating colonies.[251] To thrive, he argued, colonists needed "complete liberty," which was a guarantee that absolutist governments were unable to provide. For Algeria to succeed, Duval claimed, France had to change its Bonapartist empire into a republican regime that would allow for freedom of initiative. His critique thus sought to pull apart Napoleon III's association of "domestic empire" with "colonial empire," implying that they were intrinsically opposed enterprises that required distinct political institutions.

As these responses make clear, colonists and republicans mostly did not distinguish between Napoleon III's use of "royaume arabe" in 1863 and 1865—even though his second public letter took measures to assimilate the indigenous population into France. Duval's condemnation of both Napoleon III's "royaume arabe" and his empire, moreover, marked a new stage in this opposition. Duval's interpretation of Napoleon III's empire described its character as inherently oppressive and antiprogressive, redeploying an older liberal critique of imperial politics that proved increasingly popular in an era of rising discontent. Equally important, Duval's insistence that Napoleon III's empire was incompatible with the colonial project introduced a division between "domestic" and "overseas" empire that the emperor had rejected.

The Imperial Legacy of Napoleon III in Republican France

In 1865, amid these debates, the Senate passed a law granting the indigenous populations in Algeria French nationality while denying them citizenship on the basis of their adherence to Muslim and Mosaic law.[252] This law was greeted with mixed emotions by the Arabophiles who had long influenced Napoleon III's thinking on Algeria.[253] On one hand, the law gave Algerians an official status for the first time, and it granted them access to public service employment.[254] It also technically opened an official avenue for pursuing French citizenship, albeit one that required Algerians to renounce religious law in exchange for political rights—a prospect that the vast majority of Algerians were uninterested in and that neither the military administration nor the settlers welcomed.[255] The 1865 sénatus-consulte thus marked a definitive turn away from any idea that Algeria was an Arab nation and granted indigenous people little security in exchange. In the long run, moreover, it would affirm the idea that Islam was incompatible with French citizenship and solidify the inferior legal and political status of most Algerians living under French rule. As many in the settler community had hoped, the French state would continue to build a colonial regime designed to serve the needs of a minority European population clearly delineated from displaced and economically impoverished indigenous communities.[256]

Napoleon III would remain in power in France for five more years, but after 1865 he increasingly turned away from Algeria. He became caught up in European politics and the French expedition in Mexico; he also became ill. Moreover, from 1866 to 1868, Algeria faced a series of natural disasters (earthquakes, fires, and especially famine) whose devastating effects on Algerian communities partly resulted from French policies that had undermined indigenous ecological, economic, and social systems.[257] These disasters further weakened Algerians' resilience in the face of colonial rule and undercut whatever enthusiasm some Algerian notables might have had for Napoleon III's policies.[258] In the face of both indigenous resistance and the clear lack of enthusiasm from the colonial administration, Napoleon III's plans to improve schooling, alleviate poverty, and "liberate" the indigenous population largely evaporated.[259] His dreams of constructing a new kind of French Empire also disappeared, especially after the overthrow of Maximillian in Mexico. By the late 1860s his "empire"—apart from Cochinchina—was once again a primarily domestic affair.

On a practical level, it is thus clear that Napoleon III's initial proposed reforms failed in Algeria much like his military expedition failed in Mexico. The royaume arabe did not protect and strengthen an Arab nation any more than establishing a Latin empire brought peace, order, and "regeneration" to Mexico. Napoleon III's two major reforms—the sénatus-consultes of 1863 and 1865—had first inadvertently made it easier for settlers to claim Algerian land and then undermined the idea that Algerians had their own national identity. In both Mexico and Algeria, Napoleon III's attempt to recast the French Empire had fallen apart in the face of local resistance. Napoleon III's failures abroad also reverberated back into the metropole. The Mexican expedition especially played a key role in discrediting Bonapartist empire at home.

Napoleon III and his supporters had used ideas from the complicated, overlapping, and often internally contradictory traditions of Saint-Simonianism, romantic nationalism, Orientalism, and racial thought to explain and justify their understandings of empire in Mexico and Algeria. At the same time, they also sought to navigate between contemporary beliefs about ancient Rome, the colonial empires of the ancien régime, the revolutions of 1789 and 1848, and the first Napoleonic empire. In his attempts to project French power overseas, Napoleon III thus invoked memories of Roman expansion, French imperial greatness under Napoleon I, and France's revolutionary identity as a defender of liberty while avoiding negative narratives about revolutionary radicalism, Napoleonic warmongering, and imperial despotism. He positioned empire as a force that could impose order, create peace, and liberate nationalities around the world. At the same time, he reconciled French political control over or interference in other nations with this commitment to national liberation by invoking a vision of civilizational and racial hierarchy that he imagined in some mixture of cultural, religious, historical, and political terms. Napoleon III sometimes described this hierarchy chronologically—by contending that the French were "ahead" of Mexicans and Algerians—and sometimes instead used the motif of decay and regeneration to explain it.

These visions of empire, nation, and race in Mexico and Algeria created conceptual contradictions or uncertainties and usually did not reflect the way that most inhabitants of either Mexico or Algeria understood their own identities. Most Mexican liberals rejected the idea of latinité, and even the Mexican conservatives who had helped author the idea usually described it in less hierarchal and more Catholic terms than French officials did. And while some Algerian notables welcomed Napoleon III's proposed reforms, Napoleon III's contention that Algeria was an Arab nation always rested uneasily with the complex identities that indigenous communities embraced. This disconnect between Napoleon III's imperial vision and the self-understanding of many Mexican and Algerian people posed a legitimacy problem for an empire whose claim to sovereignty was grounded in the language of popular national self-determination—although in Algeria especially such a problem remained mostly theoretical thanks to the opposition of the settler community and the highest levels of the colonial administration.

Napoleon III's ideas about empire in fact had few, if any, permanent effects on the operations of colonial rule on the ground in either Mexico or Algeria. Even in the first half of the 1860s, before both endeavors collapsed, the vision of empire that he promoted bore little resemblance to French policy in either place. But Napoleon III's attempt to recast France as a multinational Mediterranean empire destined to regenerate other Latin peoples by exporting its Bonapartist imperial system to other parts of the world nevertheless had consequences for French political and imperial identities. If Napoleon III's vision of empire in both Mexico and Algeria was partly rooted in evocations of earlier imperial systems, it also foreshadowed the model of the "protectorate"—territories ruled through indirect influence—that British colonial advocates in particular would embrace in the last quarter of the nineteenth century.[260] As French republicans sought to both compete with Britain and justify the expansion of French overseas territory during the 1870s and 1880s, they would remain troubled by these arguments over empire and Napoleon III's attempt to tie imperial overseas expansion to Bonapartist politics.

Chapter 2

Redefining Republic and Empire in France after 1870–71

The Franco-Prussian War lasted barely more than half a year. France declared war against Prussia in July 1870, and by late January 1871 it had already lost. Violence sputtered on in the form of internal revolution and civil war for several months afterward, but even this second, more divisive wave of conflict ended by May. Despite its brief duration, however, the war and the Paris Commune that followed it fractured the French political landscape. The defeat brought an end to the empire that had ruled the country for twenty years, but the republic that replaced it did not emerge out of national consensus: it remained intact because the country's main antirepublican political groups—the Legitimists, Orleanists, and Bonapartists—failed to agree on how to set up another kind of government. Over the next ten years, intellectuals, writers, artists, and politicians worked to fill the void left by the empire's collapse by attempting to popularize alternative models of political organization and visions of the nation, often in competition with one another.[1]

These ongoing political conflicts were bound up in a broader struggle over how to remember the Second Empire, the war, and the Commune. In the years following the *année terrible*, politicians, writers, artists, and journalists produced innumerable newspaper articles, pamphlets, monuments, novels, and histories devoted to explaining the events of 1870–71.[2] These cultural productions, however, did not interpret the year in the same way. Authors, intellectuals, and artists crafted works that advanced their own perspectives, which were often tied to their respective ideological positions, personal experiences, and aesthetic preferences.

In recent years, the memory of the Franco-Prussian War has attracted new scholarly attention.[3] But while historians have emphasized the ways in which commemoration of the war became caught up in the Third Republic's divisive political culture, few have looked at the effects of these ongoing struggles over politics and memory on popular understandings of "empire" and its relationship to both domestic and overseas policies in the early 1870s. But narratives about the war and the Commune often used the events to articulate judgments about the relative value of empire and republic as forms of political organization. Republican writers, politicians, intellectuals, and artists attempted to mobilize private memories of 1870–71 into a collective discourse that would unite the French beneath the new republican state while their Bonapartist counterparts wove alternative narratives to discredit it and celebrate the empire in its place. Monarchists, on the other hand, tried to use the war's events to discredit both republic and empire. These competing accounts served to solidify a diametrical opposition between the concepts of empire and republic—even if the French continued to disagree about the content, value, and significance of the two terms. And while these arguments about "empire" and "republic" were mostly grounded in domestic political conflict, the emerging dichotomy between them created political and conceptual problems for republican intellectuals who believed that the new republic should expand its colonial empire.

The debates over the relationship between empire, republic, and the events of 1870–71 gained strength from the way that the war and the Commune intersected with ongoing political tensions. Beginning in the early 1860s, left-leaning political opposition groups had become increasingly critical of the empire's policies and institutions. With the looser press laws established in the early years of the "liberal" empire, these groups could popularize their opinions by publishing them in newspapers. More open elections also enabled them to elect more deputies to the Corps législatif—a trend culminating in 1869, when the opposition won majorities in cities across France. These opposition delegates, moreover, included radicals such as Léon Gambetta who refused to acknowledge the regime's legitimacy.[4] Napoleon III's disastrous intervention in Mexico, combined with his unpopular efforts in Italy and his policies in Algeria, had undermined the support that he had built up in the first years of his reign. In the face of this rising opposition, Napoleon III found it difficult to impose his personal will on government policy—as the mixed results of his attempt to establish a royaume arabe in Algeria made clear.

Despite the growing opposition, Napoleon III's rule was not on the verge of collapse. In response to the agitation from the left-leaning opposition during the elections, he issued liberal reforms in September 1869 meant to win over moderates and distance them from their more radical counterparts.[5] These reforms were relatively successful; multiple prominent liberals came to support the empire. In 1870 Napoleon III issued a plebiscite asking whether the French supported these reforms and a new constitution—an implicit referendum on the regime. Outside of Paris, the response was positive: most voters voted in favor of the empire, including many moderates and liberals. The most negative responses to the plebiscite came from Algeria, where most colonists voted against it.[6] The resounding success of the plebiscite enabled the empire to reestablish its legitimacy in the face of the 1869 elections that had elected so many members of the opposition. The relationship of Napoleon III's political system to overseas territory or to other types of empire remained unresolved. But in the eyes of much of the population, he had successfully defined the empire domestically as a political model that allowed for some democratic political participation and even increased overt political dissent but that continued to combine "liberty" with "order."[7]

At first, the war with Prussia only consolidated the empire's appeal. Once the conflict seemed inevitable, it attracted widespread popular support and produced a mood of political consensus.[8] Many opposition groups argued that the French needed to put aside their political differences for the duration of the conflict.[9] But this consensus only lasted while French prospects in the war seemed good. Losses frayed the empire's reputation, as it became clear that the army had a poorly structured command system, not enough soldiers, disorganized supply lines, and an insufficient number of railroads to move the troops to the front.[10]

Napoleon III's surrender after the disastrous battle of Sedan—alongside one hundred thousand of his troops—destroyed what credibility the Second Empire had left. Napoleon III's popularity had always depended partly on the myth of his uncle's military greatness, and this display of military incompetence weakened the mythic links. Much of the population in Paris, Lyon, and Marseilles took to the streets, demanding the institution of a new republic. On September 4, the liberal opposition in the Corps législatif staged a coup d'état in Paris—partly to prevent the popular, more radical revolution that seemed to be brewing in the city—and proclaimed the establishment of the Third Republic. The new provisional government primarily included moderate republicans, who quickly organized themselves into the Government of National Defense.[11]

If the French loss at Sedan marked the end of the Second Empire, it did not signal an auspicious beginning for the new republic. Outside of major cities, most people only accepted the republic as a temporary measure because the country was in crisis.[12] The new Government of National Defense even struggled to maintain the support of the urban groups that had brought it into power because those groups wanted more radical reforms than the ministers were prepared to offer. The government's decision to continue the war even though most of the army was out of commission also proved disastrous.[13] The outcome of the republic's first official elections—held in February 1871, shortly after the surrender—reflected widespread discontent; they returned a majority of Legitimist and Orleanist candidates, drawn primarily from rural areas.[14] The Third Republic's first elected legislature was thus dominated by monarchist deputies, which hardly seemed to assure the republic's future. Antirepublican deputies would dominate the government until 1879. These electoral results satisfied neither republicans nor conservative groups, who felt confined within a political system they disliked.[15]

The Parisian Left's declaration of the Paris Commune in March 1871 further destabilized the new republic. The Commune lasted barely more than two months, but its legacy left a profound mark on French politics. The government declared that the Communards were criminals and convinced the Prussians to release the French army from prisoner-of-war camps so that it could crush them. During the "Bloody Week" in May, the newly reconstituted army slaughtered at least twenty thousand Parisians and arrested nearly fifty thousand more. Many of those arrested were incarcerated in work camps in Paris or New Caledonia.[16]

Because Communards described themselves as republicans and claimed the revolutionary tradition as their own, the Commune raised particularly thorny questions for moderate republicans. Many republican deputies supported the conservative government's campaign to crush the Commune and were eager to portray Communards as either socialist radicals or degenerates to disassociate themselves from the uprising. But even though this distancing largely succeeded—most of the population remembered the Commune as a socialist, not republican, movement—some Communard policies and decisions continued to haunt republican memory and politics throughout the late nineteenth century.

The French spent the thirty years following the Commune working out exactly what the new French "republic" meant and how it should be organized. The republicans themselves disagreed about this question, as they navigated between democratic impulses, fear of the mob, belief in the guiding power of educated elites, and concern about the continued appeal of monarchism, Bonapartism, and the Catholic Church.[17] Their political opponents also lacked unity: monarchists argued about which Bourbon descendent to support, while Bonapartists disagreed about whether to defend Napoleon III. This chapter analyzes the ensuing political debates over "empire," "republic," and the legacy of the année terrible, examining how they played out across newspapers, political pamphlets, and novels published in the early years of the Third Republic. It shows that in this moment of political transition, the meanings of both "empire" and "republic" were fluid and potentially associated with defeat and civil war. It was for this reason, I argue, that republicans were so eager to define the republic against an empire that they held responsible for the disasters of 1870–71—even as such definitions raised questions about the republic's relationship with Algeria and other overseas territories.

Visions of Empire in the New Republic

In the wake of defeat and civil war, politicians, intellectuals, and writers of a variety of ideological stripes sought to determine the cause for France's embarrassing defeat and destructive civil war. These attempts were controversial, as many blamed the defeat not on German tactics but on different groups or trends in French society. Some held the entire army responsible, while others charged its generals or administrators. Others blamed Napoleon III or the Second Empire, while some held the Government of National Defense at fault for the final devastation. Still others maintained that there was something wrong with the nation itself. Due partly to these differences in opinion, even by 1880 the French had not reached a consensus on the causes for defeat. But if these debates remained unresolved, they nevertheless shaped the new ways that intellectuals and politicians thought about the meanings of "empire" and "republic."

This debate over the political and national implications of French defeat played out most explicitly in newspapers and especially political pamphlets. Pamphlets, because they were not published regularly and could be smuggled across borders, were more difficult to censor than newspapers, which after the Commune were placed under the same censorship regime that Napoleon III had used during the 1860s.[18] But both types of writing were usually deeply partisan; their authors were often politicians of different stripes. These publications thus expressed the opinions of a relatively narrow segment of highly politically engaged metropolitan elites, but the vibrancy of the conversation also reflected the expansion and ever-increasing economic and political power of the French bourgeoisie—a demographic shift that had begun under the Second Empire—along with growing literacy rates, which expanded the potential reading audience for these arguments.[19] These publications could also have different purposes. Some were aimed at the highly educated, while others sought to appeal to wider audiences. Some were intended to rally those who shared beliefs similar to those of the author, while others were intended to convince those on the fence.[20] Although these different attempts to influence popular understandings of the Franco-Prussian War and its relationship to French politics thus did not operate in the same way and did not circulate among the same people, they all contributed to a conversation about the nation's past and its future that extended beyond the halls of government and into the public sphere.

This conversation also evolved over the 1870s as writers responded to each other's arguments and reacted to political events. From 1871 to 1873, the republic was particularly unstable. The Orleanist and Legitimist deputies who dominated the National Assembly openly worked together to restore the monarchy and crown the comte de Chambord king of France. The divisions between these two groups meant that this attempt to restore the monarchy was troubled from the start—Orleanist supporters of constitutionalist monarchy conflicted with the Legitimists' counterrevolutionary convictions—but in those early years, it seemed possible that the two groups might come to a compromise position.[21] At the same time, the threat of a Bonapartist resurgence seemed remote, and Bonapartist sympathizers remained quiet.[22] In the earliest years, monarchists and republicans thus poised themselves primarily against one another. They invoked different interpretations of the Second Empire to discredit each other and promote their own forms of political organization. The nature of the debates over the war and the empire shifted in the mid-1870s, when the likelihood of a monarchical restoration receded, and the Bonapartists reemerged as a potential alternative to the republican government.[23]

Early Debates: Monarchists and Republicans

Although no political groups articulated coherent interpretations of the war and the Commune, there were common concerns that fell along political lines. In the early years of the Third Republic, the monarchist politicians, writers, and journalists who participated in these conversations were mostly Legitimists, and they usually focused less on detailing the Second Empire's problems than on undermining the republican regime.[24] Many did hold the empire responsible for the defeat, and several condemned empire as a form of political organization.[25] But for the most part, monarchists tended to dismiss Napoleon III and his military strategies out of hand before devoting most of their attention to the republic and its relationship to the Commune. A number linked the republic to radical movements and social disorder, describing republicans as "enemies of France" and the republic as "diabolical."[26]

If most monarchists thus tied the empire to French defeat and the republic to civil war, others conflated empire and republic, contending that they were the same type of government and equally discredited by recent events. One pamphlet maintained that it was "Napoleon III and the republican party that had brought the country to its unfortunate position."[27] It argued that many of Napoleon III's most reprehensible decisions—his wars with Italy, his invasion of Mexico, and his refusal to stop Prussian expansion—were made at the behest of the republicans.[28] The pamphlet concluded, "The monarchy of St. Louis, of Henry IV and of Louis XIV made us the greatest people on earth, and gave us magnificent conquests; the Republic and the Bonapartists, however, brought us the scaffold, massacres, civil war, ruin, and invasion."[29] In other words, the monarchy was responsible for France's once-powerful position in Europe, while the republic and the empire had dismantled that position.

For the most part, however, even the Legitimist writers who dominated the conversation took a conciliatory tone toward at least some republican ideas as they attempted to attract undecided Orleanists. Some even argued that republicanism was fine for countries like the United States but unsuited to France because of its violent revolutionary legacy, its incompatibility with French national character, and its break with historical traditions.[30] The Legitimist candidate to the throne, they promised, would incorporate some republican principles while avoiding the republic's most destructive tendencies. In the words of one commentator, the monarchy would strengthen France and preserve its social fabric by uniting the country with its "glorious past, [and] bringing back its traditions while keeping all of the conquests of its first revolution."[31] The author thus described the Legitimist candidate as a constitutionally minded monarch who would respect some republican traditions, even as he continued to describe his claim to the throne as based on divine right.[32] This strategy would break down in 1873 when the comte de Chambord refused to rule constitutionally, but in the meantime some monarchists sought to co-opt part of the republican platform—even as they attacked the republic itself.

Republican politicians and intellectuals' early accounts of the Franco-Prussian War, the Commune, and the Second Empire were partly shaped by these monarchist attacks on the republic. In political pamphlets and newspaper articles, they sought to prove that it was the Second Empire, and not the republic, that was to blame for the disasters of 1870–71. Some republican writers thus held Napoleon III personally responsible for these events. Eugène Spuller and Émile Dehau, two republican politicians, contended that because Napoleon III was a dictator who decided policy from above, he alone was to blame for the disasters that had torn the country apart. They argued that Napoleon III's pattern of placing his own desires over the needs of the country had weakened France and left it unprepared for war.[33] They also took aim at Napoleon III's military capabilities, claiming that his incompetence as a military commander was the most important factor in French defeat. This focus on Napoleon III's military abilities reflected republican concerns about the continued power of the Napoleonic myth of military greatness. Many republicans saw this myth as responsible for Napoleon III's rise, and they feared that he might be able to return to power if it remained intact.[34]

Most authors went beyond personal failure, however, and insisted that the defeat did not just stem from Napoleon III's personal, political, or military weaknesses but also from the fact that the empire itself was a flawed and illegitimate political system. *Le petit journal* implied that the empire's fault lay in its tendency to promote loyalty over competence. The resulting administration—built on conformity and personal connections—could not govern the country or meet the demands of waging a war.[35] Other authors charged that the empire's failures lay in its corruption and decadent culture that spread throughout the entire administration and infected the nation. Different writers envisioned this corruption in different ways: some described it as a spirit of criminality, some as sexual promiscuousness and gender transgression, and others as a degradation of political values.[36] But all agreed that as a result the empire had left the French weak, divided, and unable to unite in the face of a common enemy.[37] These authors thus tied what they saw as the empire's moral failures to the outcome of the conflict with Prussia and implied that the government had been destined to end in disaster.

Most republican writers also argued that it was the Second Empire, and not the new republic, that was responsible for the Commune. One writer contended that the empire had allowed "radicals" of all types to flourish and that these radicals had simply seized the opportunity offered by the empire's defeat to revolt.[38] The republic, on the other hand, had crushed this uprising—putting an end to the radical politics that the empire had allowed to flourish.[39] Other authors took a more theoretical approach and tried to

FIGURE 3. The cover of a republican pamphlet attacking Napoleon III. The title reads, "Beware of the Empire!" The cat's whiskers reference Napoleon III's mustache, and the image positions him as a scheming, effeminate puppet master. Jean Pilori, *Gare à l'empire* (Paris: A. Lévy, 1871). Bibliothèque nationale de France.

redefine popular understandings of the relationship between republicanism and radicalism, contending that radicalism was the necessary consequence of empire and monarchy. According to this argument, oppressive personal rule necessarily led to resentment and anger, which in turn resulted in uprisings and in legal, moral, and material disorder.[40] This explanation of the Commune cast the republic as the only political institution that could promote order and stem the rising tide of radicalism. It also discredited the monarchy by tying it to the empire and implied that the ascendancy of the Legitimists and the Orleanists would further destabilize France.

In fact, while some republican pamphlet-writers defined the empire as a unique form of political organization and attempted to discredit it alone, most tied its failures to other conservative governments. Many described the empire as a "type" of monarchy—and then argued that all forms of monarchy were intrinsically despotic.[41] Raymond d'Aiguy, an officer at Lyon's court of appeals, for example, described the Bonapartists, the Legitimists, and the Orleanists as "three monarchies" and held them responsible for "dishonoring [the nation's] name, debasing its flag, and plunging it into an abyss of ruin and devastation."[42] Writers who distinguished between Bonapartists, Legitimists, and Orleanists often claimed that all were bad; in the words of one writer, they were "synonymous with tyranny, absolutism, and despotism."[43] Only the republic, they argued, could foster the development of progress and prosperity in a way that unrepresentative regimes could not.

Although republicans and monarchists alike connected the empire to the disastrous events of 1870–71, both groups were at first most interested in defending their forms of political organization against each other. They nevertheless also rejected the official understandings of "empire" promulgated by Napoleon III throughout his reign. Napoleon III had described the empire as the moderate way between republic and monarchy. He maintained that it balanced liberty with order, based its legitimacy on the support of the people, and ensured the development of peace and prosperity. Abroad and in the colonies, he had also promoted an image of imperial grandeur while eschewing his uncle's legacy of conquest by depicting his empire as a defender of nationalities. The republican and monarchist pamphlets dismissed these claims by describing the empire as incompetent and corrupt. At the same time, critics on left and right co-opted his contention that the empire represented a "middle" way in domestic politics, arguing that their own conceptions of the republic or the monarchy were actually more moderate.

In the early 1870s, both monarchist and republican writers' treatment of Napoleon III's vision of imperial influence abroad was nevertheless not entirely coherent; while most early pamphlets held him responsible for France's defeat and condemned his military strategies, they did not usually lay out a broader condemnation of his foreign and colonial policy. In the middle of the decade, when the Bonapartists began to be perceived as a new threat, a broader condemnation of the empire's domestic and foreign policies would take shape.

Napoleon IV and the Declaration of Chislehurst

The Bonapartists mostly did not participate in the first wave of this pamphlet war over the memory of 1870–71 and its relationship to the empire and the Commune. This was partly because the group had scattered. Napoleon III was in exile and ill; there was also no organized imperialist organization within France.[44] The situation shifted in the mid-1870s. In 1873 Napoleon III died after a failed surgery to remove the kidney stones that had been plaguing him for years.[45] And in March 1874, his son, Prince Napoleon, reached the age of majority in a publicized ceremony in Chislehurst, England.[46] The Bonapartists thus were able to replace a candidate tainted by the events of the war with a charismatic young man. In the wake of this event, several Bonapartists mobilized to reclaim the empire and restore its reputation. Eugène Rouher, a key figure in Napoleon III's government, founded the group L'Appel au peuple, which worked to elect Bonapartist candidates to the National Assembly—leading to a surge made possible by the growing sense that a monarchical restoration was unlikely. He and his followers began to advocate within the Chamber of Deputies for a national plebiscite that would allow the French people to choose between republic, monarchy, and empire.[47] At the same time, new imperialist publications tried to popularize Bonapartist ideas and promote the Bonapartist cause. By 1877 there were 104 Bonapartist deputies in the National Assembly.[48]

In response to these developments, monarchists and especially republicans mobilized against what they saw as the rising threat of a Bonapartist restoration.[49] Ultimately, their concerns proved unfounded—Napoleon IV had trouble unifying his supporters, and he died fighting the Zulus in South Africa in 1879.[50] But from 1874 to 1876, a second wave of political writing about the Franco-Prussian War, the Commune, the empire, and the republic emerged.[51] This second wave of debate was distinct from the first: it was dominated by republicans and Bonapartists, both of whom attempted to construct a vision of French politics in opposition to one another. And perhaps most importantly, it was this second wave of conflicts over the relationship between the empire, the war, and the republic that solidified republican understandings of "empire" as a form of government. This vision of empire would also help shape how the republicans discussed the republic's relationship to France's overseas colonies.

Bonapartist pamphleteers writing in the mid-1870s sought to reframe the conversation about the empire, its virtues, and its relationship to the war. They wanted to combat republican and monarchist claims about imperial culpability and promote a positive vision of empire. They employed different strategies to accomplish this task. Some challenged the contention that the empire was responsible for the war and defeat and blamed both on the republicans instead. Paul de Cassagnac, one of the most influential Bonapartist deputies in the Third Republic, thus argued that it was republican deputies who had forced Napoleon III into the conflict.[52] Other authors contended that the republican-dominated Chamber of Deputies had refused to allocate funds to the army in the years leading up to the conflict, so the army's deficits were their fault.[53]

Most Bonapartist writers, however, chose not to dwell on the war. They instead tried to restore the Second Empire's reputation by emphasizing Napoleon III's nonmilitary achievements or by defining "empire" more abstractly as a system of government that could resolve issues in contemporary France. In an 1873 pamphlet, for example, a writer argued that the prevailing view of Napoleon III was inaccurate because it focused on his "unhappy struggle" but failed to remember the great things he had brought to France, including "universal suffrage, the Grand Exposition, the major thoroughfares constructed in cities, the axe brought against pauperism, the respect and glory acquired by the flag."[54] This amnesia, he maintained, was the result of "ingratitude."[55] Albert Duruy, another prominent Bonapartist politician, took a more theoretical approach that engaged even less directly with Napoleon III's record. He stated that France was not suited to either monarchy or republic because its kings were prone to "abuses" and its republics to "excesses." The empire, he declared, curbed both problems because it "borrowed the monarchy's strength of resistance and the republic's strength of initiative . . . [and was] simultaneously authoritarian and democratic."[56] It thus provided a middle way between two extremes. Duruy argued that the empire could take this middle way in industry as well as politics because it could navigate between the needs of industrialists and workers.[57] Duruy's defense of empire thus avoided referring to Napoleon III and instead attempted to show how Bonapartism could solve contemporary problems. But his idea of empire as the middle way borrowed heavily from Napoleon III's attempts to give theoretical shape to the imperial system early in his reign. And in fact, Napoleon III's vision of empire as the middle way appeared in many Bonapartist pamphlets, reflecting the fact that the Bonapartists mostly defended older ideas about empire instead of offering new ones.[58]

Many of these pamphlets grounded their portrayals of empire in the figure of Napoleon IV, whom they described as the embodiment of Bonapartist virtues. They assured their readers that he was a mature, masculine young man who was wise beyond his years.[59] Some linked him to his great uncle, noting that he "evoked . . . the great figure of Napoleon I."[60] Others emphasized his ideological purity by describing him as the "incarnation of the imperial regime" and promising that he would rule "a government regimented by a Constitution with a democratic base . . . controlled by an elective Assembly, and contained by a second Assembly."[61] Such descriptions promised that the young heir would continue the Napoleonic tradition of promoting suffrage while upholding order through authoritarian measures—another echo of Napoleon III's theory of empire.

Bonapartist pamphlets were not solely defensive; many also attacked the republican government's legitimacy. Some writers contended that the republicans' claim to represent the people was disingenuous, because they refused to organize a referendum on France's political organization. Until the republicans allowed the people to decide whether they wanted a monarchy, republic, or empire, Bonapartists declared, they could not claim that the republic was based on universal suffrage.[62] Several authors unfavorably compared the republicans' unwillingness to organize such a vote to Napoleon III's decision to allow the people to ratify the empire by plebiscite.[63] Another insisted, "Of all the regimes that have been tried in France, the empire has always been founded by the people. Only the emperor has always recognized the sovereignty of the people as the unique source of all legitimacy."[64] The republic, the author argued, had always been imposed on the people by a minority.[65] The fact that the republicans would not agree to organize a plebiscite revealed that they knew they did not have the will of the people behind them.[66]

In the mid-1870s, most Bonapartists thus sought to restore the vision of empire that Napoleon III had promulgated early in his reign—at least in terms of his internal politics. They portrayed the Bonapartist empire as a regime that expressed the will of the people, combined "liberty" with "order," and kept anarchy at bay. They also emphasized the economic prosperity that France had experienced under the Second Empire, maintaining that the empire embraced the tenets of economic liberalism without ignoring workers and the poor. They connected this vision of a restored empire to the young prince Napoleon, who would use his youth to regenerate the nation. But, notably, even as these pamphlets built on Napoleon III's propaganda about the domestic benefits of empire, they did not invoke his vision of the empire beyond the boundaries of metropolitan France. This was partly a reflection of their reluctance to discuss the Second Empire's foreign policy in the wake of French defeat. It may have also resulted from the fact that both Algeria and Mexico had been sources of controversy, not unity, at the start of the Franco-Prussian War. The empire that Bonapartists were defending was thus primarily a domestic one that carefully eschewed reference to Napoleon III's policies in Europe and overseas.

Renewed Criticisms of Bonapartism

This wave of Bonapartist defense of the empire set off a second conversation about the war and its connections to contemporary French politics among republicans and monarchists. The monarchist pamphlets published in the wake of Napoleon III's death and Napoleon IV's coming-of-age differed from earlier monarchist writings: most were written by Orleanists, and they treated the Bonapartists as a direct threat, even when they contended that imperialism's rise in popularity was only a "mirage."[67] These writers focused on explaining possible reasons behind this apparent surge in Bonapartist popularity and then worked to disabuse their readers of any remaining affection they might have for the empire.[68]

Despite the condemnations of Bonapartist empire in these longer pamphlets, the monarchist response to the Bonapartists' rise was muted in the popular press. Although some journalists identified the imperialist surge as dangerous and warned their readers that a Bonapartist restoration would have negative consequences for France, most did not directly refute Bonapartist political or historical arguments.[69] Republican writers, on the other hand, responded more vociferously in both the press and political pamphlets to the reemergence of imperial political propaganda. Many republican writers, moreover, engaged directly with Bonapartist arguments about the recent war and its relationship to both the Second Empire and the new republic. They worked to defend the republic as the legitimate government of France, to discredit the Bonapartist Appel au peuple campaign, and to elaborate on and popularize the negative view of the empire that they had put forth in the early 1870s.

To some extent, the republican condemnations of Bonapartism in the mid-1870s echoed those that had appeared earlier in the decade. Multiple republican writers reiterated earlier republican claims that Napoleon III was personally responsible for the defeat, that the empire had "corrupted" the French people, and that Bonapartism, not republicanism, was to blame for the outbreak of the Commune. These later condemnations, however, were often more inflammatory than their earlier counterparts.[70] One author thus shaped his history of the war around a biography of Napoleon III that contended he had been illegitimately conceived and was primarily skilled in conspiracy and deception. He described the late emperor as a "debauched, cold, indecisive dreamer, inclined to utopias, and of mediocre intelligence. . . . He had neither scruples nor remorse."[71] Others contended that the empire had purposefully corrupted French society; to maintain its despotic power, the imperial government had tried to make the people forget about their lost political rights by guaranteeing them material well-being. The policies of "bread and circuses" had degraded popular morality and the social fabric, leading to both French defeat and the outbreak of the Commune.[72] Still others claimed that the Bonapartists had intentionally empowered the socialist and communist groups who started the Commune.[73] While republican pamphlets in the early 1870s had described the emperor as incompetent and despotic and argued that imperial culture had weakened the French people, these later pamphlets often thus implied that Napoleon III and the imperial government had been deliberately plotting to undermine the French nation.

Republican writers in the mid-1870s did not just return to earlier condemnations of the Second Empire and Napoleon III; they also developed new arguments, some of which focused more directly on discrediting Bonapartist political philosophy. Instead of co-opting the claim that the empire represented a middle way between the republic and the monarchy, as some republican writers had in the early 1870s, later writers began to attack it.[74] The empire's position was not in the middle, republican journalist Louis Herbette insisted, but contradictory. The Bonapartists pretended to recognize "principles of religion and of the Revolution, of national sovereignty and imperial legitimism, of discipline and liberty, of hierarchy and equality, of social revolution and conservatism . . . and hundreds of others that take on innumerable combinations."[75] Because these principles were at odds with each other, he claimed that it was impossible to embrace all of them at the same time. And in fact, Herbette declared, the empire simply made use of whichever principle seemed most expedient in a particular situation. Imperialism was therefore not a moderate political philosophy marked by compromise but a chimeric one that professed to be all things to all people. The author accused both the empire and the Bonapartist coalition of drumming up support by making contradictory promises to different communities. The unifying principles that defined imperialism, he concluded, were "force" and "ambition."[76]

Republican writers used this deepened critique of Bonapartist imperialism to attack contemporary Bonapartist political practices such as Rouher's Appel au peuple campaign. They objected to Bonapartist calls for a plebiscite on the nation's political organization.[77] One writer argued that plebiscites were illegitimate because "national sovereignty is the expression of individual liberty; . . . it is inalienable and imprescriptible. The monarchy rests on the negation of national sovereignty. The Empire . . . is the abdication of national sovereignty consecrated by a vote."[78] In other words, the republic alone was based on national sovereignty because it alone allowed for the freedom of the rights-bearing individual. All other forms of political organization were unjust, which meant there was no reason to force the people to choose a type of government through plebiscites.[79] Republicans thus promoted a vision of Bonapartist politics as tyrannical and deceitful.

Republicans writing in the mid-1870s also directed more energy toward criticizing the empire's foreign policy than their earlier counterparts had. Instead of focusing on the empire's failures in the Franco-Prussian War, they tried to show that the empire's problems ran deeper and that the empire was a dangerous, bellicose regime. One writer, for example, maintained that Napoleon III had sought out wars to mask problems at home throughout his reign. At first he met with some success, but his military incompetence meant that this strategy led to disaster.[80] Another similarly reminded his readers that Napoleon III had squandered French resources by engaging in fruitless military conquests before foolishly committing to the fatal fight against Prussia.[81] Several writers pointed to Napoleon III's invasion of Mexico as key to France's defeat, claiming that the lives and resources wasted made France unable to defend itself.[82] These writers thus described the Franco-Prussian War as an example of Napoleon III's warmongering and incompetence rather than as an isolated fluke and implied that the Second Empire had been committed to endless war. They also positioned what they described as Napoleon III's overseas "adventures" as central to France's later defeat.

Some writers in fact insisted that the empire's problematic relationship to war went beyond Napoleon III and rested in the inflated military reputation of Napoleon I.[83] One writer thus acknowledged that Napoleon I had led France to some inspiring military victories but argued that his empire, like Napoleon III's, had collapsed in defeat. The two rulers were thus not as different as they seemed.[84] Historian Henri Martin took this argument even further in a pamphlet that claimed that both Napoleon I and Napoleon III created ineffective imperial systems that led France into unwinnable wars and eventually led to territorial losses.[85] A third writer offered a more expansive critique still, portraying Napoleon I as a bloodthirsty warrior who, because he was not French, looked after his own interests instead of the French nation's.[86] His rise to power and his rule, the writer argued, had been a disaster for France whose consequences had continued long afterward.[87] The argument that the Napoleonic empire was synonymous with war and defeat was not new; Napoleon III had spent most of his reign combatting it. But it became an increasingly integral part of the republican platform in the mid-1870s.

Some republican writers did not only take aim at the empire's military policies; they also went out of their way to condemn Napoleon III's "politics of nationalities," which they held responsible for France's defeat, dismemberment, and marginal position in contemporary Europe. Napoleon III's attempts to support national movements, these writers claimed, had dragged the country into conflicts in Europe and overseas, failed to win France any allies, and contributed to the unification of Germany. His contention that different peoples should have their own state, moreover, helped the Germans justify the annexation of Alsace and Lorraine. The German Empire had mobilized Napoleon III's language of nationality to argue that the German-speaking peoples who lived in those departments should belong to a newly unified Germany.[88] The foundation of the empire's foreign policy, these writers thus argued, was inimical to France's interests.

There were multiple commonalities between the republican pamphlets written in the early and mid-1870s. Later pamphlets reiterated the early charge that the empire was responsible for French defeat. Many continued to emphasize the corruption of both Napoleon III and the Second Empire while connecting Bonapartism to radical politics. Republicans' persistent focus on the empire's popular military reputation demonstrates that despite all expectation, Napoleon III's defeat at Sedan had not dismantled the Napoleonic myth of military greatness.

It is nevertheless clear that republican writers in the mid-1870s were developing new concerns. Whereas some republican writers in the early 1870s linked the empire to other forms of monarchy, republicans said almost nothing about monarchy later in the decade. Nor did they associate the empire with any other form of government: they treated it as unique. They also dealt less directly with the events of the Franco-Prussian War—unless they were addressing Bonapartist attempts to reject responsibility for defeat. At the same time, many focused on demonstrating that the empire was a defective political system that had always led France into disaster. Some writers emphasized the failures of its leaders, while others condemned its political ideology, its relationship to war, or its policies. But despite these differences, by the mid-1870s these writers were constructing an increasingly unified vision of the Second Empire. They criticized the political structures and ideologies that Napoleon III had embraced throughout much of his reign. He had portrayed the Second Empire as the middle, moderate way between republic and monarchy, and in the last years of his regime he had also described the empire as a military power, following in the footsteps of Napoleon I to create an overseas empire that could foster, instead of crush, national aspirations. The republican pamphlets turned those claims on their head. They contended that the empire was despotic, disorderly, bellicose, militarily incompetent, and never based on the will of the people. They even condemned the empire's commitment to the politics of nationality as inimical to France's best interests. They also tried to discredit the Bonapartists' contemporary efforts by describing them as dishonest. Despite the ongoing divisions amongst republicans, these writers were able to use the events of the Franco-Prussian War to discredit the empire's claims about itself and to demonstrate that it was the republic, not the empire, that embodied France's positive qualities.

This republican shift away from the specific events of the war and toward a broader condemnation of the empire was linked to shifting political patterns in France. By 1874 it was clear that the monarchists no longer posed a direct political threat to the republic, and in 1875 the National Assembly approved a series of laws that would act as a constitution—an important step toward stabilizing and legitimizing the regime.[89] As a result, republicans were under less pressure to defend their role in the war. It was now the Bonapartist resurgence that posed a direct threat to the republic's newfound stability.[90] Republicans thus had new reasons to argue that the problems with the Second Empire did not just stem from Napoleon III—who was already dead—but were endemic to imperialism itself. They therefore sought to show that all emperors, including the would-be Napoleon IV, promoted policies that undermined French interests.

If these shifts in representation reflected France's changing political landscape, they also reveal the ways in which the conceptual categories of "empire" and "republic" progressively hardened against one another in the early 1870s, especially in republican thought. Although many Bonapartists continued to emphasize the connections between the empire and certain republican ideals, republicans disavowed these connections by defining the empire and the republic in stark, contrasting terms. Republicans did not always agree on the content of these dichotomies, but the broad structural opposition became sharper as the decade progressed and as republicans no longer felt the need to defend the republic against monarchism.

Republicanism, Bonapartism, and Empire

Despite the divisions among various republican factions, a semicoherent understanding of the Second Empire took shape during the 1870s in republican political writing, evolving through debates with monarchists and Bonapartists. This "republican vision" defined the new republic as the opposite of the previous empire. This definition was inaccurate—the republic borrowed political practices and economic policies from its predecessor. But by the end of the 1870s, the republicans had popularized this view, defining "empire" as a problematic system of government that contradicted France's ideal political practices and values. Tellingly, this vision of empire began to appear not just in political pamphlets with limited audiences but also in novels and short stories written about the Franco-Prussian War. Zola's *La débâcle*—which we saw in the introduction—was not published until the 1890s, but even in the 1870s a series of novels and short stories, published by prominent writers such as Victor Hugo, Émile Erckmann, Alexandre Chatrian, and Alphonse Daudet, reiterated the opposition between empire and republic that appeared in more explicitly political writing, telegraphing it into middle-class popular culture.[91] Republicans' success in promoting this vision was due partly to these popular publications, but it was also due to the fact that by the end of the decade they had politically secured the republic against monarchist and Bonapartist challenges.[92] Even before Napoleon IV's death in 1879, the Bonapartist threat had begun to fade.

This conversation about empire and its relationship to the new republic did not focus on questions about colonial or overseas territories. Few of the pamphlets or newspapers mentioned Napoleon III's specific policies in Algeria or Mexico when they condemned his empire. In fact, many republican attempts to discredit the Second Empire focused on its effects on metropolitan France. Republican condemnations of empire at home nevertheless had consequences for how republicans imagined empire overseas. This was not because writers assumed that all empires were equivalent to Bonapartism. "Empire" certainly had uses in other national contexts that French commentators were aware of: Queen Victoria was crowned the "empress of India" in 1876, and the new German state forged in the wake of the Franco-Prussian War also called itself "the German Empire." That said, the concern that imperial practices abroad would lead to despotism at home had long been a central tenet of liberal thought; such concerns had driven early liberal criticisms of imperial expansion in both France and Britain.[93] These concerns had faded in the mid-nineteenth century following the abolition of slavery and the emergence of new theories of progress that helped bolster liberals' sense of the exceptionality of their own civilizations.[94] But Napoleon III had muddied the waters. His attempt to combine "domestic" and "overseas" empire into one unified theory of "empire" had collapsed in the face of opposition, but republican critics themselves conflated both aspects of the Bonapartist empire as they drew on these older liberal arguments to treat Napoleon III's "warmongering adventures" abroad and his despotism at home as inextricably linked. They defined both in opposition to the republic, claiming that empire had weakened France and led to its defeat.

The question of how to understand the relationship between the republic and overseas empire more specifically nevertheless remained unanswered. And it arose immediately in the years following the war, becoming especially pointed in Algeria—the territory that had attracted so much controversy under Napoleon III. Struggles over the legacy of the Franco-Prussian War, Napoleon III's domestic and overseas policies, and his ideas about the politics of nationality would affect this attempt to create a republican Algeria. But competing groups in the colony who had an interest in defending particular forms of overseas domination that benefited their personal interests would also shape these contestations over both the meaning of empire and Algeria's future.

Chapter 3

Creating a Republican Algeria

In 1877 Alphonse Daudet, the popular author known for his short stories about Algeria and the Franco-Prussian War, published a novel titled *Le nabab*. It chronicled the life of Bernard Jansoulet, a fictional character who was born into poverty in southern France, made a fortune in Tunisia, and returned to enter Parisian high society during the Second Empire. The novel used Jansoulet's life to paint a negative vision of Second Empire politics and society, describing the imperial elite as selfish, superficial, effete, and overly sexualized. Daudet indicated that the Second Empire used unethical political practices to consolidate its power, delegating authority to dishonest officials who gained their positions through bribery, personal connections, and rigged elections. The political system encouraged cronyism and scheming—values that infiltrated the upper classes. The novel's portrayal of the Second Empire thus echoed those that appeared in other republican novels in the years following the Franco-Prussian War. *Le nabab* discredited Bonapartist politics by tying the imperial government to social problems that it in turn implied were responsible for France's defeat. But Daudet linked France's "decadence" to the Second Empire's relationship with Tunisia and "the Orient" as well as to its internal politics.[1]

Daudet's novel implied that the Second Empire and Tunisia were connected on several levels. First, it indicated that many members of the imperial government were financially and politically dependent on "Oriental" rulers such as the bey of Tunis or "Orientalized" figures like Jansoulet. For Daudet, these connections were a problem: because he believed North Africans were effete and immoral, he thought that their infiltration of Parisian society amplified its decadence and corruption.[2] But, most noticeably, Daudet implied that the Second Empire and Tunisia shared values and customs: he described Tunisia as "enervating" and "depraved" and styled the Second Empire in the same terms. The novel at times conflated the empire and North Africa: at one point, Daudet even described an important French official as an "African king."[3]

Conflating the Second Empire with Tunisia drew on a long literary and political tradition of invoking the specter of "oriental despotism" to criticize French rulers as autocratic; it discredited Bonapartist politics at a moment when Bonapartism's appeal seemed to be rising once again.[4] At the same time, Daudet's portrayal also blurred the edges between Napoleonic European empire and France's relationship with its overseas territories in North Africa. Although Tunisia was not a French colony in the 1860s or 1870s, Daudet's novel implied that it acted as a client state to the Second Empire and contended that shared cynicism, laziness, selfishness, and corruption bound both together.[5] Daudet also indicated that imperial France's ties to "the Orient" were partly responsible for the rot and decay that characterized imperial society. Although Daudet's work did not explicitly condemn expansion overseas, it implied that the Second Empire's interest in North Africa and its political corruption were part of the same imperial system and that both had had devastating consequences for the nation.

The debates that transpired over the Second Empire and its relationship to the events of 1870–71 had a profound effect on republican—and liberal—discourse about France's overseas colonies in the early years of the Third Republic. Because Bonapartism remained popular among French voters throughout the 1870s, republican writers had mobilized to condemn empire as both responsible for France's decline and as at odds with the nation's values and interests. They also positioned the empire in opposition to the new republic, which they promised would repair Napoleon III's damage to the nation. France's overseas territories became entangled in this conversation about the empire's failings largely because of Napoleon III's policies toward Mexico and Algeria. His vision of a France and Mexico united by shared imperial politics and latinité, alongside his insistence that Algeria was not a "colony" but a "royaume arabe" with its own national identity, had together complicated French discourses about empire and colonization. These visions positioned the Second Empire alternatively as the head of an informally united Latin race or as a multinational entity composed of a set of distinct nations ruled by one central administration. Beneath either of these regimes, "empire" referred both to a type of domestic politics and to different ways of projecting power overseas.[6]

As we have seen, Napoleon III's attempt to cast the Second Empire as the head of a confederation of Latin empires and as a multinational "Mediterranean empire" encountered resistance in Mexico and in Algeria. Napoleon III's efforts to restructure Mexico's political system collapsed; his attempts to redefine Algeria as a royaume arabe met with little more success. Throughout the 1860s, settlers contended that Algeria was not a royaume arabe but a French colony and argued that they alone could ensure the territory's economic and political prosperity. They worked to undermine Napoleon III's imperial system, criticizing both the structure of the Algerian administration and the military's position within it by claiming that the system indulged indigenous people and hindered colonists' interests. Instead of treating Algeria as a distinct nation, they argued, the government should "assimilate" the territory and its peoples. Europeans should have the same rights and institutions as their metropolitan counterparts, while Algerians should be forced to assimilate into French culture. Colonists thus articulated an alternative vision of Algeria's purpose and ideal structure. Moreover, they made alliances with Napoleon III's republican opponents in the metropole, who saw the conflict as an opportunity to undermine Napoleon III's authority. Because of this opposition, Napoleon III never restructured Algeria or carried out most of his proposed reforms.

In fact, even before the empire's collapse, the royaume arabe had dissolved. In 1869, under pressure from settlers and the Senate, Napoleon III organized a commission to draft a constitution for the territory that overturned many of his earlier proposals.[7] The constitution conceded that the settlers were the territory's key population and treated Algeria as a colony, not an Arab nation. It also embraced an assimilationist program, established assemblies and parliamentary representation, and extended the reach of civil territory.[8] But even though the colonists had advocated for a constitution, they rejected these measures, claiming that they extended the policies of the royaume arabe. They objected to the commission's decision to maintain military territory, because they saw the military as partisan to Algerians. They also protested the extension of voting rights to foreigners and indigenous people.[9]

These arguments extended beyond Algeria; one of the colonist coalition's long-standing republican allies, Jules Favre, brought the matter to the Corps législatif in early 1870.[10] From March 7 to 9, 1870, the Corps législatif argued about Algeria's administration before voting to dissolve the territory's military organization and institute civilian rule.[11] Colonists greeted this news with satisfaction: *L'echo d'Oran* described it as the "Waterloo of the royaume arabe."[12] But if the colonists gained a number of theoretical concessions under Napoleon III, the government made few policy changes before the outbreak of the Franco-Prussian War. Colonists and republicans alike attributed this reticence to Napoleon III's ongoing commitment to his earlier vision of Algeria and continued to associate the imperial government with the royaume arabe.[13]

If Napoleon III's attempt to restructure Algeria had fallen apart by 1870, his vision of a multinational Mediterranean empire clearly remained a subject of debate. Moreover, critics of Napoleon III's imperial system often unintentionally reinforced his attempts to collapse domestic and overseas empire. They also treated domestic politics and overseas policies as intertwined, arguing that Napoleon III's misguided approach toward Algeria stemmed from Bonapartism's flaws. As Daudet's *Le nabab* shows, some republicans continued to associate Napoleon III's Mediterranean empire with his domestic imperial system throughout the 1870s.

The legacy of Napoleon III's conflation of "domestic" and "overseas" empire created both strategic and conceptual problems for republicans. After the empire's collapse, republicans had condemned domestic empire as a "decadent," "militaristic," "corrupt," and "oppressive" form of political organization. But if domestic empire contradicted the values of the new republic, what about overseas empire? What was its relationship to Bonapartist practices? Republican politicians and intellectuals did not have a clear answer to these questions; the fact that most republicans—throughout the 1870s and into the 1880s—did not use the word "empire" to describe any of France's overseas territories illustrates the pressure of these ongoing domestic political conflicts. Instead, they employed a series of different words—from "colony" to "*département*"—when referring to these places. This marked a shift from Second Empire usages: the imperial government had deployed the terms "empire," "overseas empire," "Mediterranean empire," and "colonial empire" to refer to overseas territories.

In the republic's first decade, uncertainties and tensions over "empire" had particular resonance in Algeria, unsurprisingly given its perceived importance to France and centrality to Bonapartist policy. The turmoil that broke out in the territory after the September 4 Revolution in 1870 also raised immediate questions about its political organization. Settlers and their metropolitan allies used the collapse of the Second Empire to transform the territory's administration to better align with their interests, which helped precipitate a widespread indigenous revolt. This ongoing instability in turn provoked a wider, highly politicized conversation about Algeria's organization and its relationship to France.

Ultimately, as other historians have shown, republican intellectuals and politicians came to couch their visions of empire in Algeria in the language of assimilation—the framework that Algerian colonists had long deployed to justify their demands.[14] Assimilation, as we have seen, was an idea with a history dating at least back to the Revolution; it had been invoked in the Algerian context as early as the Second Republic. Historians have often attributed its ascendancy in the early Third Republic to its association with central republican universalist tenets.[15] But in the earliest years of the Third Republic, the republicans were not politically ascendant, and the embrace of assimilation came as much out of these disagreements between republicans and the conservative groups who dominated the National Assembly as from an inherent affinity between assimilation and republican thought. Assimilation, moreover, was not the only model proposed, even by republican thinkers. The process of developing a new understanding of Algeria and its relationship to France was thus ongoing, fraught, and negotiated between settler populations and metropolitan authorities whose interests did not always align.

Much like the debates over France's political organization occurring at the same time, these arguments about empire's future in Algeria played out primarily in often polemical newspaper articles and, especially after the collapse of the Commune, political pamphlets, which were less likely to face state censorship.[16] The structure of the conversation about Algeria was even more complicated than the conversation about France's political future, however. Writers remained divided by their political beliefs, but their divergent personal investments, connections to different parts of the colonial administration, and widely varying levels of knowledge about French colonial policy also shaped their visions of empire in Algeria. Politicians, journalists, intellectuals, military officers, colonial administrators, and settlers in both France and Algeria all weighed in. The conversation thus often spanned the Mediterranean, albeit unevenly. While the wire service Havas disseminated information throughout the empire, only some of the pamphlets and newspaper articles would have circulated widely outside of the cities where they were published, let alone between colony and metropole.[17] Writers in Algeria and France also often had distinct concerns, which meant that arguments about empire took on divergent shapes in both places.

Despite these differences, the conversation about empire in both metropole and colony shared at least one key characteristic: French voices dominated it. Even during the 1860s, Algerian notables—who often played important roles in shaping French policy on the ground as colonial intermediaries—had only indirectly participated in public debates over the royaume arabe. Figures such as Abd el-Kader had loomed large, but even though some of his writing appeared in translation throughout the period, most of what was published did not comment directly on empire or its political implications. Under the Third Republic, however, Algerians were even more deliberately systematically excluded as the colonial administration became increasingly committed to defending the free speech of colonists while seeking to systematically police both the writing and speech of Algerian communities.[18]

This chapter examines the debates over Algeria and its connections to the French nation in the wake of the Franco-Prussian War and considers what they reveal about understandings of "empire" in early Third Republic France. It argues that these debates marked the first moment of a conversation about empire that continued to develop through the end of the nineteenth century. Throughout this conversation, French republicans tried to differentiate between domestic and overseas empire and explain why overseas empire did not contradict republican values even if its domestic counterpart was problematic. At the same time, they tried to show why their model of overseas "republican" colonization was superior to its Bonapartist predecessors.

War and Revolution: Algeria in 1870–71

The French defeat at Sedan and the September 4 Revolution triggered an immediate trans-Mediterranean discussion about Algeria's administrative structure. This discussion was at first driven by settlers, who took to the streets in Algerian cities to highlight their loyalty to the new republican government, protest the remains of the Bonapartist regime, and advocate for widespread change in Algeria. Their actions precipitated a whirlwind of reforms but also drew settlers into conflict with the new republican government.[19] The Mokrani (Muqrani) Revolt, which broke out in the spring of 1871, further complicated the situation. Taken together, these events further undermined the already very limited effects of Bonapartist political ideas in Algeria. A contradictory combination of settler self-interest, republican political opportunism, and ideological conviction would define the new colonial administration's hybrid political system. The contestations around these new structures would in turn have implications for the French conversation about the meaning and implications of "empire" in the years to come.

The events that led to this transformation in Algeria's administrative system were convoluted. In the weeks following the collapse of Napoleon III's government, the new republican government moved a number of republicans sympathetic to settlers' demands—including Auguste-Hubert

Warnier—into the territory's administration.[20] At the same time, colonists across Algeria organized themselves into "republican committees of national defense," much like their urban counterparts in metropolitan France.[21] But although their purported intention was to defend the country against Germany, they also staged public protests against Governor-General François Louis Alfred Durieu, who they claimed was plotting a Bonapartist coup.[22] The Republican Association of Algiers was particularly active. In circulars published in Algerian newspapers (temporarily freed from the censorship regime of the Second Empire that would be reinstated after the collapse of the Commune), its members argued that the Algerian military administration was incompatible with republican values and demanded immediate reform.[23] They succeeded in securing Durieu's resignation by early October 1870—as well as the resignation of two successive military governors-general by early November.[24]

In the face of settlers' unrest, the Government of National Defense in Tours took a series of steps to placate them. Léon Gambetta, the minister of the interior, charged Adolphe Crémieux, the minister of justice, with Algeria's affairs because Crémieux had visited the territory on multiple occasions. Crémieux and the other members of the interim government were sympathetic to colonists' distaste for the military regime—partly because they needed colonist support and partly because they themselves saw the military as a conservative institution hostile to the republic's future. On October 24, 1870, Crémieux sponsored a series of decrees to reorganize Algeria. These decrees largely dismantled the military regime and took steps toward legally assimilating the colony into the metropole.[25] They replaced the military governor-general with a civil governor-general, divided Algeria into three departments that would each elect two deputies to the National Assembly, and reorganized the consultative and superior councils that advised the governor-general, to increase settlers' influence on both.[26] Crémieux selected Henri Didier, an advocate for settler interests who had served as Algeria's deputy during the Second Republic, to serve as the new civil governor-general and promised prompt elections to fill the other positions.[27] The decrees nevertheless maintained the division between civil and military territory and granted French citizenship to Algerian Jews.[28]

Though the Crémieux decrees acceded to many colonist demands, they did not quell the rising discontent. Many colonists objected to the fact that the decrees maintained military territories and did not abolish the bureaux arabes. If they welcomed the prospect of a civil governor-general, they were frustrated by the fact that the government was to remain in the hands of the military until Didier could arrive from France—which, considering that he remained trapped in besieged Paris, would take at least several months. They were also incensed by the government's decision to grant citizenship to Algerian Jews, whom they claimed "share neither our customs nor our civilization."[29] In Algiers especially, colonists marched in the streets to protest the new measures and demand the resignation of all administrators associated with the military regime.[30]

The radical republican mayor of Algiers, Romuald Vuillermoz, a lawyer who had been deported first to Guyana and later to Algeria after the Paris uprisings of 1848, made use of these protests to send the government a series of escalating demands.[31] At first, he asked the republican government to appoint a "temporary special commissioner" to run Algeria's civil and military affairs until Didier could arrive from Paris.[32] The government in Tours did not respond to the request, leading Vuillermoz to issue an ultimatum on November 7: the government could either send a special commissioner, or the Algiers Committee of National Defense would appoint Vuillermoz to the position.[33]

When the government in Tours did not respond to the November 7 telegram, the Republican Committee of National Defense in Algiers took matters into its own hands and appointed Vuillermoz to the position of interim special civil commissioner.[34] Vuillermoz made use of his new position to transform Algeria along prosettler, republican lines.[35] His appointment also encouraged colonists to widen their ambitions. Over the next few days, multiple groups began expressing hostility toward the Tours government and demanding reform. Alexandre Lambert, the editor of *L'écho d'Oran* and another 1848 deportee who returned to Paris in 1871 as a delegate to the Commune, insisted, for example, "Algeria will not adopt that new error of old Crémieux. We say to the delegation of Tours: either Algeria will be entirely French, and ruled entirely by French law, or, if it is necessary that she is ruled beneath an exceptional regime, she will make her own colonial constitution."[36] In other words, the recently passed Crémieux decrees were illegitimate. The government should not create a new constitution for Algeria; it should either assimilate the territory into France or allow the settlers to determine the regime under which they would live. On November 13, Algiers republicans sent new demands to the interim government, insisting that settlers should have the right to name their own civil governor and appoint deputies to draft a new constitution.[37] Just a few weeks before, settlers had been advocating for a civil regime. Now they wanted the right to choose their own officials and select a new administrative structure for the colony.[38]

The government in Tours condemned the committee's actions and sent Vuillermoz multiple notes announcing that it rejected "this act of usurpation," marking a break between metropolitan and settler republicans.[39] On November 17 the interim government appointed the former prefect of Oran, Charles du Bouzet, as the new special commissioner, and many Algerian cities withdrew their support for Vuillermoz.[40] When Bouzet arrived in Algiers on November 20, Vuillermoz had to step down. But Bouzet's appointment did not end the political unrest in Algeria. He continued to conflict with Vuillermoz, who remained the mayor of Algiers.[41] Crémieux and the national government's decision to modify the decrees of October 24 in late December and early January by extending civil territory—effectively dismantling the bureaux arabes, placing military territories under the control of civilian prefects, and legally assimilating civil territory into the metropole—did not resolve tensions either.[42]

Ultimately, the national government intervened in the ongoing conflicts between Vuillermoz, the Algerian municipal council, and Bouzet by dissolving the municipal council of Algiers, dismissing the mayor, and replacing Bouzet with yet another special commissioner on February 9, Alexis Lambert, the prefect of Oran.[43] Lambert succeeded in establishing an uneasy peace in Algiers, despite the fact that the metropolitan elections brought conservatives into the national government who settlers feared would be unsympathetic to their interests.[44] Even the outbreak of the Paris Commune met with a muted response because a widespread indigenous revolt overshadowed the events in the metropole.[45]

The indigenous revolt began in early March in Kabylie when Mohamed el-Mokrani (Muhammad al-Hajj al-Muqrani), an important Kabyle leader who had long worked closely with the French government, called a council of war. Over the next few weeks, he convinced other neighboring peoples to join him.[46] In early April this revolt turned into a widespread popular uprising when Cheikh el-Haddad (Shaykh Sidi Muhammad al-Haddad)—an influential member of the Rahmaniyya, a Sufi Muslim brotherhood—declared his support and described the conflict as a jihad, or a struggle against a foreign aggressor that threatened Islam.[47] By late April, approximately two hundred thousand Kabyles had joined, and the uprising continued to spread in the provinces of Constantine and Alger.[48] Through the spring and summer of 1871, the insurgents attacked settler farms, villages, and towns in an attempt to drive European settlers out of Algeria. It was only in late October 1871 that the French military suppressed the revolt.[49]

The causes behind this insurrection were both complex and diverse. Most historians agree, however, that the political and administrative changes instituted in the late 1860s and especially in 1870–71 made indigenous Algerian elites fear for their future.[50] Many Algerian leaders had had personal relationships with Napoleon III; el-Mokrani had visited him during the festivities at Compiègne in the 1860s.[51] There were certainly tensions between local elites and Napoleon III's administration: even as his administration tried to coopt Algerian elites, it also undercut their authority and economic position over time.[52] But el-Mokrani and his allies nevertheless saw Napoleon III and his administration—especially the bureaux arabes—as a bulwark against settlers who sought to steal their land. They feared that a civilian administration would privilege the settlers' interests over their own.[53] The first months of the Third Republic had only consolidated their suspicions of civilian rule, as the republican journals had used the new freedom of the press to openly advocate for the cantonment of indigenous peoples and to argue that the new government should take a series of drastic measures to secure indigenous land. The Crémieux decrees, which undermined indigenous law and threatened to expand the scope of colonization, consolidated the impression that Algeria's indigenous inhabitants were under attack. The fact that the settlers worked to ship bureaux arabes officers—the only administrators that most indigenous communities ever interacted with—outside of the territory further compounded the situation. There were longer-term causes at work as well. The slow impoverishment of indigenous Algerians under French rule, combined with the disastrous famine of the late 1860s, contributed to the sense that there was little to lose.[54] El-Mokrani and his followers decided to act at a moment when France seemed vulnerable, before the government could consolidate a regime that they saw as antithetical to their interests.[55]

The revolt—combined with the outbreak of the Commune—changed the tenor of debates in Algeria about the territory's administration and its relationship to France. The newly elected metropolitan government decided to replace Lambert with an administrator who could wield greater authority over both the settler and indigenous populations.[56] It eliminated the position of special commissioner and appointed Vice-Admiral Louis Henri de Gueydon as "Civil Governor of Algeria."[57] At first, colonists objected to this announcement—Gueydon was a member of the military, after all, even if he was serving as Algeria's "civil governor."[58] He was also Legitimist in political orientation and close to Adolphe Thiers, the conservative president of the republic.[59] The settlers argued that his appointment represented the resurrection of imperial politics.[60] But in the face of the growing insurrection and the specter of the Versailles government's sharp repression of the Paris Commune, most unhappily acknowledged his authority. By mid-1871 the settlers' campaign to radically restructure Algeria had thus ended in a compromise solution that seemed to bridge, at least temporarily, military and civilian rule.

For approximately six months following the collapse of the Second Empire, a vocal group of settlers organized into committees of defense engaged in an ongoing political battle with the interim republican government in Tours over Algeria's future. They demanded political representation, the end of the military regime, easy access to indigenous land, and "assimilation" into France. The settlers' campaign against the last vestiges of the military administration and the royaume arabe was, overall, successful. Although they were unable to draft their own constitution for the territory or appoint all their own administrators, they secured French political and legal rights and marginalized the indigenous population.[61] They owed their success partly to the fact that the interim government needed their support and was distracted by events unfolding in the metropole. But colonists' ability to demand reforms also stemmed from the way that they had mobilized republican anti-imperial discourse. They argued that Algeria would only be truly "republican" when it adopted a civil administration, highlighting the connections between the military and the Second Empire. This strategy had its limitations, however, which became evident as divisions between "moderate" and "radical" republicans in the metropole intensified in early 1871—especially when some colonists expressed sympathy for the Communards. The conservative metropolitan government that came to power in 1871 became suspicious of settlers' calls for radical reform and settled on a hybrid system that met most of their demands but kept elements of the Second Empire's imperial system in place.

These transformations in Algeria's administration also had an important effect on the position of indigenous Algerians. Although no French administration ever treated settlers and Algerians equally, settlers' interests clearly dominated the new civil administration. This was partly because under the republican civil regime, French citizenship conveyed significantly more political and legal rights than it had beneath the military regime. Under the Second Empire, for example, neither colonists nor indigenous Algerians could select their administrators. Under the new regime, however, European settlers and Algerian Jews, as French citizens, could choose the representatives for the entire territory, which meant that those representatives would be responsive to their needs. Muslims, as noncitizens following the 1865 sénatus-consulte, had few representatives at all, and the colonial administration chose what few they had.[62] The application of other metropolitan institutions, such as trial by jury for criminal cases, also had very different implications for French citizens and Muslim Algerians. Muslims were subject to French criminal law, but as noncitizens they could not serve on juries—and as a result French citizens now had the right to be tried by a jury of their peers, while Muslims would be tried by settlers.[63] This structural inequality would only increase over time, as settlers were able to mobilize their increased influence and the logic of assimilation to transform the legal structures surrounding Algerian land. The 1873 Warnier Law, proposed by longtime settler advocate Auguste-Hubert Warnier, placed Algerian land under French civil law instead of Islamic or customary law, thereby making it significantly easier for settlers to claim.[64] But even as early as 1870, indigenous people's imagined exclusion from republican civil Algeria was evident in settler demands for the territory's organization and the government's responses, most of which were formulated as though the non-European population did not exist.[65] As historian Annie Rey-Goldzeiguer has pointed out, in the wake of the events of 1870–71, the settlers succeeded in co-opting the very word "Algerian," which in the future would be used to refer to Algeria's European population and not its indigenous one.[66]

This ideological marginalization of the indigenous population heightened in the wake of the 1871 revolt. Although metropolitan and colonist commentators disagreed about the specific causes of the insurrection, there was nevertheless a widespread consensus in both Algeria and France about what the revolt revealed about Algeria's indigenous population. *Le petit journal*, in a series of articles purportedly based on interviews that one of its journalists conducted with his "Arab friend," claimed there were two factors behind the revolt. First, the Arabs' religion "commanded them to kill Christians." The fear of French force had long kept the indigenous population from acting on this commandment—but when they saw Germany easily defeat France, they lost their fear of French military prowess. As a result, the Arabs decided to revolt against French rule and kill as many Christians as they could.[67] Versions of this argument—which conflated Algeria's Arab and Kabyle populations and insisted on their shared religious fanaticism—appeared in many newspapers and pamphlets, both reflecting and reinforcing French suspicion of Islam's political influence.[68]

This negative vision of Islam also created a consensus in Algeria and the metropole around the idea that the indigenous population was treacherous. Napoleon III had sought to center France's relationship with Algeria on an imperial relationship with an "Arab" nation. The indigenous revolt convinced many commentators across the political spectrum that the indigenous population could never be central to a French Algeria. Most came to support the settlers' contention that an expansion of European colonization was necessary to secure the territory.[69] The National Assembly's 1871 decision to punitively expropriate the land of the peoples who had revolted reflected this agreement.[70] The "Arabophile" project to defend the economic and political interests of indigenous peoples had been losing ground since the mid-1860s. The 1871 revolt consolidated the colonist position that Europeans would enable Algerian prosperity—permanently undermining the vision of Algeria as a royaume arabe or Arab nation.

The widespread belief that Napoleon III's imperial "politics of nationalities" was partly responsible for all of France's contemporary problems further consolidated this condemnation of the idea of an Arab nation. In the wake of French defeat, both republican and monarchist writers had claimed that Napoleon III's attempt to divide Europe into independent nation-states had led to the unification of Germany and the annexation of the regions of Alsace and Lorraine.[71] Multiple commentators maintained that this policy was also responsible for provoking the indigenous revolt.[72] Historian and archaeologist Eugène Beauvois, for example, argued that Napoleon III's "misapplication of the principle of nationality" was at the root of French problems in Europe and Algeria alike.[73] Charles Strauss, a lawyer and republican administrator who spent much of his career in Algeria, asserted even more directly that the "catastrophic politics of nationality" had caused France to almost lose Algeria, just as it had lost Alsace and Lorraine.[74] By directly linking the Algerian revolt to France's loss in the Franco-Prussian War, these writers insisted that creating policy based on the idea of an Arab nation would only continue to lead France toward disaster.

Theorizing Algeria's Relationship to the Republic

The indigenous revolt thus reflected a new political consensus about the importance of colonization and marked an end to the royaume arabe, but it also provoked more theoretical debates about Algeria's future and its relationship to France. Although most settlers and metropolitan politicians, journalists, and intellectuals condemned Napoleon III's royaume arabe, they disagreed about what should replace his imperial system. What would a new "republican" Algeria look like? Ongoing debates over the relative benefits of a civil or military administration, the role of the army, and the usefulness of military territory would shape the process of determining a new vision of empire—questions that the conflicts of 1870–71 had not resolved. This conversation was also couched in broader disagreements about how to remember the Second Empire, the Paris Commune, Algerian radical republicanism, and the Mokrani Revolt. Although the conversation began in Algeria, by late 1871 it extended into the metropole as well, so conflicts within France over the relative merits of republicanism, monarchy, and Bonapartist imperialism also informed it. After all, while the moderate republican Government of

National Defense had presided over Algeria's reorganization in 1870, conservative politicians—many of whom opposed the republic—dominated the elected government that came to power in 1871. These conservative politicians did not always agree with the interim government's policies toward Algeria; in 1873–74, they in fact launched an inquiry into its Algerian policies, focusing on "communard" activity in Algeria's cities and the military's handling of the insurrection. Conservative leaders thus sought to define the territory on their own terms.[75]

Conflicts in the colony and political disagreements in the metropole thus deeply influenced these more theoretical debates about empire in Algeria. That said, unlike the struggles between the settlers, indigenous communities, and the metropolitan government in 1870–71, these later debates did not, for the most part, directly affect the actual operations of colonial rule there. Their importance therefore lies not in their policy consequences but in their effects on French politics and imperial imaginaries. And while, ultimately, these arguments would help create a consensus around a model for empire in Algeria centered on assimilationist ideals, they also reveal the multiplicity of imperial visions that continued to persist after the collapse of Napoleon III's royaume arabe.

This conversation began in 1871 as a debate about the causes behind the Mokrani Revolt. If most commentators agreed that the uprising demonstrated that indigenous Algerians were untrustworthy, they disagreed about which policies had instigated its outbreak. Some maintained that the empire and Algeria's military administration were responsible, whereas others claimed the instability of the new republic and civil administration was to blame. These contrasting positions emerged from oppositional beliefs about the political conflicts that had transpired in Algeria and France following the Second Empire's collapse, and they served as a referendum on both the empire and the republic's respective relationships with Algeria.

Several writers connected to the military—alongside some journalists with Bonapartist sympathies—sought, as early as the second half of 1871, to use the Mokrani Revolt to attack the new civil administration and to defend the military administration's legacy in Algeria. In political pamphlets and newspapers published mostly in France and therefore probably aimed primarily at metropolitan audiences, these writers also often tied what they identified as the new civil administration's problems to broader failings of republican governance. Even if these writers did not defend Napoleon III or the royaume arabe, they therefore sought to show that it was the republicans who were responsible for recent Algerian conflicts. These arguments often linked Algeria's administration directly to metropolitan political questions, and they had much in common with contemporary monarchist and Bonapartist attacks on the republic within metropolitan France.[76]

Many of the writers associated with the military focused their attacks on the republican government around its decision to pass the Crémieux decree granting Algerian Jews French citizenship. For example, Louis Serre, a former soldier, argued, "Without the naturalization of the Jews . . . the revolt would have never happened."[77] He noted that Arabs "hated" the Jews because they were "soft, cowardly, and effeminate," and as a result Arabs were "humiliated" when the Jews were elevated to positions above them.[78] Serre thus invoked anti-Semitic reasoning to conclude that the decree had been a disastrous mistake and to cast doubt on the republican administration's ability to draft legislation for Algeria.[79]

Other former military officers implied that the revolt stemmed from issues that went beyond a single decree to include a broader set of problems with the new republican regime. Many pointed to the republic's decision to establish a civil administration. François Leblanc de Prébois, another former officer who had represented Algeria in the legislative assembly in 1849, maintained that the civil administration's inability to control indigenous Algerians proved that it was "weak" and "inane."[80] He argued that eliminating the military administration in a territory almost entirely composed of indigenous peoples was "an illusion"; instead of eliminating the bureaux arabes, the military should expand its authority over "civil" and "military" territories alike because it alone could ensure security.[81]

Several other authors echoed Prébois's claim that the revolts proved that a "civil government" would never be able to rule Algeria. But instead of arguing that a civil regime was weaker than a military regime, they contended that the civil regime was problematic because it was beholden to settlers' interests. In the Bonapartist *Le gaulois*, journalist Creuzat de Salvière, who had written a defense of the royaume arabe in 1865, argued that the civil government would subsume the needs of indigenous peoples to those of colonists. He maintained that settlers hated the military regime because it "interrupted their taste for domination" and saw the civil regime as "more apt . . . to enrich them." Salvière thus implied that the colonists' use of republican ideals to defend the civil regime was fraudulent; their embrace of civil government stemmed only from a desire to secure their own interests.[82] They had succeeded in duping their metropolitan republican allies, he argued, but the indigenous Algerian population was aware of their motives. The Kabyles thus revolted against the civil government because they saw that it would strip them of their privileges.[83] He concluded by warning that indigenous Algerians would keep revolting against a civil government radically opposed to their interests.[84] Salvière thus sought to counter settler arguments—advanced throughout 1870–71—that the civil administration was more "just" or "effective" than its military counterpart. Instead, he maintained, the civil regime was illegitimate, and it would undermine France's ability to hold on to Algeria.

Many of the authors who condemned the Third Republic's policies in Algeria also implied that republicanism itself was responsible for the territory's current problems. Some insisted that the settlers' radical republicanism had sparked the insurrection. Serre argued that the Algerian "radical press" and "Communard movements" alarmed indigenous Algerians and pushed them to revolt.[85] Prébois and Salvière similarly maintained that the radical settlers' printed attacks against the Second Empire and their protests against the military administration alienated Arabs in particular, who saw Napoleon III and the military as their protectors.[86]

Even though these critics of the new republican government and the civil regime were more sympathetic toward indigenous Algerians, most nevertheless agreed that colonization would ensure Algeria's future security. Jules Quinemant, a retired military officer and colonist, claimed that Arabs "could not be assimilated" or make Algeria prosperous but that the military could "move them closer to us."[87] In order to ensure Algeria's future wealth and stability, Quinemant argued, the government needed to settle former soldiers in military agricultural colonies so that the French population would "counterbalance . . . that of the indigenous."[88] These colonists, he averred, would slowly gain the respect of their indigenous neighbors who only acknowledged military force. This vision of colonization thus positioned the spread of the settler population as equivalent to the spread of the military's influence in Algeria. But instead of replacing the military government with a civil government, he proposed to displace the civil colonist population with a military one.[89] This argument had a long history that dated back to Thomas-Robert Bugeaud, the governor-general of Algeria who had conquered much of the colony under the July Monarchy, and it was not particularly popular in the early 1870s.[90] Other critics of the civil regime nevertheless advanced similar arguments, contending that the nature of the colonist population needed to change in order to end conflicts with the military administration. Prébois and Salvière thus both argued that the government should recruit colonists from rural France who would be free of the demagogy of their urban counterparts and farm more effectively.[91] These arguments conceded that the European settler community was critical to Algeria's future but could hardly have been popular among settler advocates for civil government.

Royalist newspapers in France echoed some of these criticisms of the republican policy in Algeria and the civil administration, even if they were also critical of Napoleon III and the royaume arabe. Auguste Lenthéric, a journalist who had worked at *L'akhbar* in Algeria before returning to France to cover Algerian issues for the *Gazette de France*, thus opined, "It is clear today that the politics followed by the Empire will spare us no failures. In Algeria the royaume arabe, Napoleon III's foolish utopia, has brought its fruits: the insurrection of all the tribes in the province of Alger and Constantine." He argued that the revolts in Algeria were part of a pattern of the Second Empire's weaknesses: its policies had led both to French defeat in Europe and indigenous revolt in North Africa. But he also contended that the new republican government bore responsibility for the insurrection, as it had allowed radicals to both unsettle the colonial administration and print their inflammatory opinions in newspapers.[92] While Lenthéric argued that a civil administration would help solve Algeria's problems, he warned against the influence of radical republicans on Algerian politics and suggested that if they were allowed to dominate representative institutions, they would contribute to future unrest in Algeria.[93] Even as he condemned Bonapartist policy and supported a civil administration, he therefore implied that unchecked republican radicalism would undermine French colonial rule.

Both settlers in Algeria and republican journalists in France rejected these attacks on Algeria's civil administration and offered up distinct interpretations of the turmoil of 1870–71. Most of the publications written by settlers in Algeria in fact sought to use the insurrection to further condemn the military administration by arguing that it was responsible for the recent revolt's outbreak and spread. *L'akhbar*, for example, claimed that by first mismanaging indigenous Algerians and then limiting European colonization, the military regime had set the stage for a revolt and then weakened the state's ability to suppress it.[94] Other authors went a step further and implied that the military had deliberately provoked the conflict. As *L'Alger française* argued, if the military had acted immediately, it would have been "easy to put down the revolts with a single blow," but "the military authority neglected to put its foot down on the first sparks, and now everything is on fire." The author went on to indicate that this negligence was deliberate because the military wanted to use the revolt to prove that it was critical to France's authority in the territory.[95] Settler journalists publishing in Algeria thus sought to use the uprising to show that the bureaux arabes and military government were corrupt, self-serving, and ineffective institutions that would be detrimental to Algeria's future, even if the government in France was becoming "republican." While some writers were also critical of some of the policies passed by the new republican government—especially the decision to grant citizenship to Algerian Jews, which was extremely unpopular among settlers in Algeria—they also promised that a republican civilian administration that promoted colonization would bring stability to the territory.[96]

Settlers' arguments about the military's role in recent Algerian conflicts extended into the metropolitan press, and especially to republican newspapers, partly because colonists wrote to them to express their opinions about the unfolding events. Charles Jourdan, an Algerian landowner and son of Louis Jourdan, another 1848 deportee who had returned to France in 1852 to become the editor of the influential moderate republican opposition journal *Le siècle*, wrote a series of letters in late 1871 that appeared in his father's newspaper and attacked the military's attempt to handle the revolts. In these letters, Jourdan highlighted el-Mokrani's ties to the bureaux arabes' important officers and implied that those officers may have started the revolt in the first place. He went so far as to demand an official inquiry into the military's behavior during the revolt and warned that the government would prosecute any officers who had committed crimes against the state.[97] He concluded by expressing the hope that the metropolitan government would limit the military's future influence.[98] This claim that the bureaux arabes had sanctioned and even sparked the revolts also appeared in multiple pamphlets that settlers published in the metropole.[99] Émile Thuillier, another 1848 deportee, even wrote and staged a play called *Le royaume arabe* in both Algiers and Marseille that made the same claim—although the play apparently attracted considerably more interest in Algiers than in Marseille.[100]

Many of the publications printed by settlers in Algeria that sought to discredit the bureaux arabes and the military administration by tying both to the uprising did not engage directly with questions about metropolitan France's political organization. This may have partly stemmed from the fact that in the aftermath of 1871, the press in Algeria was more heavily policed than the press in France, but it may have also reflected settler journalists' ongoing preoccupation with securing a civil administration.[101] Republican writers in the metropole, on the other hand, were much more likely to invoke the revolt to condemn not just Algeria's military administration but also the Second Empire more broadly. They sought as well to differentiate the new regime from the previous administration and lay out a vision for a new "republican" Algeria.

Many republican writers in the metropole thus linked the revolts directly to Napoleon III's attempt to reorganize Algeria into a royaume arabe.[102] Even explanations of the revolt that adopted a moderate tone often had a clear political agenda. Félix Robiou de la Trehonnais, a French historian and orientalist, maintained that many colonist attacks on the bureaux arabes, the military administration, and Napoleon III were "calumnies."[103] At the same time, however, he argued that both Napoleon III and his officers had been "seduced" by the "undeniable courage of the Arabs . . . their savage bohemian customs, and all the poetry in their patriarchal and free life."[104] He even claimed that Napoleon III and his officers shared key commonalities with the Arabs since both embraced a political system based on "absolute sovereignty." As a result of the emperor's desire to preserve this "splendid mirage of the desert," Trehonnais insisted, the imperial administration had treated Arabs too leniently and wrongly opposed the expansion of European settlements.[105] These policies led to an uncontrollable indigenous population that revolted when its Bonapartist-protected privileges were challenged. Trehonnais thus argued against the often repeated contention that Napoleon III and the bureaux arabes had been conspiring against French Algeria, but his characterization of the motivation of the Napoleonic bureaux was just as damning. After all, he implied that the imperial government and Arab tribes lived by the same patriarchal codes and had much in common. In the context of a well-developed colonial discourse that invoked those tribes as the epitome of barbarian practices and feudal values, such a comparison was highly unflattering to the Second Empire. Moreover, like other authors, Trehonnais concluded by noting that the problems with the Second Empire's administration demonstrated that Algeria's future lay in a republican civilian administration and expanded colonization.[106]

If republicans painted the Second Empire as responsible for Algeria's problems while implying that the new republic would restore the territory, they did not agree on how the republic would solve these problems or on the relationship it would have with Algeria. Many concurred that the republic would redeem past faults by granting colonists the "political liberty" intrinsic to republican government. But they at least initially had sharp disagreements about what this "political liberty" would look like and the specific relationship with France it would entail. Most republicans followed the position laid out by settler advocates such as Auguste-Hubert Warnier and Jules Duval in the 1860s, who had long contended that Algeria should be assimilated into the French nation as part of a broader campaign to dismantle the military administration and gain access to the civil rights and governmental institutions guaranteed to metropolitan citizens.[107] These theorists and politicians, like their counterparts writing in the 1860s, were less clear on the position that the indigenous population would occupy in this new "assimilated" state—although most contended that indigenous people should be forced to assimilate to French cultural and social norms without having access to French political rights.[108]

In contrast to the many writers who argued that the new Third Republic should assimilate Algeria into the French nation, however, other republican authors insisted that France should reconstitute Algeria as a semiautonomous colony. Most of the advocates for this position were settlers themselves, although metropolitan intellectuals with few direct ties to Algeria numbered among them as well. Those who made the case for Algeria's autonomy did so for different reasons. One group claimed that Algeria could never assimilate because its indigenous population would only slowly—if ever—adapt to French rule. As a result, they concluded that Algeria's administration needed to be independent so that it could govern its settlers as French citizens while subjecting the indigenous population to a different regime.[109] While some of these authors argued that assimilation should at least remain a long-term goal, others maintained that Algeria should become a semiautonomous state that could determine its own affairs while maintaining a "national link" to the republic.[110] Even if these authors did not believe that Algeria should be understood as a royaume arabe, in other words, they nevertheless maintained that Algeria's indigenous population had to be accounted for in its administration.

A second group argued, on the other hand, that France could not assimilate Algeria because the settlers' needs diverged too sharply from the needs of those in metropolitan France.[111] This group proposed yet a different model for Algeria centered on a vision of Latin unity. Instead of describing Algeria as part of a multinational Mediterranean empire, as Napoleon III had, or as an extension of France, these thinkers portrayed the territory as a new Latin nation composed of settlers from across the Mediterranean.[112] As Patricia Lorcin has shown, this vision of a new "Latin" race coming of age in Algeria would become increasingly popular in the 1880s and 1890s.[113] But it had its origins in the late 1860s and early 1870s, when republican thinkers used it to defend an autonomous vision of Algeria's future.

One of these thinkers was Paul Fawtier, a radical republican politician from Philippeville who published a pamphlet for metropolitan and settler audiences arguing that Algeria could not assimilate into France because its settler population consisted of immigrants from across the European Mediterranean.[114] He contended that these immigrants' ties to their former countries were too strong for them to become French, but that they could come together to form a new Algerian nation because such a nation would incorporate elements of their old identities instead of conflicting with them. This Algerian nation would have its own colonial parliament and constitution determined by settlers, but it would not become independent; instead, it would relate to France through a federal system. By creating a federalized state that spanned the Mediterranean and incorporated the European peoples that lived on its shores, Fawtier claimed that France would make Algeria attractive to emigrants and build alliances with other Mediterranean nations.[115]

This understanding of the benefits of building a nation of "Latin peoples" in Algeria also appeared in other works. Henri Verne, a member of the General Council of Constantine, published a pamphlet that advanced a different version of this argument.[116] Verne did not advocate for a federal system but for a modified vision of political assimilation. In his account, Algeria's future rested on a settler population that the metropole's political structures would eventually govern. However, like Fawtier, Verne insisted that the inhabitants of Algeria were different from the inhabitants of France; because they included "Latin peoples" from across the Mediterranean, they were a "new people." If the metropole acknowledged this, he promised, these settlers would build "a rich and strong Algeria" that would enable France to exercise "a strong influence over other Latin peoples."[117]

These authors' visions of a "Latin" Algeria echoed the metropolitan writers who argued in 1871 and 1872 that a Latin Alliance would allow Latin peoples to defend themselves in the face of competition from Germany, Britain, and Russia. They also reflected—even more directly—Napoleon III's vision for a "Latin" Mexico, which Napoleon III had believed would extend France's influence over other Latin nations and create a loose federation of Latin empires. The fact that multiple republican writers mobilized latinité to describe France's relationship to Algeria thus indicates that while they rejected some versions of Napoleonic empire, they did not reject all of them, as some sought to apply Napoleon's vision for Mexico to Algeria. If the royaume arabe had fallen into disfavor after 1871, latinité had not entirely.

As these divergent visions of a "republican Algeria" make clear, there was no consensus in the years after 1871 among republicans about how to imagine Algeria's relationship with France. While most commentators embraced the idea that Algeria should become part of the French nation, others argued that Algeria needed to be understood as a territory distinct from France. These latter arguments had weaknesses associated with them, however. Many authors who argued in favor of autonomy connected the idea of an autonomous Algeria to a vision of France as a decentralized and federated republic, which was discredited by its associations with Communard thought after 1871.[118] As Käthe Panick has shown, moreover, in the years following the war's conclusion, the idea of latinité or a Latin race was primarily used by republican writers to explain what they saw as the "decadence" of the French, Spanish, and Italian people. The idea thus was increasingly connected to notions of French weakness and not French strength, reflecting its associations with the Mexican expedition.[119] Perhaps partly for that reason, the calls for Algerian autonomy did not gain traction in the immediate aftermath of 1870–71 within the conservative government in power.

These diverse accounts of Algeria's problems and its potential reflected the political concerns of the people who formulated them. Many settlers had an interest in linking the recent insurrection to military incompetence because they were still seeking to eliminate the last vestiges of the military administration, and they feared that the outbreak of the revolts would convince metropolitan administrators to restore the military regime.[120] At the same time, in light of the republicans' shifting electoral fortunes in 1871, some colonists started to separate their own desires to reorganize the colony from the conflicts of domestic politics. They began to claim that their demands did not emerge from any political ideology but instead stemmed from a desire to transform Algeria into a functioning territory. As one settler journalist contended in the fall of 1871, "reconstituting the administration of Algeria on new bases is not politics, but colonization."[121] This argument sought to convince readers of all political convictions to support the administrative reorganization of Algeria. Especially in light of the strong links between many Algerian colonists and metropolitan radical republicans during the winter of 1870–71, this type of positioning represented a discursive shift and a new political strategy.

In metropolitan France, on the other hand, most authors explicitly tied their descriptions of the revolt and its implications for Algeria to domestic political debates. Indeed, the historic close ties between the settlers and the republicans ensured that Algeria and its future became entangled in wider political arguments about the viability of republicanism, monarchism, and Bonapartism in the early years of the Third Republic—even at a moment when some settlers tried to depoliticize the question of Algeria's future. Those who entered the debate about the relative value of the civil or military administration thus usually couched their arguments in a wider set of claims about France's political organization. Bonapartist and conservative commentators insisted that the republicans' changes to Algeria's administration were responsible for the insurrection. By arguing that the radical press played a key role in pushing the indigenous population to revolt, moreover, they invoked the situation in Algeria as evidence that the damage caused by radical republicans in 1871 extended beyond Paris. They thus rejected the idea that a civilian regime could rule Algeria more effectively than a military one and cast aspersions on republicanism itself by linking it to the radicalism of the Commune. Republican commentators, on the other hand, highlighted the connections between the military regime and the Second Empire, arguing that both were responsible for contemporary Algeria's problems. They sought to demonstrate that the revolt was the result of the Second Empire's negative legacy and not connected to the new republic. At the same time, they promised that the new republican regime would be able to bring peace and prosperity to the territory—even if they did not agree about what a "republican Algeria" would look like.

These commentators also expressed different views about the connections between Algeria's administrative structure and French politics. Although most conservatives bound the civil administration to the new republican government and implied that both were responsible for the indigenous revolt and Algeria's current problems, they did not usually defend the Second Empire or Napoleon III's royaume arabe. Even as they relied on some of the principles that had underwritten his policies toward Algeria—for example, that France's interests lay in defending indigenous Algerians against settler predations—they never referred to Napoleon III. In other words, even as they tied the failures of the civil regime to republicanism, they sought to distance the military regime from Bonapartism. This rhetorical strategy reflected the degree to which Bonapartism and Napoleon III had become discredited. But it also meant that these commentators struggled to present a coherent vision of Algeria's future. They argued for the continued presence of the military regime but did not connect the military's presence in Algeria to any particular understanding of Algeria's relationship to France.

Republicans, on the other hand, painted the Second Empire's collapse as a break in Algeria's history. They described the new civil administration as a natural outgrowth of republicanism and claimed that it had transformed Algeria's old "imperial" relationship to France into a new "republican" one. The new Algeria was not a separate, subject nation. Instead, it would either merge with the French nation or exist next to it as a semiautonomous "Latin" state. As a result, republicans implied, the new Algeria would align with republican values and overcome the mistakes of the past—a line of argumentation that echoed promises that republicanism in metropolitan France could redeem the country from the Second Empire's faults.

Conservative critics' inability to articulate a clear model for a new Algeria—combined with the fact that the association with radical Communard thought had discredited the republican campaign for Algerian autonomy—meant that by the mid-1870s politicians of all parties increasingly began to use "assimilation" to describe Algeria and its relationship to France. A discourse that positioned Algeria as central to France's future in the wake of the Franco-Prussian War also drove this move toward "assimilation." The idea that Algeria was critical to France was not new: Lucien-Anatole Prévost-Paradol, a prominent French liberal, had posited it in 1868 when he contended that strengthening the French presence in Algeria would enable France to counter Prussia's growing power.[122] In light of France's defeat, Prévost-Paradol's claim that France needed to increase its territory and population in order to avoid becoming a second-rate power took on new urgency.[123] Many authors began to invoke his vision of a *France africaine* when articulating their ideas about Algeria.[124]

As other scholars have shown, the idea that Algeria and France were bound together was also enforced by attempts to link the territory to the lost regions of Alsace and Lorraine that Germany had recently annexed. Even in 1871 some writers began to argue that France should use Algeria to "create a second France . . . to compensate for our diminished presence on the Rhine."[125] By transforming Algeria into three départements, a writer for *Le temps* hoped, France would be able to regain what it lost in status, population, and territory when Germany defeated it.[126] The author of the popular children's book *Le tour de la France par deux enfants* wrote a novel devoted to the subject in 1887, *Les enfants de Marcel*, which described Algeria as the "new Alsace."[127] In this vision, merging Algeria into the French nation would not only benefit settlers, who would gain the rights, privileges, and institutions that they had been denied; it would also benefit France itself by healing the dismembered national body and conjoining it with new overseas territory.[128]

The tendency to link Algeria, Alsace, and Lorraine both drove and was driven by a visible if unsuccessful campaign to encourage displaced Alsatians and Lorrainers to move to Algeria. As early as December 1870—even before Germany annexed the two regions—Auguste-Hubert Warnier began to argue that the government should encourage French citizens living under German occupation to immigrate to Algeria.[129] He claimed that many peasant families in occupied territories had no resources to rebuild their destroyed homes. If they moved to metropolitan France, they would impoverish and weaken the nation. But in Algeria, they would invigorate both colony and metropole by generating capital and increasing the population.[130]

The idea that Alsatians and Lorrainers should move to Algeria became even more popular after Germany annexed the territories and gave their inhabitants the choice between leaving and surrendering their French citizenship.[131] A movement developed to encourage the refugees to immigrate to Algeria, where they would be able to "remain French."[132] This plan eventually gained government support. In June 1871 the National Assembly voted to set aside one hundred thousand acres of the "best land" for emigrants from the new German territory of Alsace-Lorraine and promised to pay to transport them to the colony and set up "population centers" for them that would include a school, roads, water, and other basic services.[133] The Algerian administration also raised money to help with the project.[134]

Multiple groups emerged from across the ideological spectrum to facilitate emigration from Alsace-Lorraine. The Society for the Protection of Alsatians and Lorrainers raised money and advocated on the behalf of emigrants to Algeria to increase their land allotments.[135] In 1873, they even sent one of their members to Algeria in order to inspect the situation of the recent émigrés and arrange assistance for them if necessary.[136] In 1874 the comte d'Haussonville, an Orleanist with familial ties to the French prime minister, Albert de Broglie, organized an art exhibition at the Palais de la Présidence du Corps Législatif to fund Alsatians and Lorrainers "who wanted to remain French" as they emigrated to Algeria.[137]

Despite the efforts of the government and these advocacy groups, very few families from Alsace-Lorraine moved to Algeria, and many of those who did eventually left for metropolitan France.[138] These efforts nevertheless produced an enduring mythical connection between the two territories: the idea that Algeria would help make up for France's loss proved very influential.[139] As a result, the campaign helped secure popular conceptions of Algeria as an "extension" of metropolitan France. European settlers in Algeria had long campaigned for the territory's assimilation into France. This assimilation was never cemented as fully as many of them hoped—indeed, republicans' rhetorical embrace of the language of assimilation translated very unevenly into local colonial practice—but on an abstract level, the idea that Algeria was an integral component of the French nation gained increasing traction in the wake of the defeat.

Empire, Republic, Colony, and Nation

In the aftermath of the Franco-Prussian War, French republicans defended the new republic against their political opponents by arguing that the Second Empire was responsible for all of France's political misfortunes and promising that the republic alone could redeem the country. They contended that empire was an illegitimate form of political organization and promised that any return toward imperialism would ruin France's future. Such arguments threw the nature of France's relationship with its colonies into question because some writers and intellectuals continued to associate "colonies" with "empire." The relationship between these two ideas was particularly conflicted in Algeria because Napoleon III had used the territory to promote the idea of a French Mediterranean empire that would rest on Bonapartist political principles and bind multiple nations together beneath one overarching political structure. On a discursive if not a practical level, he thus transformed Algeria into a centerpiece example of Bonapartist imperial strategy.

After the Second Empire's collapse, republicans therefore worked to transform understandings of France's relationship with its overseas territories. They distinguished between France's colonial holdings and European Napoleonic empire by describing those holdings in republican terms. In the 1870s much of this conversation referred to Algeria in a complex set of conflicts and negotiations between settlers, the French government, and intellectuals of different political stripes. Tellingly, the conversation excluded indigenous Algerian voices, whose minimal influence over Bonapartist colonial policy republicans and settlers invoked as evidence of Napoleonic rule's militarism, decadence, and infatuation with aristocracies—all political problems these writers promised that the new republic would resolve in both France and Algeria. The Second Empire's legacy, the memory of French defeat in the Franco-Prussian War, and the loss of Alsace and Lorraine thus deeply informed this evolving debate about Algeria, but settler political activism and the widespread indigenous revolt shaped it too. Over the course of these arguments, most French republicans and settlers came to agree that Algeria was not a colony; instead, they contended, it should be understood as an "extension" of the French nation overseas.

The government's decision to describe Algeria as an extension of France partly came out of a longer assimilatory tradition in republican thought, but more immediate factors also shaped it. Settlers pressed for this vision because it offered them a hegemonic position within the territory and enabled them to campaign for extended political, civil, and property rights. Republican politicians in the metropole, seeking to shore up support in the National Assembly, also had an interest in placating their settler allies.[140] But while the embrace of assimilation promised concrete benefits for both settlers in Algeria and republican politicians in France, the material consequences of the embrace of the language of assimilation are difficult to trace. Debates about how to envision empire in Algeria only ever indirectly intersected with the struggles within the colony over the local organization of political power, the structure of administrative institutions, and land policy. And in France political support from Algerian settlers certainly did not translate into a legislative majority for republican politicians during the first half of the 1870s.

If redefining Algeria did not have direct practical consequences for the structure of French rule, however, it had much clearer effects on republican visions of empire and politics. Over the course of these contestations, many republicans embraced the idea that domestic politics and imperial policy were interconnected. Like their liberal predecessors of the late eighteenth century, they contended that despotic rule overseas was linked to autocratic politics at home. They thus argued that France's imperial structures should align with republican political values and practices—which meant supporting representative institutions and limiting the authority of the military and local elites. By accepting settlers' contention that they were the primary population in Algeria and granting them additional political rights, republicans could claim to have transformed the colony much as they sought to transform the metropole. This vision carried contradictions. It remained unclear exactly how and to what degree Algeria would be able to "assimilate" into France. The position of the indigenous population in this newly assimilated Algeria also remained necessarily unspecified.[141] And, on an ideological level, "assimilation" did not give republicans a language to describe France's relationship to other overseas territories. In the years to come, as republicans looked to expand French influence in other parts of the world, they would search for more comprehensive models that did not rest on the concept of assimilation.

Chapter 4

Expeditions and Expansion between Algeria and Senegal

By 1873 Auguste-Hubert Warnier, one of the vocal colonist opponents of Napoleon III's royaume arabe, had become Algiers's deputy to the National Assembly. That year, he recommended Paul Soleillet, the son of a fabric manufacturer who had spent time traveling in Algeria, to the Algiers Chamber of Commerce. Soleillet, he explained, had undertaken "with very persistent tenacity" an enterprise that would contribute to the "prosperity of Algeria" by extending the colony's commercial relations first to the Sahara and then to sub-Saharan Africa.[1] Soleillet proposed to undertake an exploratory mission to Aïn Salah, an oasis market town outside the boundaries of colonial Algeria and under the sovereignty of the emperor of Morocco.[2] In his presentation to the Algiers Chamber of Commerce in May 1873, Soleillet argued that there was a vibrant trans-Saharan caravan trade that went from the southern perspective either west toward Morocco or east toward Tripoli, thereby circumventing Algeria. He contended that French merchants could turn this trade toward the colony by making connections in key trading towns and identifying European products that the Saharan traders might want. He proposed to visit Aïn Salah with a sampling of goods to facilitate these connections and asked the Chamber of Commerce for financial and political support. Not only would his expedition enrich Algeria, he promised; it would also build relationships between the colony and the peoples who lived beyond its borders, extending French influence into Central Africa.[3]

Soleillet would cite Warnier's letter of recommendation in his numerous requests for government funding for a variety of expeditions into the 1880s—reflecting the influence that the name of this long-standing opponent of the royaume arabe wielded in colonial circles beyond his death.[4] But Soleillet's first expedition did not rest only on Warnier's support; as Jacques Valette has made clear, the Chamber of Commerce was also interested—largely because it, too, was convinced of the trans-Saharan trade's value.[5] The Chamber of Commerce in turn solicited the support of Antoine Chanzy, Algeria's governor-general, by invoking the mission's potential political and economic benefits.[6]

Through Chanzy, Soleillet gained access to a network of support in the Algerian administration. Chanzy reached out to military officers and *caïds* (*qa'ids*), indigenous Algerian leaders who worked for the French colonial administration, in the Algerian Sahara, asking them to aid Soleillet as he traveled south.[7] Chanzy's appeals to the metropolitan government, on the other hand, proved less fruitful. Although the Ministry of Public Instruction endorsed the mission, it refused to fund Soleillet's efforts.[8] Even the Paris Geographical Society declined to finance Soleillet because of his commercial aims, although one of its most illustrious members, Henri Duveyrier, who had undertaken expeditions into the Algerian Sahara during the 1850s and had ties with Warnier, sent a letter containing advice.[9]

Despite the relative lack of interest in the metropole, it was remarkable that Soleillet's expedition attracted as much support in Algeria as it did. Soleillet was drawing on a tradition of elite settler interest in the trans-Saharan trade and support for exploratory missions in the south.[10] But he lacked the skills of other explorers: he spoke no Arabic, and even as he argued that the mission would have "scientific" and "commercial" value, he had no formal training in geography or cartography.[11] E. Vignard, a colonial official who knew Arabic and was familiar with the Saharan notables whom Soleillet proposed to meet, had agreed to join the mission in the summer of 1873. But he had a falling out with Soleillet later that fall and dropped out before the expedition left Algiers.[12]

Despite his technical deficits, however, Soleillet proved able to mobilize settler elites' conviction that Algeria should be more lucrative than it was. This conviction was rooted in an orientalist narrative that described Roman Algeria as a fertile place that had fallen into decadence and positioned France as the civilizing influence that could restore its prosperity.[13] Soleillet's proposal to reestablish an ancient trading route by embarking on a scientific and commercial expedition intersected with this narrative. The enthusiasm surrounding his mission also points to the fact that even in the early 1870s, when the metropolitan government had concerns about the political implications of imperial expansion, settler businessmen and administrators were looking for ways to spread French influence beyond North Africa. Soleillet insisted that his mission did not have a "political, military, or religious character," but he also claimed that it would build connections between Algeria and the territories that surrounded it.[14] The rhetoric of "influence" also surrounded other desert expeditions by Norbert Dournaux-Duperé and Eugène Joubert, Victor Largeau, and Louis Say funded by settlers and the Algerian administration in the early 1870s.[15]

Over the past thirty years, scholars have looked at the ways in which both geographical societies and individual explorers helped propagate colonialism.[16] As they have shown, the celebration of individual explorers—and the ties between those explorers and colonial projects—was not new in the nineteenth century. Eighteenth-century elites had followed the voyages of explorers; interest in exploration was tied to the Enlightenment and the spread of scientific thinking.[17] By the late nineteenth century, however, the growth of the popular press had extended the audience for accounts of exploration. In France the press's interest in exploration partly reflected its ties with the Paris Geographical Society, which promoted many of these missions.[18] Exploration also, as historian Berny Sèbe has argued, intersected with powerful norms in European popular culture, which—thanks to the transformations of the Industrial Revolution and contemporary ideas about masculinity—was primed to structure narratives around "great men" celebrated as heroes.[19] Much scholarship has focused on the position of explorers in the popular press during the 1880s, looking especially at the figure of Pierre Savorgnan de Brazza and the way that proponents of colonialism used him to popularize overseas expansion.[20] The expeditions sponsored in the Sahara in the 1870s have been less thoroughly examined because they were less successful and occupied a less prominent place in popular culture. But as historian Jacques Valette has made clear, the relationship between advocates of colonial expansion and explorers in the 1880s had its roots in the previous decade.[21]

It was not only settler elites in Algeria, the colonial administration, and geographical societies who acted as colonial advocates in the 1870s; some moderate republican politicians who came to power in 1878—the year that the republicans consolidated their hold over the state—were also interested in colonial expansion. These politicians grouped around Léon Gambetta, and their interest in colonialism stemmed partly from their interpretation of France's defeat in the Franco-Prussian War. They were concerned that France was in danger of becoming a second-rate power, so they believed that the country needed a mechanism to increase its prestige and make up for its loss.[22] Even in 1871 republican intellectual Ernest Renan took up the point, arguing that colonization was a "political necessity of the first order."[23] Expanding its influence outside Europe, colonial advocates implied, would protect France against Germany and enable it to compete with expanding British interests in Africa and Asia.

At the same time, however, colonial expansion in the early 1870s had slippery political associations. Thanks partly to Bonapartist policy, multiple writers and politicians continued to connect colonization to "empire" more broadly. Arguments over Algeria's organization during and following the Franco-Prussian War had not led to a new consensus around these terms. Settlers had deployed a juxtaposition between Bonapartist and republican overseas policy to convince France's republican government to restructure Algeria in alignment with their own interests. What they described as a "republican" model denied Algeria's colonial structure; it was predicated on the notion that Algeria was not a colony but an extension of France overseas. This conception of Algeria granted political and civil rights to settlers but not to indigenous people, and it thus secured the settlers' hegemonic position within the territory. It also enabled the new republic to differentiate its policies in Algeria from those of the Second Empire. But because this model was based on the denial that France's policies in Algeria were colonial or imperial, it did not provide a framework for how to understand future overseas expansion.

In the second half of the 1870s, intellectuals made a series of attempts to systematically define "colonialism" and explain its benefits for France. These texts may have helped convince some republican politicians and intellectuals to embrace colonial expansionism, but they did not have a very wide audience or eliminate the term's complicated political implications. Thanks to the death of Napoleon IV in 1879 and continued divisions between the Orleanist and Legitimist parties, a monarchical or Bonapartist restoration was increasingly unlikely, but republicans remained concerned about the appeal of monarchist and imperialist ideas and divided among themselves.[24] Expeditions like Soleillet's thus offered ideological benefits to republican advocates of colonialism. As a number of historians have shown, individual explorers' ability to become compelling popular heroes in the divisive early years of the Third Republic stemmed partly from the fact that they were not publicly bound to any party and were thus positioned to present themselves as embodying the nation as a whole.[25] By tying exploration and colonialism together, republican advocates of colonial expansion could position expansion overseas as something that could transcend the politically divided history of empire in France. This vision of exploration, moreover, celebrated values that opposed those that republican politicians and intellectuals had charged defined Bonapartist imperialism. Republicans had contended that Bonapartism was a militaristic and despotic political doctrine that cultivated decadence, effeminacy, and hysteria in France. Soleillet and other explorers argued that exploration was a peaceful, masculine enterprise; they emphasized its commercial, scientific, and humanitarian benefits and did not speak about military conquest. Instead, they tied trade and influence together, and they positioned expeditions—and technocratic projects such as the construction of a trans-Saharan railroad—as a way to increase both beyond the borders of France's current colonies and protectorates, especially around Algeria and Senegal in Africa and Cochinchina and Cambodia in southeast Asia. This portrayal of exploration bore almost no resemblance to the actual practice of colonial expansion, but it became a central way that republicans spoke about it during the 1870s and early 1880s.

This conversation about exploration and colonial expansion, like the conversation about Algeria's future and its relationship to France, was both fragmented and exclusionary. In the aftermath of the Commune's collapse, the conservatives who dominated the Third Republic had reinstituted many of the measures used by Napoleon III's government to control the press, and throughout the 1870s the new republic policed settler newspapers in Algeria more closely than their counterparts in France.[26] In 1881 this practice changed, as the law passed that year to end censorship of the political press in the metropole was extended to Algeria and the colonies, but it was only applied to French-language publications directed by French citizens.[27] Tellingly, the passage of the 1881 press law coincided with the formalization of the *indigénat*, a legal code that defined a series of "crimes that only natives could commit" in Algeria and Cochinchina.[28] As historian Arthur Asseraf has explained, these two laws created a system "in which French citizens could publish freely, while Muslims were forbidden not only from publishing, but even from speaking, assembling, and moving around Algeria."[29] The administration viewed even bilingual publications owned by French citizens that employed Muslim journalists, such as Constantine's *El Mountakheb*, with great suspicion, and it pressured that newspaper to shut down.[30]

These dynamics were not the same in Senegal, the other French colonial territory that Soleillet would visit as he sought to traverse the Sahara. During the second half of the nineteenth century, Senegal had transformed from a collection of trading outposts to a center of colonial conquest. That conquest had begun during the Second Empire beneath Louis Faidherbe, the then-governor of Senegal.[31] Faidherbe's expansionary policies received mixed support from the metropolitan government, and the conquests temporarily halted after he departed in 1865. But they transformed metropolitan perceptions of the territory. In 1872 the government of the Third Republic recategorized Senegal as a *grande colonie*, entitled to the same rights and privileges that the inhabitants of Réunion and France's Caribbean territories had gained in 1848.[32] And over the 1870s, the inhabitants of Saint-Louis and Gorée (and later Rufisque and Dakar) gained the right to elect their own mayors, municipal councils, a deputy to the National Assembly, and perhaps most importantly, a General Council, which had influence not only over the budget of the towns but also over the rural interior. These rights only extended to town inhabitants, not to those who lived in newly conquered territory. But they nevertheless created a robust local political culture dominated by firms based in Bordeaux, wealthy métis families, and to a lesser extent African Muslim families, who all played a critical role in facilitating the gum and peanut trades that brought wealth into the colony.[33]

Senegal's status as an "old" colony that dated to the ancien régime, its lack of a substantive settler population, its economic dependence on trade with states in the African interior, and its need for local intermediaries to facilitate that trade thus led the Senegalese colonial regime to incorporate a more diverse array of colonial subjects into the French political community than its Algerian counterpart did. Even outside of the towns, moreover, French rule depended on collaboration with African power brokers—a fact that reflected the tenuousness of French claims to inland territory during this period.[34] That said, in the early 1880s, newspapers and other publications remained tightly controlled by the colonial administration. During the mid-1880s, the métis community was able to use the 1881 law on the press to establish two independent newspapers that circulated back to the metropole on the ships of Bordeaux trading firms. But while the Senegalese colonial administration could not ban these publications outright, it was able to exert enough political and economic pressure to shut them down.[35]

Throughout the 1870s and the 1880s, the structure of the French conversation about empire was thus designed to exclude colonial subjects in both Algeria and Senegal—even as French claims about the benevolent nature of republican imperial expansion were grounded in sanitized portrayals of the relationships that explorers such as Soleillet cultivated with indigenous communities. That said, the actions of different colonized communities in both Algeria and Senegal had direct effects on French debates about empire across this period, as this chapter will show. Moreover, even as portrayals of the heroic masculinity of the white French expert structured narratives about exploration, explorers themselves always depended on the work of indigenous colonial intermediaries such as traders and interpreters. Those intermediaries, in the words of historian Tamba M'bayo, "manage[d] the transmission of information between the French authorities and Africans" and thus "had some bearing on the interchanges between the two groups as well as the knowledge they produced."[36] An especially underqualified explorer like Soleillet was even more dependent on the interpreters that accompanied him.

This chapter considers how coverage of expeditions and technocratic projects such as the trans-Saharan railroad in North and West Africa in the late 1870s and early 1880s not only popularized the idea of colonial expansion but also transformed debates over "empire." It begins by considering the growing theoretical literature on colonization that began to circulate in the 1870s, before reflecting on how that literature intersected with popular coverage of explorers such as Paul Soleillet. Soleillet's career is particularly revealing because he was an unsuccessful explorer who nevertheless in the 1870s and early 1880s attracted settler and state support as well as an audience in the popular press. I argue that while Soleillet never became a "national hero" in the way that Brazza would in the mid-1880s, he, like other early explorers, enabled colonial advocates to differentiate between overseas colonialism and continental imperialism. At the same time, however, I show that these attempts to reconfigure colonial empire met at least initially with limited success—partly because representations of exploration were themselves unstable and partly because so many of the expeditions that the state funded in the 1870s and early 1880s ended in disaster.

Theorizing Colonization in the Early Third Republic

In the early 1870s, a growing theoretical and scholarly literature began to circulate in France that attempted to define "colonization" and explain its purpose and benefits. This literature did not appear out of nowhere. There was a long tradition of French writing on colonialism that had a mixed intellectual and political heritage; it was the scope of this later literature and its close connections with academic and political institutions that was new. Writers in the 1870s nevertheless directly borrowed from older Saint-Simonian, liberal, Catholic, and republican publications about colonialism, civilization, and politics. Many also drew directly on British theoreticians and modeled their ideas after British colonial policy. These writers invoked Britain partly because they saw it as successful but also because it enabled them to distinguish between colonial expansion and the discredited Napoleonic empire, distance their ideas from Napoleon III's, and show that colonization did not necessarily contradict republican values.

Historians have long argued about the role that this literature played in colonial expansion and the scope of its popular influence. In 1972 historian Raoul Girardet contended that the theorists writing in the 1870s formulated what he called the *l'idée coloniale*, which led to the colonial conquests of the 1880s and 1890s. More recently, other scholars have argued that most theorists in the 1870s were not calling for colonial expansion but instead wanted to change France's relationship with its extant overseas territories. Still others have insisted that colonial administrators and settlers shaped France's colonial ideology and policies—not armchair theorists in the metropole. It seems clear that much of this literature lacked a popular audience when it first appeared.[37] But it was influential among the scholarly, political, and settler circles invested in exploration and geography in the 1870s, and its assumptions—and contradictions—helped shape French popular accounts of exploration.

One of the earliest theorists was Jules Duval, the Fourierist, economist, and critic of Napoleon III's royaume arabe, who published his *Les colonies et la politique coloniale de la France* in 1864 during the Second Empire. This book, later republished in the 1870s along with *L'Algérie et les colonies françaises*, defined colonization as an "ancient" practice that consisted of "the foundation of new societies; it is an art because of the practical methods it employs, a science because of the laws it uses."[38] Although material interests impelled societies to colonize, colonization also involved "moral, religious and political interests. . . . It initiates savages and barbarians to the arts and the faith of civilization; it is the moral education of young societies."[39] Duval claimed that the French practice of colonization began with the ancient Gauls, reemerged during the Crusades, and reached its first apogee in the early modern era. He focused on explaining how France's colonies emerged and why many of them fell apart. He then turned to the eighteenth and nineteenth centuries, noting that during that period, France's colonizing efforts derailed, apart from the 1830 conquest of Algeria and the Second Empire's occupation of New Caledonia and Cochinchina. As a result, Duval argued, contemporary France ranked only fourth among the colonizing peoples: its colonies were less numerous than Britain's, the Netherlands', and Spain's.[40] He argued that France needed to adjust this imbalance to command international respect because "all colonies . . . are a source of honor for the metropole." They lent the colonizing nation prestige, moral authority, and global influence.[41]

Even in 1864 Duval thus described colonization as a unique enterprise separate from domestic political questions. Colonization, he argued, was the practice of founding new societies—and it therefore, in his view, had little to do with politics. His vision of colonization was nevertheless rooted in contradictory political ideas. He implied that for colonies to succeed, governments needed to regulate them with policies that encouraged political, economic, and religious liberty—a clear reflection of liberal values. At the same time, his belief that colonization could unite Europeans and "barbaric" peoples into one progressive civilization had its roots in Saint-Simonian thought.[42] But by demonstrating that the French had founded colonies under a variety of circumstances and systems of political organization, he indicated that Bonapartism and the Napoleonic empires were unrelated to French overseas conquests. Duval's attempts, in the 1860s, to depoliticize colonial expansion were thus themselves profoundly political: he was seeking to reject—and indeed, delegitimize—the Bonapartist reading of empire set forward by Napoleon III.

Nearly a decade later in 1874, Paul Leroy-Beaulieu, a journalist, liberal economist, and the son-in-law of Michel Chevalier (the former Saint-Simonian, chair of political economy at the Collège de France, and advocate for the Mexican expedition), published the first edition of *De la colonisation chez les peuples modernes*.[43] The work drew on Duval, but its scope was more ambitious: it tried to describe the colonizing efforts of all modern nations, not just France. Leroy-Beaulieu also worked more systematically to develop a model for colonization and a theoretical justification for the practice. Like Duval, he maintained that colonization was an act undertaken by all "civilized peoples," and he rooted its origins in ancient Greece and Rome. His narrative began in early modern Europe, examining the French, British, Spanish, Portuguese, and Dutch colonial projects. By comparing their methods of colonization, he claimed that he could elicit a theory of colonization and a model for future colonial policy.[44] He devoted the second half of the work to explaining this theory and recommending policies metropolitan governments should adopt vis-à-vis their colonies, many of which he drew from British examples.

Unsurprisingly, Leroy-Beaulieu's vision of colonialism was deeply steeped in liberal principles: he argued that, above all, colonies required economic and political "independence." From an economic standpoint, he contended that colony and metropole alike would prosper most if colonies could trade on the free market. Politically, he claimed that colonies needed to have the authority to act on internal matters independently of the central government. He insisted that settlers should elect local administrators and politicians democratically. Only once the settlers had the ability to trade and govern themselves, he argued, would the colonies prosper. If France hoped to keep its remaining colonies, he warned, the new republican government would need to increase its territories' economic and political freedoms.[45]

Leroy-Beaulieu sought to define "colony" more systematically than his predecessor. Duval—like Napoleon III and many other contemporary thinkers—had equated "colony" with "settlement." Leroy-Beaulieu, on the other hand, insisted that colonies could take three forms: commercial, plantation, and agricultural.[46] Of these three types, he maintained that agricultural (or settler) colonies were the most complex and rewarding.[47] He contended that "colonization is the expansive force of a people: it is its power of reproduction" and "the submission of the universe or of a large part to its language, ideas, and laws."[48] In other words, the establishment of agricultural colonies was beneficial because they would secure the future of France's language and culture by spreading both globally. Even though he was an economist, Leroy-Beaulieu thus saw colonization's benefits as political, cultural, and national. Like Duval, he believed that colonizing would increase France's international prestige. But he was even more concerned about the ways in which it would bolster the nation's ability to compete demographically, linguistically, and culturally with other European powers.

Although Leroy-Beaulieu explained the purpose of colonial expansion differently from Duval, both employed similar strategies to distinguish between overseas colonization and the Napoleonic empire. Leroy-Beaulieu's approach was more explicit, however, because of its comparative methodology. Whereas Duval had distinguished colonization from domestic political debates by arguing that many French governments—from monarchies to republics—had founded colonies, Leroy-Beaulieu took the argument a step further by insisting that all "civilized" peoples practiced colonization. Colonization, he maintained, was thus not tied to any political party or regime; instead, it reflected the character of the French people as a whole. And whereas Duval's work implied that military conquest within Europe was distinct from colonial expansion overseas, Leroy-Beaulieu opposed them to one another. Overseas colonization, he argued, denoted the spread of one nation across the globe in the form of small "new" societies that would come to dominate the surrounding territory. Colonial empires were thus distinct from European empires because European empires ruled over diverse preexisting societies, while colonial empires founded new ones. Tellingly, his history of colonization made no mention of metropolitan empires like the one constructed by Napoleon I.[49]

In 1874 Leroy-Beaulieu saw Algeria as the site to begin to rebuild France's colonial holdings. He argued that by adopting assimilationist policies toward the territory, France could restore its prosperity.[50] From there, he hoped,

France would expand its influence from Algeria toward Senegal, which would enable it "to dominate and civilize the entire northwest of Africa. . . . We could have there beneath our influence a territory almost as large as Europe."[51] Even in 1874 Leroy-Beaulieu thus looked beyond Algeria, hoping that France would use it to extend its colonizing efforts into new territories. He concluded by encouraging France to improve its policies toward its existing colonies and informing his readers that "the people who colonize the most are the premier people; if they are not today, they will be tomorrow."[52]

Napoleon III had sought to secure the prestige of the Second Empire in the early 1860s by promoting a vision of empire that combined his political program with overseas imperial expansion. His vision of a multinational Mediterranean empire dominated by France drew on his uncle's attempt to establish a modern version of the Roman Empire across Europe. Both Duval and Leroy-Beaulieu, on the other hand, distinguished between domestic empire and colonial expansion. The political organization of France, they implied, did not determine its relationship to the territory it conquered. This renunciation of politics was, of course, itself a political argument; these writers used it to rebuff Napoleon III's political goals and reject his vision of a multinational empire, which they saw as at odds with the colonial holdings they hoped to establish. Colonialism would not bring new nations into a wider French Empire, they argued; instead, it would allow France's culture, language, and "race" to spread across a wider geographical expanse. They thus sought to provide a foundation for justifying republican colonialism with a model that was more flexible than "assimilation"—which had emerged in the arguments over Algeria—but that remained distinct from Bonapartist imperialism. At the same time, however, these descriptions of colonization offered no clear way to explain the relationship between colonies and metropole. Although Duval and Leroy-Beaulieu prescribed policies that the metropolitan government should use to regulate its colonies, they did not explain the mechanisms that bound them together. By avoiding the term "empire," these writers lacked a vocabulary to describe the political structure that connected France to its overseas territories.

If liberal and republican thinkers who formulated theories of colonization in the 1860s and 1870s avoided using "empire" to describe France's relationship with its colonies, some conservative theorists did use the term. Abbot Pierre-Auguste Raboisson, a conservative Catholic writer, published one of the most influential of these texts in 1877. Instead of separating "empire" and "colony" like Duval and Leroy-Beaulieu, Raboisson linked the concepts. He argued, "The grandeur and prosperity of colonies makes the grandeur and prosperity of empires. As a result, it is of paramount importance that

France possesses great and prosperous colonies."[53] Raboisson indicated that while all empires did not possess colonies, the strongest empires had extensive ones. Moreover, he claimed, when these empires lost their colonies, their influence collapsed.[54] Raboisson's formulation had two consequences. First, it indicated that colonies and empires existed in an interdependent relationship and defined colonies as a necessary attribute of imperial formations. Second, it implicitly described France as an "empire."

Raboisson also defined the term "colony" differently from Duval and Leroy-Beaulieu. He argued that colonization was "the effective action of a state on a territory (possessed through treaties or conquests) to appropriate its productions and assimilate its inhabitants."[55] By assimilating inhabitants, he claimed, an empire "extended its homeland, multiplied its citizens" if it "communicated to its colonies' inhabitants its spirit, its heart and its faith."[56] Like Duval and Leroy-Beaulieu, Raboisson thus portrayed colonization as the extension of France. But whereas both Duval and Leroy-Beaulieu had argued that colonization above all signified the "settlement" of one group of people in new territory, Raboisson implied that it involved bringing new groups of people beneath one overarching state and assimilating them into French culture.[57]

Most notably, Raboisson's account of colonization and colonial practices did not distinguish between European conquests or imperial structures and their overseas counterparts. Instead, it confounded them. Raboisson used the term "colony" to refer to any territory conquered by an "empire." He described Alsace, Scotland, and Ireland as "colonies" of France and England because they were territories inhabited by different peoples later assimilated by the conquering state. He in fact invoked the Alsatians' devotion to France under German rule to demonstrate how effective French colonizing efforts could be. From this perspective, France's relationship with Alsace or Austria-Hungary's relationship with the Czechs was equivalent to France's relationship with Algeria.[58] Both represented conquered territories that a state sought to administer and incorporate.

In some ways, Raboisson's vision of the relationship between empire and colony had more in common with Napoleon III's 1860s ideas than with the models embraced by his contemporary theorists. Napoleon III had also collapsed "domestic" and "overseas" empire: he had sought to restructure France's relationship with Algeria and extend the country's influence overseas to invoke the memory of Napoleon I's extensive European conquests. But Raboisson's vision also remained distinct from Napoleon III's. Napoleon III had tied the structure of France's government to its relationship with its overseas territories, while Raboisson did not discuss France's political organization. Even more importantly, Napoleon III defined his empire as a multinational entity: he promised that it would respect the customs, beliefs, and practices of its inhabitants. For Raboisson, on the other hand, empire eliminated differences between peoples, encouraging conquered peoples to adopt the customs, beliefs, and practices of the conquering state. Notably, he argued that to improve its relationship with its colonies, France should encourage their inhabitants to convert to Catholicism. Once Algeria and Cochinchina's indigenous inhabitants adopted France's religion, he implied, they would become productive citizens.[59]

Raboisson's vision of the relationship between empire and colony had several features that would have made it controversial during the 1870s. He described Alsace as a colony at a moment when most politicians were describing it as an integral part of the nation. He argued that France's problems with colonization dated to the Revolution and implied that republicanism was at odds with colonial expansion.[60] But Raboisson was not an outlier in the conversation about colonization: he was an active member of the newly formed Société des études coloniales et maritimes, one of the few organizations in the 1870s devoted to popularizing the colonies.[61] His account of colonization thus demonstrates that in the 1870s some thinkers continued to associate European empire with colonial expansion and perceived them as politically intertwined.

Raboisson's explanation of the relationship between colony and empire was marked by contradictions—partly because he explained what he meant by "colonization" more clearly than what he meant by "empire." At times he used "empire" interchangeably with "nation," but he also used the term to refer to any state that had conquered territory. He certainly did not equate "empire" with "Napoleonic empire," nor did he imply that an empire needed an emperor. Conservative values and skepticism of republicanism shaped his vision of empire, but it remained politically ambiguous. This text's acceptance of Bonapartist ideas about empire, however, reveals that republicans' attempts to discredit empire as a form of political organization and to separate it from colonial expansion continued to face challenges.

These attempts to define colonization in the early 1870s thus did not resolve arguments about colonialism's political implications or even consistently distinguish between colonialism overseas and European imperial politics. But they did offer more robust theoretical frameworks for thinking about the operations and benefits of colonial expansion. Some of these frameworks, especially Leroy-Beaulieu and Raboisson's claim that colonialism could assume forms that did not involve European settlers, inflected colonial advocates' accounts of exploration in the 1870s. These advocates imagined the mechanisms of colonial control they were establishing flexibly, if vaguely. The insistence across these texts that colonial expansion could secure France's international standing and cultural influence also appeared in popular coverage of exploration.[62] At the same time, colonial advocates were able to use exploration and other technocratic projects to avoid the political contradictions that characterized these theoretical texts.

The Politics of Geography and Trans-Saharan Expeditions

The belief that exploration could facilitate overseas expansion and transcend France's political divides itself had a complicated history. During the 1860s the Paris Geographical Society, organized beneath politician Prosper de Chasseloup-Laubat, geographer Charles Maunoir, and colonial theorist Jules Duval, came to see exploration and colonial expansion as linked. They looked with alarm at the popularity of David Livingstone, the British explorer working in Africa.[63] Napoleon III shared these concerns about Britain and an interest in exploration as a way of advancing French influence, which partly reflected the ties between the society and his government. Chasseloup-Laubat particularly was both minister of the navy and the colonies and the society's president, and he served as the impetus for the mission entrusted to Ernest Doudart de Lagrée and Francis Garnier to explore the Mekong River from 1866 to 1868.[64] The society, in turn, promoted the mission with the aim of further extending France's growing possessions in Indochina.[65]

The Geographical Society's ideas about exploration converged with Bonapartist policy in Algeria too. Henri Duveyrier, who won the society's most influential prize and became the model French explorer after his expeditions among the Touareg (Tuareg) people in southern Algeria during the early 1860s, had ties to the Algerian Saint-Simonian community. Throughout the first part of his career, he was in close communication with Ismaël Urbain, one of the architects of Napoleon III's royaume arabe, although Duveyrier was more critical of Islam and more supportive of the settler community than Urbain.[66] But his vision of exploration as a peaceful encounter between East and West and his conviction that France's future in Algeria and in the Sahara would have to be grounded in persuasion of the indigenous community—instead of in force against it—owed much to the line of Saint-Simonian thinking that also structured Napoleon III's ideas about the royaume arabe.[67] The relationship between the society and Napoleon III was not without its tensions during the Second Empire; Jules Duval remained one of the royaume arabe's most influential critics. But at least around the subject of exploration, cultural influence, and overseas expansion, the government and the society's respective visions seem to have coincided.

Despite the Paris Geographical Society's ties to the Second Empire and its policies in Indochina, the society's reputation did not suffer after the Franco-Prussian War. Chasseloup-Laubat was one of the few high-profile political figures associated with Napoleon III's regime elected to the National Assembly in 1871.[68] The ability of the society and Chasseloup-Laubat to reinvent themselves after the war stemmed partly from the fact that neither was associated with some of the Second Empire's most controversial overseas policies: the attempt to restructure Algeria as a royaume arabe or the Mexican expedition. Bonapartist influence lingered in the society into the 1870s (Bonapartists were slightly overrepresented in the membership, and Roland Napoléon Bonaparte would actually become president of the society in 1910), but it included republicans and monarchists as well. The society was thus well positioned to argue that the vision of colonial expansion that it offered, like the expeditions that it sponsored, transcended political divisions and represented national interests.[69]

If anything, the Franco-Prussian War augmented the Paris Geographical Society's prestige. In the war's wake, republicans agreed that the defeat originated in France's education system, which, they felt, failed to inculcate young men with a patriotic understanding of their own country. Numerous stories circulated about troops less familiar with French geography than the invading German soldiers, due to either their lack of maps or their inability to read the maps they had. In response to these narratives, republicans sought to make geography a key component of the school curriculum.[70] Increased enthusiasm for geography did not just appear in schools; over the 1870s, regional geographical societies spread across France. By 1881 France had more geographical societies than any other European country, and a larger number of overall members as well: ninety-five hundred, up from about six hundred in 1871.[71] And while these geographical societies emphasized national geography, they promoted overseas exploration and colonial expansion too. Given the intellectual ties between the geographical societies and republican reformers, it is unsurprising that both reforms to the geography curriculum and funding for expeditions to Africa increased dramatically from 1878 to 1884, the same moment when the republicans consolidated their control over the state.[72]

Paul Soleillet's ability to convince geographical societies, government agencies, and members of the colonial administration to fund his expeditions in 1870s France partly reflects their convergence with those groups' overseas ambitions. But Soleillet's success was also due to his ability to weave together these circulating discourses about geography, science, and commerce to promote a model of "humanitarian" empire that seemed to simultaneously align with republican values and transcend debates over the politics of empire, even as it sharply diverged from the actual practices of French imperial rule. This model—like the discourses it built on—converged with some actual Bonapartist ideas about empire, but it positioned colonial expansion against the understanding of Bonapartist imperialism that republican politicians and intellectuals had constructed in the Franco-Prussian War's wake.

The potential appeal of this vision of empire to colonial advocates was apparent even in the dynamics surrounding Soleillet's first expedition to Aïn Salah, the oasis market town on the border of French colonial Algeria. With the support of the Algiers Chamber of Commerce and Governor-General Chanzy, Soleillet embarked on an underfunded expedition in December 1873. He met with mixed success. When he arrived at the outskirts of Aïn Salah, city leaders denied him entrance because he lacked a letter of recommendation from the emperor of Morocco.[73] Even more troublingly, he found few merchants interested in his pack of European goods, which raised questions about the degree to which it would be possible to turn the Saharan trade toward Algeria—the basic premise of his mission.[74]

Despite these failures, on his return to Algiers, Soleillet met with accolades. The Algiers chamber's president announced that Soleillet had "lifted a veil and now we can finally form a judgment on these territories that are still mysterious to us." Chanzy similarly contended that Soleillet had "rendered an incontestable service to national commerce."[75] The chamber and Chanzy also suggested that the expedition had proven fruitful enough to warrant a second attempt. Tellingly, neither would fund it, but they asked the Ministry of Foreign Affairs to obtain a letter from the emperor of Morocco that would enable Soleillet to enter Aïn Salah; they also recommended Soleillet to the minister of commerce.[76] Their support may have partly reflected the fact that Soleillet's expedition looked more successful in the face of the disaster that met Norbert Dournaux-Dupéré's mission, who was murdered along with his companions in a different part of the Algerian Sahara in April—a turn of events that raised questions about the efficacy and safety of individual expeditions.[77]

In the weeks following Soleillet's return, however, the Algerian administration's support declined. Vignard, who had proposed to accompany Soleillet to Aïn Salah, objected to Soleillet's official report to the Chamber of Commerce, which had also appeared in *L'akhbar* and *La vigie algérienne*, two prominent Algerian newspapers. Vignard wrote several articles to *La vigie algérienne* contesting Soleillet's account, characterizing him as an incompetent liar who should never have been entrusted with a mission in the first place and contending that "anyone who knows M. Soleillet and is familiar with his degree of instruction knows that the idea of giving him a scientific mission is ridiculous."[78] Worse, by the end of the summer, military officials in the Algerian Sahara noted that a number of Muslim notables had registered complaints against Soleillet. These leaders had lent Soleillet money or resources, and Soleillet had repaid none of his debts.[79] Because these notables perceived Soleillet as a government agent, officials warned, the debts were creating unrest. Even in 1877, a General de Loverdo, commander of the subdivision of Médéa, wrote to the governor-general of Algeria to say that "the indigenous community still distrusts isolated explorers supported by the government since Soleillet's expedition."[80] Complaints from Algerian notables thus undercut Soleillet's ability to weave his own narrative about his success as an explorer.

The resulting decline in the administration's support meant that Soleillet could not complete a second expedition to Aïn Salah. Remarkably, however, Soleillet's failures in Algeria did not end his career. Thanks to Chanzy and the initial recommendation of the Algiers Chamber of Commerce, the Ministry of Commerce gave Soleillet a small subvention to undertake another expedition; it also recommended him to chambers of commerce across France.[81] Settler support thus gave Soleillet a metropolitan audience. And in a series of meetings with chambers of commerce, public conferences, private letters, and publications, Soleillet extended the scope of his original mission's ambitions and positioned those new ambitions within a wider vision of French colonialism in Africa.

For his second expedition, instead of promising to return to Aïn Salah, Soleillet proposed to undertake a longer mission between Senegal and Algeria. This expedition would take him through the Sahara and the region south of it, the Sudan, neither of which were under French sovereignty.[82] The idea of undertaking an expedition between Algeria and Senegal was not new; in the early 1860s the Paris Geographical Society had established a prize for the first explorer who completed the journey.[83] Soleillet was thus aligning himself with a prestigious project endorsed by the primary geographical society in France. He also positioned his exploration as the first step toward building deeper connections between the two colonies.[84]

In Soleillet's descriptions of the benefits of his proposed expedition, he reiterated many points that he and his supporters had made when he had planned to visit Aïn Salah. Commercial benefits remained a central theme—unsurprisingly, given that he was asking for money from chambers of commerce. He promised that his expedition would attract caravans from the Sahara to Algeria; he also argued that it would establish access to the Sudan, a territory that he depicted as prosperous, densely populated, barbaric, and isolated from European influence. The Sudan, he promised, was thus a promising market for European goods.[85]

Soleillet also further developed his explanation of how his missions would spread French civilization and influence. He tied this explanation to a vision of France's future in Africa. As he noted in a letter to the minister of commerce, France would not "make new conquests by force, but we can and we should subject to our influence the populations who live within the natural sphere of attraction between our two colonies."[86] He argued that peaceful strategies—rather than the threat of violence—would enable France to obtain this preponderant position. Fear of conquest, he maintained, was undermining French commercial and political influence in the territories that bordered Algeria. Expeditions led by individual explorers without military ties would allay these fears, creating trust and commercial relations.[87] The government could build on explorers' work by constructing a trans-Saharan railroad to facilitate communication and exchange between Algeria and Senegal; at the same time, it should also establish consulates within regional African powers. These consulates would resemble France's consulates in Europe, but they would also "peacefully penetrate [Africa] with our commerce, our industry, our civilization, and our customs."[88] According to this vision, then, exploratory missions such as his were part of a broader national project that would allow France to establish a preponderant position in Africa—even as it respected the autonomy of the peoples who lived there.

Soleillet justified the need for this expansion by appealing to the specter of European—and especially British—competition in an argument that tied political and commercial interests together. As it stood, he remarked, even though France had two African colonies, "neither French commerce nor French civilization was preponderant" there; instead, France's rivals undercut its position by spreading their influence between Algeria and Senegal. This undermined the prosperity of both colonies and threatened to progressively isolate them from one another. Connecting France's colonies was thus critical to securing future French prosperity and prestige in Africa.[89]

At the same time, Soleillet contended, French influence south of the Sahara would not only benefit France; it would also benefit Africans. While Soleillet contended that the Sudan especially was a fertile and potentially prosperous place, he maintained that the continued practice of slavery rendered its inhabitants miserable.[90] Soleillet invoked the persistence of slavery as a sign of African barbarism, but he contended that he "believed in civilization through commerce." Over time, he argued, commercial relations between France and the peoples of the Sudan would end slavery and lead them into a higher state of civilization.[91]

Notably, even as Soleillet insisted that France should respect the independence of the peoples who lived between Algeria and Senegal, he proposed to radically reshape the territory's politics, culture, social practices, and even topography. A trans-Saharan railroad, he argued, would not only facilitate trade with the peoples who lived in the Sahara and the Sudan while connecting Algeria with Senegal; it would also provide French engineers and scientists with access to the desert. Ultimately, French scientific knowledge would transform the desert itself, restoring it to a woodland—which Soleillet believed was its original form. Soleillet tied this project to the abolition of slavery in the Sudan; he argued that French merchants could buy enslaved peoples, use them as requisitioned laborers or apprentices, and then grant them freedom after they had transformed the desert. Under this system, the French would abolish slavery, fertilize the Sahara, and create there a vast community of loyal formerly enslaved peoples.[92]

The vision of peaceful expansion that Soleillet sold to metropolitan chambers of commerce resembled neither the history of French colonialism in Algeria nor the contemporary policies of the republican administration there. As other scholars have shown, French rule in Algeria was, from the beginning, based on violence.[93] And, tellingly, even as Soleillet claimed that his vision of France's future in Africa was pacific, humanitarian, and commercial, it was in fact ambitious, expansionist, and interventionist. This vision of expansion may not have been based on military conquest, but it depended on political, economic, and cultural domination. Even as Soleillet avoided using the word "empire," he made use of logics that defenders of empire had long invoked to reconcile expansionism with human rights: interimperial competition, the civilizing mission, and scientific development. His invocation of slavery as a sign of African barbarism also drew on British and French abolitionist traditions. Abolitionists in the first part of the nineteenth century described slavery as evidence of the barbarity of colonialism, but after European powers abolished the slave trade, they used the persistence of slavery in Africa to justify interfering in African societies.[94] At the same time, Soleillet's argument that explorers could peacefully spread French influence while avoiding the violence of conquest drew from the vision of exploration put forward by Henri Duveyrier and other leaders of the Paris Geographical Society.[95] His contention that the French state should connect Algeria with Senegal, on the other hand, built on the work of colonial theorists such as Paul Leroy-Beaulieu.

Soleillet's vision of expansion pulled together these threads to work against the negative associations with "empire" that developed after the Franco-Prussian War. Republican politicians had argued that empire was problematic because it was militaristic and despotic; they had held up Napoleon III's overseas expansionist policies as the expression of his domestic political values. Soleillet's vision of France's future in Africa was, if anything, more expansionist than Napoleon III's, but because he claimed it would be based on "commerce," which liberals saw as antithetical to militarism, it could avoid the charges of warmongering and despotism that had greeted Napoleon III's overseas adventures. This form of expansionism, Soleillet implied, would also be more efficient than conquest. By building relations between free—if unequal—people, France would gain subordinate allies even as it avoided the costs of having to administer them.

Soleillet's message, whether naive or deliberately misleading, was at least somewhat popular among French chambers of commerce; they invited him to speak, and Lyon's chamber gave him five thousand francs.[96] Five thousand francs would not have fully funded even a small expedition, but as Pierre Savorgnan de Brazza undertook his first mission to Gabon in 1874 with ten thousand francs, it was a substantial foundation for one.[97]By May 1875, however, news of Soleillet's debts to Muslim notables in Algeria began to circulate in the metropole, and the minister of commerce sent a confidential note to all chambers recommending against further subsidies.[98] Soleillet continued to promote his proposed expedition and the idea of a trans-Saharan railroad, but he struggled to raise the funds that he needed.

The controversies over Soleillet's behavior in Algeria did not haunt him in the metropole for long, however. In 1877 republicans' success in national elections ushered new officials with closer ties to the Paris Geographical Society into government ministries.[99] At the same time, King Leopold II of Belgium's 1876 international geographical conference in Brussels increased explorers' prestige. As scholars have shown, Leopold II used the conference to create an International Association for the Exploration and the Civilization of Africa—a philanthropic cover that Leopold II used to conquer and brutally rule a personal empire in Central Africa.[100] But even if the association barely met a handful of times, it helped consolidate the consensus surrounding the utility of missions led by individual explorers among those sympathetic to colonial expansion.[101]

The association's account of exploration's benefits also converged with the vision of colonial expansion that Soleillet was propounding. In his address to the Paris Geographical Society about the conference, the society's president, Camille Clément de la Roncière-le-Noury, noted that the association would promote "methodological exploration of central Africa, with the double purpose of reducing the slave trade and opening new avenues for science."[102] The society's secretary-general, Charles Maunoir, further explained in his annual report that the association agreed that exploration would contribute to European knowledge, create new commercial ties between Europe and Africa, and initiate the "civilization" of Africa. According to this vision, exploration thus had commercial and scientific benefits for Europeans, but it was essentially a humanitarian enterprise.[103] The association also contributed to the notion that exploration was a European-wide endeavor, which further detached it from the divisive political history of empire in France.

The understanding of exploration embraced by the association little resembled the violence that some of the most famous explorers such as Henry Morton Stanley were using in Central Africa, let alone the dynamics of European imperial rule. And it is clear that at least some of the propagators of this vision, such as Leopold II, deliberately used the rhetoric of peaceful exploration duplicitously. But these domestic and international developments nevertheless helped at least temporarily legitimize the vision of scientific, commercial, and industrial colonial expansion that Soleillet had been promoting in his conferences. Soleillet capitalized on this; in his publications, he began to invoke Leopold II's endorsement of expeditions led by individual explorers.[104] And despite reservations expressed by important geographers about his abilities, Soleillet's continued efforts began to meet with some success. In January 1877 the Ministry of Public Instruction awarded him a subvention of five hundred francs, and the Ministry of the Navy and the Colonies offered him free transportation to Senegal.[105] Paul Dalloz, the editor of *Le moniteur universel* and *Le monde illustré*, commissioned Soleillet to publish accounts of his travels, an arrangement modeled after Stanley's relationship to the *New York Herald*. *Le monde illustré*'s explanation of the arrangement ended by remarking, "Who knows? We may have found our Stanley," a comment that highlights the transnational nature of discourses about exploration.[106]

Soleillet's ability to solicit support and funding for his explorations also reflected the fact that his project directly intersected with the ambitions of Louis Brière de l'Isle, the governor-general of Senegal, who wanted to take up Faidherbe's legacy of military conquest and extend Senegal's borders into the Sudan and toward Algeria. Over the second half of the 1870s, Brière de l'Isle used a variety of methods—from diplomatic missions to "defensive" military expeditions—to extend French influence inland.[107] Perhaps unsurprisingly, when Soleillet arrived in Saint-Louis, Brière de l'Isle awarded him five thousand francs.[108] But it was not Brière de l'Isle alone who supported funding Soleillet's mission. Wealthy métis trading families with representatives on the colony's Administrative Council (which predated the more independent General Council created in 1879) in fact encouraged the governor-general to increase the amount of the award. Gaspard Devès, the head of an influential métis family and representative from Saint-Louis, spoke at length in praise of Soleillet, hoping that his mission would augment commerce between "us and the peoples of the Sudan," although he suggested that Soleillet would need a local assistant to develop these relations effectively.[109] Other métis representatives such as Jean-Jacques Crespin and Jean Béziat also supported the mission in the name of promoting trade, reflecting Soleillet's ability in the late 1870s to represent different visions of colonial expansion to different groups of people.

In 1878 Soleillet's second expedition (this time from Senegal through Timbuktu to Algiers) like his first met with limited success. He never made it to Timbuktu; he ended his trip in Ségou, the center of the Toucouleur Empire in the Sudan beyond Senegal's borders that had already been visited by two French explorers—Eugène Mage and Louis Quentin—in the 1860s. According to his letters to Brière de l'Isle, Ahmadou, the powerful Toucouleur ruler, blocked Soleillet's passage to the Niger River. With limited resources, he decided to return to Saint-Louis.[110] But even though he failed to reach his destination, the reports that he sent to the Ministry of Public Instruction and to Brière de l'Isle won him a new level of financial support and visibility in France.

In these reports, Soleillet described his methods of exploration and his reception in Ségou; he also included a description of the terrain and an ethnographic account of the "races" living there. In a letter that the Ministry of Public Instruction found impressive enough to publish in *Le journal officiel*, he positioned himself as a simple traveler "without escort, without arms, with a mule, the most peaceful of all mounts. I am accompanied by a single servant who serves me as both guide and interpreter. I dress and eat like the indigenous people. I do not even have a tent; I lodge in their huts, and when it is necessary to sleep outside, I do so like the blacks."[111] This strategy, he noted, brought him the "sympathy of the people and their chiefs" but did not diminish respect for him or for France; Ahmadou himself had saluted Soleillet's French flag.

The letter thus built on the vision of exploration that Soleillet had promoted in his conferences and publications; it implied that peaceful expeditions like his could build relationships with Africans and gain their respect—even as they consolidated geographical and ethnographic knowledge. Soleillet also described the explorer as an unassuming but courageous, masculine figure who could forgo material comforts and inhabit a

Journal des Voyages

ET DES AVENTURES DE TERRE ET DE MER

N° 200. — Prix : 15 centimes | Bureaux : 7, rue du Croissant.

Abonnements. — PARIS, 8 fr. — DÉPARTEMENTS, 10 fr. — ÉTRANGER, 12 fr. — Dimanche 8 Mai 1881.

TEXTE. — Actualités géographiques : Paul Soleillet à Médine. — Les Robinsons de la Guyane (suite). — L'Ukraine. — Aventures périlleuses de Narcisse Nicaise au Congo (suite). — Chronique des voyages et de la géographie.

ILLUSTRATIONS. — Paul Soleillet à Médine : Le voyageur vit arriver les soldats sans émotion. — Les Robinsons de la Guyane : Ce forçat n'était pas, ne pouvait pas être seul. — Fumeurs d'opium en Chine. — L'Ukraine : Vues et paysages. — Aventures périlleuses de Narcisse Nicaise au Congo : Nicaise sortit de la hutte en criant victoire.

ACTUALITÉS GÉOGRAPHIQUES. — Paul Soleillet à Médine : Le voyageur vit arriver les soldats sans émotion. (Page 275 col. 3.)

200

FIGURE 4. An artist's sketch of Paul Soleillet leaning on a doorway in the Sudan. The image invokes his own self-description, positioning him as a courageous, masculine figure who is both at home with—and towering over—his African hosts and French soldiers alike. "Paul Soleillet à Médine," *Journal des voyages et aventures de terre et de mer* (Paris: Imprimerie Charaire et fils, 1881), 224. Bibliothèque nationale de France.

paternalistic position in the liminal space between cultures and peoples. Soleillet did not draw a consistent racial divide between himself and the different groups he interacted with; he noted that the Moors in particular "could not be distinguished from other Mediterranean peoples; as a native of Provence, I myself belong to this race and every day I encounter Moors who remind me of the features of my friends from Avignon or my acquaintances from Arles, Aix, or Marseille." He also followed Faidherbe in comparing the Bambara, on the other hand, to "our Auvergnats of France."[112] What set him apart, he explained, was his knowledge and expertise, which he generously dispensed to the Sudan's inhabitants. In this letter, Soleillet thus positioned himself as an objective, high-minded observer who could transcend racial prejudice; his lack of prejudice is in fact meant to operate as one of the characteristics that marks him as superior to the people he describes. He also offered a vision of republican colonialism, which he mobilized implicitly in contradistinction to older, exploitative imperial systems built on the labor of enslaved peoples, holding instead that European commerce, education, science, and civilization would attract the respect—and obedience—of indigenous peoples if Europeans treated those peoples with "sympathy." Even as Soleillet differentiated this vision of republican colonialism from earlier antecedents, he thus based it on a clear vision of civilizational hierarchy that echoed the Saint-Simonian thinking that Napoleon III and his followers had invoked in Algeria and Mexico. Soleillet's denial of his own racial prejudice sought to both naturalize and legitimize this hierarchy.

Soleillet's trip to Ségou marked the beginning of his career's apogee. After publishing his letter, the ministry sent Soleillet a subvention of ten thousand francs to continue his journey. Because he only received notice of the subvention after he had returned to Saint-Louis, he could not use it, but it represented a higher level of government support.[113] Soleillet also attracted an increasing amount of attention in the metropolitan press.[114] After returning to France, he was asked to speak at conferences across the country about his recent expedition, the town of Ségou, the peoples of the Sudan, and his vision of colonial expansion.[115] Both Brière de l'Isle and wealthy members of the Senegalese métis community were also impressed by Soleillet—or at least continued to believe that his work intersected with their ambitions. They paid for his trip back to France to recover his health and promised him twelve thousand francs if he were willing to undertake an additional expedition. Jean-Jacques Crespin in particular remained convinced that Soleillet's work would be "extremely advantageous for the development of the colony's commercial influence"—a view that echoed Soleillet's understanding of colonial expansion, even as it intersected with Crespin's own economic interests.[116] Brière de l'Isle's support, on the other hand, was less a response to Soleillet's vision of colonialism than a reflection of the fact that Soleillet's projects served his expansionary goals.[117] By 1879 Soleillet had thus finally attracted support from the metropolitan and colonial administration as well as from elites in Saint-Louis and the press, either because they found him or his vision of exploration useful.

The Trans-Saharan Railroad and Expansion without Empire in Africa

The Ministry of Public Instruction's new support for Paul Soleillet partly reflected the government's growing interest in the trans-Saharan railroad. Scholarship on the railroad has disagreed on the government's seriousness about the project. Did it really intend to build a railroad across the Sahara? Or was the project a scheme to convince the public to consent to colonial expansion? Whatever its level of commitment, in the late 1870s and early 1880s the administration invested more than a million francs in exploratory missions for the trans-Saharan railroad that generated a large amount of publicity.[118] And from the beginning, both the project's planners and newspapers reporting on it couched the trans-Saharan railroad in the same language of paternalistic, peaceful overseas expansionism that Soleillet had used to describe his expeditions.

The government's embrace of the project was not due directly to Soleillet. In 1875 Adolphe Duponchel, the chief engineer of bridges and roadways, published a treatise advocating for the construction of a trans-Saharan railroad that cited Soleillet's and other explorers' work. As an engineer, Duponchel was a credible advocate for the project, and the Ministry of Public Works commissioned him to undertake a formal study. At the same time, prominent figures such as Ferdinand de Lesseps, who had developed the Suez Canal, began to endorse Duponchel's ideas.[119] The new republican government's interest was partly due to the project's convergence with the administration's decision to stake its reputation on constructing a network of railroads across France—a plan spearheaded by Charles de Freycinet, the minister of public works.[120] But Duponchel and his supporters' description of the trans-Saharan railroad was also ensconced in colonial language. Duponchel positioned the railroad as a project that would "open the markets of the Sudan" and transform the area between Algeria and Senegal "into a French India."[121] The project, he maintained, was therefore "in the interest of civilization and humanity" as well as "our commerce and our industry." Duponchel thus echoed the conviction of Algerian settlers, the colonial administration, métis trading elites in Senegal, and explorers such as Soleillet that the Sudan was prosperous and that industrial, commercial, and cultural influence—rather than military conquest—would deliver it into French hands.[122] Like Soleillet, Duponchel also invoked the specter of European imperial competition, warning that the British were also interested in extending their influence into Africa and might soon leave France behind.[123]

Both colonial advocates and the government responded positively to Duponchel's study. Paul Leroy-Beaulieu reviewed the book in *Le journal des débats* and praised its vision for "colonizing the Sudan," which, he maintained, would open "an avenue of glory, influence, and [enable France] to once again hold a great place in the world."[124] Charles de Freycinet sent a proposal to the president of the republic, Jules Grévy, promising that a railroad would open the Sudan, which was "at the door of Algeria and Senegal" and had "all the riches of India and America," to French commerce while ending the slave trade. But it also argued that explorers needed to map out the territory between Algeria and Senegal before the project proceeded. Freycinet proposed to create a commission of experts to organize these expeditions and give them "precise instructions."[125] Grévy accepted the proposal in July 1879, and the commission met later that month. Headed by Freycinet himself, it brought together engineers, members of the Paris Geographical Society, military officials, politicians, and explorers—including Soleillet.[126]

Ferdinand de Lesseps, one of the commission's most prominent members, opened the first meeting by reading a letter from Henri Duveyrier (who could not attend the session), which defined the project's framework. Duveyrier echoed Duponchel's positive assessment of Saharan commerce's value, but he also warned that the Touareg who lived in the Sahara would see the railroad as "their ruin." The French would have to work closely with the Touareg and "offer them tangible advantages" to build a railroad through their territory.[127] At the same time, he argued, exploratory missions would need to appear "peaceful" and avoid a "military character" so as not to frighten indigenous communities and lead them to view the explorers and the railroad through the lens of conquest.[128] While it might be possible to conquer the region, he acknowledged, it would be impossible to subdue the Touareg who lived there, and prolonged fighting would eliminate the commerce that the French hoped to attract.[129]

The members of the commission seem to have accepted Duveyrier's insistence that the expeditions and the trans-Saharan railroad needed to avoid the appearance of conquest, even as they also agreed that the railroad would spread French control over the territory it crossed. But they argued about what a "peaceful" expedition looked like. While some deputies such as Lesseps insisted that individual explorers such as Soleillet should lead missions, others—including military officials and several engineers—contended that the missions required multiple experts protected by army officers and indigenous troops. Such expeditions, they maintained, would bring back more specific information and enjoy greater security in the face of indigenous hostility.[130] Several republican politicians, on the other hand, worried that larger parties would look like military expeditions "with the character of conquest."[131] Jacques Lucet, a senator from Algiers, especially criticized the decision to place Colonel Paul Flatters at an expedition's head, as he had a "great military reputation" in Algeria.[132] Lucet's concerns may have partly reflected ongoing conflicts over the role of the military in Algeria's administration, but they also intersected with the commission's uncertainty about what "peaceful" colonization was supposed to look like. Duponchel responded to these disagreements by questioning whether expeditions were necessary. "The Touaregs and the Arabs have the taste for geography," he noted, "they are used to taking great voyages . . . and they can recognize topographic points better than we can." The commission should simply ask these indigenous Algerians—whose geographic expertise Duponchel positioned as superior to French explorers'—for information.[133] His suggestions were ignored, however; the commission was convinced that French explorers were critical to the project's success, reflecting its members' assumptions about who could have geographic expertise. Duveyrier finally resolved the argument by contending that the Flatters mission would appear peaceful if its members presented themselves as commercial agents.[134] And in the end, the commission sponsored two exploratory expeditions; the larger Flatters mission in the northern Sahara, and a small mission led by Soleillet from Senegal to Timbuktu.[135] Both missions, they agreed, would rely on "diplomatic methods."[136]

The commission's commitment to "peaceful" colonial expansion was nevertheless complicated by the fact that the Ministry of the Navy and Colonies had taken responsibility for constructing the railway's Senegal-Niger branch. Bernard Jauréguiberry, the minister of the navy, and Brière de l'Isle, the governor of Senegal, were planning from the beginning to use the railroad as an excuse to occupy the Western Sudan militarily. They had identified Ahmadou's Toucouleur Empire as a challenge to their expansionary goals, and they were determined to destroy it. At the same time, they, too, insisted publicly on their pacific intentions—demonstrating that even colonial officials bent on outright military conquest felt obliged to use the language of peaceful expansion in the early 1880s.[137]

The coverage of the trans-Saharan railroad project in the press was largely positive, and it echoed many of the themes that appeared in the commission's debates. Journalists on both the left and the right echoed the commission's consensus that the railroad could serve as a lucrative boost to French commerce and as vehicle of "civilization and progress."[138] But while the journals agreed that the it would extend French influence in Africa, they offered contradictory visions of what that influence would look like. An author in

Le journal des débats argued that the project would bring civilization to territory "ravaged by elephants and monkeys [and] sterilized by barbaric tribes always at war with one another" and acknowledged that it might force the French to "militarily occupy the Sahara" at strategic points. This account made colonization sound like military conquest, and it conflated the inhabitants of the Sudan with wild animals. While it used the language of the civilizing mission, it applied that language to the territory rather than the people who lived there—a divergence from the humanitarian pretentions of the project's organizers.[139] Most journalists, however, insisted on the mission's benevolent intentions. Victor Meunier, writing in *Le rappel*, insisted that the trans-Saharan railroad would enable the French to colonize "along reassuring lines of peace, work, and justice" that reflected the country's "democratic benevolence." Fortunately, he argued, the French "do not have the prejudice of color," which would enable them to act as "saviors of inferior races."[140] Meunier thus positioned the colonial expansion proposed by the government as a reflection of its republican politics and enlightened, unprejudiced perspective, even as he justified French control of the Sudan by appealing to principles of racial hierarchy—the same rhetorical move that Soleillet had deployed in his official reports.

Despite substantial government support, both Flatters's and Soleillet's missions ended in failure. Soleillet was robbed shortly after leaving Senegal, forcing him to return to Saint-Louis. He would have been murdered without the intervention of Saad Buh, an important religious figure who had developed close relations with the Senegalese administration.[141] The Flatters mission also returned early after encountering resistance from the Touareg population.[142] In the face of these failures, the commission met in the summer of 1880 to decide how to proceed. Duponchel again questioned the value of the expeditions and suggested that the government was putting the explorers at risk. This time, General Victor Colonieu and Louis Say—who both had experience in Algeria—echoed Duponchel's concerns about Flatters's mission especially. Say insisted that government representatives needed to reach out to the Touareg before the Flatters expedition could return, a suggestion that called into question the ability of exploratory missions to build relations with indigenous communities.

Most of the commission, however, remained convinced that Soleillet and Flatters should continue their respective missions. They agreed that the expeditions had already returned useful results; they were also concerned about British competition. As a result, the commission voted to renew funding for both expeditions, and Soleillet was invited to meet with Léon Gambetta and Jules Grévy.[143] The failures of the first expeditions do not seem to have dampened enthusiasm for the trans-Saharan railroad—or for Flatters or Soleillet—in the French press either. Before his departure for Saint-Louis, members of the Parisian press held a banquet to celebrate Soleillet.[144] And after he left, metropolitan newspapers continued to cover his movements, describing him as a "courageous explorer" who would "achieve the conquest of Africa for universal civilization."[145]

Soleillet's position in Senegal, on the other hand, had become more complicated. When Soleillet had returned to Saint-Louis in April 1880 after the robbery, Brière de l'Isle was out of town. Soleillet and his three companions—his interpreter Boubaker Kann Diallo and two men that Saad Buh had sent to accompany Soleillet—either asked or were asked to testify about the incident by the colonial administration. According to Soleillet, he never heard back from the governor about how the interview was supposed to take shape, so he asked Senegal's recently constituted General Council (a locally elected body dominated by métis families and Bordelais trading houses) to listen to his testimony instead. Soleillet claimed that the local colonial administration then subsequently unfairly asked him to testify about the incident a second time.[146] According to Parfait-Louis Monteil, the director of political affairs in Senegal, on the other hand, Soleillet should never have testified in front of the General Council at all. He maintained that Soleillet's case was outside the scope of the council's responsibilities and that Soleillet obstructed the real investigation by refusing to allow his three companions to testify without being personally present himself. Moreover, Monteil complained, Soleillet treated the process "with great animosity" and launched an unjustified complaint with the powerful Bordelais trading house Maurel and Prom.[147]

Whatever Soleillet's reasons, by choosing to testify to the General Council, reaching out to Maurel and Prom, and resisting the demands of the Senegalese colonial administration, he inserted himself directly into an escalating conflict between Brière de l'Isle and almost all of the most influential groups in Saint-Louis.[148] The conflict centered partly on the question of the relative authority of appointed colonial administrators and Senegal's newly established elective institutions; it also reflected the fact that Brière de l'Isle's policy of colonial conquest at times conflicted with the commercial interests of both Bordelais firms and wealthy métis and African Muslim trading families.[149] Starting in 1879, some of these métis families began to support a press campaign in the metropole to discredit Brière de l'Isle by portraying him as a supporter of slavery; they would successfully force his resignation in 1881.[150] Soleillet's third attempt to enter the Sudan and cross the Sahara thus from the beginning lacked unified support from local colonial institutions in Senegal.

Unsurprisingly, the new Flatters and Soleillet expeditions were even less successful than the first. The Flatters expedition was massacred in the Sahara.[151] Soleillet's departure from Saint-Louis, on the other hand, was delayed by conflict in the Sudan and then derailed by an argument with Brière de l'Isle over an article that Soleillet published in a metropolitan newspaper criticizing the governor's expansionary politics.[152] Soleillet had discovered that a mission organized by Brière de l'Isle and led by General Joseph Galliéni had secretly intended to destroy Ahmadou's empire instead of negotiate with it, as the Senegalese administration had claimed. In his letter, Soleillet maintained that colonial administrators had "lied," and he held their policy responsible for Galliéni's failures.[153] Brière de l'Isle complained to the Ministry of Public Works, which in turn revoked its support for Soleillet's expedition. Once again, Soleillet was forced to return to France, leaving his mission unaccomplished—a turn of events that highlighted how much Soleillet's career had always depended on the goodwill of local colonial administrators and pointed to the limits of the metropolitan government's commitment to his vision of peaceful colonial expansion.[154]

In the wake of the Flatters expedition's massacre, the government showed little interest in pursuing the trans-Saharan railroad. This partly reflected the fact that news of the Flatters expedition intersected with the beginning of a protracted conflict with the Bey of Tunisia.[155] But many key members of the commission also concluded that exploration and technocratic projects—at least in the Sahara—would not lead to the spread of French influence. In the commission's final meeting, the governor-general of Algeria insisted that to build a railroad across the Sahara, the government would first have to "solidify French domination over the Sahara" and "support [the trains] with military posts." The rest of the commission agreed, arguing in its final report that France could only build the trans-Saharan railroad once it "permanently and definitively occupied the Algerian Sahara."[156] The failures of the Flatters mission in particular thus raised doubts about the efficacy of the vision of expansionism embraced by Soleillet and many other colonial advocates in the late 1870s. While it eschewed violence and was less politically problematic than military conquest, it had also proven expensive and unsuccessful.

A New Model of Colonial Expansion?

By the end of the 1870s, with their hold over France's government more secure, some republican officials and intellectuals embraced the idea that overseas expansion was necessary to secure French prestige and influence in the face of British and German expansionism. But for these republican thinkers, the legacy of the Napoleonic empire and Napoleon III's conflation of "overseas" and "European" empire remained troubling. Republicans had devoted much attention to attacking empire and placing it in opposition to the new republic. As a result, they avoided describing overseas territories as "an empire" and sought to develop robust theories that could explain why maintaining or even expanding these territories was in line with republican values. But some colonial theorists continued to associate the two formations, and those such as Duval and Leroy-Beaulieu who avoided the term "empire" struggled to find a different theoretical vocabulary to describe the form of political organization that would structure France's relationship with its overseas territories. As a result, the relationship between "empire" and "colonies" remained conflicted and ambiguous within republican discourse itself and in republican debates with antirepublican theorists.

In the 1870s some members of the new republican government and the colonial administration turned to the Paris Geographical Society and to explorers such as Soleillet to envision what they described as a new model of colonial expansion. While they did not explicitly compare this model of colonial expansion to Napoleon III's imperial ideas, they positioned it in opposition to the understanding of empire that republican politicians were consolidating in the 1870s, even as they sometimes borrowed from the actual ideas about overseas colonial rule that Napoleon III used to shape his empire in Algeria and Mexico. This type of colonial expansion, they promised, would be "peaceful" and avoid the military conflict and despotism that republicans claimed had characterized Napoleonic imperial projects—as well as the exploitative practices used by the ancien régime. Instead, the new colonial expansion would be based on commerce, science, and technology. Its pacific qualities themselves would stand as a reflection of French civilizational and racial superiority (which colonial advocates continued to invoke, even as some of them denounced the "prejudice of color" that they claimed had characterized the ancien régime and the Napoleonic empire). French explorers would act as paternal figures toward indigenous people, attracting their respect by handing down knowledge and cultivating prosperity. Exploration and colonialism would thus express France's best qualities, even as it increased its prestige on the world stage. They would align with republicans' commitment to science, to commerce, and to democratic politics—even as they transcended divisive political debates that continued to characterize Third Republic France.

This vision of overseas expansion left important questions open. What would "peaceful" colonialism look like? How would the state control territory that it did not militarily control? What position would the inhabitants of the territory occupy vis-à-vis France? The advocates of exploration did not clearly address these issues, and at times they offered contradictory answers to them. Some suggested that exploration and projects like the trans-Saharan railroad would lead to limited military occupation; others argued that these territories would remain technically independent but closely allied to France. This vagueness was not necessarily problematic for colonial advocates in France, however; it enabled readers to envision colonialism in whatever terms might most appeal to them. Tellingly, it was only in Senegal—where these different interpretations could have policy implications—that the contradictions in Soleillet's promises about the benefits of his work became problematic. Would exploration lead to increased trade? Or to formal conquests? As métis and African Muslim traders came to see their commercial interests as at odds with Brière de l'Isle's military conquests, the answers to those questions became increasingly important. For observers back in France, the obvious failures of the trans-Saharan railroad project were more troubling than its contradictions; it threw the efficacy of this vision of "peaceful" expansion into question, at least in Algeria and Senegal. The discourse of exploration had implied that indigenous people would naturally respect explorers who embodied a restrained masculine strength grounded in European science and commerce. Soleillet's and Flatters's experiences raised troubling questions about these assumptions.

Soleillet struggled to find both government and private funding for additional missions in Africa after the trans-Saharan railroad project dissolved. This partly reflected his personal limitations and his ongoing conflict with Brière de l'Isle, but it also stemmed from his association with the project.[157] The government did not abandon its support for all explorers in the 1880s, however. Brazza's meteoric career would reach its height several years later, and the ideas about exploration he used converged with those deployed around and by Soleillet—they, too, worked to undo the association between colonial expansion and autocratic politics. But at the same time, the republican government came to embrace colonial conquest more openly, which colonial advocates would find new vocabularies to defend.

CHAPTER 5

New Colonial Vocabularies and Overseas Conquest in Vietnam

On January 24, 1886, Émile Lonchampt, a reserve army officer and a member of the Société d'émulation de Cambrai, organized a conference in Paris devoted to examining what he described as the *politique coloniale* of Louis XV. The conference focused on Joseph-François Dupleix's efforts to establish a colony in India. Lonchampt's speech highlighted Dupleix's achievements. He claimed, for example, that Britain was later able to assert its authority over India only because its administrators copied Dupleix's innovative governing strategies. And although Lonchampt acknowledged that France lost its major Indian outposts, he insisted that Dupleix's life showed—contrary to what he saw as popular belief—that eighteenth-century France was just as effective at colonizing as Britain. France's colonial failures did not stem from a lack of aptitude but from the government's poor management and the people's inability to appreciate "valiant explorers" such as Dupleix who "worked for the glory of their country" and embodied "male courage."[1]

Lonchampt also made it clear that he believed Dupleix's history was relevant to problems facing contemporary France. Even now, he insisted, "intrepid explorers" were extending French influence into new territories. Much like Dupleix, he feared, these figures had inadequate government and popular support. This lack of support imperiled both the explorers' safety and the success of their missions. It was also dangerous to France's future.

Only by embracing politique coloniale, Lonchampt warned, would France be able to maintain its position in Europe: unless it pursued a ruthless path of overseas expansion, it would fall behind its neighbors. He acknowledged that some republicans might object to the prospect of violently conquering and subjugating other peoples on ideological grounds, but he insisted with a kind of Darwinian logic, "All people . . . are subject to the general law of terrestrial life that dictates that the great inevitably devour the small. . . . One can dream of an ideal world where justice presides over the destiny of nations and of an ethereal vision which sees people as brothers. . . . I do not believe in such a brilliant mirage."[2] France's commitment to these ideals, Lonchampt implied, delivered its colonies into British hands and Alsace and Lorraine into German ones. Instead of dreaming of universal fraternity, France should address the law of "terrestrial life" by securing itself against its enemies.[3]

Lonchampt's interest in France's former colonies and his tendency to connect them to contemporary problems was echoed throughout the 1880s, particularly in scholarly circles but also in political debates, newspaper articles, journals, and textbooks.[4] A wealth of literature emerged devoted to France's past and present colonies and to what commentators increasingly described as politique coloniale. Much like the theorists of the 1870s, writers usually described colonialism as a long-standing practice that many European states employed in overseas territories. This description enabled writers to avoid explaining the relationship between colonies overseas and empires like Napoleon's in Europe. But if these writers' understandings of colonialism intersected with their 1870s counterparts', important differences remained. Far more writers were interested in the topic in the 1880s, and more of them sought to define colonialism systematically. Later writers were also not calling for reforms in extant colonies but demanding aggressive colonial expansion. Tellingly, Lonchampt cast even exploration in different terms than most colonial advocates used in the 1870s. In his account, exploration was not a practice that would connect indigenous peoples to France in unequal but peaceful and mutually beneficial ways; instead, it led to military conquest and domination.

International events partly drove both this new interest in colonialism and the belief that colonial expansion was an apolitical enterprise critical to France's future. During the early 1880s, the sense of European competition over African territory increased, which led to the 1884–85 Berlin Conference.[5] It focused on establishing the rights of European powers to Africa and determining how European states could lay claim to territory there. But by laying out rules for "colonial conquest," the meeting solidified the consensus that war, conquest, and domination outside of Europe were morally justified and different from their counterparts within Europe. At the same time, the conference convinced politicians and intellectuals across Europe that colonization was necessary for any state hoping to maintain its international influence. In the following years, the speed of European conquests dramatically increased.[6]

In light of this international interest in colonial expansion, French writers and politicians' insistence on politique coloniale's importance is perhaps unsurprising.[7] But the centrist republicans who consolidated their hold over the republic in 1879 did not simply react to changing international norms—they also contributed to them. Jules Ferry, France's prime minister from 1880 to 1881 and from 1883 to 1885, orchestrated multiple new overseas conquests during his tenure. In 1880 he encouraged the annexation of Tahiti and neighboring islands. In 1881 he fabricated a crisis with the bey of Tunisia to justify sending troops across the border to "secure" Algeria and then declare Tunisia a protectorate. He also encouraged explorations in the Sudan, the Congo, and Madagascar with an eye toward expanding France's holdings in Africa. And, finally, he spearheaded the conquest of northern Vietnam from 1883 to 1885. The French government's policies thus played a role in provoking the events that led to the 1884–85 conference and reflected the accelerated pace of colonial conquests that occurred in its aftermath.[8]

The perceived limits of less aggressive ways of extending France's influence overseas through exploration or technocratic projects such as the trans-Saharan railroad partly drove centrist republicans' embrace of overseas military conquest in the 1880s. Pressures—often conflicting—from the military as well as from business, trading, missionary, and settler interests both in the metropole and in Algeria, Senegal, and Vietnam—also played a role. But the embrace additionally stemmed from centrist republicans' attempts to buoy their political support by claiming that a France aligned with republican values would "prevent a second Sedan" and resist the military disasters of the Second Empire.[9] In the second half of the 1880s especially, centrist republican politicians argued that while the republic could not immediately avenge itself against Germany, conquests overseas would increase its strength by training the army, expanding France's commercial networks, and enhancing its prestige. Over time, these thinkers argued, such conquests would make it possible for France to regain its lost provinces. They would also enable France to keep British ascendancy in check. This argument built on claims made about the benefits of colonialism in the 1870s, and it contributed to the growing interest in politique coloniale among moderate republicans.[10]

The contention that colonial conquests would increase France's prestige and allow it to win back its lost provinces was nevertheless controversial.

Nationalists condemned the idea.[11] And even if many republicans argued that politique coloniale was essential to their party's domestic legitimacy and France's international reputation, military conquest rested uneasily with some republican principles—especially with the republic's theoretical commitment to supporting liberty among peoples and fraternity between nations. Lonchampt's call for action made some of these contradictions apparent. He dismissed the principles in question by describing them as idealistic, impractical, and dangerous in the face of European competition. But the fact that he felt the need to mention them at all makes it clear that the association in republican thought between conquest, subordination, and ancien régime and imperial governments had not disappeared. Even as supporters of colonial expansion such as Lonchampt argued that domestic politics had no bearing on colonialism—which they described as a matter of national prestige and security—other republicans still saw overseas expansion and domestic politics as intertwined. In fact, many still associated colonial conquest with authoritarian forms of political organization and drew connections between the new "colonial empire" that republican France was building and the older "Bonapartist empire" that had led France to defeat. These disagreements led to a series of contestations over the purpose, history, and morality of politique coloniale.

These debates over politique coloniale coalesced around the government's decision to invade northern Vietnam in the mid-1880s and wage war against the Hué court that ruled the territory. The conflict's complications first sparked debates in the Chamber of Deputies about its costs and methods. Moderate republicans defended Ferry's policies, while some leftists and conservatives questioned their means and purpose. Ultimately, discontent with Ferry's actions in what the French called "Indochina" spread across the Chamber of Deputies, enabling the opposition to bring down his government in March 1885.[12] And the debate in the Chamber of Deputies reverberated beyond the halls of government into the public sphere in newspapers, journals, pamphlets, and scholarly treatises. These texts' arguments about Vietnam partly reflected those circulating in the Chamber of Deputies, but many connected their arguments to questions about the purpose and politics of politique coloniale. The debates about Vietnam—and the discussion about politique coloniale that they provoked—thus marked a moment when "colonialism" became an object of widespread discussion in the metropole.

These 1885 arguments over colonial expansion were particularly visible thanks to the 1881 law that eliminated censorship on the political press, which made it easier for newspapers especially to publish articles that were critical of government policies. Newspapers generally had a wider distribution than the political pamphlets that had often dominated earlier French debates over empire due to the existing censorship laws. This reach only expanded after 1881; many of the Parisian papers began to reach audiences across France because the Hachette company started to distribute them by rail. The three mass dailies that described themselves as politically neutral—*Le petit journal*, *Le petit parisien*, and *Le matin*—commanded the largest audiences. That said, the political press also gained a significantly wider readership in the wake of the 1881 law.[13] The law thus both made it easier for French writers and journalists to express a wider range of opinions on the government's policies in Vietnam and ensured that those arguments circulated more widely—at least in France—than many of the earlier contestations over Mexico, Algeria, and Senegal and their relationships to France had.

If the explosion of newspapers after 1881 meant that a growing number of people in France could read about these debates over empire, the structure of the debates themselves remained both hierarchical and exclusionary. This was partly because even as the audience for newspapers expanded, most French journalists continued to share a relatively elite background.[14] But it was also because the arguments over colonial conquest in Vietnam were—even more than earlier arguments over Mexico, Algeria, and Senegal—deeply rooted in the metropole. Outside of a handful of French military and colonial officials, very few people actually in Vietnam directly weighed in.

The metropolitan structure of these arguments was partially the result of practical issues, such as the long distance of Vietnam from France; anything not sent over government telegraph was necessarily delayed. It additionally reflected the fact that at least some groups in Mexico, Algeria, and Senegal had more long-standing ties and established communication networks with France than most people even in Cochinchina, the part of southern Vietnam that the French had formally ruled since 1863. Linguistic divides also played a role. Few people spoke French in independent northern Vietnam, and in Cochinchina, too, French was relatively rare during the early 1880s—for a variety of complicated reasons. Most members of the southern Vietnamese elite were reluctant to send their children to the handful of French-language schools established by the colonial administration, which, by most accounts, were underfunded and minimally effective anyway.[15] That elite itself had been profoundly unsettled by the introduction of French rule; the most highly educated mandarins who had been central to the Hué administration had fled Cochinchina for the north when the French established control, creating both a power and cultural vacuum.[16] Most of the local intermediaries willing to work with the French were Vietnamese Christians, who generally supported French expansion due to the Hué court's history of religious persecution. Some of those intermediaries did speak French and in fact wrote books that helped shape French perceptions of Vietnam and influenced French colonial policy there.[17] But even figures who developed especially close ties with French officials or visited France—such as Truong Vinh Ky and Huyn Tinh Cua—did not primarily focus their attention on either describing Vietnam to the French or on promulgating the use of French in Vietnam. Instead, they devoted most of their energies to promoting *quoc ngu*, the romanized script for writing Vietnamese developed by European missionaries. They simultaneously sought to eliminate the use of both Chinese script and *nom*, the Vietnamese ideographic script, in order to reduce Cochinchina's ties to both China and Confucianism.[18] The French colonial administration, which was deeply worried about China's influence in Cochinchina, supported this goal, and began printing an official government newspaper in quoc ngu with the assistance of Christian Vietnamese intermediaries during the 1860s.[19] By the early 1880s, these policies had begun to lead to the growing adoption of quoc ngu in Cochinchina, but they did not lead to a wider embrace of the French language.

Forms of public expression also remained relatively closely controlled by the colonial administration. While the 1881 law on the press was promulgated in Cochinchina, it only applied to publications written in French by French citizens; all other publications were subject to prepublication censorship.[20] Even the Cochinchinese-elected colonial council—created in the early 1880s—did not really serve as a forum for the discussion of expansionary policy during these early years in the way that it sometimes did in Senegal. The colonial council had some of the same influence over the local budget that its Senegalese counterpart had, and it included Vietnamese elites, but settlers dominated it by design.[21] In the early years especially, moreover, many of the Vietnamese councilors complained about the fact that much of the discussion that took place on the council remained untranslated, raising questions about how able they were to weigh in. When they did enter the conversation, moreover, they primarily focused their attention on shaping French policies within Cochinchina itself. This focus at least partly reflected the structural interests of many of the Vietnamese councilors; in Senegal, many members of colonial council were involved in trade with the areas that the French colonial administration was seeking to conquer, which gave them a vested interest in French military policy. In Cochinchina, on the other hand, the councilors mostly included a mixture of elite landowners and Christians, who were at least in the early 1880s primarily concerned about educational policies, the structure of cantonal and communal colonial administration, and the French government's decision to sell opium to raise revenues. Settlers' dominant position on the council also meant that the Vietnamese councilors struggled to influence French policy even in many of these areas.[22]

The situation in northern Vietnam itself was still more complicated, as the French state was engaged in active warfare against the Hué court, which primarily sought to resist French incursions by requesting military support from the Chinese Empire, the traditional power broker in the region, rather than by appealing to the French public—at least partly because it was clear that the French had not dealt with the court in good faith.[23] And while the French relied on Vietnamese troops and officers recruited from the south, they lacked the powerful local allies they had mobilized in Mexico, who had been able to use their knowledge of the French language and their international ties to help shape both the invasion and French discourses around it.[24]

If Vietnamese voices were thus relatively absent from these arguments over expansion in Vietnam, the actions of different groups in Vietnamese society played a critical role in shaping French conversations about empire. French politicians and journalists responded directly to the military and diplomatic strategies employed by the Hué court to resist French rule; indeed, the disasters that accompanied the invasion made it clear that despite colonial advocates' rhetoric, France was not able to easily or inexpensively project power across the globe. But the fact that the arguments over empire in Indochina were so centered in the metropole itself meant that they often remained even more detached from what was really happening in Vietnam than the arguments over empire in Mexico, Algeria, or Senegal had been. They also had, if possible, even fewer effects on the actual shape of French imperial rule in the territory. These debates were thus important not because they had measurable consequences for French colonial policy in Vietnam or elsewhere but because of their effects on French republican politics.

The parliamentary debates in 1885 over France's conquest of northern Vietnam have received extensive scholarly attention and are accepted as a "turning point" in France's colonial history because they marked both the first and last moment of major opposition to colonial expansion in the metropole before the interwar period.[25] Even though opponents to Ferry's politique coloniale brought down his ministry, they did not stem growing support for colonial conquest. Multiple historians have sought to explain the reasons behind the opposition's failures. Some have pointed to the divisions in the groups that opposed expansion.[26] Others have argued that Ferry's opponents mostly had practical, rather than ideological, concerns; they only saw Ferry's policies in Vietnam as problematic when they failed.[27] But if scholars have highlighted the opposition's weakness, they have devoted less attention to examining why proponents of colonial empire took that opposition so seriously. Long after it became clear that the opposition would not surrender northern Vietnam, proponents of colonial expansion continued to attack critics of politique coloniale.

This chapter examines the arguments that emerged during France's conquest of Vietnam over the republic's expansionary policies. It looks at the ideological concerns that underpinned the arguments justifying or condemning the conquest and considers how the conversation about politique coloniale intersected with disputes over the meaning, value, and history of "empire" and its relationship to the republic. I show how the memory of Napoleon III and France's defeat during the Franco-Prussian War continued to shape republican conversations about colonial expansion into the 1880s. For much of this period, critics of politique coloniale could mobilize the memory of Napoleon III to attack their opponents' ideas—partly because he was responsible for investing France in Cochinchina and Cambodia during the 1860s. In response to these critics, defenders of politique coloniale sought to develop a vocabulary that would legitimize the practice in public eyes. By examining the connections between disputes over Vietnam and arguments about the political organization of the French state, I highlight how the memory of the Second Empire helped shape a republican discourse about colonial conquest.

The chapter begins by examining the parliamentary debates over Vietnam and the reactions that those debates provoked in newspapers, journals, and political pamphlets, emphasizing the role played by political ideology and memory in this conversation. It then turns to the theoretical literature that emerged in response to these debates and analyzes how different authors sought to define politique coloniale and provide it with a theoretical basis and history. Through this analysis, I demonstrate that the historical relationship between "empire" and "republic" remained a problem for republicans as they sought to justify new overseas conquests in the 1880s. At the same time, I show how republicans were increasingly able to elide those connections by controlling the perceived domestic political implications of colonial conquest.

The Conflict over Indochina, 1883–85

The republican government's decision to launch a large invasion of northern Vietnam in 1883 marked a heightened degree of investment in Southeast Asia. But the Second Empire had initiated French involvement there by conquering territory and sponsoring explorations during the 1850s and the 1860s that were ostensibly peaceful in intent. The explorers were usually naval officers, however, so such expeditions always had a military character. Much like in Algeria, republican policies in Vietnam built on patterns established during the Second Empire—even if republican officials did not acknowledge these continuities.

In 1857 Napoleon III had sent troops into Cochinchina as an addendum to the larger invasion of China during the Second Opium War. This military action was ostensibly supposed to protect French Catholic missionaries and the local Christian population from persecution at the hands of the Vietnamese emperor, Tu Duc.[28] But French officers at least initially found little support among the Vietnamese Christians they were sent to protect. Instead of winning a quick victory, they engaged in a protracted conflict from 1858 to 1862.[29] Over time, they were able to make use of the internal instability in the Vietnamese Empire in order to gain some ground, and in 1863 they forced Tu Duc to sign a treaty that ceded three of his southernmost provinces to France, granted freedom of navigation to all French ships, opened up major cities to French trade, paid the French government an indemnity, and declared religious freedom throughout his empire.[30] As the concessions make clear, the Second Empire's interest in the territory had a religious component, but it centered on securing French commerce in Southeast Asia while increasing the government's prestige domestically and internationally.[31]

If the 1863 treaty met most of the Second Empire's goals, it did not end the conflict. The French administration continued to antagonize the Hué court by annexing more territory—a measure that the governor of Cochinchina, Admiral Pierre-Paul de La Grandière, was already envisioning in 1864—and by trying to establish trade with China.[32] During the late 1860s and early 1870s, moreover, officers Ernest Doudart de Lagrée and Francis Garnier spearheaded expeditions up the Mekong, Red, and Yangtze Rivers to increase France's economic influence in northern Indochina and China. These expeditions increased French interest in trading with the Chinese province of Yunnan during the last years of the Second Empire and the first years of the Third Republic, even as they added to tensions with the Chinese and Vietnamese governments.[33]

These tensions came to a head in 1872 and 1873 during the first crisis over Tonkin. In 1872 the French trader Jean Dupuis led an expedition up the Red River to illegally sell arms to the Chinese. On his return, Vietnamese mandarins in Hanoi detained him, so he asked Governor-General Admiral Marie-Jules Dupré for assistance. Dupré sent Francis Garnier to Hanoi, ostensibly to negotiate with the mandarins.[34] Instead, Garnier joined forces with Dupuis; they seized Hanoi's citadel and issued a proclamation declaring that the Red River was open to international trade. In the ensuing conflict, Garnier was killed.[35] The metropolitan government was uninterested in supporting a military conflict, however, so it ordered the French troops to withdraw and used the incident to negotiate a new treaty with the Vietnamese government that consolidated France's hold over Cochinchina and increased its trading privileges in Tonkin, although the treaty was never really enforced.[36] The 1872–73 conflict thus reflected the interest of colonial administrators in extending French control in Indochina during the early years of the Third Republic and the unwillingness of the metropolitan government to engage in protracted military conflict to conquer new territory. At the same time, it highlighted the determination of at least some highly positioned officials at the Hué court to resist French incursions into Vietnamese territory.[37]

At the beginning of the 1880s, metropolitan attitudes toward Vietnam began to change in response to developments in Southeast Asia. To counterbalance growing French power in Cochinchina and local challenges to imperial authority in the northern borderlands, Vietnamese emperor Tu Duc began to cultivate closer ties with China. He also sought aid from the Black Flags, a semi-independent army commanded by Liu Yong Fu and composed of soldiers of fortune from Guangxi, China.[38] At the same time, the British started advancing toward Yunnan from Burma.[39] The belief that France's ability to control territory overseas would determine its future influence and prosperity convinced many centrist republicans that securing France's position in Indochina against British and Chinese competition (which naval and colonial officials in Southeast Asia continually invoked in their correspondence) was critical.[40] As a result, when local officials again instigated a conflict, the republican government responded more vehemently than it had in 1873.

In April 1882 the governor-general of Cochinchina, Charles Le Myre de Vilers, sent naval officer Henri Rivière to Hanoi to enforce French trading rights guaranteed in the 1874 treaty.[41] Like Dupuis and Garnier in 1873, Rivière used the troops accompanying him to capture the city's citadel, which he held for a few days before the metropolitan government ordered him to surrender it. The incident thus resolved quickly, but even as the Hué court continued to negotiate with Le Myre de Vilers and the French minister of foreign affairs for a peaceful solution, Tu Duc also became increasingly convinced that the Vietnamese Empire could only stave off French conquest by resisting new incursions with military force.[42] He thus appealed to the Chinese government for military assistance in the event of a conflict. In response, Chinese administrators agreed to send arms to support the Black Flags and move an army into the northern provinces of Tonkin.[43]

The incident also sparked debates in France. Some republican politicians—including Prime Minister Charles Duclerc—began to advocate for a military intervention in Vietnam. They framed this military intervention as defensive and insisted that its objectives would include protecting French commerce and enforcing the 1874 treaty. But they also made it clear that France could only accomplish these objectives if it occupied the country.[44] Many politicians nevertheless remained wary of funding another overseas conflict so soon after the expensive conquest of Tunisia, and they also remained unenthusiastic about the prospect of an open conflict with China. Because the Chinese emperor had traditionally exercised rights of sovereignty over Vietnam, the threat of a conflict was real.[45] Eight months of uneasy peace followed as the Hué court sought to negotiate its position between France and China. At the same time, Governor-General Le Myre de Vilers, Bernard Jauréguiberry (the head of the naval ministry who had also sought to spearhead expansion in Senegal), and Frédéric Bourée (the French minister in Beijing) all proposed contradictory plans to address the conflict with the Chinese government. Both Bourée and Le Myre de Vilers suggested negotiating an agreement with China that would divide Vietnam into Chinese and French zones of influence, whereas Jauréguiberry insisted that the French government should impose a protectorate by using military force.[46] When Jules Ferry assumed the position of prime minister in February 1883, the group advocating for a military intervention gained new influence in the Chamber of Deputies.[47]

This shift in French political leadership had repercussions in Vietnam. Rivière—now hopeful for metropolitan support—renewed his attacks against Vietnamese forces, and in May he died in battle with Vietnamese and Black Flag troops.[48] News of his death reached France at the end of the month. When the minister of the navy announced that Rivière was dead, the Chamber of Deputies voted unanimously to approve war credits that would underwrite a military intervention.[49] Ferry promised that with new troops, funds, and supplies, the army would consolidate its hold over Vietnam.

Rivière's death also led to demands across multiple newspapers and other publications for revenge to protect French "honor."[50] This contrasted with the public reaction to the news of Garnier's death in 1873 and Flatters's death in 1881, which were more muted. French writers argued for the conquest of all Vietnam, which would, they promised, bring trading benefits to France even as it secured the country's national prestige.[51] Many centrist and right-leaning newspapers claimed that the incident reflected the government's regrettable lack of commitment to its overseas territories and contended that moving forward, France would need to protect its "external prestige, moral force, and commercial markets" regardless of public opinion.[52] These arguments about colonialism's benefits echoed those made by explorers such as Soleillet and by the Paris Geographical Society in the late 1870s, but those earlier groups had claimed that "influence"—and not conquest—would best deliver trade and prestige to France.

Calls for revenge and conquest, however, were not unanimous. Several journalists used the incident to criticize the government's policies in Vietnam. Radical-socialist Henri Rochefort compared the government's strategies in Vietnam unfavorably to Pierre Savorgnan de Brazza's "peaceful" conquest of the Congo, thus invoking the model of exploration that the republican government had at times embraced and questioning why the government was not using it in Vietnam.[53] But only *Le petit parisien*, the popular daily, attacked the premise of France's presence in Vietnam by describing it as a dangerous "adventure"—the term that the republican opposition had used to describe Napoleon III's overseas expeditions. This adventure, the anonymous journalist warned, would lead to a "war six thousand leagues from France" and was likely to become the republic's "Mexico."[54] Although the journalist did not condemn the government's quest to avenge Rivière, he implied that France's presence in Vietnam was problematic and compared the country's strategies there to Napoleon III's overseas policies. This perspective was not widespread, but the memory of Mexico and "Napoleonic adventures" would continue to hang over the republican government's policies in Vietnam.

Despite these criticisms, Rivière's death appeared to create a consensus within the government and the educated public about the necessity of extending investment in Vietnam. France's renewed military efforts in the territory were initially successful, partly because Emperor Tu Duc died suddenly in July 1883 without a clearly designated heir, creating a dynastic crisis. Four emperors succeeded him in little less than a year, and the Hué court remained deeply divided about how best to respond to the threat posed by the French.[55] As a result, in June 1884 the French government was able to force the weakened Vietnamese court to sign the Pâtenotre Treaty, which established a French protectorate over Tonkin and Annam.[56] But the agreement did not end the conflict with China, which moved into a higher key after the failure of the 1884 Li-Fournier Convention.[57] The quest to avenge Rivière thus marked the beginning of a protracted conflict between the French army, Vietnamese mandarins, the Black Flags, and regular Chinese troops that lasted two years.[58] Over the second half of 1884, Ferry had to appeal to the Chamber of Deputies several times for more money and men. While the deputies continued to approve these bills, discontent over growing expenses began to rise on both the right and the left. This discontent would crystalize in response to the "crisis" of Lang Son in March 1885.[59]

The French had captured the city of Lang Son in February 1885 after months of fighting with Chinese and Black Flag troops.[60] In March, however, the Chinese counterattacked, and the French fled, abandoning their supplies and many of their cannons.[61] It was a relatively inconsequential defeat, especially as it occurred after Ferry had secretly entered into peace negotiations with Chinese authorities, although it weakened Ferry's bargaining position and temporarily undermined the French resident-general's authority at the Hué court.[62] But because no one knew about the extent of the loss or the negotiations, the arrival of the telegram announcing the defeat—sent by Louis Brière de l'Isle, who had been moved from Senegal to Vietnam—sparked a firestorm of controversy.[63] Ferry announced the news on March 30, using the occasion to ask for a credit of two hundred million francs to "avenge [France's] loss" and "safeguard [its] honor."[64] Republican radicals Georges Clemenceau and Alexandre Ribot insisted that parliament could not discuss the question of credits until it held an inquiry to determine responsibility for recent events.[65] Clemenceau went so far as to contend that France's defeat at Lang Son proved that the Ferry ministry was untrustworthy, which meant, "the Chamber no longer has ministers before it, but defendants . . . accused of high treason."[66] Conservatives, led by Bonapartist Jules Delafosse, agreed. Even many centrist republicans who had long supported Ferry's actions in Vietnam voted against him. In response, Ferry's cabinet resigned.[67]

The government's response to Lang Son was nevertheless equivocal. A new ministry headed by Henri Brisson, a deputy from the Left, took power in April 1885. When the new minister of foreign affairs, Charles de Freycinet, proposed to send two hundred million francs and eight thousand soldiers into Tonkin, most of the chamber—including 46 of the 147 radical republicans—voted for the measure, demonstrating that they were willing to support intervention as long as Ferry was not behind it.[68] The Ferry ministry's collapse also did not interrupt peace negotiations with China, which concluded provisionally with a cease-fire on April 4, 1885.[69] China and France signed the Tsientsin Treaty two months later on June 11, 1885, leading China to formally withdraw its soldiers and its claims to sovereignty over Vietnam.[70] Even though the opposition brought down Ferry's government over its policies in Tonkin, it thus voted for measures that had emerged directly from his policies.

The peace treaty did not end the fighting in Vietnam, however. After the Chinese troops withdrew, the Vietnamese emperor, Ham-Nghi, fled the capital with some of his advisers and launched a revolt against French rule in response to French military officers' continued attempts to insult and undermine the monarchy, eliminate the protectorate, and establish direct colonial administration in northern Vietnam.[71] In response, a highly placed mandarin named Phan Dinh Phung launched the Can Vuong, or Aid the King, movement, calling on Vietnamese scholars and administrators to revolt against French rule.[72] The French sought to discredit the movement by replacing Ham-Nghi with a new ruler, Dong Khanh, whom they believed would be more malleable. But Dong Khanh had little popular legitimacy, partly because Ham-Nghi eluded capture for several years.[73] It was only in 1888 that the French were able to find him and exile him to Algeria. And despite French efforts to reach out to Vietnamese mandarins, popular revolts persisted until 1892.[74] As a result of this concentrated resistance to the extension of French colonial control, Brisson could not recall troops from the territory—or impose direct colonial administration—and the ensuing conflict provoked renewed parliamentary debates over France's position in northern Vietnam.[75] Even though the opposition was motivated by concerns over money and manpower, its members began a conversation about France's policies in Tonkin and politique coloniale's connections to republicanism and Bonapartist imperialism.[76] Defenders of politique coloniale drew on colonial theories articulated by thinkers such as Paul Leroy-Beaulieu to explain the practice of republican colonialism, justify it politically, and define it as essential to France's future. Leftists and conservatives, on the other hand, argued that politique coloniale was endangering France. They also sought to discredit politique coloniale by tying it to the Second Empire.

Jules Ferry made one of the first attempts to explain politique coloniale and justify its practice in July 1885, several months after his ministry collapsed. In his much-cited speech to the Chamber of Deputies, he defined politique coloniale as a system that rested on a combination of "economic principles and interests, humanitarian beliefs of the highest order, and political considerations." These factors, he explained, were interdependent. He claimed that all countries in Europe—no matter their political organization—were expanding their reach in Asia and Africa. They were also introducing protective tariffs that would close off their empires to French goods. If France did not join in colonial expansion, he insisted, it would become unable to compete politically and economically overseas or within Europe.[77] Abstaining from colonial conquest would lead to a "decadence" and cause the nation to fall "from the first rank of nations to the third or fourth."[78] Ferry therefore described politique coloniale as a national, economic, moral, and military mission that transcended party affiliations and conflicts but still converged with republican politics and moral principles. He contended that France's decision to dominate others would contribute to the republican mission of spreading liberty and justice across the world. He also drew directly on the language of racial inequality to differentiate between conquest within Europe—which he implied was suspect—and conquest overseas.[79]

Ferry's defense of politique coloniale borrowed heavily from earlier thinkers. His insistence that politique coloniale was an apolitical endeavor critical to France's future echoed Duval's and Leroy-Beaulieu's claims about colonization's benefits.[80] But Ferry was more focused on defending military conquests, and in the process he proffered more elaborate descriptions of racial hierarchy and its relationship to "civilization" and "civilizing processes." The idea that France had an obligation to "civilize" the people it conquered was not new. But Ferry's juxtaposition of "superior" and "inferior" races drew sharper racial lines than many of his leftist republican and Saint-Simonian predecessors, who tended to criticize the "prejudice of color" as an ancien régime, British, or Spanish colonial problem—even as they themselves appealed implicitly to ideas about racial hierarchy to defend colonial expansion.

Ferry's explicit invocation of the idea of racial hierarchy at least partly reflected the growing influence of racial science in the mid-1880s. Racial science was not new, and, as we have seen, it had begun to become institutionalized in France as early as the 1850s in the Société d'anthropologie and the Muséum national d'histoire naturelle. But the government of the Third Republic envisioned the spreading of education, secularism, and science across France as central to the defense of republicanism itself, and it offered anthropologists a new level of support and visibility, funding, for example, the establishment of a new École d'anthropologie during the mid-1870s.[81] Ferry—along with many other moderate republican politicians in the 1880s—had personal connections to some of the members of these anthropological organizations thanks to his role as minister of public instruction, and he spoke enthusiastically about their work.[82]

By the mid-1880s most of the intellectuals associated with these newly prominent anthropological institutions had come to embrace a neo-Lamarckian vision of human inequality and evolution. This "racial paradigm," as historian Carole Reynaud-Paligot has explained, combined biological, cultural, and environmental understandings of race; it included a belief in "a hierarchy of human races according to morphological characteristics understood to be closer to or further from those of animals; a hierarchy of human societies' cultural characteristics; and the idea that intellectual and moral character could be inherited."[83] There was thus somewhat greater consensus among anthropologists about how to understand "race" in the 1880s than there had been in the 1860s, although anthropologists still disagreed about the relative importance of the role of heredity and environment in shaping human difference, about how to categorize peoples into different racial groups, and about the significance of the racial differences they identified.[84]

In his speech, Ferry did not reference these ongoing arguments. Instead, he relied on the prestige of the new racial science to dismiss the idea of human equality as impractical and irrational, while simultaneously gesturing toward some neo-Lamarckian ideas to shore up his contention that racial inequality could justify colonial conquest. Because neo-Lamarckians thought that acquired characteristics could be inherited, most continued to believe that racial hierarchies were not permanent, although many also maintained that "superior" peoples would be able to "progress" better than their "inferior" counterparts.[85] Ferry's contention that France's right to conquest rested on its duty to "civilize" the conquered explicitly invoked this notion of Lamarckian progress, as it implied that France would make conquered peoples less "inferior" over time. But at the same time, Ferry's insistence that the world could be divided between "superior" peoples who had the right to conquer and "inferior" ones who were destined for subjugation raised questions about what such progress would look like and whether it was in fact possible. Ferry's vision also deviated from the views of at least some anthropologists and other intellectuals working within the paradigm of the new racial science, who did not necessarily draw connections between their beliefs in racial inequality and colonial conquest.[86]

Deputies on the right and the left objected to Ferry's vision of politique coloniale. Some rejected Ferry's contention that politique coloniale would benefit France economically. Others claimed that overseas conquest would weaken France instead of enabling it to compete with its neighbors, as Ferry had suggested.[87] But most critics went beyond practical problems and objected to Ferry's attempts to align overseas conquest with republican principles. They took issue with his claim that politique coloniale was morally and politically justifiable because it reflected "superior" races' rights over their "inferior" counterparts'. Georges Périn, a radical deputy from Haute-Vienne, contended that Ferry's claims that France would "civilize" inferior peoples was obfuscation; in fact, the civilizing mission was a cover for greedy, ruthless theft. His fellow radical, Camille Pelletan, argued that "the civilizing mission" could not be used to justify conquest because violence and civilization were at odds. Georges Clemenceau even claimed that Ferry had borrowed his ideas about racial inequality from German intellectuals, implying that they were prejudiced, unscientific, and a violation of republican principles.[88] Most deputies—including Pelletan and Clemenceau—did not reject Ferry's racism altogether, but they objected to his division of the world into two categories of "inferior" and "superior" and to his equation of racial inequality with the right of conquest.[89]

Some deputies linked not only the idea of racial inequality but politique coloniale itself to other forms of political organization—especially the discredited Second Empire. Leftist deputy Émile Vernhes, for example, insisted that colonial conquest was "not an act of republican politics." On the contrary, it represented the continuation of imperial strategies and values in the Third Republic. "Since 1870," he complained, "the majority of ministers . . . have acted like Napoleon III, who, fearing above all the demands for domestic political liberty, threw himself . . . into Mexico and other expeditions. This sovereign thus sought to use war to create a diversion. . . . You practice the same system."[90] Vernhes—who had been a fierce critic of Napoleon III and spent much of the Second Empire in exile—thus argued that like Napoleon III, the Third Republic used conquests abroad as a distraction from political matters at home and that such conquests were key components in political systems that sought to deny rights to French citizens.

Vernhes's effort to tie the republic's politique coloniale to Napoleon III and the Second Empire was echoed by other deputies. Edgar Raoul Duval, who convened with the conservatives, also connected the republic's colonial expeditions to the Mexican expedition, warning that Vietnam would end in a repetition of 1870–71.[91] Monarchist Armand de Baudry d'Asson, on the other hand, remarked that politique coloniale showed that "the Republic means war."[92] He thus deployed the old republican critique of the empire—"the empire means war"—against Ferry. Clemenceau, on the other hand, claimed that a republic that embraced politique coloniale would be even worse than the Second Empire. The Second Empire, he contended, had at least promised to pursue peace; politique coloniale was a promise of unending conflict.[93]

Frédéric Passy, a prominent liberal economist, proposed a different imperial comparison by drawing parallels between politique coloniale and Germany's policies in Alsace-Lorraine. He noted that republicans condemned "the crimes committed in European conquest" while pretending that they "not only had the right but the duty to dominate, enslave, and exploit other peoples who . . . have their own personality and nationality . . . and are not less attached to their independence. . . . These territories are the life, the body, and the blood of these poor people, they are their Alsace and their Lorraine."[94] By annexing territories around the world and subjecting their inhabitants to French rule, Passy averred, France was acting like the German

Empire. If centrist republicans wanted to insist that Germany had committed a crime by annexing Alsace and Lorraine, they could not steal territory from other peoples. He noted that although advocates of politique coloniale asserted that France needed to expand to remain a great power, "great peoples" protected the independence of others.

Even though most deputies voted to continue France's investment in Vietnam, some on the left and the right thus at least verbally rejected both the policies that Ferry's ministry had embraced there and the language of politique coloniale in which they were couched. They contended that politique coloniale—with its emphasis on military conquest—did not align with republican principles but that it instead was an enterprise that converged more clearly with Bonapartist and German imperial values. Such imperial enterprises, they argued, had also endangered France before and would do so again.

Public Arguments over Indochina and Politique Coloniale

These debates over Lang Son and politique coloniale spread beyond the Chamber of Deputies. The parliamentary debates themselves were reprinted in pamphlets and newspapers, and they entered a wider conversation about politique coloniale that played out in the political and popular press across France. Both advocates and opponents of politique coloniale joined this conversation to explain their ideas about France's future in Southeast Asia and the purpose of politique coloniale. The participants had widely varying knowledge of what was happening in Vietnam, and their proposals had, if anything, even fewer direct effects on the structure of French colonial rule in Vietnam than the proposals made by deputies in the French legislature. The conversation's importance thus lies in what it reveals about French conceptions of empire at a moment that many historians have identified as a turning point in the French government's pursuit of colonial conquest. Namely, it demonstrates that during the mid-1880s it was not just politicians but also a wider group of French elites who continued to see potential intersections between colonial conquest abroad and autocratic or Bonapartist politics in the metropole and worried about what those intersections revealed about contemporary republican politics. The specter of Napoleon III thus continued to loom over conversations about republican colonialism across France.

Although many moderate republicans had abandoned the Ferry ministry in the wake of Lang Son, most centrist republican newspapers continued to defend the government's actions. In the crisis's immediate aftermath, they employed several strategies to convince their readers that the Ferry ministry's policies in Vietnam had not irrevocably failed, most of which did not engage directly with theories of politique coloniale. These defenders of Ferry's policies tended to minimize Lang Son's consequences while invoking the event as a reason for all political parties to rally around the flag and invest more resources in securing Tonkin—the position that most journalists had taken after Rivière's death.[95] They called on the new ministry to continue Ferry's efforts in Southeast Asia under the banner of national honor.[96] At the same time, they tried to depoliticize these debates over France's expansionary policies in Indochina by describing them as "national" issues that should transcend party politics—a strategy that likely reflected their concerns about the fact that many politicians who had condemned Ferry's policies in the Chamber of Deputies had done so by either maintaining that the policies were "not republican" or by connecting them directly to Bonapartist or German imperial politics.

Some centrist republican journalists were more critical and condemned the invasion of Tonkin.[97] Former prime minister and moderate republican Jules Simon declared that Tonkin offered France no strategic or economic benefits, so expansion there was "not in the interest" of the nation.[98] Novelist and journalist Henri Escoffier, publishing under the pen name Thomas Grimm, argued that no part of Indochina would benefit France. Instead of conquering territory so far afield, France should spread its influence in North Africa, which was more economically productive and better positioned strategically. Escoffier thus contended that after signing favorable peace treaties with China, France should pull its resources out of the territory.[99] Despite these criticisms, neither Simon's nor Escoffier's visions of France's colonial future differed from that of Ferry's supporters.[100] Even if they objected to Tonkin's conquest, they did not disavow colonial expansion. Instead, they differentiated between more and less useful colonies and contended that Tonkin fell into the latter category.

Several prominent economists also criticized the government's policies in Vietnam and politique coloniale—reflecting larger divides among economists over colonial expansion. They maintained that despite promises made by politique coloniale's supporters in the Chamber of Deputies, colonization would never increase trade enough to make conquered territories profitable. Catholic intellectual René Lavollée declared that it was expensive to conquer territory and to preserve French control over it. Even in Algeria, France had always lost money.[101] Liberal Yves Guyot, who would be elected as a radical deputy later in 1885, warned that the colonies were so expensive that they would hinder France's development of metropolitan infrastructure necessary to stay competitive within Europe.[102] He argued that the moderate republicans worried about "civilizing the Cochinchinese" when they lacked the money to pay instructors to educate their own citizens. Instead of fretting about "policing" the colonies, he maintained, France should focus on building its own infrastructure.[103]

Journalists on the left and the right also took on a more critical attitude toward the government's policies in Vietnam and politique coloniale. In their articles, they echoed arguments set forth by their counterparts in the chamber. Several insisted that the government had been duplicitous in promoting the conquest of Vietnam.[104] They also maintained that republicans' politique coloniale was undermining national security. Orleanist and former prime minister Albert de Broglie, in a speech to the Senate that was later printed and distributed in pamphlet form, contended that the attempt to conquer colonies overseas when France was already weakened was nonsensical.[105] Colonies, he insisted, were a "luxury" that would compromise France's position on the continent, as a weakened France would have to use more of its limited resources to assert its authority overseas.[106] France would find it difficult to control the people it had conquered, he warned, and it would also struggle to hold its conquests against its European rivals. It was not an accident, he argued, that Germany was encouraging France's embrace of politique coloniale. The Germans were pleased to see that France's overseas struggles had already diminished its military power and alienated its British ally.[107] Eventually Germany would declare war and take all of France's new colonies for itself.[108] The republican government might dream of creating a "colonial empire"—a term he noted appeared in a recent "government publication"—but such an empire was destined to end in disaster.[109] This belief that politique coloniale would compromise France's position within Europe and that Bismarck was encouraging the policy with that result in mind appeared in a numerous pamphlets and newspaper articles across the political spectrum.[110]

Leftist republicans were particularly likely to criticize politique coloniale by insisting that it violated republican principles and moral values—much like their allies in the Chamber of Deputies. Charles-Ange Laisant, for example, the editor of *Le petit parisien* and a radical deputy, insisted that the politicians who embraced colonialism were "republicans in name" but "reactionaries in fact." He invoked moderate republicans' activities in Tunisia, Tonkin, and Madagascar as evidence that their politics contradicted "democratic principles." These expeditions, he claimed, were "ruinous" for the public because they sacrificed "honor, French blood, the financial equilibrium, [and] national defense" to the needs of "high finance."[111] Laisant thus implied that politique coloniale undermined the practice of democracy in

France itself as it sacrificed the needs of the people to the selfish demands of one class.

Louis Guétant, who would later go on to join the Ligue des droits de l'homme, focused more on the effects of politique coloniale on colonized peoples. He argued that politique coloniale was the "official organization of international brigandage," involving the "exploitation of the weak" and the destruction of "the independence of young peoples who are forming their nationalities," so that France could take their riches.[112] Claiming that France would "civilize" the indigenous population was an absurd pretext that allowed it to "steal [these peoples'] liberty and their country."[113] The only examples of "civilization" that France had shown thus involved "massacring prisoners" and "destroying private property." France's behavior in Tonkin and Madagascar—and even Algeria—proved that the republic's support for "liberty and independence" was a lie.[114] This behavior was particularly embarrassing, he argued, because France had protested so loudly against Germany's behavior in Alsace-Lorraine.

Like some leftist republicans in the Chamber of Deputies, Guétant drew parallels between the moderate republicans' politique coloniale and the Second Empire. He noted that, ironically, many of the deputies who supported France's colonial expeditions had opposed Napoleon III's expedition to Mexico in the name of the Mexican people. But after they rose to power, they engaged in the same behavior that they previously condemned. This political shift was embarrassing for republicans, but it also would endanger the country, as the results of Napoleon III's disastrous attempts to extend French influence overseas showed. Guétant noted that after the Franco-Prussian War, many politicians came to see Algeria as "compensation" for France's loss. However, he asserted, Algeria actually "played a role" in the defeat. If Napoleon III had not overinvested there, France "would not have needed to be compensated" in the first place. All societies that built empires eventually succumbed to "decadence," so France should focus on strengthening itself at home instead of trying to conquer distant colonies.[115]

Comparisons between Ferry's ministry and the Second Empire appeared in multiple popular daily and left-leaning journals. Some writers implied that blind optimism marked both regimes. An article in the daily *Le petit parisien*, for example, claimed that the moderate republicans cried, "To Peking!" with as much enthusiasm and as little preparation as the Bonapartists before them had shouted "To Berlin!" at the outset of the Franco-Prussian War.[116] Another article in *La presse* similarly described the Ferry ministry as "a poor imitation of the Empire" that had collapsed the same way as its predecessor had in 1870.[117] Other writers drew parallels between the two regimes' moral flaws. In the

FIGURE 5. This political cartoon appeared in a republican satirical journal. It compared Ferry to Bazaine, a military officer close to Napoleon III who, as a marshal of France, was defeated by the Prussian army at Metz, the turning point in the Franco-Prussian War. Alfred Le Pétit, "Ferry et Bazaine," *Le grelot*, April 5, 1885, 3. Bibliothèque nationale de France.

socialist *La justice*, Stephen Pichon argued that the government's conquest of Vietnam had been undertaken with even more "cynicism and bad faith than the Empire itself would have permitted."[118] He thus implied that the problems that many republicans had attributed to the imperial government also affected the republican regime. Henri Rochefort proclaimed in an even more inflammatory tone, "I do not wish to do Napoleon III the dishonor of comparing him to Jules Ferry. If the former committed the odious folly of declaring war on Germany, at least he went in person to Sedan. . . . Ferry did not even risk his insect shell for an instant during this expedition."[119] In this account, Ferry and his ministers were more corrupt than their imperial counterparts because they sent others to die overseas without risking themselves.

These parallels were hyperbolic; they compared the Ferry ministry to the Second Empire to attack the ministry's credibility. Other journalists on the left and the right made more direct connections between the two regime's strategies and respective relationships to overseas territory by complaining that both devoted too many resources to expensive, never-ending overseas expeditions. In *La justice*, Léon Millot argued that the Second Empire and the Third Republic undertook "warlike expeditions that will haunt us forever." He noted with despair, "After the experience of Crimea, China, Mexico, and Germany, we have thrown ourselves at Tunisia, Madagascar, and Tonkin."[120] He thus implied that the Second Empire and the Third Republic shared destructive core programs. He concluded by insisting that France would only find stability and prosperity by giving up overseas conquest. Multiple writers also continued to describe Vietnam as an "adventure"—the term that republicans and monarchists had used to condemn the Mexican expedition and tie it to France's defeat during the Franco-Prussian War.[121]

Leftists' and conservatives' criticisms of the Ferry ministry's policies were thus—unsurprisingly—more pointed than those of their moderate republican counterparts. They began from the premise that the architects of the Ferry ministry's strategies in Vietnam were incompetent and criminal; they also held not only Ferry but the centrist republicans who dominated the Chamber of Deputies responsible for France's problems overseas. Leftist writers were especially likely to argue that France should not have been in Tonkin and Annam in the first place and to insist that all of Ferry's colonial conquests—including Tunisia and Madagascar—were equally problematic.[122] But both leftists and conservatives sought to discredit the Ferry ministry's behavior in Vietnam by associating it with the Second Empire and Napoleon III. Conservative commentators often in fact used this comparison to demand regime change. Novelist Élémir Bourges argued that the events proved that France's decision to "abandon itself to the spirit of rebellion and democracy" had undermined its ability to wage war.[123] Writing under a pen name, monarchist Léon Lavedan similarly contended that the republic had weakened the army and that its only legacy would be the Paris Commune and military defeat at the hands of the Chinese Empire.[124] Philosopher Étienne Vacherot went so far as to proclaim that the events proved that France required a prince to guide it.[125] Increasingly displaced by centrist republicans, conservatives hopefully compared the Ferry ministry's collapse to 1870 and envisioned a new, conservative government taking its place.

Despite these attacks on Ferry's policies in Tonkin and politique coloniale, most commentators promoted similar strategies in response to France's recent defeat at Lang Son. Nearly all critics argued that France needed to send in more troops, supplies, and money to recoup its losses, even if they differed on how they proposed to follow up on this aid. Republicans who supported Ferry were more likely to demand an expansion of France's efforts in the territory, calling in some cases for an invasion of Beijing. Conservatives offered a more modest vision of France's future in Indochina, but they agreed that France needed to win the immediate conflict to safeguard its honor.[126] Some also suggested that after defeating its enemies, France would need to remain in the territory; in *Le gaulois*, for example, monarchist Henry de Pène argued that France could not "abdicate" its responsibilities in East Asia. After all, France was a "Catholic nation" and could not abandon the Christians in Vietnam to persecution at the hands of their own government—an argument that reflected the long-standing influence of Napoleon III's initial justification for conquering territory in Indochina starting in the 1860s.[127] And even leftists who argued that Ferry's investment in overseas territories and his promotion of politique coloniale was leading France toward disaster did not usually claim that France should adopt new strategies in Tonkin. Some implied that eventually France should consider withdrawing from the territory—but even those writers did not propose a clear exit strategy. Most leftist and conservative journalists thus proposed a vision for Tonkin's future that did not deviate markedly from the one proposed by Ferry himself.

Colonial Theory and the Republic

Even though conservative and leftist criticisms had few effects on France's position in Indochina, the contention that politique coloniale weakened France, violated republican principles, and aligned the Third Republic with the Second Empire troubled supporters of colonial expansion. In the face of these arguments, colonial advocates produced new texts in the second half of the 1880s that tried to defend politique coloniale, a term they claimed was often used but seldom understood.[128] This literature was mostly written by intellectuals with connections to overlapping republican colonial advocacy groups and to the growing number of French learned societies focused on colonial issues that were taking shape in the second half of the 1880s.[129] Some of these figures had made their careers in the colonies; others had ties to politicians invested in colonial expansion such as Jules Ferry or to colonial industries and enterprises.[130] Whatever their relationship to empire, all sought to appeal to narrow, well-educated audiences, although some were more scholarly and others more popular in orientation. These writers' explanations of politique coloniale did not always align with Ferry's—partly because they were not all committed to defending his conquests. But like Ferry, they tried to demonstrate that colonial expansion transcended domestic political divisions to weaken potential connections between republican colonialism and Bonapartist imperialism.

A number of writers, including economist Charles Gide, who had succeeded colonial advocate and royaume arabe opponent Jules Duval as the head of the procolonial journal *L'économiste française*, and Gabriel Charmes, a journalist who wrote for the prestigious *La revue des deux mondes* and *Le journal des débats*, positioned politique coloniale as apolitical by claiming that all major European powers—republics and monarchies alike—had embraced it.[131] Jean Marie Antoine de Lanessan, a naval physician, naturalist, and member of the Société d'anthropologie who would later become the governor of Indochina, similarly insisted that colonization was a "universal movement . . . pushing all the nations of Europe toward territory that civilization has not yet conquered."[132] Politicians had not created this movement, he argued; instead, it was a "natural" outgrowth of human development, which meant it was not subject to political or moral debates. It resulted from the fact that Europe had entered a new "scientific" stage of civilization defined by growing markets and industrialization.[133] Multiple writers thus echoed Ferry's claim that politique coloniale had nothing to do with domestic politics: instead, it was a phenomenon transforming Europe that France ignored at its peril.[134] This insistence that colonization was a pan-European phenomenon that transcended political divides was not new; Leroy-Beaulieu's description of colonialism had been predicated on the idea. But writers in the 1880s were especially likely to describe colonization as a "necessary" or "natural" facet of modern life and to warn their readers of other countries' colonial ambitions.

Other authors sought to render politique coloniale apolitical by grounding it in narratives about French history. Alfred Rambaud, a professor of history at the Sorbonne with ties to Ferry, thus contended in his lengthy collaborative historical account of French colonization that France was one of the oldest colonizing countries.[135] He averred that explorations and encounters with other peoples had always been a key element of French national identity.[136] Aristide Couteaux, a journalist who worked to disseminate republican and scientific principles by writing pamphlets for popular audiences under the pen name Jacquillou, similarly insisted that colonial expansion was "independent of any form of government."[137] It represented a "politics of the nation" that was "traditional" to all governments that have "cared about the prosperity, the grandeur, and the glory of the country." The republic had thus simply embraced expansionist policies that France's most effective leaders had always promoted.[138]

Many defenders of politique coloniale also sought to deflect attacks that colonial expansion was "antirepublican" or "Bonapartist" by highlighting its benefits for the nation. These defenders often articulated their understandings of these benefits in diametrical opposition to their critics' attacks on politique coloniale. Lanessan thus argued that colonial expansion would enable France to secure resources and markets that would eventually improve its material wealth. He noted that critics of politique coloniale rightly stressed that conquering colonies could be expensive, but he argued that these critics also underestimated the economic benefits that these colonies would bring.[139] Rambaud and journalist Jules Bossière, on the other hand, were more cautious. Bossière acknowledged that poorly run colonies could cost the metropole money. He contended, however, that well-run colonies would bear the costs of their own administration while providing France with natural resources.[140] Rambaud similarly conceded that modern colonies might never produce as much wealth as their eighteenth-century predecessors but maintained that they would increase trade in important new markets.[141] Neither of these authors saw colonies as a likely source of income, but they assumed that colonized territories would indirectly help industry and trade.

Other writers insisted that politique coloniale would strengthen the military. Louis Vignon, a professor at the fledgling École coloniale and a former chief of staff for the Ministry of Commerce with family connections to the moderate republican leadership of the 1880s, explained, for example, that France's colonies had always supported the nation in times of war, so there were historical reasons to believe that conquests would increase France's continental security—not weaken it, as some opponents of politique coloniale had long claimed.[142] Alfred Rambaud, objecting to critics' contentions that France's engagements overseas would limit the number of troops it could draw on during a European conflict, similarly argued that France's colonies would extend the "theater of war" and force France's opponents to send their troops around the world. Moreover, the colonies would add soldiers to France's armies as "citizens of color" came to form a "colonial army" that could fight in "intertropical wars."[143]

Some writers also repeated the argument that politique coloniale would increase France's cultural and intellectual influence. Vignon argued that colonization would "bring [France's] name, its language, [and] its ideas to distant places," which would secure the nation's "moral and intellectual grandeur."[144] Gide similarly claimed that colonization could solve France's problems with its declining population, which were undermining its position as one of the world's "greatest" nations. In the past, a "small but civilized people" such as the Greeks could conquer large empires, but in a world where all peoples were becoming "equal," the economic prosperity, military power, and intellectual influence of each nation would be "mathematically proportional to the number of its population."[145] In order to secure France's future influence, Gide argued, France needed to expand in Asia and especially in Africa, where it could "adopt and assimilate people from foreign races" in order to increase the size of its population. One day, he promised, these peoples would come to "speak our language, read our books and our journals, nourish themselves on our ideas, [and] associate themselves with our history and our political destiny."[146] With such a large adopted population, he implied, France would remain among the ranks of the greatest nations. Vignon and Gide's claim that colonization would spread French culture thus directly echoed claims of earlier writers such as Duval, Leroy-Beaulieu, and others associated with the Paris Geographical Society. But while Duval and Leroy-Beaulieu had claimed that colonization would spread French culture because French settlers would bring it with them, colonial advocates such as Gide were less likely to center their visions of colonialism on the movement of French people—a fact that reflected the growing turn away from the model of settler colonies as France conquered more territory that settlers would find difficult to live in during the 1880s.

Although many of these writers thus argued that colonization was an apolitical enterprise that benefited the nation, some defenders of colonization also sought to reconcile politique coloniale with republican principles by maintaining that it contributed to the larger republican project of spreading liberty and promoting progress.[147] Charles Gide, for example, noted that while "humanitarians" insisted that colonization amounted to "oppression" and "robbery," their arguments suffered from a misunderstanding. Although it was true that "men of all races . . . must be considered equal in rights," some "political organisms" were still "inferior" and "defective." The "rights of individual barbarians" could not be violated, but the "rights of barbarian states . . . were not sacred." By differentiating between individuals' and states' rights, Gide could argue that invading and forcibly ruling "barbarian states" aligned with republican ideas. Overthrowing such states would enable their indigenous inhabitants to "pass from barbarism into civilization." As a result, these conquests contributed to the "general good of humanity."[148] Conquest and domination could thus coexist with a national commitment to individual liberty and equality.

Other defenders of politique coloniale justified its status in republican thought by distinguishing between republican colonial expansion and its antecedents. They acknowledged that early European colonization had been problematic but maintained—on highly dubious historical grounds—that contemporary colonizers employed new methods and pursued different goals. Arthur Bordier, a professor of medical geography at the newly established École d'anthropologie in Paris, for example, conceded that "colonization in the past had mostly been a work of destruction."[149] But the new politique coloniale "would not destroy but revitalize races . . . [and] substitute the spirit of conquest with peaceful association."[150] Republican colonial conquest was thus distinct from monarchical or imperial colonial conquest: it did not rely on exploitation but instead promoted peace and prosperity.[151] Aristide Couteaux echoed this argument, claiming that the republic's politique coloniale did not involve war at all. Instead of attacking peaceful societies—like the colonial powers of the seventeenth and eighteenth centuries—the republic was "repressing the brigandage committed by hordes of savages on the frontiers of our overseas possessions." Couteaux thus claimed that the republic was behaving like a police force instead of as an invading army; its incursions and conquests were intended to impose order, which would benefit France and the indigenous population.[152]

For the most part, the scholarly and journalistic defense of colonization echoed many of the themes that appeared in Ferry's speech. This is perhaps unsurprising because these writers both influenced and were influenced by Ferry for much of the 1880s. They defended politique coloniale by describing it as a "national politics" that would improve France's global mercantile, military, political, and cultural position. But, at the same time, they defined politique coloniale's relationship with domestic political questions in sometimes contradictory ways that went beyond Ferry's views. Some figures such as Gabriel Charmes divorced politique coloniale from republican political values, which he implied were irrelevant.[153] Charmes described the republicans' theoretical commitment to promoting liberty and fraternity as foolish in a world where political dominance lay in the hands of the strongest. He thus indicated that the republicans' values—while adequate for shaping France's domestic policy—had little place in colonial conquest. Politique coloniale, he averred, required strategic planning instead of moral principles.

Most republicans, however, differentiated between republican colonial conquests and imperial or monarchist conquests, even if they simultaneously contended that politique coloniale was apolitical. Unlike its monarchist and imperial predecessors, they argued, republican France was not conquering territories to amass power or riches. Instead, it was spreading French culture and values to "uncivilized" peoples. As a result, these conquests were not despotic; they would organize uncivilized societies, improve their material well-being, and introduce them to the principles of liberty, equality, and fraternity. The republic's politique coloniale would thus promote human progress by exposing societies around the world to republican ideals. The argument that republican colonialism would operate differently from its historical antecedents was also not new. Paul Soleillet, the Paris Geographical Society, and supporters of the trans-Saharan railroad had all promoted a vision of a "peaceful" republican colonialism based on trade and French "influence." But, generally speaking, they had argued that republican colonialism was different because it would not depend on military conquest; these later authors were contending that republican colonialism was different even though it depended on military conquest.

These thinkers' ability to distinguish between republican conquest and monarchical or imperial conquest was, like Ferry's, predicated on a belief in racial hierarchy. In his speech to the Chamber of Deputies, Ferry had insisted that "superior races" had rights over "inferior races" such as the Vietnamese. The political opposition had condemned this language as antirepublican, even if they did not reject the idea of racial hierarchy itself.[154] And, notably, most other defenders of politique coloniale substituted the words "culture" or "civilization" for the word "race"—which was closer to the way that Soleillet and members of the Paris Geographical Society had invoked the idea of racial inequality without explicitly naming it during the late 1870s.[155] This vocabulary allowed republicans to distance themselves from "the prejudice of color," which they often continued to associate with the British, the Germans, or ancien régime slave owners, even as they reified similar hierarchical structures. But, at the same time, these commentators reiterated Ferry's claim—which some journalists and deputies had objected to—that colonial conquest was just if the conquerors were "superior" to the conquered and planned to "improve" the peoples now under their control. Because these thinkers classified all peoples who were not of European descent as "inferior," they, much like Ferry, were able to justify French conquest in Asia or Africa. That said, these thinkers' use of this obfuscating language points to the persistent tensions in nineteenth-century republican thought around the role of explicitly racist logic within the colonial project.

Bonapartist Empire and Colonial Conquest

The Third Republic's decision to invade, conquer, and occupy Tonkin and Annam unleashed a debate that played out both in the Chamber of Deputies and in the press over politique coloniale, its relationship to republican politics, and its implications for the French nation. Both right-wing and left-wing critics of France's policies overseas sought to discredit politique coloniale not, for the most part, by citing its negative effects on Vietnamese people but by claiming that autocratic rule abroad would lead to despotism at home—a pattern, as a number of scholars have pointed out, that had characterized liberal anticolonial thinking beginning in the eighteenth century.[156] These critics sought to make the association between colonialism and despotism real by associating politique coloniale with Napoleon III and the Second Empire. Their criticisms gained enough support to overturn Ferry's government and push some centrist republicans out of the Chamber of Deputies in the elections of 1885, even if the opposition proved unwilling to end Ferry's policies.

In response to these contentions that colonial conquest was antirepublican and aligned with Bonapartist principles, supporters of politique coloniale defended their ideas in numerous publications that simultaneously defined the policy as apolitical and in line with republican principles. Many argued that republican colonial empire had as little to do with the Second Empire as republican colonial conquest had to do with French colonies under the ancien régime. This rhetorical move echoed ideas about colonial expansion offered by explorers such as Paul Soleillet and the Paris Geographical Society in the late 1870s. But most of those figures had envisioned republican colonialism as domination without military conquest; by the 1880s, colonial advocates were arguing that military conquest, too, could align with republican principles. Their publications were aimed at elites and did not have a popular audience, but they helped shift the political conversation around politique coloniale at this historical moment.

As approval for colonial expansion grew during the 1890s, the memory of the Second Empire, Mexico, and France's defeat in the Franco-Prussian War would begin to fade from the conversation about France's politique coloniale. Increasingly, French politicians, journalists, and intellectuals came to see continental empire and colonial conquest as distinct. This dichotomy did not emerge organically, however, and it was not without its contradictions.

In fact, it was partly because of the way critics mobilized the memory of the Second Empire during the 1880s that republican commentators formulated their defenses of politique coloniale in the way that they did. The republican defense of colonial expansion thus evolved out of the shadows of France's problematic relationship to Napoleon III and the empire that he had failed to construct.

CHAPTER 6

Defending a "Colonial Empire" in Republican France

In 1894–95 debates erupted in both the Chamber of Deputies and the press over the invasion of Madagascar. At first glance, these debates echoed the arguments over the 1885 military setbacks in Vietnam. The military expeditions had much in common; both originated under Jules Ferry during the mid-1880s. Much as he had in Vietnam, Ferry invoked a history of missionary work, along with trading and diplomatic agreements, to justify his government's attempts to claim rights over the Merina (or "Hova" in most contemporary French sources) government of Queen Ranavalona III and Prime Minister Rainilaiarivony.[1] The Merina government controlled central Madagascar, and over the nineteenth century it had gradually extended its influence over neighboring territory. At the same time, it had sought to preserve its independence from European powers by navigating between the British, the French, and later the Americans.[2] In 1883, prodded by lobbying from French traders in Réunion, who resented Merina restrictions on their ability to trade and purchase land, Ferry claimed that France's traditional rights in Madagascar were threatened, so he launched a military invasion with the goal of curbing British and American influence and establishing a French protectorate.[3] The initial invasion seemed successful; the Merina sent diplomatic missions to Britain and the United States, asking them to intercede, but neither was willing to, and the French were able to force the queen to sign a treaty of protectorate.

A few years later, in 1890, France secured British and German acceptance of its rights to the island.[4]

The treaty itself quickly became a source of conflict, however, as the French resident-general, Charles Le Myre de Vilers—the same colonial official who had been central to the campaign to expand French territory in Indochina—sought to increase French control over the island even as Prime Minister Rainilaiarivony tried to limit French influence. In 1894 the French government demanded an expansion in the terms of the protectorate, which the Merina government refused.[5] In response, the Chamber of Deputies voted to fund an expedition to the island led by General Jacques Duchesne. The accompanying report justified this decision by claiming that the Merina government had never abided by the 1885 treaty and acted in "bad faith." It also insisted that the French were simply enforcing the terms of the protectorate and guaranteeing their rule "against all future resistance."[6]

The metropolitan press was initially supportive of the expedition. An article in *Le monde illustré*, a popular illustrated journal, was not entirely unsympathetic to the queen, claiming that she had "grace," "distinction," and "intelligence," but it also contended that a "curious mix of barbarism and civilization" characterized her court. It noted that the queen's salon, for example, was furnished "in a European style" but "without taste," with a mirrored wardrobe placed next to a piano.[7] The article thus implied that the queen's court—or at least its interior decorating—was laughable; it had the trappings of European "civilization," but those elements were just for show because the queen did not understand them. What's more, the article insisted that the queen exercised "no real political authority." Instead, she spent her days "gossiping with princesses and women of honor while chewing betel nut or playing lotto or checkers"; real power lay in the hands of conspirators who could not enforce order or even take care of their own soldiers, who lived on the brink of starvation. These conditions, the author insisted, endangered French nationals, who faced "an impossible situation" because of the "implacable hostility of the old Anglo-Hova party" and "banditry that has emerged out of the Hova administration's anarchy and exactions." The Merina government, the article concluded, was thus inefficient, corrupt, despotic, dependent on the practice of slavery, and dominated by the British—an image designed to discredit Merina protests against French authoritarianism, draw attention away from their European-style government and school systems, which French readers might interpret as "civilized," and enable the author to claim that the republic would bring security, justice, and order to Madagascar.[8] Like Paul Soleillet in the 1870s, the article also redeployed the language of European antislavery movements to highlight European superiority and justify colonial expansion.

FIGURE 6. The portrait of Queen Ranavalona III that accompanied the article echoed the author's description of her as a "thoughtful," "demure," and largely powerless woman; she sits on a throne, but she looks away from the viewer, and her crown sits on the table beside her. "S. M. Ranavale III, Reine de Madagascar," *Le monde illustré*, September 29, 1894, 13. RetroNews, le site de presse de la BnF (1631–1950).

The invasion did not go smoothly; Duchesne's expeditionary force ran into setbacks from the start. When French troops encountered the Malagasy army, they met limited resistance. But if almost no French troops died in combat, nearly six thousand of the fifteen thousand soldiers sent to the territory died of disease.[9] Moreover, almost as soon as France succeeded in forcing the Merina government to agree to its terms, a popular uprising erupted. The movement, often referred to as the *menalamba*, or "red shawl," uprising, took the form of a guerrilla war. The uprising was a reaction not only against the French but also against the centralizing reforms of the Merina government; its adherents targeted foreign missionaries and indigenous Christians.[10]

In 1896 chaos spread across the island as the French tried and failed to exert control. In the face of this upheaval, the French government sent in Colonel Joseph Gallieni to serve as governor-general; he eventually succeeded in suppressing the revolt.[11] Much like his counterparts Henri Roussel de Courcy and Louis Brière de l'Isle in Vietnam (where Gallieni had also served), he was deeply suspicious of the indigenous monarchy from the start, reflecting ongoing republican suspicions of "local aristocracies" that, if anything, had been further sharpened by Napoleon III's cultivated relationships with Arab notables. A few months after arriving in Madagascar, he deposed and exiled Queen Ranavalona III.[12] After some argument, the French government decided to formally end the protectorate and transform Madagascar into a colony.[13]

France's invasion of Madagascar thus ended with French control over the territory, but it consumed more resources and lives than predicted. The government found itself investing both money and men in an expensive and unpopular expedition, as the army's high mortality rate clearly stemmed partly from poor government planning. The Ministry of War had not even supplied the invading troops with enough porters to carry supplies or sufficient medicine to treat those who fell ill. Worse still, conflicts between the Ministry of War and the newly established independent Ministry of the Colonies complicated the treatment of sick soldiers. To avoid having to collaborate with colonial officials, army officers shipped sick soldiers to France instead of bringing them to nearby Réunion. Many died on the journey because of the heat and unsanitary conditions.[14]

The problems that accompanied the invasion of Madagascar received considerable attention in the press. To some extent, this coverage echoed the debates over Vietnam that occurred a decade previously. Journalists from the leftist, rightist, and popular presses came together to attack the government's policies and practices. The right-leaning *La revue hebdomadaire*, for example, described the invasion of Madagascar as "poorly prepared, organized, and conducted" and accused both the minister of war and the minister of the colonies of incompetence.[15] The popular *Le monde illustré* similarly wondered how the government "could have thrown itself into this deadly campaign with so little thought or foresight."[16] The left-leaning *Le rappel* complained that the expedition had been organized in a way that "delivered our troops to all of the forces of destruction posed by a murderous climate" instead of putting them in a position to fight the Merina.[17] These journals thus implied that the government—and especially the Ministry of War—had acted incompetently and endangered the lives of French soldiers.

Many journalists contended that these mistakes warranted immediate consequences. The popular *Le petit parisien* condemned the expedition's "incapable organizers" and averred that they had committed an "unpardonable crime" that "mocked" the nation.[18] A journalist writing for the conservative *Le gaulois* argued that the deputies needed to determine who was responsible for "the thoughtless waste of French resource and the sacrifice of so many of its children."[19] The leftist *La justice* agreed that parliament should launch an inquiry into the expedition.[20] The insistence that the administration's behavior was not simply foolish but criminal had also characterized the criticism of the Tonkin expedition in 1885.

The Ministry of War's decision to repatriate troops through the Suez Canal in the middle of the summer was the object of particular criticism.[21] In the Senate, Arthur Ranc, the head of the Gauche démocratique parliamentary group, wanted to question the ministry over the incident; journalists on the right and the left supported these efforts. The centrist *Le temps, the* conservative *Le Figaro*, and the left-leaning *La justice* all accused the ministry of corruption and heartlessness. They implied that the minister of war had sent ill troops home on ships—even though he knew that it would kill them—because he was hoping that if they died in France instead of in Réunion, they would not be counted as casualties. The ministry had thus sacrificed soldiers' lives, these journalists contended, in a misguided attempt to seem less incompetent.[22] Other writers attacked ministerial rivalries; radical journalist and politician Camille Pelletan, for example, argued that the Ministry of War refused to send soldiers to Réunion because the island was beneath the auspices of the Colonial Ministry, and the Ministry of War feared that the Colonial Ministry would invoke any resources it used to care for French soldiers to make claims on the riches of Madagascar.[23]

The press coverage of the invasion of Madagascar was far from uniformly condemnatory, however. Many of the journalists writing for the *Le journal des débats* and *La liberté*, in particular—conservative republican newspapers—claimed that the expedition's problems were minor and that the government was not responsible for them. One article, for example, argued that the intensity of the criticism over Madagascar did not reflect the events that had transpired but socialist meddling. The socialists, the author implied, were not interested in soldiers' welfare; instead, they wanted to use Madagascar to divide republicans and discredit the government.[24] Gaston Calmette, writing for *Le Figaro*, alternatively claimed that the discontent was due to British propaganda.[25] These journalists were not uncritical of all the ministry's decisions, but they believed that the repatriation incident did not merit as much attention as it was receiving.[26]

The invasion of Madagascar thus provoked a debate in the press that echoed the arguments over Vietnam in the mid-1880s. In both cases, metropolitan French voices who often had relatively little information about what was happening overseas dominated the conversation.[27] And, at the same time, the main points of controversy also centered on a colonial military expedition's effects on France and France's soldiers—with a few exceptions, journalists and politicians were less concerned about the effects of military conquest on people in Vietnam or Madagascar. But there were important differences too. During the earlier arguments over Vietnam, a wide coalition of journalists and politicians on the left and the right had invoked Indochina as evidence of politique coloniale's flaws. They associated it with the Second Empire and implied that Napoleon III's embrace of colonial conquest was responsible for leading France to defeat at Sedan in 1870. Together, these criticisms forced the proponents of colonial expansion to articulate more elaborate theoretical defenses for their expeditions.

In 1895, on the other hand, there was less debate over the merits of colonial conquest. In August and September, many journalists and some politicians condemned the Ministry of War's tactics and strategies. A few still used the events in Madagascar to link the Third Republic to the Second Empire and describe both as incompetent. François Coppée, the nationalist poet, thus argued, "Beneath the Empire that you saw fall and beneath the Republic acclaimed by the naive and the ridiculous . . . you can see the same faults, the same lack of foresight . . . the same frivolousness in the heart of politicians when it comes to spending the blood and the gold of France."[28] Others held up the conflict between the Ministry of the Colonies and the Ministry of War as evidence of broader political problems in the Third Republic.[29] Still others—especially on the right—insisted that the incident reflected badly on the Chamber of Deputies.[30] However, most journalists did not question the value of conquering Madagascar. And although a few journalists on the left still contended that politique coloniale was incompatible with republican principles by associating it with Bonapartist and German imperialism, most critics avoided entering a discussion about the drawbacks of colonial expansion—even if they questioned the government's strategies.[31]

In this context, Georges Clemenceau's reaction to the events of Madagascar is revealing. In 1885 Clemenceau helped shape the Left's opposition to the Tonkin expedition by articulating an expansive critique of politique coloniale, which he insisted violated republican principles. In 1895 he remained critical of the Madagascar expedition but argued against it in different terms. In an open letter to Arthur Ranc published in *La justice*, he expressed support for the decision to question the minister of war on his policies.[32] He condemned the Ministry of War's "criminal destruction of lives" and claimed that the French people had the right to know "what inept ideas or negligence . . . led to the decimation . . . of our unhappy soldiers." Much like in 1885, Clemenceau also described the problems with Madagascar as part of a broader problem with republican politics. He argued that the republic itself was corrupt and even contended that "Republican politics have consisted . . . of changing men and formulas in order to maintain all of the errors of empire." But although he questioned the ministry's methods and implied that they revealed the republic's political flaws, he did not say that the government should have avoided invading Madagascar. Instead of calling for the republic to refrain from colonial expansion, he insisted that the republic needed broad-sweeping domestic reforms.[33] This perspective was echoed by multiple critical journalists on the left. They suggested that the conflict had revealed problems in the Ministry of War, the army, and perhaps even in the republic, but they did not use the incident to criticize colonial expansion.

Notably, while journalists criticized the behavior of the government at large and the Ministry of War in particular, they remained convinced of the inevitability and benefits of victory.[34] Once word reached France of General Duchesne's success at Antananarivo (Tananarive in contemporary French sources), *Le gaulois* insisted that the French should thank "our brave soldiers, their eminent commanders, and their general" for bringing the expedition to a successful close. The author went on to conclude that the expedition—despite its problems—had brought honor both to the army and to France.[35] Although the leftist *La lanterne* continued to condemn the Ministry of War after victory was assured, it too praised Duchesne and his army for their successes.[36] Journalists thus distinguished between the army's administration and the army itself and celebrated the conquest of Madagascar even if they criticized the way that the conquest had been conducted.[37]

The conflicts over Madagascar reveal that many commentators from across the political spectrum remained suspicious of the Third Republic and of the republican coalition that governed it during the 1890s. Many were quick to portray the government and the army as corrupt and incompetent. More generally, they argued that the government—either in the form of the Ministry of War or the Chamber of Deputies—was too engaged in petty internal struggles to wage war effectively. But, at the same time, these conflicts also show how competing views of colonial conquest had faded from the center of the debate. While some journalists continued to compare the Third Republic to the Second Empire, the majority did not imply that colonial conquest itself was a Bonapartist or imperialist practice.[38] They simply used the government's botched efforts as an opportunity to criticize the governing political coalition.

In this chapter, I reflect on how this growing political consensus around colonial conquest affected French discourses about empire during the mid-1890s. I show that this consensus—which, as other scholars have demonstrated, emerged out of political conflicts in the Third Republic, the growing influence of increasingly sophisticated racialized and racist thought, competition with other European powers, and pressure from interest groups both in the colonies and in the metropole—helped, in the minds of republican commentators, to depoliticize colonial expansion and separate it from domestic issues. And, as a result, it was during the 1890s that a growing number of French writers and politicians began to use the terms *empire colonial* and *empire d'outre-mer*, or overseas empire, to describe France's overseas territories. This broke with most usage in the earlier years of the Third Republic; throughout the 1870s and even into the early 1880s, most colonial advocates had avoided using the term "empire" to refer to France's overseas territories—partly because it had been so discredited by Napoleon III, who had used "empire" to refer both to his domestic political system and to France's relationship with overseas territories. Colonial advocates had devoted considerable attention to detaching colonial expansion from Bonapartist empire, and they had therefore avoided using anything that might sound like Bonapartist vocabulary to describe their colonial projects.

The chapter's analysis focuses on how prominent colonial advocates imagined this new term—colonial empire—across a variety of political pamphlets, academic writing, and more popular publications. To some extent, I argue, these texts' embrace of colonial empire reflects the degree to which the memory of Bonapartism had faded by the end of the nineteenth century. But, at the same time, most colonial advocates who used the term continued to try to control its political implications by either demonstrating that it aligned with republican ideals or by arguing that it transcended domestic politics—the same techniques that republican advocates of colonial expansion had been using since the 1870s. In fact, the visions of colonial empire that these texts propounded had their roots in early Third Republic ideas about colonialism, which were themselves constructed in opposition to republicans' beliefs about what Bonapartism represented. Some colonial advocates also borrowed from or referenced actual Bonapartist imperial practices—reflecting the fact that even as "empire" became a safer conceptual category for republicans to openly embrace, republican colonial ideas continued to be inflected by conflicting domestic political traditions.

A New Colonial Synthesis? Political Crisis and Imperial Conquest

The turn to the term "empire colonial" in the 1890s to describe France's conquered territories stemmed partly from international influence. British colonial theorists had for some time used "colonial empire" to refer to Britain's overseas conquests. During the 1880s and 1890s French advocates of politique coloniale saw Britain as a competitor and as a model.[39] Colonial advocates who used the term were thus adapting it from a different national context. Given the complex history of empire in France, however, the term's embrace nevertheless marks an important shift.

This growing use of "empire coloniale" to describe France's colonies was especially remarkable in light of the controversy that had surrounded politique coloniale in 1885, when the Chamber of Deputies brought down Jules Ferry's government over his policies in Tonkin.[40] The crisis over Tonkin illuminated the conflicts in moderate republicans' embrace of politique coloniale and revealed that many on the left and the right continued to associate colonial conquest with Bonapartism and other imperial structures, even if they did not reject colonialism itself. But, in the years that followed, political advocacy for colonial conquest spread across most political parties and cultural platforms.

Multiple factors contributed to the metropolitan political consensus that arose around colonial conquest in the late nineteenth century. As other scholars have shown, the political crises of the 1880s and the 1890s simultaneously altered the Third Republic's political configuration and moved colonial expansion away from the center of political controversy. As a result, for most of the decade, a governing coalition that saw colonial conquest as a tool that could unite a divided nation and increase France's international prestige ruled the country. This vision of colonialism's advantages was hardly new—Napoleon III had described it in much the same terms. But, in the 1890s, these ideas did not encounter effective opposition.

The growing enthusiasm for colonialism during the 1890s stemmed partly from the Boulanger Affair and its aftermath. Georges Boulanger, a general and minister of war, had challenged the elitist, moderate republic in the late 1880s by promoting populist political engagement, criticizing the Third Republic's political institutions, and advocating for revanche against Germany.[41] These tactics drew on Bonapartism's political legacy and attracted support from the Left and the Orleanist and Bonapartist Right.[42] When Boulanger was elected deputy of Paris in January 1889, the moderate republican leadership and press expected a Bonapartist-style coup d'état.[43] Instead,

Boulanger hesitated and ultimately fled the country, and *Boulangisme* died out over the next two years—well before Boulanger committed suicide in 1891.[44]

Boulangisme's collapse had multiple political effects. It strengthened the centrist republican supporters of colonial expansion while weakening radical, Bonapartist, and monarchist critics. Some monarchists and the majority of Catholics—reacting both against the demagogic character of Boulangisme and in accordance with an order from the Vatican—rallied to the republic and its colonial policies.[45] The Legitimist and Orleanist parties fractured and realigned, and their successors were mostly willing to work within the republic's legal and political framework.[46] The Bonapartists, too, were increasingly marginal; the death of Napoleon IV in 1879 had already weakened Bonapartism as a political movement. His uncle and heir had then alienated most of the party by associating himself with the republicans. The rise—and fall—of Boulanger thus only consolidated the growing sense that the Bonapartists were increasingly irrelevant.[47] As a result, the Third Republic emerged with a strong political center with renewed concerns about popular violence and revolution and a commitment to defending the political order and to extending France's reach overseas.[48]

The legacies of Boulangisme also affected the discourse surrounding overseas conquest. First, the fear of revolution led moderate leaders on both the right and the left to view colonial expansion as a way to unite a populace prone to political division and disorder.[49] Much like Napoleon III in the 1860s, they saw colonial expansion as an attractive strategy to redirect popular bellicose sentiment and strengthen France's military reputation while avoiding the dangerous European war that revanchism threatened. And at the same time, the problematic specter of Napoleonic empire, which opponents of colonial expansion had invoked to criticize the republic's activities overseas for much of the 1870s and 1880s, faded along with Bonapartism itself. Republicans' concerns about mass politics and the weakness of their former political opponents thus worked together to strengthen the appeal of colonial expansion and unsettle the ability of its opponents to criticize it.

The Dreyfus Affair threatened this confluence of moderate republicans and conservatives that had marked much of the 1890s in the second half of the decade, creating a new rift in the French political order and again redrawing the lines between Left and Right.[50] For several years, anti-Dreyfusard nationalists used the affair to inflame popular sentiment against the Third Republic and its institutions. For most of 1898, Dreyfus's defenders were on the defensive; some of them lost their seats to rising nationalist and anti-Semitic groups in the Chamber of Deputies.[51] Conservative republicans split on the issue, and a number joined the nationalists and the remaining monarchists in opposition to the republic.[52] At the same time, however, the anti-Dreyfusards struggled to unite into a coherent political coalition.[53] Moreover, as they turned to violence and threatened revolution, they pushed their opponents to make common cause against them.[54] Socialists, radicals, and leftist republicans thus united to form the government of republican defense, or the Bloc des gauches. In the wake of the affair, this new coalition consolidated political control over the Chamber of Deputies, while the conservatives and nationalists found themselves politically marginalized.[55] The Dreyfus Affair thus reordered the political alliances that had characterized the early 1890s while raising moderates' fears about the threat posed by the right to the republic's stability.[56]

The Dreyfus Affair had contradictory consequences for France's colonies. Its effects were perhaps most dramatic in Algeria, where anti-Semitic groups came to wield a large degree of influence over local politics, which they used to disenfranchise Algerian Jewish voters en masse. These groups also led a campaign of targeted violence against Algeria's Jewish population that exceeded the level of violence in metropolitan France.[57] Anti-Semitic candidates defeated their opponents nearly across the board in the Algerian elections of 1898; enthusiasm for anti-Semitism was so extensive that settlers elected Édouard Drumont, one of the leaders of the anti-Dreyfusard movement in France, to represent them in the Chamber of Deputies.[58] Algerian settlers thus helped give the French anti-Semitic movement a wider political stage in the metropole.[59] But even as settlers cultivated close connections to anti-Semitic groups in France, many also demanded greater political and financial autonomy in the name of the new "Latin" race that they argued was taking shape in the European settler community in Algeria. These demands—along with the vision of Algeria as a territory that belonged to a "Latin" people of European immigrants from France, Italy, Spain, and Malta—had their antecedents in the early 1870s, as we have seen. This language also echoed Napoleon III's rhetoric of latinité, although Napoleon III had used that rhetoric to justify intervening in Mexico, whereas the settlers used it to define a European Algerian identity that was connected to but distinct from France and differentiated from Algeria's Jewish and Muslim populations.[60]

The popularity of this anti-Semitic and autonomist settler movement had consequences for the structure of French rule in Algeria; it put an end to the metropolitan government's attempt, starting in 1891, to pass reforms that would have loosened the economic and political hold of the settlers over Algeria, protected indigenous property, and invested Algeria's indigenous populations with at least some additional local political power.[61] The metropolitan government, faced with the threat of unrest in both France and Algeria, set aside these reforms and instead granted European settlers even greater influence over the colony's finances and administration.[62] The aftermath of the affair thus further consolidated the hegemonic position of European settlers in Algeria, even as it also contributed to some concern in the metropole about the settlers' violence and their loyalty to France.[63]

If the affair thus both cemented and raised questions about the settler colonial regime that was taking shape in Algeria, it also echoed in other parts of the empire, sparking debates about overseas territories' administrative structure, especially over the role played by Catholic missionaries and army officers. But these debates were limited in scope; the Bloc des gauches, which came to power in the wake of the Dreyfus Affair, curbed the anticlericalism that was a key part of the group's domestic political platform in overseas colonies.[64] Arguments over the army's position in the republic also do not seem to have threatened the republic's commitment to expanding its colonial influence and securing its hold over already conquered territories.[65] These dynamics have led some scholars to argue that the affair—much like the other scandals of the 1890s—served to direct political attention away from France's policies in its overseas territories. Most of France's colonies remained outside of the center of controversy, and it seemed as though politique coloniale no longer served as one of the key conceptual categories through which politicians articulated their conflicting visions of the future of the nation and republic.[66] Indeed, by the time the Fashoda Incident broke out in 1898 in the middle of the Dreyfus Affair, colonial conquest appeared to be the only subject on which the warring republican and nationalist factions could agree.[67] Even the post-Dreyfus transfer of political power to the Bloc des gauches did not affect the government's attitude toward colonial expansion.

A reaction against political division at home thus partly drove this turn toward colonial conquest among moderate and conservative politicians and intellectuals in the wake of Boulangisme and the anti-Dreyfusard movement. But during the 1890s, advocates of colonial expansion also drew on some of the ideas that Boulangists and anti-Dreyfusards had popularized, including discourses of racial science, degeneration, and nationalism.[68] As we have seen, racial thinking had long played an important and contradictory role in French colonial thinking.[69] Napoleon III had drawn on a Saint-Simonian vision of racial progress to defend his plan to restructure France's relationship with Mexico and Algeria, while colonists in Algeria especially had used an alternative system of racial classification to mobilize against that plan. In the late 1870s, explorers such as Paul Soleillet had used liberal ideas about enlightened white masculinity to justify "peaceful" expansion in Africa; Jules Ferry, on the other hand, had invoked an explicit vision of racial hierarchy to legitimize the conquest of Tonkin that drew on neo-Lamarckian ideas promulgated by anthropologists and other racial theorists. Over the late 1880s and 1890s, explanations of racial difference rooted in some combination of biology and culture became even more prominent in metropolitan France.[70] These explanations of racial difference were not necessarily Darwinian—Lamarckian notions of material progress remained influential—but they applied principles borrowed from evolutionary biology to explain society and politics.[71]

As historian Emmanuelle Saada and others have shown, the growing influence of racial science in the metropole did not directly affect administrative or legal practices in the colonies; French administrators do not seem to have been particularly conversant with anthropological racial theories, and the earliest references to racial criteria in French colonial law date from the 1920s.[72] But these discourses did affect metropolitan French ideas about the political implications of colonial expansion in two ways. On one hand, an ever-larger number of politicians used the language of Darwinian competition to justify France's overseas colonial expansion. They insisted that all nations were competing with one another for influence and that the most powerful of these nations would come out on top.[73] Unless France extended its borders and expanded its population, it would find itself unable to keep up with its British and German rivals. In its substance, this argument was not new—as we have seen, journalist Lucien-Anatole Prévost-Paradol had articulated a version of it in the late 1860s. But it became both more widespread and tied into biologized ideas about racial degeneration in the 1880s and 1890s.[74]

On the other hand, a growing number of thinkers also relied on these increasingly prominent "scientific" discourses about racial inequality to differentiate between conquest within Europe and overseas colonial conquest. By arguing that the peoples living in Africa were both biologically and culturally inferior to Europeans, republicans could argue in favor of democratic political practices in Europe and nondemocratic domination of non-Europeans overseas. Ferry had met with controversy when he tried to invoke this vision of racial inequality in the mid-1880s. Most republican colonial advocates—such as Soleillet—had instead embraced culturally encoded language to defend racist hierarchies while condemning "the prejudice of color" as unrepublican and un-French. By the 1890s, however, Ferry's ideas had moved into mainstream republican thought.

There were several factors that contributed to the growing visibility of racial science in metropolitan France during the 1890s. It partly stemmed from the efforts of anthropologists themselves, who had argued that "racial evolutionism and applied anthropology" could be placed "in the service of the state" and forged close ties with the republican political establishment.[75] But this visibility also partially reflected the fact that the Dreyfus Affair helped consolidate a split in French racial thinking between the republican Left and the nationalist Right. Both sides shared "a depreciating view of non-Western civilizations and a belief in the power of heredity and the unequal perfectibility of human races."[76] But they disagreed on the role played by race and evolution within Europe itself. Many anthropologists had long implied that race and evolution functioned differently in European and non-European spaces, maintaining, for example, that improvements in milieu or environment would have a greater effect on "civilized" races than on their "uncivilized" counterparts, which meant that "civilized" Europeans would be able to "advance" across the Lamarckian evolutionary spectrum in a way that "uncivilized" non-Europeans could not.[77] That said, French anthropological institutions also provided a platform—albeit a limited one—for Georges Vacher de Lapouge, an "anthroposociologist," as he called himself, to popularize his reinterpretations of mid-nineteenth-century racial theorist Arthur Gobineau's ideas about racial degeneration. Lapouge synthesized these ideas with some elements of Darwinian evolutionism, maintaining that racial hierarchy and racial conflict could explain European relationships with non-Europeans, social hierarchies within European countries, and conflicts between European states. His writing had a limited audience in France, but it directly inspired nationalist and anti-Semitic leaders.[78]

During the Dreyfus Affair, most anthropologists rejected Lapouge's understanding of race's operations within Europe and the anti-Semitism of the anti-Dreyfusards. But their rejection of anti-Semitism and Lapouge's ideas about racial degeneration did not lead them to question their belief that a racial hierarchy structured the relationship between European and non-European peoples.[79] And by the end of the Dreyfus Affair, the use of "race" to explain France's internal social structure or position within Europe had become, for the most part, the right-wing nationalist position. The use of racial science to describe relationships with peoples outside of Europe—which at least some republicans in the 1880s had still associated with the ancien régime and the practice of slavery, even if they embraced racist beliefs about human hierarchy—had, on the other hand, become more politically acceptable within the leftist republican camp.[80]

As other scholars have shown, however, the idea that racial hierarchies were at least partially biologically encoded and potentially unmutable nevertheless continued to sit uneasily with republican justifications for colonial expansion. Republicans claimed that they had a moral right to colonize overseas because they would bring "civilization" to the peoples who lived there. But if the peoples who lived there were biologically inferior, as republicans increasingly claimed, how could a new "civilization" or "culture" improve their status? This tension had marked Ferry's attempts to justify colonial conquest in the 1880s, and it would continue to mark republican thought about colonial conquest.[81] Even though applying the language of racial science to republican colonial conquest created potential contradictions (as Todd Shepard has suggested, these contradictions were perhaps a reason that racial categories were not encoded in French law before Vichy), it helped justify a vision of global racial inequality that secured the popularity of politique coloniale and supported new attempts to outline a comprehensive vision of a republican colonial empire.[82]

The political crises that marked the late 1880s and the 1890s thus helped contribute, in different ways, to the emergence of a more prominent interest in colonial expansion among a wider section of French society. The rise of racial science and continued political conflict also offered rationales for defending that expansion. This interest was further consolidated by perceived competition in overseas territories on the part of other European powers—especially Britain—and by the emergence of new groups and societies committed to promoting France's colonies. The "colonial lobby," as this loose alliance of groups came to be known, was far from unified. Its members lacked a clear ideology and a united set of goals. But they formed a group of politicians, businessmen, settlers, missionaries, writers, and intellectuals who came together to popularize France's colonies and secure their importance.[83]

The role of the colonial lobby in France's overseas empire has been a subject of historiographical debate. Some scholars have contended that the colonial lobby was largely responsible for imposing France's empire on an uninterested public.[84] Others have claimed this argument overstates the colonial lobby's role in promoting support for French colonization, especially in the late nineteenth century. They have argued that enthusiasm for colonialism spread beyond a narrow spectrum of interested parties, thereby contesting the argument that colonialism was imposed from the top down.[85] Still others have noted that referring to the different groups who supported colonization as one "lobby" can obscure the divisions between their goals.[86]

Lobbying groups certainly played an important role in driving many of France's colonial conquests during the 1880s and 1890s.[87] Many of these groups also tried to increase awareness of and enthusiasm for France's overseas territories at the end of the nineteenth century. While they sometimes worked at cross-purposes with one another, advocates for colonial expansion nevertheless contributed to colonialism's growing popularity in the 1890s—even if they did not agree on how to understand colonialism or its relationship to the nation and the republic.[88] These groups did not "impose" colonialism on an unwilling population, but they began to popularize a conversation about overseas territories and their connection to the French republic that would continue across a wider span of media and a larger public during the twentieth century.

During the 1890s in particular, colonial advocates and lobbying groups produced a rush of new publications, all seeking to define what many increasingly described as France's colonial or overseas empire and explain that empire's relationship to republican values and the French nation for ever wider audiences. These attempts to popularize the colonies have received an enormous amount of historiographical attention. Multiple scholars have looked at how colonial advocates in France mobilized scholarship, popular publications, material culture, expositions, and spectacle to "sell" the colonies to the French people and to reify the ideas about racial and civilizational hierarchy on which colonial systems were structured.[89] As they have shown, these representations were able to circulate across France, thanks partly to the continued growth of the popular and political press in the wake of the 1881 law. The conversation about colonial empire nevertheless remained a fractured one, dominated for the most part by French elites who had widely varying levels of familiarity with the colonies themselves. Indeed, it was still relatively difficult for those in the metropole without direct connections to the colonial administration or the military to gather good information about what was happening in many parts of the empire, especially in places where French authority was new and indigenous communities had fewer connections with the metropole.[90] These representations of the French Empire were thus highly curated, and they do not tell us much about how the empire functioned. Instead, they reveal how French politicians and intellectuals imagined "empire" and its implications for French politics and the French nation.

The Emergence and Development of "Colonial Empire"

The extensive scholarship on the French embrace of colonial conquest in the late nineteenth century has focused on the question of how republican colonial advocates sought to reconcile republican or liberal commitments to human rights and democratic politics with colonial practices of violence, subjugation, and domination.[91] But it has devoted less attention to explaining how republicans' attempts to promote colonial conquest intersected with older ideas about empire and colonization, which had often initially been promulgated by their political adversaries. Texts published by several prominent colonial advocates at the end of the nineteenth century, including Arthur Girault, Paul Leroy-Beaulieu, Jean Marie Antoine de Lanessan, and Joseph Chailley-Bert, make it clear that "empire" abroad no longer raised the specter of "empire" or autocracy at home in the 1890s as threateningly as it had even in the 1880s. All four authors used the term "empire colonial" to describe France's relationship with its overseas territories, reflecting the new consensus around the benefits of colonial conquest. But even if these texts employed different terminology to describe overseas territories and projected greater confidence about colonialism's future, their arguments echoed those of earlier colonial advocates. These visions of colonial empire continued to reflect a conflicted relationship with Bonapartist legacies, and these authors, like their earlier counterparts, still sought to control empire's domestic political implications by describing it as either a specifically republican or more broadly national project. Empire's complex political history in France thus continued to shape these authors' ideas.

Arthur Girault, a moderate republican and professor of law, became one of the most influential voices in this discussion about colonial empire and its relationship to republicanism and nation, reflecting the importance of legal thinking in late nineteenth-century colonial theory.[92] In 1895 he published *Les principes de la colonisation et de législation coloniale*, which came to operate as the theoretical foundation for French colonial legislation and administration.[93] The book—published in five subsequent editions over the next fifty years—sought to defend colonial empire on legal grounds.[94] The book's introduction described colonization, laid out a system for classifying colonies, and endorsed the value of colonialism in ideological, economic, and political terms. At the same time, it also proposed a foundation for colonial legislation. This colonial legislation, Girault explained, would structure France's colonial empire by binding colonies to the nation in a manner consistent with republican political principles.[95] In order to articulate this vision, Girault drew on a complex mixture of social Darwinist thought, a familial vision of society, and republican ideals.[96]

Girault's introduction began by defining the practice of colonization. Like many other colonial theorists, he contended that colonization was an act only undertaken by "civilized" peoples who moved to a territory "occupied by a savage . . . or half-savage population." These "civilized" peoples would then create new infrastructure, "improve" the territory they settled in, and "civilize" the indigenous peoples they encountered. He insisted, "It is this civilizing action, this double *culture* of the land and its inhabitants that constitutes . . . the work of colonization."[97] Colonization thus did not necessarily have to involve a large settler population; instead, it referred to the spread of "civilization" to lands that had previously remained "barbarous or savage." Any type of colony could carry "civilizing consequences."[98]

Girault appealed to multiple logics to justify colonial expansion. First, he argued that "superior men" had a "natural right" to procure as many goods and as much space for themselves as they could. He acknowledged that this expansion often had an initially devastating effect on indigenous peoples. But he insisted that subsequent generations benefited from European rule. Moreover, he contended, colonization would also directly benefit France by preventing internal conflicts, improving the "moral character" of the country's citizens, and increasing France's global influence. It would thus allow France to compete against its European rivals. Finally, he argued, colonization spread commerce and industrialization across the world while preventing war between different European powers. It thus contributed to "human progress."[99] Girault therefore partly drew on the social Darwinist language of survival of the fittest in order to provide a "scientific" defense of colonization; he argued that France had a right to the territory of "weaker peoples" and implied that France itself would be "weakened" if it did not exercise that right.[100] At the same time, he made use of the language of the civilizing mission to describe colonization as a moral project that adhered to republican principles. These two lines of reasoning were not consistent with one another, but they worked together to detach colonization from any associations it might have with political tyranny or Bonapartist imperialism by depicting the practice first as "scientific" or apolitical and secondarily as republican.

Girault's discussion of colonial legislation worked to further bolster this vision of a specifically republican colonization and a republican colonial empire. He contended that countries could invoke three colonial principles or models to structure the legal relationship between colony and metropole. These principles would not necessarily translate directly into legislation, and they would not be applied the same way in each colony.[101] Instead, each would provide an ideological framework that would accommodate individual differences.

Girault argued that the first of these principles—subjugation—had been popular in the seventeenth and eighteenth centuries. This model understood colonies as a means to enrich the metropole; European nations exploited the territories that they conquered to recuperate the greatest amount of wealth possible.[102] During the Revolution, however, he claimed, many people had come to see this model as tyrannical. Revolutionaries had insisted that all races were equal and that "birth into a civilized race" did not confer superiority or legal rights over those born into "less civilized" ones.[103] Revolutionaries' condemnation of the exploitative practices that characterized "subjection," he implied, spread across Europe. As a result, he claimed—without evidence—that almost no contemporary European countries used subjugation to structure the relationship between metropole and colony.

The second principle, according to Girault, was "autonomy." Unlike "subjugation," which he implied was morally and politically dubious, Girault described autonomy as a "virile" and "hardy" colonial model. Colonizing nations that embraced the principle of autonomy, he argued, intended to enable colonies to become independent. The government would "guide the first steps" of the new colony but then would progressively "abandon" their affairs to them. Ultimately, the diplomatic tie would "rupture," and the colony would become a new state. This model was "not entirely foreign" to France, Girault maintained, but it found its full expression in Britain.[104] Girault expressed some admiration for Britain's embrace of autonomy, but he also used the negative language of "abandonment" to describe it. Moreover, he contended, such a policy could not be instituted in France.

Instead, Girault insisted, France should embrace the third and final principle of "assimilation" and use it to structure its colonial empire. This principle—which he argued belonged to the "Latin races"—sought to slowly transform France's colonial possessions through economic development and "civilizing" processes so that they could become an extension of the French nation overseas. "Assimilation," Girault warned his readers, did not mean that all parts of the empire would be treated identically. Nor did it indicate that France's colonies would be immediately assimilated into the nation-state. It also did not enable the colonies' inhabitants to exercise any political rights. Instead, "assimilation" represented a goal that could only be achieved over time.[105] Notably, in subsequent editions, Girault described colonial assimilation as increasingly further in the future.[106]

As historian Samia El Mechat points out, Girault's presentation of his principles of colonization created a vision of French colonial empire that on a theoretical level fell in line with republican politics and values. By arguing both that the ancien régime had used the principle of "subjugation" to structure its relationship with its colonies and that revolutionary thinkers had objected to this model, Girault avoided engaging with the idea that empire itself could contradict republican political principles. The problem was not with conquest or overseas expansion but instead with the principle of subjugation—a principle he maintained that the Third Republic had replaced with the much fairer "assimilation."[107] Indeed, Girault situated assimilation as central to republican politics; he argued that its influence in colonial politics had always been tied to "the triumph of republican ideas." Over the nineteenth century, he maintained, France had embraced assimilation when the republicans were in power—only to abandon the principle once they fell out of power.[108] A colonial empire that used assimilation to structure its relationship with its colonies would thus by definition operate according to republican principles.

Girault's association of assimilation with republicanism was not unique; French settlers in Algeria and politicians in France had long connected assimilation to the French Revolution, even if administrative assimilation had also been central to Napoleon's regime in Europe and, at times, to the ancien régime as well.[109] But, as we have seen, the history of the republic's relationship to assimilation was more complicated than Giraud's breezy synthesis implied. Both settlers' demands for assimilation in Algeria and the republican policy that took shape there partly in response to those demands had long been predicated on the deliberate exclusion of most Algerians. French administrators in other parts of the empire, too, spoke the language of assimilation, but in both theory and practice they had commingled it with association.[110] Indeed, historian Osama Abi-Mershed has argued that the myth that the late nineteenth-century republican colonial empire consistently operated according to the principle of assimilation had its origins not in actual colonial policy but in the writings of colonial theorists such as Girault.[111] Girault's contention that subjugation had been only used by the ancien régime rested on even more dubious historical ground, as republican colonial rule had consistently rested on a distinction between those with access to rights and those without them.[112]

How would Girault's imagined republican colonial empire operate? Girault addressed this question by invoking a familial metaphor to describe the empire and its evolving relationship to the French nation. Throughout his introduction, he compared France's colonies to children who required parental guidance due to their "uncivilized state." At first, they would not be able to exercise political or civil rights because they could not yet exercise them responsibly. As France provided them with guidance and resources, they would slowly become more self-sufficient and "civilized," gaining additional freedoms. Once they neared adulthood—a moment that would occur once "Europeans are numerous enough or the indigenous peoples are sufficiently civilized"—France would grant them new rights and responsibilities.

Finally, once the colonies became fully adult, they would be invested with complete political rights. Notably, however, these rights did not include independence—instead, the colonies would merge into the French nation-state and become overseas provinces.[113] Their inhabitants would become citizens, invested with the same rights enjoyed by their metropolitan counterparts. In this vision, France's colonial empire was thus a family in which children would become equal partners on assuming adulthood. Once this happened, the "empire" itself would disappear, to be a replaced by an expansive French nation-state that had spread across the globe.

Girault's familial model for colonial empire enabled him to articulate a commitment to the principle of assimilation while justifying the republic's actual practice of denying colonized people political rights and representation. The French empire was "republican," he implied, because it promised to eventually incorporate colonized peoples into the nation. They would only live beneath French control until they reached "maturity" and could join the ranks of their "civilized brethren." France's empire was thus republican because it was destined to disappear; its authoritarian structures were temporary measures intended to allow colonies to eventually enjoy political rights and freedoms. In the meantime, imperial practices might contradict republican values—but if they led to assimilation, they were the legitimate expression of the republican state. Girault's vision of empire justified through indefinitely deferred rights had deep republican roots.[114] At the same time, his contention that this model of colonization belonged to "Latin" peoples echoed back to Napoleon III's vision of an allied set of "Latin" empires.

Girault's attempt to reclaim the term "empire" and align it with republican political principles by both differentiating it from its antecedents and promising its future disappearance built on claims made by colonial advocates such as Arthur Bordier and Aristide Couteaux, who had attempted to defend politique coloniale in the 1880s; these ideas also appeared in other contemporary works.[115] But some thinkers writing in the 1890s also envisioned empire as a more permanent part of the French state; still others did not necessarily seek to align it with republican political principles at all. In 1901 Paul Leroy-Beaulieu published a new edition of *De la colonisation chez les peuples modernes* that envisioned a French colonial empire in both more permanent and less explicitly republican terms. This text built on older editions of Leroy-Beaulieu's extensive account of the history of Europe's colonies by doubling the text devoted to describing French, British, German, Belgian, and Russian colonization and extending the theoretical part of the work.[116] At the same time, it also deployed the term "empire" to explain these countries' respective relationships to their overseas territories. The term had not been entirely absent from Leroy-Beaulieu's 1874 edition, but in 1901 it played an increasingly central role as a conceptual category. Comparing the 1901 edition to the 1874 edition thus illuminates how the thinking of one of the most influential early colonial advocates shifted over the late nineteenth century. In the intervening years, Leroy-Beaulieu had in fact become an even more prominent public figure, elected first to Michel Chevalier's seat in the Académie des sciences morales et politiques and subsequently his chair in the Collège de France.[117] He did not write for a popular audience, but he retained close ties to the political and intellectual elite; in the 1890s he was among the most visible of French economists.[118]

In the new preface, Leroy-Beaulieu began by describing France's newly conquered overseas territories in congratulatory terms. He noted that the French colonial movement had expanded over the past decade and that popular enthusiasm for the colonies had grown alongside it.[119] The colonies, he implied, had prevented France from falling into decadence. He argued, "At the moment when public opinion seemed resigned to the situation in metropolitan France created by the sad events of 1870–1871, we had before us . . . immense spaces . . . the embryo of a colonial empire."[120] This colonial empire, he suggested, had compensated for the territory lost during the Franco-Prussian War while securing the country's future. Without such an empire, France would be "sequestered" in a small part of the world; its economic and moral influence would become increasingly limited.[121] According to this logic, France's empire served as an auxiliary to the nation: it was critical to both national recovery and survival.

Leroy-Beaulieu did not define "colonial empire" in his work. And in many ways, his vision of the relationship between France and its colonies echoed his earlier arguments.[122] There were some important distinctions, however. In 1874 Leroy-Beaulieu had emphasized the importance of "settlement colonies," which he insisted would spread France's influence across "unpopulated territories" around the world. And even though he had suggested that France should consider extending its control from Algeria south toward Senegal, he had focused on encouraging the government to develop its existing colonies—especially Algeria.[123] By 1902, however, Leroy-Beaulieu had embraced colonial conquest, and he argued that France should focus on conquering "commercial" colonies and "colonies of exploitation"—not territory for settlement.[124] To some extent, this shift reflected the changes in France's colonial holdings over the previous three decades. Most of France's new territories did not attract settlers.[125] It also perhaps reflected Leroy-Beaulieu's frustration with the settler society that was taking shape in Algeria, which he saw as exploitative.[126] But this shift also affected the way that Leroy-Beaulieu described the shape of the empire as a whole. In 1874 Leroy-Beaulieu had claimed that colonies were destined to become independent; they were temporary additions to the nation-state that would develop into allied countries over time. France would not colonize to create a permanent political union but to spread influence throughout the world.[127] In 1902, on the other hand, he argued that many of France's new "commercial" colonies would never gain independence. Without settler populations, he argued, "advanced civilization" was unlikely to remain in these places once Europeans left. European supervision alone could keep the indigenous peoples from lapsing back into "barbarism." As a result, these territories would remain dependent on France. To rule them effectively, France would have to develop a political and administrative infrastructure that would connect them to the nation in a beneficial way.[128]

If Leroy-Beaulieu did not define "colonial empire," his 1902 edition articulated a new model for French colonial holdings that envisioned them as a permanent and institutionalized part of France. He used the term "empire" to capture that permanence and institutionalization. This model hinged on a modified understanding of the "civilizing mission" that had long driven much of France's colonial policy. Like Ferry and Girault, Leroy-Beaulieu insisted that "civilized" peoples had a "right" to rule over peoples whose "civilizations" were either "decrepit" or "ignorant and weak" and to spread French ideas and their culture across such territories.[129] But while Ferry and Girault had argued that the "civilizing presence" of France would "improve" the peoples that they conquered, Leroy-Beaulieu promoted a vision of unchanging human inequality that could only be remedied by permanent political and cultural domination. Leroy-Beaulieu thus drew on the strain of Lamarckian racial thinking that held that non-Europeans would not be able to "progress" in the way that Europeans could to justify a system that would enable France to exert political and institutional control over distant places and peoples without integrating them into the French nation or enabling them to develop into independent nations.[130] Instead, they would remain under "tutelage."

Leroy-Beaulieu's vision of French empire had much in common with Girault's. This commonality is unsurprising, not least because Girault had drawn on older editions of Leroy-Beaulieu's work when drafting his book. Notably, both drew on the language of racial inequality and social Darwinism to create a vision of empire detached from domestic political questions. They positioned colonial conquest as part of an evolutionary competition to determine which peoples would be able to survive. Political and moral principles had little relevance in such a vision of human society. But while

Girault claimed to combine this evolutionary thinking with republican ideas by articulating a commitment to the principle of assimilation, Leroy-Beaulieu sought to detach empire and colonization from domestic political questions. Unlike Girault's, his vision of a French empire was thus a permanent one—although Girault, too, had suspended his proposed "assimilation" to the distant future.

In his 1897 *Principes de la colonisation*, Jean Marie Antoine de Lanessan, the former governor-general of Indochina, articulated an even more extreme version of this argument. A naval physician with long-standing ties to the Société d'anthropologie, Lanessan had spent more time in France's colonies than Girault or even Leroy-Beaulieu, who owned a farm and winery in Tunisia that he regularly visited; Lanessan had also served as a member of the Chamber of Deputies since 1881.[131] In the 1880s Lanessan had relied on economic arguments to justify colonial expansion. By the end of the nineteenth century, he had come to rest his vision of colonial empire on an even more hierarchical strain of Lamarckian thinking than the one invoked by Leroy-Beaulieu.[132] Lanessan insisted that racial inequality had driven human history; it explained which peoples had expanded over new territory and which had contracted or disappeared.[133] He claimed that conflicts between peoples over territory were inevitable and implied that modern colonization was the extension of this underlying natural law. As a result, he acknowledged, like Girault, that colonization was undeniably "savage"; moreover, "the degeneration or the destruction of one of the races in contact" inevitably followed. This destruction was not necessarily violent—it might take the form of "miscegenation" or "displacement"—but it was the inevitable consequence of contact. Colonization thus did not "improve" colonized peoples but reflected the conflict over resources and land that drove human history. At the same time, however, this destruction was not purposeless. While it might negatively affect colonized peoples, the spread of civilization across the world contributed to the "progress of humanity."[134]

In this vision of colonial expansion, Lanessan drew on the evolutionary notion of "survival of the fittest" to argue that racial conflict was central to human history. Colonization thus did not require moral or political justification; it simply reflected human nature. At the same time, however, he also used a positivist notion of "progress" that implied that colonization would contribute to a broader project of civilization.[135] Lanessan thus did not abandon the idea of the "civilizing mission" but reoriented it. Instead of spreading civilization to different *peoples* around the world, he implied, colonization spread civilization to different *territories*. Moreover, instead of benefiting the specific groups of people that fell beneath French control, it benefited humanity as a whole. This understanding of the civilizing mission was also implicit in Leroy-Beaulieu's work, and it was not new; it had appeared in the press coverage of the trans-Saharan railroad at the beginning of the 1880s. But, by the 1890s, it echoed more widely across colonial theorists' works.[136]

Girault, Leroy-Beaulieu, and Lanessan thus articulated overlapping but distinct visions for France's empire, its future, and its relationship to the French nation. However, all of them developed these visions indirectly: they did not actively define empire and its significance. Economist Joseph Chailley-Bert, a member of the Chamber of Deputies, an instructor of comparative colonization at the Institut d'études politiques de Paris, and the prominent secretary of the Union coloniale, a commercially oriented pro-colonial pressure group, and the editor of its newspaper, sought to define the term more directly.[137] In 1901 he published an article that distinguished between colonial empire, politique coloniale, and *mise en valeur* (development).[138] Many people, he warned, failed to differentiate between these different terms, which had undermined France's ability to compete overseas. Politique coloniale, he contended, described the conquest of colonies, while mise en valeur denoted the process of development that would enable them to become profitable. He used colonial empire, on the other hand, to refer geographically to France's overseas holdings.

If Chailley-Bert used "empire" as a geographic term, he also employed it to articulate a particular vision of France's overseas territories and their relationship to the nation. In fact, he deployed the term partly to avoid using the word "colonies," which he felt was widely misused. Unlike Girault and Leroy-Beaulieu, who used "colony" to refer to all of France's overseas territories, Chailley-Bert argued that the term should only refer to territories dominated by settlers. Almost none of France's new conquests fit this description because indigenous peoples made up the majority of their respective populations. Indochina, Madagascar, and even Algeria were thus not colonies but French possessions. Referring to them erroneously as "colonies" had unfortunate consequences because it led the public and politicians to treat these territories identically to old settler colonies such as Réunion and the Antilles.[139] Instead of grouping France's overseas territories together as colonies, he thus united them under the term "empire," which he saw as less bound up in problematic practices.[140]

One of the main problems with treating French possessions as colonies, Chailley-Bert insisted, was that it led colonial administrators to ignore the indigenous populations of each colony. He contended that French policy needed to "recognize the differences in race, genius, aspirations, and needs between indigenous inhabitants and their European masters" and provide each group with a distinct set of institutions.[141] The Third Republic had not recognized this need. Its colonial policies continued to follow those developed under the ancien régime and during the Revolution, which had been aimed first at settlers and later at formerly enslaved peoples. These policies had sought to integrate these inhabitants into the metropole. He argued that in territories occupied by settlers and "Africans," whom he claimed lacked "any culture of their own," these methods were relatively effective. But he maintained that territories such as Algeria and Indochina were inhabited by "whites" and "yellows" who were "too intelligent and anchored in their civilizations" to be integrated into France.[142] For the most part, he argued, colonial administrators had either treated this problem with "indifference" or foolishly attempted to assimilate populations that could not be assimilated. Only under the Second Empire had the government sought to deal with it directly by establishing bureaux arabes that provided indigenous peoples with their own administration. Chailley-Bert noted that there were problems with the bureaux arabes but suggested that the republican government should follow this model to create a true "indigenous policy."[143]

Like Girault, Chailley-Bert thus connected the Third Republic's current colonial policies to the French Revolution. But while Girault used that connection to argue that republicans had created a new kind of polity that transcended empire's traditional associations with despotism and exploitation, Chailley-Bert positioned the connections between revolutionary and contemporary republican policy as problematic. For Chailley-Bert, "republican empire" had not solved the imperial problems of the ancien régime. Instead, revolutionary legacies had led republicans to embrace a model of empire that was inapplicable to most of France's overseas territories.

Chailley-Bert's critique of "assimilationist" policy was not unique. In the 1890s a number of colonial policymakers and administrators were beginning to criticize assimilationist ideas and to advocate (much like the Arabophiles during the Second Empire) for some form of "association" instead.[144] Chailley-Bert's nostalgia for some Second Empire institutions, such as the bureaux arabes, is less than surprising in this light. But Chailley-Bert's vision of a French Empire based on association and his belief that indigenous peoples, rather than white settlers, would be critical to France's overseas territories converged even more directly with Napoleon III's.[145] Chailley-Bert described an ideal French Empire as a differentiated space that would enable conquered peoples to live according to their respective "civilizations" while remaining subjugated in a field of French power, a vision that echoed some of the features of Napoleon III's multinational Mediterranean empire. His vague descriptions of these subjugated "civilizations" also echoed the contradictions, gaps, and racism that had led Napoleon III to describe Mexico as a "Latin nation" and Algeria as an "Arab" one. In other words, even as Chailley-Bert implied that the term "empire" was politically neutral, his vision of empire expressed certain Bonapartist qualities.[146]

Girault, Leroy-Beaulieu, Lanessan, and Chailley-Bert all played important roles in shaping French colonial theory during the late nineteenth and early twentieth centuries. During this period, all also began to use the term "empire" to describe France's relationship with its overseas territories. At the same time, their respective visions of this empire remained distinct, partly because their understandings of colonization, the "civilizing mission," and race diverged. Girault argued that non-Europeans were both "uncivilized" and "racially inferior." But he maintained that France would be able to institute reforms that would improve "uncivilized races" and integrate them into France itself. Leroy-Beaulieu and Lanessan, on the other hand, implied that "civilization" could not address racial inequality so easily; some peoples, they argued, were too biologically and culturally inferior to internalize its practices. The purpose of colonization was not to civilize "inferior peoples" but instead to spread "civilization" to new parts of the globe.[147] As we have seen, this disagreement over whether all peoples were equally capable of evolution was not isolated to these theorists; it marked neo-Lamarckian racial theory in nineteenth-century France.[148] Chailley-Bert's thinking operated somewhat differently. For Chailley-Bert, the problem was not that some peoples were too inferior to adopt "civilization." He argued that the most "uncivilized" people the French had conquered—which he described as enslaved peoples from Africa—had integrated into French society. The problem arose when France encountered "more sophisticated societies" because they would resist French ideas and practices. In his work, Chailley-Bert thus usually focused on what he called "civilizational" rather than "racial" differences, instead of invoking neo-Lamarckian evolutionary theory that mapped race and civilization on top of one another in the way that Girault, Leroy-Beaulieu, and Lanessan did. His work nevertheless remained grounded in racist thinking; he invoked long-standing European understandings of racial hierarchy that located sub-Saharan Africa at the bottom, Asia and North Africa in the middle, and Europe at the top to criticize French colonial policy, and he described his vaguely delineated "civilizations" in racialized terms. But his emphasis on the importance of cultural difference made him more skeptical than Girault, Leroy-Beaulieu, and Lanessan that France's conquered populations would recede before or merge into France's "superior culture." And in some ways, he had even less faith in colonization's ability to spread "French civilization" than Lanessan.

These different understandings of colonization, the civilizing mission, and race led each of these thinkers to articulate distinct visions for colonial empire, how it should operate, and how it should relate to the French nation. Girault defined colonial empire as an explicitly republican set of legal measures and institutions that bound colonies to the metropole and would increasingly fold that empire into the French nation. Leroy-Beaulieu and Lanessan, on the other hand, defined colonial empire as an apolitical and permanent institutional and administrative structure that would enable France to ensure the continual presence of "civilization" in the territories that it had conquered. Chailley-Bert also defined colonial empire as apolitical; for him, the term referred to all of France's overseas possessions without implying that they could all be treated as settler colonies. At the same time, however, Chailley-Bert also used the term to articulate a vision of an open political structure that would incorporate many peoples and places into it. If Chailley-Bert thus sought to distance empire from domestic politics, he—and even Girault to some degree—nevertheless used the term in ways that were reminiscent of Napoleon III. Chailley-Bert in particular also endorsed some specific Bonapartist policies. This echo demonstrates the degree to which fears about Bonapartism's political influence had faded by the end of the nineteenth century even as it highlights the way that Bonapartist ideas about empire continued to echo in republican colonial theory. Republicans no longer saw Bonapartists as a political threat, but their ideas about empire remained marked by Bonapartist influence.

Popularizing Colonial Empire

The growing organization of colonial advocacy groups ensured that these theoretical accounts of empire saw wider distribution than earlier colonial theory written in the 1870s and 1880s. As a result, these publications created a more influential and comprehensive—if still conflicted—set of discourses about France's colonies and their relationship to the republic and the nation. But they still addressed a narrow audience of specialists, scholars, and politicians. During the 1890s a growing body of popular literature on colonialism also emerged that worked—albeit less directly—to defend "colonial empire" in wider public circles. Like their political and theoretical counterparts, these works did not define colonial empire in the same way. But they popularized the term and highlighted its benefits for the nation.

These popular representations of colonial empire took different forms, including novels, histories aimed at schoolchildren, colonial exhibitions, encyclopedias, and atlases.[149] In 1896, for example, historian Maurice Wahl published "an illustrated history" of France's colonial empire for schools that chronicled its establishment, described the empire's expansiveness, and highlighted its benefits. France had established this empire, he acknowledged, randomly and through force. However, he insisted, the government had had no time for reflection on strategy: all European powers were seeking to establish colonial empires in the contemporary world.[150] France's task was to give shape to this conquered territory by educating administrators, creating colonial institutions, encouraging emigration, and constituting a colonial army. Such measures, he claimed, would enable France to create a colonial empire that would enrich and strengthen the nation.[151] Wahl did not explain what shape this empire would take but described it as a permanent annex to the state that would enable France to spread its ideas and values across the world. Wahl's vision of colonial empire thus reflected the views of influential colonial theorists such as Leroy-Beaulieu and Lanessan who treated empire as an expression of national interests that transcended questions of specific political values and ideologies.

Les colonies françaises: Petite encyclopédie coloniale, edited by Maxime Petit, which was published in multiple editions during the early twentieth century, similarly aimed to popularize the colonial empire by acquainting readers with the "value" of France's colonial possessions. In the introduction, economist François Bernard argued that colonial empire was a necessary political structure that contained the process of colonization, which he described as a "natural" human impulse that had defined human history. However, it was also oppressive and violent. States thus needed to oversee colonization to "regulate the relationship" between colonists and indigenous peoples.[152] By asserting sovereign authority over colonized territories and integrating them into an overarching imperial structure, France was thus protecting indigenous communities while spreading its civilizing influence around the globe. After all, Bernard warned, if France did not conquer territories, Britain would do so instead—and Britain was less adept at "integrating and civilizing" its colonial subjects than France.[153] Ultimately, each of France's colonies would gain an increasing degree of administrative autonomy—even as the peoples who lived there integrated progressively into French society.[154]

Like other contemporary French colonial theorists, the contributors to *Les colonies françaises* thus invoked the language of social Darwinist competition to describe colonization as a process that defined human nature. At the same time, they posited the state's involvement in that process—and the institution of empire itself—as a way of integrating morality, "civilizing" force, and liberal principles into encounters that otherwise would be destructive for indigenous peoples.[155] This vision of empire drew on circulating solidarist ideas that were popular among republican thinkers in the late nineteenth century, which described "civilization" as a moderating force that could temper "natural competition" between peoples.[156] By equating "civilization" with "empire," *Les colonies françaises* could thus contend that "empire" would organize colonized territories in ways that aligned with the republican discourse of universal rights and justice—even as it also strengthened the nation.

Wahl's and Petit's accounts of France's colonial empire certainly do not represent the scope of popular work published about colonial expansion at the turn of the century. But they show how debates over the relationship between colonialism, empire, republicanism, and the nation crept into texts aimed at nonspecialist audiences. At the same time, they also demonstrate how the terminology of "colonial empire" structured France's relationship with its colonies—even if writers and politicians often failed to agree on its meaning.

For much of the 1870s and 1880s, colonial expansion and colonial empire had remained a subject of political controversy: politicians, writers, and intellectuals disagreed over its meaning, benefits, and consequences for France, and many linked empire to the discredited regime of Napoleon III. Even in the 1890s, many of these debates remained unsettled. Writers, politicians, and intellectuals continued to argue about some of the same questions that their predecessors had argued about in the 1860s. Should the government assimilate colonies into the metropole? Should it subject them to the law of free trade? How should colonies be administered? Should the state leave indigenous political structures intact or replace them with direct administration? Should it promote settler colonization? How should France treat indigenous peoples? But the argument about colonial empire's benefits for France and its relationship to the legacy of Napoleon III seemed settled.[157] Most writers had come to agree that colonial empire was necessary to the French nation and to the republic itself.

By the end of the 1890s, France's writers and thinkers had thus begun to popularize the term "colonial empire" and highlight its importance to the French nation. But they had not necessarily defined it coherently. Indeed, they failed to agree on some basic points. They argued about whether the colonial empire would remain permanently annexed to France, eventually fold into the French nation, or break apart into new, independent nations. They also debated about whether the empire was in line with republican ideals or whether republican ideals were irrelevant to colonial politics. And they continued to disagree about the significance and legacy of earlier imperial models. Ironically, at the same time that thinkers articulated visions of colonial empire that escaped the charges of Bonapartism, despotism, incompetence, and decadence lobbied against it in the 1880s, some looked more self-consciously toward the Second Empire's imperial system to describe the structure of empire and its relationship to France. In other words, at the moment when most republican French politicians and intellectuals agreed that continental and colonial empire were unrelated, republican colonial theorists were continuing to find some value in the imperial policies of Napoleon III.

Conclusion

The Imperial Paradoxes of French Republicanism

In 1908 Ben Ali Fékar, an Algerian jurist who had completed his legal education in France, published an article advocating for better political representation for Algerian Muslims in *La revue du monde musulman*, a specialist publication aimed at a primarily French audience.[1] He began by laying out the history of Muslim representation in French Algeria before turning to describe the "current system," which, he noted, strictly limited Algerians' ability to express their needs to the administration even at the local level.[2] He noted that it was "rather curious to note that the current legislation, which should be more liberal, has shown itself to be far less favorable to the question of indigenous representation than the imperial regime."[3] In other words, the republican government had adhered less consistently to liberal principles than the Second Empire of Napoleon III that it had replaced. Fékar concluded by contending that "the liberalism traditional to French politics" demanded that the republic make "large concessions" to Algerian Muslims, including the extension of education and the right to vote.[4] Fékar thus mobilized both the specter of the Second Empire and republicans' ostensible commitment to liberal politics to defend his demands to transform the structure of the Algerian colonial administration.

Fékar was a member of the Young Algerians movement, a group of French-educated Algerian Muslims who, in the words of historian Michelle

Mann, were "less an organized political party than a small and eclectic, loosely organized network of mutual acquaintances."[5] Few Muslim Algerians had access to a French-style education, but those who had were drawn together, first in bilingual sports clubs established in the 1890s and then, after 1901, thanks to the passage of the law that allowed for the free creation of associations, in Franco-Muslim Cultural Circles.[6] The Young Algerians were deeply influenced by the Young Turk Revolution of 1908, which had—at least initially—sought to create a liberal, constitutional government that would revitalize the Ottoman Empire in the face of encroaching European imperial power. They were also even more directly inspired by the Young Tunisians movement.[7]

Most Young Algerians did not seek to dismantle the colonial regime in Algeria, at least in the early twentieth century. That said, members of the group took a wide range of positions on Algeria's future and its relationship to France, which make them difficult to generalize about.[8] Many Young Algerians consistently expressed their devotion to France, and it seems clear that at least some of them accepted the logic of the civilizing mission that they had learned in French schools; they described themselves as *évolués* and condemned the "backwardness" of Algerian society while praising French liberalism.[9] But even writers who took explicitly pro-French positions also condemned the exploitative, authoritarian, and exclusionary political structures under which Algerians lived, and they proposed a variety of reforms that they suggested the republic should follow if it actually wanted to "assimilate" Algeria and transform it into an extension of France overseas. And some of them—like Ben Ali Fékar—grounded those demands for political transformation in a particular vision of the relationship between republican politics and colonial policy that drew on a long-standing set of French debates about "empire," its history, and its relationship with domestic political ideologies.

As we have seen, throughout the second half of the nineteenth century, French understandings of empire remained contested and fraught. In the 1860s Napoleon III had promoted an understanding of empire that positioned the term simultaneously as a particular political system within France and as a way of organizing territory overseas. Even during the Second Empire, this vision of empire was unstable. Napoleon III himself described empire's operations in different terms in Mexico and Algeria. In Mexico, Napoleon III had envisioned empire as a shared set of domestic policies that could connect—or federate—nations belonging to the "Latin" race; in Algeria, he had imagined empire as a political structure that could incorporate multiple nations within it. Both of these visions proved unpopular in Mexico and in Algeria, and neither was ever really instituted.

Ironically, however, the controversies that engulfed Napoleon III's attempt to impose an empire on Mexico and his proposed imperial reforms in Algeria helped reinforce the idea that empire could be understood both as an overseas and domestic project. The angry settlers in Algeria who forged links with republicans in France to thwart Napoleon III's attempts to transform the territory, together with the political opposition that condemned Napoleon III's policies in Mexico, Algeria, and France, connected the empire's domestic and overseas policies and cast both in negative terms. Napoleon III's problematic imperial policies overseas, critics argued, echoed his problematic imperial policies in France.

The collapse of the Second Empire during the Franco-Prussian War further sharpened republicans' criticisms of empire, which they increasingly described as a corrupt, despotic, decadent, and illegitimate form of political organization that contradicted France's ideals of human rights and national identity. They posited empire in opposition to the new Third Republic, arguing that it alone could represent the nation and enable it to recover from defeat. This opposition distanced the Third Republic from both the Second Empire and the Franco-Prussian War. At the same time, however, this line of argumentation complicated the new republic's relationship with its overseas territories, partly because multiple writers and thinkers continued to associate "colonies" with "empire."

The ramifications of this solidifying vision of the differences between empire and republic were especially complex in Algeria because Napoleon III had treated the territory as the centerpiece for his vision of an empire that would rest on Bonapartist principles and bind multiple nations together under one imperial structure at home and abroad. On a discursive, if not on a practical or effective level, he thus transformed Algeria into a centerpiece example of Bonapartist imperial strategy. In the early years of the Third Republic, settlers were able to make use of metropolitan republicans' campaign to discredit Bonapartist empire to demand the reshaping of Algeria in a way that suited their own ambitions. They argued that a "republican" Algeria would not be a "colony" at all but an extension of France across the Mediterranean. At the same time, they pressed the metropolitan government to pass laws that marginalized Algeria's indigenous populations and made it easier for colonists to claim their land—partly by associating protections for indigenous communities with the government of Napoleon III. This vision of Algeria also had some advantages for republicans back in France. By accepting settlers' contention that they were the primary population in Algeria and by granting them additional political rights, republicans could claim to have transformed the colony—removing the Second Empire's despotic systems and replacing them with more democratic ones—much as they sought to transform the metropole. "Assimilating" Algeria into the metropole also obfuscated Algeria's relationship to empire by positioning the territory as a constitutive part of the national body. Republicans could thus distance the territory from Napoleon III's vision of a multinational Mediterranean empire.

Settlers' ability to defend this reading of empire and republicanism in Algeria was tied up in the fact that for much of the second half of the nineteenth century, it was difficult for most Muslim Algerians to participate in French debates over empire and Algeria's future—even if they spoke French. The public sphere that these debates emerged in was expanding in the late nineteenth century, but, as we have seen, it was not a neutral space where anyone could speak.[10] In the early Third Republic, settlers were particularly well positioned to promote their ideas about empire and republicanism thanks to their ties with metropolitan republican politicians. Muslim Algerian voices, on the other hand, were even more thoroughly marginalized during the Third Republic than they had been during the Second Empire. Indeed, French republicans and settlers invoked the minimal influence of a handful of Algerian elites over Bonapartist colonial policy as evidence of Napoleonic rule's militarism, decadence, and infatuation with aristocracies—all political problems these writers promised that the new republic would resolve in both France and Algeria. These patterns of exclusion were formalized in the 1881 laws on the indigénat and freedom of the press, which enabled settler speech while restricting Algerians'.[11] These laws—combined with the collapse of Algerian education systems under French rule—ensured that there were few newspapers and publishing houses where Algerian writers could publish their ideas in French, let alone in Arabic.[12]

Even if settlers proved able to largely exclude Muslim Algerians from debates about empire, Algeria, and its future, efforts to distinguish between "republican" and "Bonapartist" Algeria remained troubled. The ongoing arguments over the colony show that contradictory visions of empire in Algeria continued to persist well after the collapse of Napoleon III's regime. These attempts to reenvision Algeria as a part of France had another problem too: they did not provide a language for justifying overseas colonial expansion. Even during the 1870s, some settlers, colonial advocates, geographic societies, and explorers thus turned to a different set of strategies for envisioning France's relationship with its overseas territories. Several writers tried to develop theories of "colonization" to convince elites of the value and importance of overseas expansion. These theories detached "empire" from Bonapartism, although the models of colonization they invoked were often contradictory and at times reinscribed contemporary associations between colonial expansion and autocratic politics. At the same time, geographic societies and explorers such as Paul Soleillet sought to develop what they envisioned as a republican model for colonial expansion, which they described as a peaceful, masculine, and scientific endeavor that promoted trade and aligned with republican values. They defined "republican colonialism" in opposition to what they described as the militaristic, despotic, and effeminate characteristics of Napoleon III's imperialism, even if in practice republican colonialism was always far from peaceful and sometimes borrowed from Bonapartist traditions. Republican attempts to reimagine empire this way nevertheless met with limited success—partly because this vision of republican empire so little resembled actual colonial practice and perhaps also because so many of the expeditions funded by the state in the 1870s ended in disaster.

During the 1880s republican colonial advocates and politicians increasingly turned away from the rhetoric of a peaceful republican colonialism and began to endorse outright colonial conquest. This shift in rhetoric led to an argument about France's conquest of Vietnam that began in the Chamber of Deputies but spread into the public sphere. During this period, republican proponents of colonial expansion defended conquest by describing it as part of politique coloniale, a practice that they promised would strengthen France's economy, international influence, and national character. At the same time, opponents of expansion on both the left and the right remobilized the memory of Napoleon III and the Second Empire to criticize politique coloniale and associate it with French defeat and imperial despotism. The strength of this opposition to colonialism pushed supporters of politique coloniale to construct a more robust defense of the practice. On one hand, they differentiated between conquest in Europe and conquest in Asia and Africa by drawing on the language of racial or cultural inequality and appealing to the idea of the "civilizing mission." At the same time, at least some continued to argue that republican colonial expansion—even when it took the form of violent conquest—was distinct from its historical predecessors because it did not aim to exploit and destroy the peoples it conquered. Instead, it would spread French culture and values and introduce conquered peoples to the principles of liberty, equality, and fraternity. These ideas appeared not only in political pamphlets and theoretical texts but also increasingly in popular publications as well.

Due to the efforts of colonial propagandists and the changing political and intellectual climate, by the 1890s the conflicts surrounding colonial expansion and even "empire" seem to have largely dissipated. Indeed, republican politicians, colonial theorists, journalists, and writers began to use the term "colonial empire" to refer to France's overseas colonies. The growing popularity of the term partly reflected the degree to which the problematic memory of Napoleon III had faded. As a result, republicans were less concerned about possible associations between the republic's overseas empire and Napoleon III's Second Empire. But this usage also reflected the fact that racialized thinking had drawn clearer lines between conquest and empire in Europe and conquest and empire overseas. Even in the 1880s some republican thinkers had associated the German Empire's annexation of Alsace and Lorraine with the French Republic's conquest of Vietnam. But by the 1890s such comparisons seemed increasingly remote. Race theory seemed to have solved the conflicts over whether "colonial empire" was a positive national attribute or a political problem.

If a new consensus had developed around the benefits of "colonial empire" by the end of the nineteenth century, colonial theorists and politicians continued to fail to agree on what the term meant, the nature of its relationship to republican politics, and its connections to the French nation. Some writers described the colonial empire as a republican project, while others insisted that it was an apolitical national strategy that did not need to be reconciled with republican political principles. At the same time, they disagreed about whether the empire would fold into the French nation, remain permanently annexed to it, or eventually break off into independent nations. If "colonial empire" was mostly no longer seen as problematic, these continuing debates demonstrate that writers continued to disagree about how to reconcile the republic's theoretical commitment to democratic practices and national sovereignty with its commitment to dominating territory overseas.

Even at the end of the nineteenth century, moreover, when the memory of Napoleon III and continental empire seemed to have lost its power in arguments over empire, republican ideas about colonial empire remained marked by Bonapartism's imperial legacies, albeit in different ways. At least some republican colonial advocates continued to borrow from actual Bonapartist imperial practices to describe the vision of the empire that they wanted to build. But, at the same time, republicans' conflicted relationship with indigenous monarchies and protectorate colonial rule in Vietnam and Madagascar may have been haunted not just by monarchy's fraught history in France but also by the specter of Napoleon III's royaume arabe and his perceived close relationships with Algerian elites.[13] Colonial models that seemed too close to Bonapartist imperialism remained fraught. In fact, most of the competing visions that emerged in the 1890s had their roots in earlier republican attempts to differentiate their imperial projects from the vision of Bonapartism they had constructed in the years after the Second Empire's collapse by turning to particular readings of revolutionary thought. Republican understandings of empire thus borrowed from multiple domestic political traditions, but they also clearly emerged out of contestations with other political groups.

The slow evolution in republican understandings of empire and its relationship to republicanism and the nation in fact emerged in dialogue with a range of ideological and political movements, including romantic nationalism, Saint-Simonianism, liberalism, neo-Lamarckian racial theories, and social Darwinism. The memory of the Franco-Prussian War, the loss of Alsace and Lorraine, tensions within the republican political tradition, and the demands and actions of settlers and colonized peoples further shaped the conversation. The growing European-wide interest in colonial conquest and expansion also played a role in shaping French understandings of empire: it helped drive and legitimize the practice while further disconnecting it from domestic political debates.

This conversation about empire and its meanings also had its own consequences. First, the conversation had some limited, indirect effects on conquered peoples living under French rule—mostly because discourses of empire helped legitimize colonial conquest and economic exploitation. Moreover, because the debates about empire intersected with arguments about "association" and "assimilation," the conversation also had theoretical implications for colonized people's rights and identities. Indigenous groups occupied different places in Napoleon III's multinational empire, the early Third Republic's assimilated Algeria, and the later Third Republic's expansive colonial empire. These distinct visions of empire also promised colonized peoples very different futures. But if these alternative imperial models had important theoretical consequences, their policy effects remained quite limited because of the complicated and fraught relationship between colonial theory, colonial policy, and colonial practice. Large gaps remained between both the empire and the republic's rhetoric about the colonies and their actual operations.

The conversation about "empire" had more direct effects on the development of republican thinking over the late nineteenth century. On the most basic level, republican writers, thinkers, and politicians were able to mobilize particular understandings of "empire" to secure republicanism's political ascendancy. In the 1860s and 1870s they promoted a negative vision of empire to discredit Bonapartism and promote republicanism as a more legitimate political model. "Empire" thus served as the foil against which they defended republican principles and politics. At the same time, especially in the 1880s and 1890s, republicans' ability to articulate a new vision of "colonial empire," associate that vision with republican ideals, and enact that vision by conquering large swaths of overseas territory, helped them demonstrate the success and strength of republican policies in the court of French public opinion.

"Empire" did not simply help republicans promote republicanism in late nineteenth-century France, however. It also at times challenged the boundaries and content of republican ideology. This was partly because empire could be associated both with Bonapartism and with overseas conquest for much of the nineteenth century. As a result, especially in the first decades of the Third Republic, critics of colonial expansion could attack the republic's colonial expeditions by associating them with the Second Empire and contending that they contradicted republican principles. Some even claimed that advocates of colonial expansion were not republicans at all and instead represented a continuation of older autocratic traditions. In response to these accusations, republican supporters of colonial expansion had to demonstrate that colonial empire and republicanism were compatible. And even if the charge that colonial empire was "not republican" subsided, the political instability of "empire" as a conceptual category persisted. This was problematic because "republican ideology" itself was far from coherent in the late nineteenth century: republicans argued about the promises and dangers of democratic practices, the meaning and application of republican citizenship, and the republic's relationship with war and conquest.[14] Debates about empire and its relationship to France continued to illuminate and at times accentuate these tensions.

Finally, debates about "empire" also had important consequences for French understandings of the nation and national identity. Throughout his reign, Napoleon III had embraced and promoted "the politics of nationality" and argued that each "people" should have its own nation-state. He reconciled his commitment to the "politics of nationality" with his desire to build an expansive empire by describing empire as either an entity that would incorporate multiple nations within it or as a political system that could federate nations together. After the Franco-Prussian War, republicans identified Napoleon III's commitment to "the politics of nationality" as one of the causes of French defeat. Instead of treating France's overseas territories as semi-independent nations, they turned to a revolutionary republican universalizing vision of the French nation that envisioned it as an open political structure, which could incorporate territories and peoples located all over the world. From the beginning, however, this expansive vision of the French nation had its limitations: even as republicans described the nation as universal, they insisted that indigenous peoples had to adopt cultural markers of Frenchness in order to join it. As a result, even in Algeria most republicans never seriously considered incorporating indigenous peoples into the nation itself.

In light of these contradictions—which became increasingly obvious as the republic conquered a growing number of overseas territories—numerous writers, politicians, and theorists began describing France's colonies as separate from the French nation. Instead of joining the national body, these colonies would exist beneath a separate imperial structure that would help other races "grow up." This vision of the relationship between empire and nation had something in common with Napoleon III's. But while Napoleon III had envisioned France as a part of his empire—he positioned it as the central nation-state among others—most republicans envisioned the French nation as outside of the empire that they were constructing. They treated the empire above all as a political, economic, and cultural asset of the French nation; it was a sign of national strength, an opportunity for national commerce, and the symbol of France's international prestige. By the late nineteenth century, empire had thus become a critical component of French national identity while remaining outside the boundary of the nation itself.

This conversation about empire and its relationship to republicanism and national identity continued into the twentieth century, as the writing of the Young Algerians makes clear. They sought to challenge both the reading of the relationship between republicanism and empire defended by settler communities in Algeria and the structure of the debates about empire themselves, which had been designed to exclude them. So, like the settlers before them, who had reached out to republicans in the metropole to oppose Napoleon III's royaume arabe, the Young Algerians sought to build alliances across the Mediterranean with *indigénophile* politicians and intellectuals who were critical of the colonists' hegemony in Algeria.[15] These attempts at alliance building also reflected the fact that many Young Algerians thought it was unlikely that the local colonial administration—which they saw as beholden to entrenched settler interests—would even listen to their proposed reforms.[16] So, they published in French journals, wrote petitions to the metropolitan government, and even sent delegations to France to explain their ideas.[17] In 1912 in particular, after the government extended military recruitment to include Muslims, a Young Algerians delegation went to Paris and met with Théodore Steeg (the minister of the interior), Georges Clemenceau, and Raymond Poincaré (the prime minister), invoking the idea of the republican citizen-at-arms to demand that military service should be accompanied by citizenship rights.[18]

To some extent, given their intended audience, the Young Algerians' argumentative strategies are unsurprising. They positioned themselves as good republicans, devoted to France and its political ideas, and they focused their criticisms on both the settler community and the colonial administration, which they maintained did not live up to those principles. They thus sought to win over people in metropolitan France by directing their criticisms elsewhere. But, at the same time, their attacks on the colonial regime in Algeria also threw the relationship between republicanism and empire back into question. In the 1870s French republicans had sought to distance themselves from the Second Empire's regime in both Algeria and France—which they had described as despotic, decadent, and effeminate—by creating a republican regime that they defined in opposition to the Second Empire, even if in practice they borrowed from the empire's policies. But in 1908 Ben Ali Fékar directly questioned this idea. Far from eliminating the vestiges of the Second Empire's despotism, he maintained, republicans had created an imperial system that was even more autocratic than the one it had replaced. And on top of that, he argued, because the French had not sought to assimilate Algeria's Muslims, it had failed to assimilate Algeria, which remained bound to France through an imperial system.

Even Young Algerians thinkers who did not directly invoke the legacy of the Second Empire consistently pointed toward this disconnect between the republic's professed political principles and the structure of imperial rule in Algeria, questioning, for example, whether "the French nation, that has sacrificed so much to bring foreigners the ideas of liberty, justice, and civilization, could deny their most basic benefits to a people whom fate has placed beneath its tutelary wing?"[19] In a widely reproduced speech, Émir Khaled, the grandson of Abd el-Kader, suggested that the republican government in Algeria had in fact been particularly oppressive, noting that the French people should understand that "when a part of a nation is without voice and without the rights of representation beneath a republican constitution, it can be even more oppressed than when all groups must obey a single leader."[20] An empire under an emperor, he thus implied, would be less exploitative than the republic's current system. At the same time, he maintained, he could not believe that France, which "exported its ideas" to other countries, would "limit its liberalism to its European territory."[21] The authors of these accounts did not contend that it was impossible to square French imperial rule with republican principles, nor did they position colonial empire itself as the problem. Instead, they took the rhetoric of assimilation that republicans and settlers had long invoked in Algeria on its face, describing Algeria and France as part of the "same nation," while highlighting the distance between that rhetoric and the actual practice of French rule, which they described as "not republican." They also implied that if France did not extend its republican principles to the territory, the state would remain hypocritically in violation of its own endorsed positions. Young Algerians writers thus implicated metropolitan France in the structure of Algeria's future, even if they blamed settlers and the colonial administration for its present form.

The Young Algerians campaigns received relatively favorable coverage in the French press in the years leading up to World War I, perhaps reflecting the success of the Young Algerians' strategy of distinguishing between the colonial administration's practices in Algeria and the ideals of French republicanism.[22] But even though the Young Algerians delegation was received warmly by senior government officials in 1912, neither the national government nor the colonial administration followed through on any of the Young Algerians' proposed reforms. This failure reflected the distance between the position of the Young Algerians, who wanted the government to immediately extend rights to Muslim Algerians, and that of their Parisian allies, who believed that those rights should be deferred to some unspecified future point.[23] It may have also reflected the fact that even if the specter of Napoleonic imperialism could still be invoked to embarrass the republican regime in the early twentieth century, republicans had sufficiently discursively disaggregated continental and overseas empire, at least in their own minds, and they no longer worried that imperial despotism overseas would threaten republican rule at home.

That said, this embrace of "colonial empire" had clear limitations. If colonial advocates began to use the term "empire" in the 1890s, the French government only adopted it under the fascist Vichy regime (at the same moment that racial categories consistently entered French law), indicating that republican ambivalence about empire had not entirely disappeared, even in the early twentieth century.[24] Criticism of republican colonial practices did not disappear either. In the decades after World War I, a new wave of criticism—originating especially from groups in the colonies and the Communist Party—would highlight the contradictions between republican promises and imperial practices.[25] These voices remained relatively marginalized in the interwar years, but they would become much stronger after 1945, as peoples in France's colonies increasingly demanded access to full citizenship rights and attacked the premise of empire itself.[26] In response to this criticism, republicans would again seek to redefine empire and rearticulate its relationship to the French nation—partly by turning away from the term "empire" and toward the alternative constructions of "France Overseas," the "French Union," and the "French Community."[27] In doing so, they would again renegotiate the complex relationship between the republic, the nation, and overseas territory. But because they failed to establish a political system that would grant equal political and social rights to its diverse members, "empire" would once again become a problem for republicans instead of a source of political and national strength. Nineteenth-century colonial conquests would lead ultimately to the collapse of the republic's imperial imaginaries in the 1950s and 1960s.

Abbreviations

AMAE	Archive du ministère des affaires étrangères, La Courneuve
AN	Archives nationales de France, Pierrefitte-sur-Seine
ANOM	Archives nationales d'outre-mer, Aix-en-Provence
SG	Archives de la Société de géographie, Bibliothèque nationale de France, Paris
SHD	Service historique de la défense, Vincennes

Notes

Introduction

1. Frederick Brown, *Zola: A Life* (New York: Farrar Straus Giroux, 1995), 641.

2. Émile Zola, *La débâcle* (Paris: Culture Commune, 2014), 19.

3. Zola, *La débâcle*, 20.

4. G. Espé de Metz, *Vers l'empire*, (Paris: Librairie Ambert, 1913), 8, 22, 81, 195.

5. Sudhir Hazareesingh, "Napoleonic Memory in Nineteenth-Century France," *MLN* 120, no. 4 (September 2005): 757.

6. Sudhir Hazareesingh, *From Subject to Citizen: The Second Empire and the Emergence of Modern French Democracy* (Princeton, NJ: Princeton University Press, 1998), 27.

7. Venita Datta, "'L'appel au soldat': Visions of the Napoleonic Legend in Popular Culture of the Belle Epoque," *French Historical Studies* 28, no. 1 (2005): 2.

8. Karine Varley, *Under the Shadow of Defeat: The War of 1870–71 in French Memory* (New York: Palgrave Macmillan, 2008), 84.

9. Dominic Lieven, *The Russian Empire and Its Rivals* (New Haven, CT: Yale University Press, 2000), 288.

10. Aimé Césaire, *Discourse on Colonialism*, trans. Joan Pinkham (New York: Monthly Review Press, 2000), 36. W. E. B. Dubois made a similar argument in 1947. See Robert Bernasconi, "When the Real Crime Began: Hannah Arendt's *The Origins of Totalitarianism* and the Dignity of the Western Philosophical Tradition," in *Hannah Arendt and the Uses of History: Imperialism, Nation, Race, and Genocide*, ed. Richard H. King and Dan Stone (New York: Berghan Books, 2007), 55, and A. Dirk Moses, "Empire, Colony, Genocide: Keywords and the Philosophy of History," in *Empire, Colony, Genocide: Conquest, Occupation, and Subaltern Resistance in World History* (New York: Berghan Books, 2008), 9.

11. Hannah Arendt, *The Origins of Totalitarianism* (New York: Harcourt, 1968), 125.

12. Arendt, *Origins of Totalitarianism*, 224, 245.

13. Richard King and Dan Stone, "Introduction," in King and Stone, *Hannah Arendt and the Uses of History*, 6, 9, 13.

14. Andrew Bacevich, *The Imperial Tense: Prospects and Problems of American Empire* (Chicago: Ivan R. Dee, 2003); Craig Calhoun, Frederick Cooper, and Kevin Moore, eds., *Lessons of Empire: Imperial Histories and American Power* (New York: New Press, 2006).

15. Ilya Gerasimov, Sergey Glebov, Jan Kusber, Marina Mogilner, and Alexander Semyonov, "New Imperial History and the Challenges of Empire," in *Empire Speaks Out: Languages of Rationalization and Self-Description in the Russian Empire*, ed. Ilya Gerasimov, Jan Kusber, and Alexander Semyonov (Leidan: Brill, 2009), 4.

16. See Fred Myers, *The Empire of Things: Regimes of Value and Material Culture* (Santa Fe, NM: School of American Research Press, 2001); Lori Khatchadourian, *Imperial Matter: Ancient Persia and the Archaeology of Empires* (Berkeley: University of California Press, 2016); Frederick Cooper, *Citizenship, Inequality, and Difference* (Princeton, NJ: Princeton University Press, 2018); Julia Hell, *The Conquest of Ruins: The Third Reich and the Fall of Rome* (Chicago: University of Chicago Press, 2019).

17. Patrick Wolfe, "History and Imperialism: A Century of Theory, from Marx to Postcolonialism," *American Historical Review* 102, no. 2 (1997): 391, 393.

18. Jane Burbank and Frederick Cooper, *Empires in World History: Power and the Politics of Difference* (Princeton, NJ: Princeton University Press, 2010), 8.

19. Gary Wilder, *The French Imperial Nation-State: Negritude and Colonial Humanism between the Two World Wars* (Chicago: Chicago University Press, 2005), 10.

20. Ann Laura Stoler and Carole McGranahan, "Introduction," in *Imperial Formations*, ed. Ann Laura Stoler, Carole McGranahan, and Peter Perdue (Santa Fe, NM: School for Advance Research Press, 2007), 8, 10.

21. Stoler and McGranahan, "Introduction," 4.

22. Frederick Cooper and Ann Laura Stoler, eds., *Tensions of Empire: Colonial Cultures in a Bourgeois World* (Berkeley: University of California Press, 1997); Frederick Cooper, *Colonialism in Question: History, Theory, Knowledge* (Berkeley: University of California Press, 2005); Matthew Fitzpatrick, ed., *Liberal Imperialism in Europe* (New York: Palgrave Macmillan, 2012); Stefan Berger and Alexei Miller, eds., *Nationalizing Empires* (New York: Central European Press, 2015).

23. Hazareesingh, *From Subject to Citizen*; Matthew Truesdell, *Spectacular Politics: Louis-Napoleon Bonaparte and the Fête Impérial, 1849–1870* (New York: Oxford University Press, 1997).

24. Osama W. Abi-Mershed, *Apostles of Modernity: Saint-Simonians and the Civilizing Mission in Algeria* (Stanford: Stanford University Press, 2010); Michel Levallois, *Ismaÿl Urbain: Royaume arabe ou Algérie franco-musulmane: 1848–1870* (Paris: Riveneuve, 2012); Gavin Murray-Miller, *The Cult of the Modern: Trans-Mediterranean France and the Construction of French Modernity* (Lincoln: University of Nebraska Press, 2017).

25. Jennifer Pitts, "Political Theory of Empire and Imperialism: An Appendix," *Empire and Modern Political Thought*, ed. Sankar Muthu (New York: Cambridge University Press, 2012), 373; Sheldon Pollock, "Empire and Imitation," in Calhoun, Cooper, and Moore, *Lessons of Empire*, 176.

26. Patricia Lorcin, "Pax Romana Transposed: Rome as an Exemplar for Western Imperialism," in *The Routledge History of Western Empires*, ed. Robert Aldrich and Kirsten McKenzie (New York: Routledge, 2014); Bonnie Effros, *Incidental Archaeologists: French Officers and the Rediscovery of Roman North Africa* (Ithaca, NY: Cornell University Press, 2018); Jessica Biddlestone, "France in Roman Africa: Antiquity and the Making of French Algeria and Tunisia" (PhD diss., Northwestern University, 2019).

27. Sudhir Hazareesingh, *The Legend of Napoleon* (London: Granta Books, 2004); Venita Datta, *Heroes and Legends of Fin-de-Siècle France: Gender, Politics, and National Identity* (New York: Cambridge University Press, 2011).

28. Alice Conklin, *A Mission to Civilize: The Republican Idea of Empire in France and West Africa, 1895–1930* (Stanford, CA: Stanford University Press, 1997); Wilder, *French Imperial Nation-State*; Nicolas Bancel, Pascal Blanchard, and Françoise Verges,

La république coloniale (Paris: Hachette littératures, 2006); Joan Scott, *The Politics of the Veil* (Princeton, NJ: Princeton University Press, 2007).

29. Frederick Cooper, *Citizenship between Empire and Nation: Remaking France and French Africa, 1945–1960* (Princeton, NJ: Princeton University Press, 2014), 4.

30. Sankar Muthu, *Enlightenment against Empire* (Princeton, NJ: Princeton University Press, 2003); Cooper, *Colonialism in Question*; Jennifer Pitts, *A Turn to Empire: The Rise of Imperial Liberalism in Britain and France* (Princeton, NJ: Princeton University Press, 2005).

31. David Prochaska, *Making Algeria French: Colonialism in Bône, 1870–1920* (New York: Cambridge University Press, 1990); Conklin, *Mission to Civilize*; J. P. Daughton, *An Empire Divided: Religion, Republicanism, and the Making of French Colonialism, 1880–1914* (New York: Oxford University Press, 2006), 10.

32. Geoff Eley, "Nations, Publics, and Political Cultures: Placing Habermas in the Nineteenth Century," in *Habermas and the Public Sphere*, ed. Craig Calhoun (Cambridge, MA: MIT Press, 1992), 289–339; James Van Horn Melton, *The Rise of the Public in Enlightenment Europe* (Cambridge: Cambridge University Press, 2001).

33. Emmanuelle Sibeud, "Une libre pensée impériale? Le comité de protection et de défense des indigènes, 1892–1914," *Mil neuf cent: La revue d'histoire intellectuelle* 27, no. 1 (2009): 67.

34. Clyde Thogmartin, *The National Daily Press of France* (Birmingham, AL: Summa Publications, 1998), 65.

35. Martyn Lyons, *Reading Culture and Writing Practices in Nineteenth-Century France* (Toronto: University of Toronto Press, 2008), 48.

36. Tony Chafer and Amanda Shakur, eds., *Promoting the Colonial Idea: Propaganda and Visions of Empire in France* (New York: Palgrave, 2002); Edward Berenson, "Making a Colonial Culture? Empire and the French Public, 1880–1940," *French Politics, Culture and Society* 22, no. 2 (2004): 127–49; Pascal Blanchard, Sandrine Lemaire, and Nicolas Bancel, *Culture coloniale en France: De la révolution française à nos jours* (Paris: CNRS, 2008).

37. Censorship also remained in place in France after 1881 for works that threatened the moral order. See Thomas J. Cragin, "The Failings of Popular News Censorship in Nineteenth-Century France," *Book History* 4 (2001): 71; Dean de la Motte and Jeannene Przyblyski, "Introduction," in *Making the News: Modernity and the Mass Press in Nineteenth-Century France*, ed. Dean de la Motte and Jeannene Przyblyski (Amherst: University of Massachusetts Press, 1999), 4; Philipp Zessin, "Presse et journalistes 'indigènes' en Algérie coloniale (années 1890–années 1950)," *Le mouvement social* 236, no. 3 (2011): 36.

38. Elizabeth Clark, *History, Theory, Text: Historians and the Linguistic Turn* (Cambridge, MA: Harvard University Press, 2004), 110.

39. Assmann distinguishes between three kinds of memory: cultural, communicative, and collective. Communicative memory is formed by individuals of a social exchange while it is taking place. This memory gives the participants a sense of mutual experience that they draw on to identify themselves as members of the group that shared in the exchange. Formed through interaction, communicative memory therefore resides in individuals and is inherently temporally limited. Memory, however, can also be objectified in buildings, images, monuments, and texts. Assmann refers to this as "cultural memory" and argues that it also affects the way that people

understand the past and their own identity. He stresses that communicative and cultural memories often exist simultaneously and both are subsumed under the term "collective memory." See Jan Assmann, "Communicative and Cultural Memory," in *Cultural Memory Studies: An Interdisciplinary and International Handbook*, ed. Astrid Erll and Ansgar Nünning (New York: Walter de Gruyer, 2008), 110.

40. Claude Nicolet, *L'idée républicaine en France* (Paris: Gallimard, 1982), 16–18; Jeremy Jennings, *Revolution and the Republic: A History of Political Thought in France since the Eighteenth Century* (New York: Oxford University Press, 2011), 75, 77, 200–202.

41. Naomi Schor dates universalism back to the medieval belief that because France was the "elder daughter of the Church," it was the site of Christian universalism. See Naomi Schor, "The Crisis of French Universalism," *Yale French Studies*, no. 100 (2001), 46.

42. Rogers Brubaker, "The French Revolution and the Invention of Citizenship," *French Politics and Society* 7, no. 3 (1989): 43; Michael Rapport, *Nationality and Citizenship in Revolutionary France: The Treatment of Foreigners 1789–1799* (London: Oxford University Press, 2000), 13.

43. Michael Broers, "The First Napoleonic Empire, 1799–1815," in Berger and Miller, *Nationalizing Empires*, 115.

44. Joan Landes, *Women and the Public Sphere in the Age of the French Revolution* (Ithaca, NY: Cornell University Press, 1988); Lynn Hunt, *The Family Romance of the French Revolution* (Berkeley: University of California Press, 1992); Joan Scott, *Only Paradoxes to Offer: French Feminists and the Rights of Man* (Cambridge, MA: Harvard University Press, 1996).

45. Suzanne Desan, "Foreigners, Cosmopolitanism, and French Revolutionary Universalism," in *The French Revolution in Global Perspective*, ed. Suzanne Desan, Lynn Hunt, and William Max Nelson (Ithaca, NY: Cornell University Press, 2013), 87.

46. Broers, "First Napoleonic Empire," 103.

47. Robert Forster, "The French Revolution, People of Color, and Slavery," in *The Global Ramifications of the French Revolution*, ed. Joseph Klaits and Michael H. Haltzel (New York: Cambridge University Press, 1994), 90, 98.

48. Cooper and Stoler, *Tensions of Empire*; Conklin, *Mission to Civilize*; Sue Peabody and Tyler Stovall, eds., *The Color of Liberty: Histories of Race in France* (Durham, NC: Duke University Press, 2003); Wilder, *French Imperial Nation-State*; Scott, *Politics of the Veil*; Dino Costantino, *Mission civilisatrice: Le rôle de l'histoire coloniale dans la construction de l'identité politique française* (Paris: La Découverte, 2008); Martin Staum, *Nature and Nurture in French Social Sciences, 1859–1914 and Beyond* (Montreal: McGill-Queen's University Press, 2011)

49. C. L. R. James, *The Black Jacobins: Toussaint L'Ouverture and the San Domingo Revolution* (New York: Vintage, 1989); Laurent Dubois, *A Colony of Citizens: Revolution and Slave Emancipation in the French Caribbean, 1787–1804* (Chapel Hill: University of North Carolina Press, 2004); Jeremy Popkin, *You Are All Free: The Haitian Revolution and the Abolition of Slavery* (New York: Cambridge University Press, 2010).

50. Laurent Dubois, "An Enslaved Enlightenment: Rethinking the Intellectual History of the French Atlantic," *Social History* 31, no. 1 (2006): 14.

51. Miranda Spieler, "The Legal Structure of Colonial Rule during the French Revolution," *William and Mary Quarterly* 66, no. 2 (2009): 374.

52. Philip Dwyer, "'Citizen Emperor': Popular Ritual, Popular Sovereignty and the Coronation of Napoleon I," *History* 100, no. 339 (2015): 56.

53. For this debate, see Stuart Woolf, "French Civilization and Ethnicity in the Napoleonic Empire," *Past and Present* 124, no. 1 (1989): 96–120; Geoffrey Ellis, "The Nature of Napoleonic Imperialism," in *Napoleon and Europe*, ed. Philip G. Dwyer (London: Pearson Education, 2001), 97–117; S. J. Woolf, "Napoleon and Europe Revisited," *Modern and Contemporary France* 8, no. 4 (August 2000): 469–78; Broers, "First Napoleonic Empire," 100–102.

54. Martyn Lyons, *Napoleon Bonaparte and the Legacy of the French Revolution* (New York: Palgrave Macmillan, 1994); Philip G. Dwyer and Alan Forrest, "Introduction," in *Napoleon and His Empire: Europe, 1804–1814*, ed. Philip Dwyer and Alan Forrest (New York: Palgrave Macmillan, 2007), 3; David P. Jordan, "Napoleon as Revolutionary," in Dwyer and Forrest, *Napoleon and His Empire*, 34.

55. Edward Said, *Orientalism* (New York: Vintage Books, 1978).

56. Yves Laissus, *L'Égypte, une aventure savante, 1798–1801* (Paris: Fayard, 1998).

57. Todd Porterfield, *The Allure of Empire: Art in the Service of French Imperialism* (Princeton, NJ: Princeton University Press, 1998), 73.

58. Patrice Bert, "Les contingences orientalistes de l'expédition de Bonaparte," in *L'orientalisme des Saint-Simoniens*, ed. Michel Levallois and Sarga Moussa (Paris: Maisonneuve & Larose, 2006), 39.

59. Juan Cole, *Napoleon's Egypt: Invading the Middle East* (New York: St. Martin's, 2007), 15–20, 165–68.

60. Michael Broers, *The Napoleonic Empire in Italy, 1796–1814: Cultural Imperialism in a European Context?* (New York: Palgrave Macmillan, 2005).

61. Woolf, "French Civilization and Ethnicity," 107; Isser Woloch, "The Napoleonic Regime and French Society," in Dwyer, *Napoleon and Europe*, 70.

62. Dubois, *Colony of Citizens*, 350, 352, 382.

63. Philippe Girard, "Rêves d'Empire: French Revolutionary Doctrine and Military Interventions in the Southern United States and the Caribbean, 1789–1809," *Louisiana History* 48, no. 4 (2007): 407–8.

64. Miranda Spieler, *Empire and Underworld: Captivity in French Guiana* (Cambridge, MA: Harvard University Press, 2012), 41–50.

65. Michael Broers, Peter Hicks, and Agustin Guimerá, eds., *The Napoleonic Empire and the New European Political Culture* (New York: Palgrave Macmillan, 2012).

66. Ellis, "Nature of Napoleonic Imperialism," in Dwyer, *Napoleon and Europe*, 100.

67. Ute Planert, "Conscription, Economic Exploitation and Religion in Napoleonic Germany," in Dwyer and Forrest, *Napoleon and His Empire*, 138.

68. Michael Broers, "Policing the Empire: Napoleon and the Pacification of Europe," in Dwyer, *Napoleon and Europe*, 153.

69. Stuart Woolf, "The Construction of a European World-View in the Republican-Napoleonic Years," *Past and Present* 137, no. 1 (1992): 78.

70. Nelly Schmidt, "Schoelchérisme et assimilation dans la politique coloniale française: De la théorie a la pratique aux Caraïbes entre 1848 et les années 1880," *La revue d'histoire moderne et contemporaine* 35, no. 2 (1988): 306.

1. The Second Empire's Imperial Ideologies in Mexico and Algeria

1. René de Saint-Félix, *Le voyage de S. M. L'Empereur en Algérie* (Paris: Eug. Pick, 1865), 95, 98–99.

2. Guy Pervillé, *La France en Algérie, 1830–1954* (Paris: Vendémiare, 2012), 47.

3. Napoleon III, *Les idées napoléoniennes*, 6th ed. (Paris: Henri Plon, 1860), 22, 30, 133.

4. Roger Price, *The French Second Empire: An Anatomy of Political Power* (New York: Cambridge University Press, 2001), 267.

5. Napoleon III, *Les idées napoléoniennes*, 110; *La politique impériale exposée par les discours et proclamations de l'Empereur Napoléon III* (Paris: Henri Plon, 1868), 78, 84, 145, 159, 191, 283, 301; James McMillan, *Napoleon III* (New York: Routledge, 1991), 74.

6. Napoleon III employed the language of nationality—not expansionism—to annex Nice and Savoy after the Italian Wars. See Sylvie Aprile, *La Deuxième République et le Second Empire, 1848–1870* (Paris: Pygmalian, 2010), 289.

7. Napoleon III, "Discours d'ouverture de la session législative de 1868," in *Œuvres de Napoléon III* (Paris: Amyot, 1869), 5: 298; Annie Rey-Goldzeiguer, *Le royaume arabe: La politique algérienne de Napoléon III, 1861–1870* (Alger: Société nationale d'édition et de diffusion, 1977), 127.

8. Candan Badem, *The Ottoman Crimean War* (Boston: Brill, 2010), 65; Leila Tarazi Fawaz, *An Occasion for War: Civil Conflict in Lebanon and Damascus in 1860* (Berkeley: University of California Press, 1994), 110; Andrew Arsan, "There Is, in the Heart of Asia . . . an Entirely French Population: France, Mount Lebanon, and the Workings of Affective Empire in the Mediterranean, 1830–1920," in *French Mediterraneans: Transnational and Imperial Histories*, ed. Patricia Lorcin and Todd Shephard (Lincoln: University of Nebraska Press, 2016), 95.

9. Patricia Lorcin, *Imperial Identities: Stereotyping, Prejudice, and Race in Colonial Algeria* (New York: I. B. Tauris, 1995); Benjamin Brower, *A Desert Named Peace: The Violence of France's Empire in the Algerian Sahara* (New York: Columbia University Press 2009); Osama W. Abi-Mershed, *Apostles of Modernity: Saint-Simonians and the Civilizing Mission in Algeria* (Stanford, CA: Stanford University Press, 2010); Jennifer Sessions, *By Sword and Plow: France and the Conquest of Algeria* (Ithaca, NY: Cornell University Press, 2011); Michel Levallois, *Ismaÿl Urbain: Royaume arabe ou Algérie franco-musulmane?; 1848–1870* (Paris: Riveneuve éditions, 2012).

10. Gavin Murray-Miller, "A Conflicted Sense of Nationality: Napoleon III's Arab Kingdom and the Paradoxes of French Multiculturalism," *French Colonial History* 14 (2014): 1–39.

11. Ann Laura Stoler and Carole McGranahan, "Introduction," in *Imperial Formations*, ed. Ann Laura Stoler, Carole McGranahan, and Peter Perdue (Santa Fe, NM: School for Advanced Research Press, 2007), 4.

12. Frederick Cooper and Ann Laura Stoler, "Between Metropole and Colony," in *Tensions of Empire: Colonial Cultures in a Bourgeois World*, ed. Frederick Cooper and Ann Laura Stoler (Berkeley: University of California Press, 1997), 1–56; Gary Wilder, *The French Imperial Nation-State: Negritude and Colonial Humanism between the Two World Wars* (Chicago: Chicago University Press, 2005); Jane Burbank and Frederick Cooper, *Empires in World History: Power and the Politics of Difference* (Princeton, NJ: Princeton University Press, 2010); Krishan Kumar, "Nation-States as Empires,

Empires as Nation-States: Two Principles, One Practice?," *Theory and Society* 39, no. 2 (2010): 119–43.

13. Price, *French Second Empire*, 172–73, 177, 181.

14. *Le petit journal* was less expensive than other newspapers published at the time, and while other newspapers had at most fifty thousand readers, it had more than six hundred thousand readers by the end of the 1860s. See Thomas J. Cragin, "The Failings of Popular News Censorship in Nineteenth-Century France," *Book History* 4 (2001): 77. See also Sudhir Hazareesingh, *From Subject to Citizen: The Second Empire and the Emergence of Modern French Democracy* (Princeton, NJ: Princeton University Press, 1998), 20.

15. J. Bonnardot, "La presse algérienne sous le Second Empire," *La revue d'histoire du XIXe siècle*, no. 184 (1949): 27.

16. Gavin Murray-Miller, *The Cult of the Modern: Trans-Mediterranean France and the Construction of French Modernity* (Lincoln: University of Nebraska Press, 2017), 204.

17. Maria Adamowicz-Hariasz, "From Opinion to Information: The *Roman-Feuilleton* and the Transformation of the Nineteenth-Century French Press," in *Making the News: Modernity and the Mass Press in Nineteenth-Century France*, ed. Dean de la Motte and Jeannene Przyblyski (Amherst; University of Massachusetts Press, 1999), 178.

18. *Le Mobacher* hired indigenous Arabic-language speakers to translate its articles into Arabic, but it still represented a government perspective. See Zahir Ihaddaden, *Histoire de la presse indigène en Algérie*, 3rd ed. (Algiers: ANEP, 2010), 14; Philipp Zessin, "Presse et journalistes 'indigènes' en Algérie coloniale (années 1890–années 1950)," *Le mouvement social*, no. 236 (2011): 35.

19. Erika Pani, "Juárez vs. Maximiliano," in *American Civil Wars: The United States, Latin America, Europe, and the Crisis of the 1860s*, ed. Don Doyle (Chapel Hill: University of North Carolina Press, 2017), 175.

20. Price, *French Second Empire*, 182.

21. Cooper and Stoler, "Introduction," in *Tensions of Empire*, viii.

22. Matthew Truesdell, *Spectacular Politics: Louis-Napoleon Bonaparte and the* Fête Impérial, *1849–1870* (New York: Oxford University Press, 1997), 7.

23. Napoleon III, "Message à l'Assemblée législatif, 31 octobre 1849," in *Œuvres de Napoléon III: Mélanges* (Paris: Henri Plon, 1862), 305.

24. Napoleon III, "Préambule de la constitution, 14 janvier 1852," in *Œuvres de Napoléon III*, 334.

25. Napoleon III, *Les idées napoléoniennes*, 137.

26. Hazareesingh, *From Subject to Citizen*, 27.

27. Arsène Houssaye, *L'empire, c'est la paix* (Paris: Plon frères, 1852); Céline Domény, *L'empire, c'est la paix* (Paris: Heu, 1852); Hector Bonnetat, *L'empire, c'est la paix* (Paris: Imprimerie Typographie de Bureau, 1852).

28. Napoleon III, *Les idées napoléoniennes*, 148; William Echard, *Napoleon III and the Concert of Europe* (Baton Rouge: Louisiana State University Press, 1983), 5.

29. David Baguley, *Napoleon III and His Regime: An Extravaganza* (Baton Rouge, LA: Louisiana State University Press, 2000), 171.

30. Napoleon III, *Les idées napoléoniennes*, 136.

31. Price, *French Second Empire*, 267.

32. Napoleon III, *Les idées napoléoniennes*, 120. These ideas date from 1839, but William Echard has argued that this early commitment to the politics of nationality structured Napoleon III's foreign policy for most of his reign, even if he was willing to sacrifice it when necessary. See Echard, *Napoleon III and the Concert of Europe*, 162, 164.

33. Napoleon III, *Les idées napoléoniennes*, 123; "Discours de l'empereur à l'ouverture de la session législative, 1 mars 1860" and "Discours de l'empereur à l'ouverture de la session législative, 5 novembre 1863," in *La politique impériale*, 324, 327, 410.

34. Napoleon III, *Les idées napoléoniennes*, 135, 70.

35. Philip G. Dwyer and Alan Forrest, eds., *Napoleon and His Empire: Europe, 1804–1814* (New York: Palgrave Macmillan, 2007); Geoffrey Ellis, "The Nature of Napoleonic Imperialism," in *Napoleon and Europe*, ed. Philip G. Dwyer (London: Pearson Education, 2001), 97–117.

36. Roger Price, *Napoleon III and the Second Empire* (New York: Routledge, 1997), 29.

37. Aprile, *La Deuxième République*, 289–91.

38. Price, *French Second Empire*, 120; McMillan, *Napoleon III*, 93. Napoleon III's simultaneous embrace of liberalism and colonial expansion reflected the wider intersection of liberalism and imperialism at this historical moment. See Jennifer Pitts, *A Turn to Empire: The Rise of Imperial Liberalism in Britain and France* (Princeton, NJ: Princeton University Press, 2005), 21.

39. Scholars continue to argue over the causes of the invasion. See Alfred Hanna and Kathryn Hanna, *Napoleon III and Mexico* (Chapel Hill: University of North Carolina Press 1971), 19; Michele Cunningham, *Mexico and the Foreign Policy of Napoleon III* (New York: Palgrave, 2001), 34; Shirley Black, "Napoleon III and European Colonization in Mexico: The Substance of an Imperial Dream," in *Hispanic-American Essays in Honor of Max Leon Moorhead*, ed. William S. Coker (Pensacola, FL: Perdido Bay Press, 1979), 133; Jean-François Lecaillon, *Napoléon III et le Mexique: Les illusions d'un grand dessein* (Paris: Éditions L'Harmattan, 1994), 39; Guy-Alain Dugast, *La tentation mexicaine en France au XIXe siècle: L'image du Mexique et l'intervention française*, vol. 1 (Paris: Éditions L'Harmattan, 2008), 12.

40. Charles Hale, *The Transformation of Liberalism in Late Nineteenth-Century Mexico* (Princeton, NJ: Princeton University Press, 1989), 3–19; Mark Wasserman, *Everyday Life and Politics in Nineteenth Century Mexico: Men, Women, and War* (Albuquerque: University of New Mexico Press, 2000), 112; Zachary Brittsan, *Popular Politics and Rebellion in Mexico: Manuel Lozada and La Reforma, 1855–1876* (Nashville, TN: Vanderbilt University Press, 2015), 37–44.

41. Nancy Barker, "Monarchy in Mexico: Harebrained Scheme or Well-Considered Prospect?," *Journal of Modern History* 48, no. 1 (March 1976): 61.

42. Nancy Barker, *The French Experience in Mexico, 1821–1861: A History of Constant Misunderstanding* (Chapel Hill: University of North Carolina Press, 1979), 179.

43. Napoleon III to Flahaut, October 9, 1861, AN 400 AP 63, quoted in Nancy N. Barker, "The Factor of 'Race,' in the French Experience in Mexico, 1821–1861," *Hispanic American Historical Review* 59, no. 1 (February 1979): 79.

44. Cunningham, *Mexico and the Foreign Policy of Napoleon III*, 108.

45. Lecaillon, *Napoleon III et le Mexique*, 57.

46. Robert Duncan, "Political Legitimation and Maximilian's Second Empire in Mexico, 1864–1867," *Mexican Studies* 12, no. 1 (1996): 30–31.

47. Kristine Ibsen, *Maximilian, Mexico, and the Invention of Empire* (Nashville, TN: Vanderbilt University Press, 2010), 4.

48. Lecaillon, *Napoleon III et le Mexique*, 104; Erika Pani, "Intervention and Empire: Politics as Usual?," in *Malcontents, Rebels, and Pronunciados: The Politics of Insurrection in Nineteenth-Century Mexico*, ed. Will Fowler (Lincoln: University of Nebraska Press, 2012), 247.

49. Wasserman, *Everyday Life and Politics*, 120.

50. Gary Moreno, "Rage against the Monarchy: American Reaction to French Intervention in Mexico," *Journal of the West* 47, no. 3 (2008): 50. Nancy Barker argues that Napoleon III began to lose interest in the venture in 1863 due to growing opposition at home and changes in European diplomacy. He had offered the throne to the archduke to secure an alliance with Austria, but when Maximilian took the throne in 1864, the alliance had fallen through. See Nancy Barker, "France, Austria, and the Mexican Venture, 1861–1864," *French Historical Studies* 3, no. 2 (1963): 245.

51. Napoleon to Forey, June 12, 1863, in *La politique impériale*, 396.

52. Whether Napoleon III believed that this new government reflected the will of the Mexican people remains a subject of debate, but his representatives and allies had an interest in establishing a new government. Nancy Barker, "The French Legation in Mexico: Nexus of Interventionists," *French Historical Studies* 8, no. 3 (1974): 417; Cunningham, *Mexico and the Foreign Policy of Napoleon III*, 149.

53. Lecaillon, *Napoléon III et le Mexique*, 82.

54. Price, *Napoleon III and the Second Empire*, 43.

55. Black, "Napoleon III and European Colonization in Mexico," 133–55; Cunningham, *Mexico and the Foreign Policy of Napoleon III*, 6; Erika Pani, "Dreaming of a Mexican Empire: The Political Projects of the 'Imperialistas,'" *Hispanic American Historical Review* 82, no. 1 (2002): 1; Douglas Richmond, *Conflict and Carnage in Yucatán: Liberals, the Second Empire, and Maya Revolutionaries, 1855–1876* (Tuscaloosa: University of Alabama Press, 2015), xiv; Edward Shawcross, *France, Mexico, and Informal Empire in Latin America, 1820–1867* (New York: Palgrave Macmillan, 2018), 4.

56. Charles Hale, *The Transformation of Liberalism in Late Nineteenth-Century Mexico* (Princeton, NJ: Princeton University Press, 1989).

57. Martin S. Staum, *Labeling People: French Scholars on Society, Race, and Empire, 1815–1848* (Montreal: McGill-Queen's University Press, 2003), 13.

58. Pierre-André Taguieff, *Le couleur et le sang* (Paris: Mille et une nuits, 2002), 19–21; Carole Reynaud-Paligot, *La république raciale, 1860–1930* (Paris: PUF, 2006), 9.

59. Nélia Dias, "The Visibility of Difference: Nineteenth-Century French Anthropological Collections" in *The Politics of Display: Museums, Science, Culture*, ed. Sharon Macdonald (New York: Routledge, 1998), 36; Nancy Stepan, *Picturing Tropical Nature* (London: Reaktion Books, 2001), 113.

60. Reynaud-Paligot, *La république raciale*, 30–51; Alice Conklin, *In the Museum of Man: Race, Anthropology, and Empire in France, 1850–1950* (Ithaca, NY: Cornell University Press, 2013), 23. A major work that would later come to help structure European racial thinking—Arthur Gobineau's *Essai sur l'inégalité des races humaines*—met with a

mixed reception in the 1850s. Jan Goldstein, "Toward an Empirical History of Moral Thinking: The Case of Racial Theory in Mid-Nineteenth-Century France," *American Historical Review* 120, no. 1 (2015): 4.

61. Napoleon III shared anthropologists' interest in ancient France, but his regime had concerns about anthropologists' polygenist theories, which the Catholic Church condemned, and their republican and anticlerical principles. Paul Broca—who organized the Société d'anthropologie in 1859—carefully positioned anthropology as apolitical. See Carole Reynaud-Paligot, *De l'identité nationale: Science, race et politique en Europe et aux États-Unis* (Paris: PUF, 2011), 114.

62. Sue Peabody and Tyler Stovall, "Race, France, Histories," *The Color of Liberty: Histories of Race in France*, ed. Sue Peabody and Tyler Stovall (Durham, NC: Duke University Press, 2003), 2.

63. Barker, "Factor of 'Race,'" 67.

64. Magali Carrera, *Imagining Identity in New Spain: Race, Lineage, and the Colonial Body in Portraiture and Casta Paintings* (Austin: University of Texas Press, 2003), 148; Miguel Angel Aviles-Galan, "Measuring Skulls: Race and Science in Vicente Riva Palacio's *México a través de los siglos*," *Bulletin of Latin American Research* 29, no. 1 (2010): 86; Joshua Lund, *The Mestizo State: Reading Race in Modern Mexico* (Minneapolis: University of Minnesota Press, 2012), ix.

65. Dugast, *La tentation mexicaine en France*, 112; Barker, "Monarchy in Mexico," 55; Guy Martinière, "L'expédition mexicaine de Napoléon III dans l'historiographie française," *La revue d'histoire moderne et contemporaine* 21, no. 1 (1974): 144.

66. Dugast, *La tentation mexicaine en France*, 176, 197, 213; Barker, "Monarchy in Mexico," 56.

67. Dugast, *La tentation mexicaine en France*, 300, 290.

68. Mathieu de Fossey, *Le Mexique* (Paris: Henri Plon, 1857), 473; H. du Pasquier de Dommartin, *Les États-Unis et le Mexique: L'intérêt européen dans l'Amérique du Nord* (Paris: Librairie de Guillamin, 1852), 74; "Note Mexique," AN 400 AP 63; F. Lavallée, "Étude sur le Mexique," *La revue des races latines* (September 1859): 86.

69. Stève Sainlaude, "France's Grand Design and the Confederacy," in Doyle, *American Civil Wars*, 108.

70. Alexis de Gabriac, "Note de M. de Gabriac sur les mines du Mexique, 1861," AMAE, MD Mexique, 10:1–6; Dubois de Saligny to Thouvenel, April 28, 1861, 28, AMAE CP Mexique, 54:266–70; Dubois de Saligny to Thouvenel, July 17, 1861, AMAE CP Mexique, 55:88–93; Nancy Barker, *French Experience in Mexico*, 195.

71. Ibsen, *Maximilian, Mexico, and the Invention of Empire*, 2.

72. Parts of this pamphlet were translated into an article that appeared in *Le journal des débats*. See "France," *Le journal des débats*, September 13, 1842, 1–2.

73. Pani, "Juárez vs. Maximiliano," *American Civil Wars*, 174.

74. Some conservatives shared their concerns with either Estrada or the French Legation. See Ignacio Aguilar to General Woll, June 1853–October 1864, AMAE PA-AP Woll, 1:1–31; Francisco J. Miranda to Estrada, November 4, 1861, AMAE CP Mexique, 56:318–19; J. D. Ulibarri to Estrada, November 29, 1861, AMAE CP Mexique, 58:17–19; "Manifesto del General Don Manuel Robles Pezuela, Escrito pocas horas antes de ser fusilado," March 22, 1862, AMAE CP Mexique, 60:239; Leonardo Marquez to Saligny, May 26, 1862, AMAE CP Mexique, 58:454–57.

75. Barbara Tenenbaum, "Development and Sovereignty: Intellectuals and the Second Empire," in *Los intelectuales y el poder en Mexico / Intellectuals and Power in Mexico*, ed. Roderic Ai Camp et al. (Berkeley: University of California Press, 1991), 82; Pani, "Dreaming of a Mexican Empire," 11.

76. Napoleon III to Flahaut, October 9, 1861, AN 400 AP 63.

77. Napoleon III to Forey, in *Affaires étrangères: Documents diplomatiques* (Paris: Imprimerie impériale, 1862), 190; Napoleon III to Forey, June 12, 1863, in *La politique impériale*, 396. The unpublished copy of the 1862 letter mentions Maximilian by name: "If the Mexicans prefer monarchy, it is in France's interest to support them, and in that case General Almonte can put forward Archduke Maximilian as the French candidate." See Napoleon III to Forey, July 14, 1862, AN 400 AP 62.

78. This idea also echoed in Napoleon III's supporters' speeches. See "Discours prononcé par M. Billaut, Ministre sans portefeuille, dans la séance du corps législatif du 26 juin 1862," in *Archives diplomatiques: Recueil de diplomatie et d'histoire*, vol. 3 (Paris: Amyot, 1862), 175. For Napoleon III's relationship to Saint-Simonianism and Saint-Simonian racial thought, see Hazareesingh, *From Subject to Citizen*, 25, and Abi-Mershed, *Apostles of Modernity*, 161.

79. Prosper Enfantin, *Colonisation d'Algérie* (Paris: P. Bertrand, 1843), 499; Stepan, *Picturing Tropical Nature*, 85.

80. Napoleon III to Flahaut, October 9, 1861, AN 400 AP 63; Napoleon III to Forey, June 12, 1863, in *La politique impériale*, 396; "Discours d'ouverture de la session de 1867, 14 février 1867," *La politique impériale*, 471. Napoleon III's contention that empire was a civilizing force first appeared in 1839, but his use of that idea to argue for empire outside of France was new. See Napoleon III, *Les idées napoléoniennes*, 11.

81. Forey, "Mexicains!," November 3, 1862, and Forey, "Manifeste à la nation mexicaine," June 12, 1863, AN 400 AP 62, dossier 1.

82. "Proclamation du Général Almonte," April 1862, AMAE CP Mexique, 57:544.

83. Shawcross, *France, Mexico, and Informal Empire*, 207.

84. He published it with Montholon, the French minister in Mexico City. See Hanna and Hanna, *Napoleon III and Mexico*, 80.

85. Emile Masseras, *Le programme de l'empire* (Mexico City: Libreria Mexicana, 1864), 17, 22.

86. Masseras, *Le programme de l'empire*, 28.

87. Patricia Lorcin, "Rome and France in Africa: Recovering Colonial Algeria's Latin Past," *French Historical Studies* 25, no. 2 (2002): 297–99; Patricia Lorcin, "Pax Romana Transposed: Rome as an Exemplar for Western Imperialism," in *The Routledge History of Western Empires*, ed. Robert Aldrich and Kirsten McKenzie (New York: Routledge, 2014), 413–15.

88. Käthe Panick, *La Race Latine: Politischer Romanismus im Frankreich des 19. Jahrhunderts* (Bonn: Ludwig Röhrscheid Verlag, 1978), 158, 162.

89. Martinière, "L'expédition mexicaine," 147; Maike Thier, "The View from Paris: 'Latinity,' 'Anglo-Saxonism,' and the Americas, as Discussed in *La revue des races latines*, 1857–1864," *International History Review* 33, no. 4 (2011): 632.

90. Aims McGuinness, "Searching for 'Latin America': Race and Sovereignty in the Americas in the 1850s," in *Race and Nation in Modern Latin America*, ed. Karin Rosemblatt et al. (Chapel Hill: University of North Carolina Press, 2003), 99–102;

Michel Gobat, "The Invention of Latin America: A Transnational History of Anti-Imperialism, Democracy, and Race," *American Historical Review* 118, no. 5 (2013): 1345–75.

91. Shawcross, *France, Mexico, and Informal Empire*, 236.

92. Amotz Giladi, "The Elaboration of Pan-Latinism in French Intellectual Circles, from the Turn of the Nineteenth Century to World War I," *Journal of Romance Studies* 14, no. 1 (2014): 59.

93. John Leddy Phelan, "Pan-Latinism, French Intervention in Mexico (1861–1867) and the Genesis of the Idea of Latin America," in *Conciencia autenticidad y históricas*, ed. Juan Antonio Ortega y Medina (Mexico: UNAM, 1968), 279; Michael Drolet, "Nature, Science, and the Environment in Nineteenth-Century French Political Economy: The Case of Michel Chevalier," *Modern Intellectual History* 15, no. 3 (2018): 711–45.

94. Guiterrez de Estrada to General Woll, May 25, 1864, AMAE PA-AP Woll, 9:251.

95. Shawcross, *France, Mexico, and Informal Empire*, 140.

96. Michel Chevalier, *L'expédition du Mexique* (Paris: E. Dentu, 1862), 86.

97. Chevalier, *L'expédition du Mexique*, 89.

98. Félix Ribèyre, *Histoire de la guerre du Mexique* (Paris: Dentu, 1863); Charles Martin, *Précis des événements de la campagne du Mexique en 1862* (Paris: C. Tanera, 1863), 275; Charles Dupin, "Du Mexique, dans ses rapports avec le règne," September 19, 1863, AN AB XIX 171; Adolphe Biarnes, *Le droit des gens, la France et les Yankees* (Nantes: V. de Courmaceul, 1866), 31.

99. Napoleon III to Flahaut, October 9, 1861, AN 400 AP 63; Thouvenel to Flahaut, September 19, 1861, in *Le secret de l'empereur*, vol. 2 (Paris: Calmann Lévy, 1889), 167–70; Auguste-Saint-Hilaire Mercier de Lacombe, *Le Mexique: L'Amérique du Nord et l'Europe* (Paris: Charles Douniel, 1861), 41; Auguste-Saint-Hilaire Mercier de Lacombe, *Le Mexique et les États-Unis* (Paris: E. Dentu, 1863), 72; J. M. Hidalgo, "Introduction," *La question du Mexique devant les Cortès d'Espagne: Discours prononcés au Sénat et au Congrès* (Paris: Laine & Havard, 1863), 8–9; Henry de Valori, *L'expédition du Mexique réhabilitée au triple point de vue religieux, politique, et commerciale* (Paris: E. Dentu, 1864), 32; Michel Chevalier, *Le Mexique: Ancien et moderne* (Paris: Librairie Hachette, 1864); *L'empire mexicain et son avenir considéré au point de vue des intérêts européens* (Paris: E. Dentu, 1865); *La question du Mexique au point de vue providentiel* (Paris: Impr. de Dubuisson, 1865), 9.

100. Paul Gaulot, *L'expédition du Mexique* (Paris: Paul Ollendorff 1906); Christian Schefer, *La grande pensée de Napoléon III: Les origines de l'expédition du Mexique* (Paris: M. Rivière, 1939); Phelan, "Pan-Latinism, French Intervention in Mexico," 279–98; Barker, "Factor of 'Race,'" 64–80; Jacques Chonchol and Guy Martinière, *L'Amérique latine et le latino-américanisme en France* (Paris: L'Harmattan, 1985).

101. This discourse tended to use the looser definition of "race" often found outside anthropology. See Urbain Deschartes, "Des races et leur mission," *La revue des races latines* (March 1860): 9–30. For a more comprehensive account, see Thier, "View from Paris," 630.

102. The perceived relationship between indigenous communities and latinité was confused and undertheorized. For the contention that the Spanish had destroyed

indigenous civilizations, see Fossey, *Le Mexique*, vii; Francis Lavallé, *Études Historiques sur le Mexique* (Paris: N. Chaix, 1859), 1:31; Agénor de Gasparin, *L'Amérique devant l'Europe: Principes et intérêts* (Paris: Michel Lévy frères, 1862), 421; Chevalier, *Le Mexique*, 261; and Biarnes, *Le droit des gens*, 12. For the contention that indigenous communities might integrate into the Latin race, see Dommartin, *Les États-Unis et le Mexique*, 27; J. Passame Domenech, *L'Empire mexicaine: La paix et les intérêts du monde Mexique* (Mexico City, 1866), 5; and F. de la Barreyrie, *Révélations sur l'intervention française au Mexique de 1866 à 1867* (Paris; Weil & Bloch, 1868), iii. For a wider discussion of French perceptions of Mexican indigenous peoples, see Dugast, *La tentation mexicaine en France*, 240–44.

103. Phelan, "Pan-Latinism, French Intervention in Mexico," 280; Thier, "View from Paris," 629.

104. Napoleon III to Forey, July 14, 1862, AN 400 AP 62; Napoleon III to Forey, June 12, 1863, in *La politique impériale*, 396. See also Emile Chabal, "The Rise of the Anglo-Saxon: French Perceptions of the Anglo-American World in the Long Twentieth Century," *French Politics, Culture, and Society* 31, no. 1 (2013): 27.

105. Thouvenel to the comte de Flahaut, September 19, 1861 and September 26, 1861, in *Le secret de l'empereur*, v. 2, 167–170, 174–176; Mercier de Lacombe, *Le Mexique, l'Amérique du Nord et l'Europe*, 41. See also Barker, "Factor of 'Race,'" 80.

106. Masseras, *Le programme de l'empire*, 12.

107. Mercier de Lacombe, *Le Mexique*, 29. Emmanuel Domenech, a missionary who later became Maximilian's press secretary, echoed this view. See Emmanuel Domenech, *L'empire au Mexique et la candidature d'un prince Bonaparte au trône mexicain* (Paris: Dentu, 1862), 130.

108. Dommartin, *Les États-Unis et le Mexique*, 44; L.-M. Tisserand, "Situation de la race latine," *La revue des races latines* 22, no. 51 (1860): 162. For a discussion of the trope of "decay" in *latinité*, see Thier, "View from Paris," esp. 629–30.

109. *La France, le Mexique et les États Confédérés contre les États-Unis* (Paris: E. Dentu, 1863), 6. (This work is variously attributed to Ernest Rasetti, Michel Chevalier, or both.) See also Dommartin, *Les États-Unis et le Mexique*, 5; Ribèyre, *Histoire de la guerre du Mexique*, 29.

110. Chevalier, *Le Mexique*, 495.

111. "Protestation de la Commission Permanente du Congrès National Mexicain contre l'intervention française," July 3, 1863, AN 223 AP 16.

112. Benito Juárez, "Proclamation," June 10, 1863, AMAE PA-AP Rouher, 4:521–22; Benito Juárez, "Proclamation," March 2, 1863, AMAE CP Mexique, 60:105–6; Benito Juárez, "Circulaire," June 10, 1863, AMAE CP Mexique, 60:151–52. These accusations were echoed by the head of the Mexican legation in Paris, and they appeared in some Mexican journals as well that French officials sent back to Paris. See A. de la Fuente to Thouvenel, March 7, 1862, AMAE CP Mexique, 58:258–68; "Translation of El Siglo XIX," June 30, 1862, AMAE CP Mexique, 59:131–2.

113. José Uraga, "Proclamation," January 23, 1862, SHD GR7 G1; Jésus Ortega to Saligny, June 10, 1862, AMAE CP Mexique, 59:36–37; "Le Moniteur républicain de Mexico: Résumé," (1862) AMAE PA-AP Rouher, vol. 10.

114. "Colonisation française," *El Monitor Républicano*, July 1, 1862, AMAE PA-AP Rouher, 4:536–539; Manuel Doblado, "Le Général Doblado Gouverneur de l'État de Guanajuato à Ses Concitoyens," and "Dernier Proclamation du general Doblado," November 9, 1863, AN 223 AP 16. This proclamation also was published in *L'estafette*, a French-language Mexican journal. See Manuel Doblado, "Un Manifeste," *L'estafette*, August 3, 1863.

115. Napoleon to Forey, April 14, 1863, and Forey, "Manifeste à la nation mexicaine," June 12, 1863, AN 400 AP 62, dossier 1.

116. "Convention signé à Miramar du 12 mars 1864 et des articles secrets" (1864), AMAE MD Mexique, 10:211–20.

117. Napoleon III to Maximilian, October 2, 1863, in Egon César Comte Corti, *Maximilien et Charlotte du Mexique, 1860–1865* (Paris: Librairie Plon, 1927), 398. French propaganda often pointed to the "fanaticism" of Hernán Cortés and other early Spanish imperialists in their accounts of Mexico's contemporary problems. See Martin, *Précis des événements de la campagne du Mexique*, 94; *L'empereur du Mexique* (Paris: E. Dentu, 1864); A. Malespine, *Solution de la question mexicaine* (Paris: E. Dentu 1864), 7; Chevalier, *Le Mexique*, 555; *La question du Mexique au point de vue providentiel*, 18

118. Shawcross, *France, Mexico, and Informal Empire*, 194; Pani, "Juárez vs. Maximiliano," 179.

119. Pelagio Antonio de Labastido, "Lettre pastorale," October 8, 1863, AMAE CP Mexique, 60:334–37; Felipe Raygosa, "Protestation des Évêques," December 21 and 26, 1863, and Tribunal suprême de Justice de l'Empire, "Protestation," December 30, 1863, SHD, Vincennes, GR7 G1.

120. Forey, "Manifeste à la nation mexicaine," June 12, 1863, AN 400 AP 62, dossier 1; "Revue de Mois," *L'estafette*, September 17, 1863, AMAE CP Mexique, 60:414–15. This theme also appeared in Maximilian's proclamations. See Maximilian, "Mexicains!," May 22, 1864, SHD, Vincennes, GR7 G1.

121. Domenech, *L'empire au Mexique*, 129; Lacombe, *Le Mexique*, 66.

122. Eugène Lefèvre, *Le Mexique et l'intervention européen* (Mexico: I. Cumplido, 1862), 423; Edgar Quinet, *L'expédition du Mexique* (London: W. Jeffs & Ghisletti, 1862), 12; Malespine, *Solution de la question mexicaine*, 27; Léonce Détroyat, *L'intervention française au Mexique* (Paris: Amyot, 1868), iii.

123. *La question mexicaine et la colonisation* (Paris : E. Dentu, 1864), 17. See also Lucien Biart, *Le Mexique d'hier et le Mexique de demain* (Paris : E. Dentu, 1865), 2; Lacombe, *Le Mexique*, 4; Barker, "Monarchy in Mexico," 55; Black, "Napoleon III and European Colonization in Mexico," 135.

124. *La question mexicaine et la colonisation*, 27, 29.

125. Adolphe de Belleyme, *La France et le Mexique* (Paris: Dentu, 1863), 20. The Corps législatif, or Legislative Body, was the lower house of the French legislature during the Second Empire.

126. Gasparin, *L'Amérique devant l'Europe*, 422.

127. Henry Moreau, *La politique française en Amérique* (Paris: E. Dentu, 1864), 157; "Le Ministère public et le barreau," *Œuvres de Berryer: Plaidoyers*, vol. 4 (Paris: Émile Perrin, 1885), 439. See also Malespine, *Solution de la question mexicaine*, 15.

128. Gaël Nofri, *Napoleon III, Visionnaire de l'Europe des Nations* (Paris: Éditions François-Xavier de Guibert, 2010), 378; Napoleon III, "Discours d'Ouverture de

la Session Législative de 1868," in *Oeuvres de Napoleon III* (Paris: Henri Plon et Amyot, 1869), 5:298.

129. Rey-Goldzeiguer, *Le Royaume Arabe*, 128.

130. John Ruedy, *Modern Algeria: The Origins and Development of a Nation*, 2nd ed. (Bloomington: Indiana University Press, 2005), 68.

131. Sessions, *By Sword and Plow*, 179. See also Sankar Muthu, *Enlightenment against Empire* (Princeton, NJ: Princeton University Press, 2003); Pitts, *Turn to Empire*; Dino Costantino, *Mission civilisatrice: Le rôle de l'histoire coloniale dans la construction de l'identité politique française* (Paris: La Découverte, 2008).

132. Jennifer Pitts, "Republicanism, Liberalism, and Empire in Postrevolutionary France," in *Empire and Modern Political Thought*, ed. Sankar Muthu (New York: Cambridge University Press, 2012), 267–70.

133. Sessions, *By Sword and Plow*, 185–201.

134. Brower, *Desert Named Peace*, 11.

135. Judith Surkis, *Sex, Law, and Sovereignty in French Algeria, 1830–1930* (Ithaca, NY: Cornell University Press, 2019), 30.

136. Sessions, *By Sword and Plow*, 206.

137. Brower, *Desert Named Peace*, 21.

138. Surkis, *Sex, Law, and Sovereignty*, 19.

139. James McDougall, *A History of Algeria* (New York: Cambridge University Press, 2017), 74.

140. Ruedy, *Algeria*, 51.

141. For detailed accounts of these debates, see Lorcin, *Imperial Identities*; Abi-Mershed, *Apostles of Modernity*; and Surkis, *Sex, Law, and Sovereignty*.

142. Abi-Mershed, *Apostles of Modernity*, 160.

143. Lorcin, *Imperial Identities*, 20, 51, 55, 104, 157.

144. Levallois, *Ismaÿl Urbain: Royaume arabe?*, 230.

145. Miranda Spieler, *Empire and Underworld: Captivity in French Guiana* (Cambridge, MA: Harvard University Press, 2012), 43.

146. Officers of the bureaux arabes were usually versed in local languages and customs. In territory inhabited by both colonists and tribes, they were supposed to ensure order and security. As a rule, they were subject to little state regulation. This lack of regulation could lead to abuse, as many colonists claimed. See Abi-Mershed, *Apostles of Modernity*, 77–95.

147. Ian Coller, *Arab France: Islam and the Making of Modern Europe, 1798–1831* (Berkeley: University of California Press, 2011), 197; Naomi Davidson, *Only Muslim: Embodying Islam in Twentieth-Century France* (Ithaca, NY: Cornell University Press, 2012), 3.

148. Michel Levallois, *Ismaÿl Urbain: Une autre conquête de l'Algérie* (Paris: Maisonneuve & Larose, 2001), 1: 634.

149. Abi-Mershed, *Apostles of Modernity*, 9.

150. Michel Levallois, "Essai de typologie des orientalistes saint-simoniens," in *L'orientalisme des Saint-Simoniens*, ed. Michel Levallois, Sarga Moussa, Emile Temime, and Patrice Bret (Paris: Maisonneuve & Larose, 2006), 94–96.

151. Surkis, *Sex, Law, and Sovereignty*, 65.

152. Pamela Pilbeam, *Saint-Simonians in Nineteenth-Century France: From Free Love to Algeria* (New York: Palgrave Macmillan, 2014), 155.

153. McDougall, *History of Algeria*, 154.

154. Levallois, *Ismaÿl Urbain: Royaume arabe?*, 233.

155. Abi-Mershed, *Apostles of Modernity*, 32.

156. Rey-Goldzeiguer, *Le royaume arabe*, 124–26; Stacey Renee Davis, "Turning French Convicts into Colonists: The Second Empire's Political Prisoners in Algeria, 1852–1858," *French Colonial History* 2 (2002): 100.

157. Pervillé, *La France en Algérie*, 46.

158. McDougall, *History of Algeria*, 118.

159. Rey-Goldzeiguer, *Le royaume arabe*, 78.

160. Georges Spillman, *Napoleon III et le royaume arabe*. (Paris: Académie des sciences d'outre-mer, 1975), 16.

161. In 1851 Napoleon III, then president of the Second Republic, issued a plebiscite asking whether the French wanted him to declare himself emperor. In metropolitan France, more than 80 percent answered "yes," while in Algeria barely 50 percent of the population agreed. See Rey-Goldzeiguer, *Le royaume arabe*, 123.

162. Charles-Robert Ageron, *Histoire de l'Algérie contemporaine, 1830–1988* (Paris: PUF, 1990), 27.

163. Ruedy, *Modern Algeria*, 71.

164. Kimberly Bowler, "'It Is Not in a Day That a Man Abandons His Morals and Habits': The Arab Bureau, Land Policy, and the Doineau Trial in French Algeria, 1830–1870" (PhD diss., Duke University, 2011).

165. Spillman, *Napoleon III et le royaume arabe*, 19; Pervillé, *La France en Algérie*, 52.

166. McDougall, *History of Algeria*, 77–93.

167. *Grâce d'Abd el-Kader, accordée par le prince Louis-Napoléon, dans la visite qu'il lui fit au château d'Amboise* (Paris: Chassaignon, 1852); Abd el Kader, *Lettre aux français* (Paris: Éditions Phébus, 1977, 2007), 199.

168. Smaïl Aouli, Ramdane Redjala, and Philippe Zoummeroff, *Abd el Kader* (Paris: Fayard, 1994), 430–33.

169. "Lettre d'Abd el Kader" (1852), AN AB XIX 3630, dossier 2; "Lettres d'Abd el Kader" (1855 and 1858), AN 192/MI.

170. Auguste Dupont, *La clémence impériale et l'émir Abd-el-Kader* (Paris: Bailly, 1852); "Abd el-Kader," *Le moniteur universel*, October 1, 1852; "Détails sur la captivité d'Abd-el-Kader," *L'écho rochelais*, October 26, 1852; "Abd el-Kader à Paris," *La gazette de France*, October 31, 1852; "Abd el-Kader," *Le moniteur universel*, October 31, 1852; "Abd el-Kader," *Le gazette de France*, November 1, 1852; "Entrevue Abd-el-Kader," *Le pays*, November 1, 1852; "Abd-el-Kader," *La presse*, November 1, 1852; Henry Cauvin, "L'Émir Abd-el-Kader," *Le constitutionnel*, November 2, 1852; "Séjour d'Abd-el-Kader à Paris," *Le journal des villes et des campagnes*, November 3, 1852; "Paris," *Le journal des débats politiques et littéraires*, November 4, 1852, 1; "Abd el-Kader à Paris," *Le courrier de Saône-et-Loire*, November 6, 1852; Eugène de Civry, *Napoléon III et Abd-el-Kader, Charlemagne et Witikind* (Paris: P. Martinon, 1853); Eugène Vayssettes, *Trois mois sous la tente et régénération du peuple arabe par l'instruction* (Alger: Bourget, 1859), 29. Some newspapers objected to this portrayal of Abd el-Kader, contending that he was uncivilized because he had multiple wives. See "La cinquième femme d'Abd-el-Kader," *L'Argus des théâtres*, April 30, 1852.

171. "L'émir Abd-el-Kader," *Le moniteur universel*, November 23, 1852; "Corps législatif, procès-verbal de la séance du mardi 30 novembre 1852," *Le moniteur universel*, December 2, 1852.

172. Albert Hourani, *Arabic Thought in the Liberal Age, 1798–1939* (Cambridge: Cambridge University Press, 1983), 63.

173. Fawaz, *Occasion for War*, 90, 97.

174. Fawaz, *Occasion for War*, 94–99.

175. "Affaires de Syrie," *Le constitutionnel*, July 31, 1860; L. Alloury, "France," *Le journal des débats politiques et littéraires*, August 2, 1860; "Affaires de Syrie," *Le constitutionnel*, August 4, 1860; "Nouvelles étrangères," *Le moniteur universel*, August 4, 1860; Maxime Vauvert, "Abd el-Kader," *Le monde illustré*, August 4, 1860; "Chronique Général," *Le courrier de Bourges*, August 8, 1860; Mangin, "Syrie," *Le phare de la Loire*, August 1, 1860; Jules Lecomte, "Courrier de Paris," *Le monde illustré*, September 1, 1860.

176. "Bulletin Politique," *Journal de la ville de Saint-Quentin et de l'arrondissement*, July 22, 1860; J. Mahias, "Beyrouth," *La presse*, July 27, 1860; *Le courrier de Saône-et-Loire*, August 8, 1860; *Mémorial de la Loire et de la Haute-Loire*, August 9, 1860.

177. F. Camus, "La dépêche de Beyrouth," *Le journal des débats politiques et littéraires*, July 19, 1860. See also "Bulletin du jour," *La presse*, August 6, 1860.

178. Charles-Robert Ageron, "Une mythe politique français: Abd-el-Kader souverain d'un 'royaume arabe' d'Orient," *Genèse de l'Algérie algérienne* (Paris: Éditions Bouchène, 2005), 41.

179. *Abd-el-Kader: Empereur d'Arabie* (Paris: E. Dentu, 1860)

180. Ageron, "Une mythe politique français," 47.

181. "Affaires de Syrie," *Le constitutionnel*, July 21, 1860; "Paris," *Le sémaphore de Marseille*, July 22, 1860; Félix Ribeyre, "Bulletin politique," *Le journal de la ville de Saint-Quentin et de l'arrondissement*, July 27, 1860; L. Pieaud, "Nouvelles de Syrie," *Mémorial de la Loire et de la Haute-Loire*, July 27, 1860; Georges Zimmer, "Affaires de Syrie," *Le constitutionnel*, August 11, 1860; A. Barlatier, "Correspondance particulière du Sémaphore," *Le sémaphore de Marseille*, August 12, 1860; Jules Duval, "Au moment," *Le journal des débats*, August 23, 1860.

182. Ageron, "Une mythe politique français," 41.

183. "Partie officielle," *Le moniteur universel*, August 6, 1860.

184. Arsan, "There Is, in the Heart of Asia," 82–87, 92.

185. Fawaz, *Occasion for War*, 113–15.

186. Levallois, "Essai de typologie," 106.

187. *Voyage de leurs majestés en Algérie, Septembre 1860* (Paris: Au Bureau de l'illustration, 1860), 15.

188. Levallois, *Ismaÿl Urbain: Royaume arabe?*, 244.

189. Robert Aldrich, "French Imperial Tours: Napoléon III and Eugénie in Algeria and Beyond," *Royals on Tour: Politics, Pageantry and Colonialism* (Manchester University Press, 2018), 38–55.

190. ANOM, Aix-en-Provence, ALG GGA/1I85.

191. Abi-Mershed, *Apostles of Modernity*, 166.

192. "Convocation à Paris de chefs indigènes," ANOM F80 1678; Rey-Goldzeiguer, *Le royaume arabe*, 183.

193. Abi-Mershed, *Apostles of Modernity*, 162, 166.

194. See Michel Levallois's comprehensive accounts of Ismaël Urbain's life and work, *Ismaÿl Urbain: Une autre conquête de l'Algérie* and *Ismaÿl Urbain: Royaume arabe ou Algérie franco-musulmane?*

195. Levallois, *Ismaÿl Urbain: Une autre conquête*, 212.

196. Abi-Mershed, *Apostles of Modernity*, 15.

197. Ahmed Bouyerdene, "Abd el-Kader et Ismaÿl Urbain, deux voies convergentes?," in *Les Saint-Simoniens dans l'Algérie du XIXe siècle*, ed. Michel Levallois and Philippe Régnier (Paris: Riveneuve éditions, 2014), 217.

198. Levallois, *Ismaÿl Urbain: Royaume arabe?*, 225.

199. Ismaël Urbain, *L'Algérie pour les algériens* (Paris: Michel Lévy Frères, 1861); Ismaël Urbain, *L'Algérie française: Indigènes et immigrants* (Paris: Challamel Aîné, 1862).

200. Urbain, *L'Algérie française*, 10.

201. Levallois, *Ismaÿl Urbain: Royaume arabe?*, 364.

202. Napoleon III to Pélissier, February 6, 1863, in *La politique impériale*, 391, 393.

203. Napoleon III to Pélissier, February 6, 1863, 394.

204. This definition of "colony" was common in the 1860s; it was shared by champion of "association" Ismaël Urbain and Jules Duval, an assimilationist who opposed the royaume arabe. See Levallois, *Ismaÿl Urbain: Royaume arabe?*, 323, and Jules Duval, *Les colonies et la politique coloniale de la France* (Paris: Arthus Bertrand, 1854), v.

205. Saint-Félix, *Le voyage*, 110.

206. Saint-Félix, *Le voyage*, 110.

207. Napoleon III to Pélissier, February 6, 1863, in *La politique impériale*, 394.

208. Napoleon III to Pélissier, February 6, 1863, 394.

209. Napoleon III, *Les idées napoléoniennes*, 70; Echard, *Napoleon III and the Concert of Europe*, 163.

210. "Proclamation aux habitants de l'Algérie" May 3, 1865, in *La politique impériale*, 436.

211. Saint-Félix, *Le voyage*, 110.

212. Abi-Mershed, *Apostles of Modernity*, 31.

213. Algeria was inhabited by a diverse set of people who did not all identify as Arab—as even Napoleon III's supporters acknowledged. But French attempts to classify indigenous peoples mostly reflected European norms and ideas about "the Orient." See Lorcin, *Imperial Identities*, 17.

214. David Prochaska, *Making Algeria French: Colonialism in Bône, 1870–1920* (New York: Cambridge University Press, 1990), 85–86.

215. Rey-Goldzeiguer, *Le royaume arabe*, 123, 189; Pierre Darmon, *Un siècle de passions algériennes: Une histoire de l'Algérie coloniale* (Paris: Fayard, 2009), 268.

216. Didier Guignard, "Le Senate de 1863: La dislocation programmée de la société rurale algérienne," in *Histoire de l'Algérie à la période coloniale*, ed. Abderrahmane Bouchène et al. (Paris: La Découverte, 2012), 77; Lorcin, *Imperial Identities*, 77. A *sénatus-consulte* was an act by the Senate with the force of law behind it.

217. Jean-Jacques Pélissier, "Rapport à l'empereur," ANOM ALG GGA/1EE26; Urbain to Lacroix, February 21, 1863, in Levallois, *Ismaÿl Urbain: Royaume arabe?*, 371.

218. As quoted in Charles Ageron, *Politiques coloniales au Maghreb* (Paris: Presses universitaires de France, 1972), 63. See also "Lettre de l'empereur," *L'indépendant de Constantine*, February 17, 1863.

219. *Le courrier d'Algérie*, February 13, 1863. *La Gironde*, a republican newspaper in Bordeaux, repeated the claim. See *La Gironde*, February 23, 1863; *La presse*, February 24, 1863.

220. Marcel Lucet, *Colonisation européenne en Algérie: Légitime défense* (Constantine and Paris: Challamel aîné 1863), 5, 11; Réméon Pescheux, *Réfutation algérienne: Vive l'Algérie! malgré la brochure "Indigènes et immigrants"* (Constantine and Paris: Challamel, 1863), 5; Jules Vinet, *La crise algérienne: Quelques mots sur la colonisation* (Paris: E. Dentu, 1863), 3.

221. Levallois, "Essai de typologie," 97, 106.

222. Auguste-Hubert Warnier, *L'Algérie devant l'empereur* (Paris: Challamel aîné, 1865), 4–18; 289. See also Louis de Baudicour, *Histoire de la colonisation de l'Algérie* (Paris: Challamel, 1860), 492, and Henry Didier, *Le gouvernement militaire et la colonisation en Algérie* (Paris: E. Dentu, 1865), 15, 17.

223. Levallois, *Ismaÿl Urbain: Royaume arabe?*, 369; Lorcin, *Imperial Identities*, 96.

224. *L'Algérie devant le budget* (Paris: Dentu, 1868), 6, 44; Auguste-Hubert Warnier, *L'Algérie devant le Sénat, indigènes et immigrants* (Paris: Dubuisson, 1863), 4; Vinet, *La crise algérienne*, 5.

225. Gavin Murray-Miller, "Imagining the Trans-Mediterranean Republic: Algeria, Republicanism, and the Ideological Origins of the French Imperial Nation-State," *French Historical Studies* 37, no. 2 (2014): 327–28.

226. *La presse*, February 16, 1863; Abi-Mershed, *Apostles of Modernity*, 170. Fourierism was an early utopian socialist movement.

227. Frédéric Lacroix, *L'Algérie et la lettre de l'Empereur* (Paris: Challamel, 1863), iv, 3, 7, 10–12.

228. Lacroix, *L'Algérie et la lettre*, 43.

229. Urbain to Lacroix, February 14, 1863, as quoted in Levallois, *Ismaÿl Urbain: Royaume Arabe?*, 366.

230. Rey-Goldzeiguer, *Le royaume arabe*, 251–52.

231. "Résumé politique des évènements survenus depuis le 18 mars jusqu'au 15 juin, 1864," ANOM, F80 1679

232. "Rapport à sa Majesté l'Empereur," March 3, 1863, ANOM, ALG GGA/11H33.

233. Rey-Goldzeiguer, *Le royaume arabe*, 253–60.

234. Abi-Mershed, *Apostles of Modernity*, 180.

235. Napoleon III, *Politique de la France en Algérie* (Paris: Imprimerie impériale, 1865), 1.

236. He referred to them as "this warlike, intelligent, and mobile nation." See Napoleon III, *Politique de la France*, 2.

237. Napoleon III, *Politique de la France*, 3.

238. Napoleon III, *Politique de la France*, 22, 24–25, 37–39.

239. Joseph Guérin, *L'akhbar*, November 9, 1864; Warnier, *L'Algérie devant l'empereur*. Guérin launched a campaign against the letter in *L'akhbar*, which was one

of the most prominent newspapers in Algeria. See Levallois, *Ismaÿl Urbain: Royaume arabe?*, 598–99.

240. Marquis de Laborde de Montpézat, *De la domination française en Algérie* (Paris: Henri Plon, 1865); Luc-Pierre Riche-Gardon, *Devoir et droit providentielle des peuples: Le peuple arabe peut-il être français?* (Paris: L. P. Riche-Gardon, 1865); Didier, *Le gouvernement militaire et la colonisation en Algérie*; Alexandre Duvernois, *Le régime civil en Algérie, urgence et possibilité de son application immédiate* (Paris: J. Rouvier, 1865).

241. Émile Cardon, "L'Émir Abd-el-Kader," *Le Figaro*, July 9, 1865; H.-Marie Martin, "Abd-el-Kader," *Le constitutionnel*, July 12, 1865; Mangin, "Courrier de Paris," *Le phare de la Loire*, July 20, 1865; Gustave Bertrand, "Semaine théâtrale," *Le ménestrel*, July 23, 1865; L. Dutailly, "Une soirée avec Abd-el-Kader," *La France*, July 28, 1865; Léo de Bernard, "Abd-el-Kader au musée d'artillerie," *Le monde illustré*, July 29, 1865; "Abd-el-Kader à Paris," *Journal de Montélimar*, July 29, 1865.

242. Clyde Thogmartin, *The National Daily Press of France* (Birmingham, AL: Summa Publications, 1998), 53.

243. Émile de Girardin, "La paix partout, la paix toujours," *La presse*, July 23, 1865.

244. Alexander Dartigue, "Revue des journaux," *Le sémaphore de Marseille*, April 25, 1865; *La gazette de France*, May 2, 1865; A. Barlatier, "Algérie," *Le sémaphore de Marseille*, May 2, 1865; "Bulletin du jour," *Le temps*, May 8, 1865; Jules Duval, "Dissolution fatale de la Société arabe," *L'économiste française*, August 10, 1865. See also Levallois, *Ismaÿl Urbain: Royaume arabe?*, 575–77.

245. Ageron, "Une mythe politique français," 52–53.

246. Rey-Goldzeiguer, *Le royaume arabe*, 401.

247. Luis Ballesteros, *L'Émir Abd-el-Kader et l'Algérie* (Paris: Retaux frères, 1865).

248. Rey-Goldzeiguer, *Le royaume arabe*, 399.

249. Jules Duval, *Réflexions sur la politique de l'empereur en Algérie* (Paris: Challamel aîné, 1866), 13, 29, 30, 96.

250. Duval, *Réflexions sur la politique*, 172.

251. Duval, *Réflexions sur la politique*, 170. See also Vinet, *La crise algérienne*, 3; Arsène Vacherot, "L'Algérie sous l'empire: Les indigènes et la colonisation," *La revue des deux mondes* 81 (September 1869): 189. These authors were drawing on common liberal beliefs about the operations of settler colonies. See Pitts, *Turn to Empire*, 17.

252. Judith Surkis, "Propriété, polygamie et statut personnel en Algérie coloniale, 1830–1873," *La revue d'histoire du XIXe siècle* 41 (2010): 29.

253. It echoed ideas that appeared in Urbain's publications. See Urbain, *L'Algérie française*, 6–10.

254. Laure Blévis, "La citoyenneté française au miroir de la colonisation: Étude des demandes de naturalisation des 'sujets français' en Algérie coloniale," *Genèses* 53 (2003–4): 28, and "Naturalisation ou citoyenneté: Les ambiguïtés du sénatus-consulte de 1865," in *Les Saint-Simoniens dans l'Algérie du XIXe siècle: Le combat du français musulman Ismaÿl Urbain*, ed. Michel Levallois and Philippe Régnier (Paris: Riveneuve éditions, 2016), 283.

255. Surkis, *Sex, Law, and Sovereignty*, 56.

256. Patrick Weil, *How to Be French: Nationality in the Making since 1789* (Durham, NC: Duke University Press, 2008), 217.

257. Kamel Kateb, *Européens, 'indigènes' et juifs en Algérie (1830–1962): Représentations et réalités des populations* (Paris: INED, 2001), 58.

258. Rey-Goldzeiguer, *Le royaume arabe*, 545.

259. Abi-Mershed, *Apostles of Modernity*, 197.

260. Shawcross, *France, Mexico, and Informal Empire*, 14.

2. Redefining Republic and Empire in France after 1870–71

1. Bertrand Taithe, *Citizenship and Wars: France in Turmoil, 1870–1871* (New York: Psychology Press, 2001), 172.

2. An 1896 bibliography of all the novels, histories, and memoirs published after the war came to over six hundred pages. See Barthélémy-Edmond Palat, *Bibliographie générale de la guerre de 1870–1871* (Paris: Berger-Levrault, 1896).

3. Catharine Savage Brosman, *Visions of War in France: Fiction, Art, Ideology* (Baton Rouge: Louisiana State University Press, 1999); Michele Martin, *Images at War: Illustrated Periodicals and Constructed Nations* (Toronto: University of Toronto Press, 2006); Karine Varley, *Under the Shadow of Defeat: The War of 1870–71 in French Memory* (New York: Palgrave Macmillan, 2008).

4. Roger Price, *The French Second Empire: An Anatomy of Political Power* (New York: Cambridge University Press, 2001), 348, 383.

5. Napoleon III, "Proclamation de l'empereur aux Français à l'occasion du plébiscite," April 13, 1870, *Archives diplomatiques: Recueil de diplomatie et d'histoire*, vol. 1 (Paris: Amyot, 1870), 418.

6. Price, *French Second Empire*, 397.

7. Napoleon III, "Proclamation de l'empereur," 418.

8. Quintin Barry, *The Franco-Prussian War, 1870–71*, vol. 1 (Solihull, UK: Helion, 2007), 17.

9. Eugène Dufeuille, "France," *Le journal des débats politiques et littéraires*, July 17, 1870; "Corps Législatif," *Le Figaro*, July 17, 1870.

10. Geoffrey Wawro, *The Franco-Prussian War: The German Conquest of France in 1870–1871* (New York: Cambridge University Press, 2003), 136.

11. William Smith, *The Second Empire and the Commune: France, 1848–1871* (London: Longman, 1996), 59.

12. Price, *French Second Empire*, 394.

13. Taithe, *Citizenship and Wars*, 10; Alan Forrest, *The Legacy of the French Revolutionary Wars* (Durham, NC: Duke University Press, 1989).

14. Peter Starr, *Commemorating Trauma: The Paris Commune and Its Cultural Aftermath* (New York: Fordham University Press, 2006), 19.

15. Taithe, *Citizenship and Wars*, 172.

16. David A. Shafer, *The Paris Commune: French Politics, Culture, and Society at the Crossroads of the Revolutionary Tradition and Revolutionary Socialism* (London: Palgrave, 2005).

17. Philip Nord, *The Republican Moment: Struggles for Democracy in Nineteenth-Century France* (Cambridge, MA: Harvard University Press, 1995), 251; Pamela Pilbeam, *Republicanism in Nineteenth-Century France* (London: Macmillan, 1995), 272.

18. Thomas J. Cragin, "The Failings of Popular News Censorship in Nineteenth-Century France," *Book History* 4 (2001): 59.

19. Sudhir Hazareesingh, *From Subject to Citizen: The Second Empire and the Emergence of Modern French Democracy* (Princeton, NJ: Princeton University Press, 1998), 167–68.

20. Martyn Lyons, *Reading Culture and Writing Practices in Nineteenth-Century France* (Toronto: University of Toronto Press, 2008), 48.

21. Paul Baquiast, *La Troisième république, 1870–1940* (Paris: L'Harmattan, 2002), 19.

22. Kevin Passmore, *The Right in France from the Third Republic to Vichy* (New York: Oxford University Press, 2013), 37.

23. Alan Grubb, *The Politics of Pessimism: Albert de Broglie and Conservative Politics in the Early Third Republic* (Newark: University of Delaware Press, 1996), 240.

24. Jérôme Grévy, *La république des opportunistes* (Paris: Perrin, 1998), 24.

25. Alfred de la Guéronnière, *L'homme de Sedan devant l'histoire* (Paris: Chez tous les librairies, 1872), 6.

26. Ludovic Hamon, *Les ennemis du peuple ou les périls de la France: Les voix amies* (Paris: B. Musset, 1872), 72.

27. Renaud d'Allen, *L'empire, la république, la monarchie devant la nation* (Marseille: H. Seren, 1871), 4.

28. D'Allen, *L'empire*, 8.

29. D'Allen, *L'empire*, 14. See also *Napoléon III et la politique contemporaine* (Espira-de-l'Agly: P. Jammet, 1872), 6.

30. Henri de la Broise, *République ou monarchie?* (Laval: Mary-Beauchêne, 1871), vi, 36, 42, 52; C. Cambier, *République, empire ou royauté* (Paris: Victor Palmé, 1871), 7–9, 10, 147; *Monarchie et république* (Lyon and Paris: Félix Girard, 1871), 6; Hamon, *Les ennemis du peuple*; Le Comte le Serrec de Kervily, *La république en France* (Paris: E. Dentu, 1872); A. Labat, *République et monarchie ou le salut de la France* (Paris: A. Hennuyer, 1871), 4.

31. Labat, *République et monarchie*, 9, 11.

32. Grubb, *Politics of Pessimism*, 66.

33. Eugène Spuller, *Histoire de Napoléon III* (Paris: A. le Chevalier, 1872), 23; Émile Dehau, *Napoléon III ou la honte nationale* (Paris: Imprimerie Auguste Vallée, 1871), 35; H. Bellamy, *République ou monarchie* (Angoulême: Imprimerie de T. Maignant, 1871), 11; Achille Eyraud, *République ou monarchie* (Paris: E. Dentu, 1872), 22; Léon Feer, *République et royauté: De la nécessité d'établir le gouvernement de la France sur la base républicaine* (Paris: E. Lachaud, 1871), 8.

34. Jean Pilori, *Gare à l'empire* (Paris : A. Lévy, 1871), 5; Félix Oger, *Les Bonaparte et les frontières de la France* (Paris: Germer-Baillière, 1872), 35.

35. Thomas Grimm, "Le choix des députés," *Le petit journal*, February 4, 1871.

36. Feer, *République et royauté*, 20–21; Auguste Dalichoux, *1871: Les premières phases d'une décadence*, 3rd ed. (Paris: Rue de Seine, 1871), 15; *La république et la monarchie* (Lille: Camille Robbe, 1873), 57; Eugène Bazin, *1870–1871* (Paris: Sauton, 1872), 6; Jean-Baptiste Vitteaut, *À Monsieur Gambetta: Réflexions sur les causes de notre décadence et les conditions essentielles de la démocratie* (Paris: J. Dejussieu, 1872), 7, 19.

37. "Paris.—3 février," *Le siècle*, February 4, 1871.

38. F. Boussenot, *Les légendes politiques et leur influence sur l'imagination du peuple français* (Paris: Librairie d'Amyot, 1872), 27.

39. Ernest Paradis, *Monarchie et république par un paysan* (Paris: André Sagnier, 1873), 27.

40. *République et monarchie* (Paris: E. Lachaud, 1872), 30, 11; *La république et la monarchie*, 44; E. Jourdeuil, *Du césarisme en France* (Paris: Librairie Muzard, 1871), 15, 22, 31; Bazin, *1870–1871*, 133; Eugene Courmeaux, *République ou royauté* (Reims: Chez tous les librairies, 1871), 19, 386; Eyraud, *République ou monarchie*, 44, 79, 119.

41. Albert Osmonville, *Ce que coûte un monarque* (Lyon: Jevai & Bourgeon, 1871), 5; Émile Second, *Histoire de la décadence d'un peuple, 1872–1900*, 2nd ed. (Paris: Librairie André Sagnier, 1873), 141.

42. Raymond d'Aiguy, *Guerre de 1870 et ses conséquences* (Lyon and Paris: Félix Girard, 1871), 57. See also Jourdeuil, *Du césarisme en France*, 5.

43. G. Barthélemy, *Route des Bonapartistes, Légitimistes, et Orléanistes* (Paris: E. Lachaud, 1871), 14; *La république et la monarchie*, 20.

44. Grubb, *Politics of Pessimism*, 130.

45. Édouard Leduc, *Louis-Napoleon Bonaparte: Le dernier empereur* (Paris: Publibook, 2010), 106.

46. Charles Blachier, *Le prince impérial* (Paris: Guérard, 1877), 67.

47. Jean-Claude Lachnitt, *Le prince impérial: Napoléon IV* (Paris: Perrin, 1997), 234, 195.

48. Grubb, *Politics of Pessimism*, 32.

49. Passmore, *Right in France*, 37.

50. Price, *French Second Empire*, 465.

51. The most important of these journals was *L'ordre*, which was managed by Eugène Rouher, one of Napoleon III's advisers, along with *Le pays* (later called *L'autorité)*, which was edited by Paul de Cassagnac, another key supporter. Other journals included *L'estafette*, *Le petit caporal*, *La nation*, *Le droit du peuple*, and *La patrie*. See Lachnitt, *Le prince imperial*, 244.

52. Paul de Cassagnac, *Histoire populaire abrégée de Napoléon III* (Paris: Lauchaud & Burdin, 1874), 70, 75.

53. Albert Duruy, *Comment les empires reviennent* (Paris: E. Lachaud, 1875), 64, 82; Alfred d'Alembert, *Quatrième dynastie: Le bonapartisme—son passé, son avenir* (Paris: E. Lachaud, 1873), 69; F. Derecq, *Les légions napoléoniennes* (Paris: Chez tous les librairies, 1874), 13; A. Chatel, *Électeurs aux urnes! Appel au peuple* (Paris: Typographie Tolmer & Isidor Joseph, 1876), 55; Fernand Giraudeau, *Vingt ans de la despotisme et quatre ans de liberté*, 3rd ed. (Paris: Lauchaud & Burdin, 1874), 124.

54. Constant Perrin, *Pourquoi Napoléon IV* (Paris: E. Dentu, 1873), 9. See also Comte de la Chapelle, *Les représentants de l'appel au peuple* (Paris: Amyot, 1875), 8, 11.

55. Perrin, *Pourquoi Napoléon IV*, 32.

56. Duruy, *Comment les empires reviennent*, 26.

57. Duruy, *Comment les empires reviennent*, 29, 52, 53,

58. Chatel, *Électeurs aux urnes*, 53; *Lettre d'un électeur à un député: De l'appel au peuple, mars 1876* (Paris: E. Lachaud, 1876), 3; Alexandre Bradier, *Les bienfaits d'empire* (Paris: E. Lachaud, 1876), 27; Gustave Cuneo d'Orant, *Le peuple et l'empereur*, 2nd ed. (Paris: E. Lachaud, 1875), 3.

59. Cassagnac, *Histoire populaire abrégée de Napoléon III*, 76; Blachier, *Le prince impérial*, 72.

60. Léonce Dupont, *La majorité du quatrième Napoléon* (Paris: E. Dentu, 1874), 19.

61. Alexis Doinet, *Une mission à Chislehurst* (Bordeaux: Imprimerie Bordelaise, 1873), 15, 6.

62. Giraudeau, *Vingt ans de la despotisme*, 135. See also Doinet, *Une mission à Chislehurst*, 11; Duruy, *Comment les empires reviennent*, 98; and *La déclaration de Chislehurst et ses conséquences logiques* (Versailles: Imprimerie G. Beaugrand & Dax, 1874), 4.

63. Ad Caillé, *Impérialistes et royalistes* (Saint-Maixent: Imprimerie de la Sèvre, 1873), 9; Comte H. de Charency, *Le bonapartisme et la démocratie: Extrait du* Messanger de l'Orne (Aleçon: E. de Boise, 1875), 5; Édouard Boinvilliers, *Les droits et les devoirs de l'impérialiste* (Paris: E. Lachaud, 1875), 30.

64. D'Orant, *Le peuple et l'empereur*, 6.

65. D'Orant, *Le peuple et l'empereur*, 63.

66. *La déclaration de Chislehurst et ses conséquences logiques*, 48.

67. *La majorité du prince impérial et l'appel au peuple, par un conservateur* (Paris: E. Dentu, 1874), 5.

68. *Les doctrines et les faits de l'empire proposés à la méditation des catholiques bonapartistes* (Agen: Imprimerie Demeaux, 1876), 35; *Le parti bonapartiste et ses hommes par un conservateur* (Paris: Librairie André Sagnier, 1875), 7; *Napoléon IV et Henri V*, 2nd ed. (Paris: Chez tous les librairies, 1873), 28.

69. Francis Charmes, "Paris: Mardi 17 mars," *Le journal des débats*, March 18, 1874; Grubb, *Politics of Pessimism*, 198.

70. Édouard Talbot, *Silence! Hommes de décembre, laissez passer la justice de l'histoire*, 3rd ed. (Auch: Imprimerie Charles Lecocq, 1877), 7.

71. *Le dernier empire* (Paris: E. Dentu, 1875), 19. See also Charles Garnier, *Histoire abrégée du dernier empire* (Lyon: Imprimerie Louis Perrin & Martinet, 1875), 12.

72. Louis Herbette, *Bonapartisme et bonapartistes* (Paris: André Sagnier, 1875), 69, 74, 82; Bellamy, *L'empire: Causerie* (Angoulême: Lougel, 1875), 18; Georges Jehan, *Les abus du despotisme* (Paris: Imprimerie Moderne, 1877), 6; Talbot, *Silence!*, 16; Garnier, *Histoire abrégée du dernier empire*, 5.

73. One anonymous writer even poised the Commune as a Bonapartist plot to reinstate the empire. See *Assez de l'empire! II: Les bonapartistes démasqués* (Paris: Le Chevelier, 1875), 29. For other examples of republicans who argued that the Bonapartist party aligned with communists, see Bellamy, *L'empire*, 21; Jules Girard, *Les charlatans de l'appel au peuple* (Paris: Le Chevalier, 1874), 19; Jehan, *Les abus du despotisme*, 10; Garnier, *Histoire abrégée du dernier empire*, 15; Herbette, *Bonapartisme et bonapartistes*, 58. Writers based this argument on the fact that several vocal Communards with communist sympathies had flocked to the Bonapartists after the Commune's destruction. See Passmore, *Right in France*, 40. For examples of socialist or communist pro-Bonapartist writing, see *L'empire et le socialisme* (Paris: Amyot, 1872); Albert Richard and Gaspard Blanc, *L'empire et la France nouvelle: Appel du peuple et de la jeunesse* (Brussels: Victor Devaux, 1872); Yves Guyot, *La vérité sur l'Empire* (Paris: Librairie du suffrage universel, 1875), 4, 21; Aristide Couteaux, *Les traitres* (Paris: Germer-Baillière, 1877), 15.

74. Herbette, *Bonapartisme et bonapartistes*, 13.

75. Herbette, *Bonapartisme et bonapartistes*, 55.

76. Herbette, *Bonapartisme et bonapartistes*, 23. See also André Lefèvre, *Petit histoire de Napoléon I* (Paris: Librairie du suffrage universel, 1875), 31.

77. Henri Béraud, *Comment les bonapartistes pratiquent l'appel au peuple* (Paris: Chez tous les librairies, 1874), 4.

78. Eugène Laffineur, *Constitution et appel au peuple* (Paris: Armand Le Chevalier, 1873), 7.

79. Laffineur, *Constitution et appel*, 11. See also Girard, *Les charlatans de l'appel*, 7.

80. Bellamy, *L'empire*, 7. See also Talbot, *Silence!*, 18.

81. *Assez de l'empire! I: Catéchisme de l'appel au peuple* (Paris: Le Chevalier, 1875), 18.

82. J. Chanaud, *Le premier et le second empire: Simples réflexions d'un ouvrier* (Paris: Libraire universelle de Godet Jeune, 1876), 50; M. George, *Ce que coûte un empire* (Paris: Imprimerie moderne, 1877), 4.

83. Bellamy, *L'empire*, 4.

84. Talbot, *Silence!*, iii.

85. Henri Martin, *Les Napoléon et les frontières de la France* (Paris: Germer-Baillière, 1877), 8, 11. See also Chanaud, *Le premier et le second empire*, 17; *Le dernier empire*, 5, 8, 20.

86. Lefèvre, *Petit histoire de Napoléon I*, 5.

87. Lefèvre, *Petit histoire de Napoléon I*, 29.

88. This argument also appeared in monarchist critiques of Bonapartism. See A. Neptune, *Le temps*, July 16, 1870; Cambier, *République, empire ou royauté*, 19, 20; *Napoléon III et la politique contemporaine*, 149; Herbette, *Bonapartisme et bonapartistes*, 54; *Le parti bonapartiste et ses hommes par un conservateur*, 17; *Le dernier empire* (Paris: E. Dentu, 1875), 32; *Les doctrines et les faits de l'Empire*, 11.

89. Grévy, *La république des opportunistes*, 27.

90. Robert Gildea, *Children of the Revolution: The French, 1799–1914* (New York: Allen Lane, 2008), 250.

91. Victor Hugo, *L'année terrible* (Paris: Michel Lévy Frères, 1872); Erckmann-Chatrian, *Histoire du plébiscite racontée par un des 7,500,000 oui* (Paris: Hetzel, 1872); Alphonse Daudet, "Les fées de France," "La mort de chauvin," "La partie de billard," "La défense de Tarascon," "La dernière classe," "Paysage d'insurrection," and "L'enfant espion," in *Œuvres complètes illustrées*, vols. 3–4 (Paris: Libraire de France, 1931); Émile Zola, *Son Excellence Eugène Rougon*, in *Œuvres complètes: La république en marche*, vol. 7, ed. Henri Mitterand (Paris: Nouvelle Monde Éditions, 2003).

92. Taithe, *Citizenship and Wars*, 172.

93. Sankar Muthu, *Enlightenment against Empire* (Princeton, NJ: Princeton University Press, 2003), 9; Jennifer Pitts, "Republicanism, Liberalism, and Empire in Postrevolutionary France," in *Empire and Modern Political Thought*, ed. Sankar Muthu (New York: Cambridge University Press, 2012), 272.

94. Jennifer Pitts, *A Turn to Empire: The Rise of Imperial Liberalism in Britain and France* (Princeton, NJ: Princeton University Press, 2005), 240.

3. Creating a Republican Algeria

1. Alphonse Daudet, *Le nabab: Mœurs parisiennes*, 26th ed. (Paris: C. Charpentier, 1878), 61, 228, 353.

2. Daudet, *Le nabab*, 131.

3. Daudet, *Le nabab*, 313.

4. Roger Price, *The French Second Empire: An Anatomy of Political Power* (New York: Cambridge University Press, 2001), 465.

5. Daudet, *Le nabab*, 433.

6. Napoleon III, "Lettre," in *La politique impériale exposée par les discours et proclamations de l'empereur Napoléon III* (Paris: Henri Plon, 1868), 394.

7. Annie Rey-Goldzeiguer, *Le royaume arabe: La politique algérienne de Napoléon III, 1861–1870* (Alger: Société nationale d'édition et de diffusion, 1977), 659.

8. "Procès-verbaux de la Commission chargée d'élaborer le Projet de Constitution de l'Algérie," in Commission de la Constitution de l'Algérie, 1867–1870, ANOM F80 2041: 4–10; Michel Levallois, *Ismaÿl Urbain: Royaume arabe ou Algérie franco-musulmane?; 1848–1870* (Paris: Riveneuve éditions, 2012), 778.

9. Rey-Goldzeiguer, *Le royaume arabe*, 663.

10. Osama W. Abi-Mershed, *Apostles of Modernity: Saint-Simonians and the Civilizing Mission in Algeria* (Stanford, CA: Stanford University Press, 2010), 160.

11. Guy Perville, *La France en Algérie, 1830–1954* (Paris: Vendémiaire, 2012), 59.

12. As quoted in Daniel Rivet, "Le rêve arabe de Napoléon III," in *L'Algérie des Français*, ed. Charles-Robert Ageron (Paris: Seuil, 1993), 65.

13. Levallois, *Ismaÿl Urbain: Royaume arabe?*, 804; Price, *French Second Empire*, 397.

14. David Proschaska, *Making Algeria French: Colonialism in Bône, 1870–1920* (New York: Cambridge University Press, 1990), 183–84; Perville, *La France en Algérie*, 61; Patricia Lorcin, *Imperial Identities: Stereotyping, Prejudice, and Race in Colonial Algeria* (New York: I. B. Tauris, 1995), 7.

15. Raymond Betts, *Assimilation and Association in French Colonial Theory, 1890–1914* (Lincoln: University of Nebraska Press, 2005); Abi-Mershed, *Apostles of Modernity*, 9; Jennifer Pitts, "Republicanism, Liberalism, and Empire in Postrevolutionary France," in *Empire and Modern Political Thought*, ed. Sankar Muthu (New York: Cambridge University Press, 2012), 263.

16. Thomas J. Cragin, "The Failings of Popular News Censorship in Nineteenth-Century France," *Book History* 4 (2001): 59.

17. Clyde Thogmartin, *The National Daily Press of France* (Birmingham, AL: Summa Publications, 1998), 55.

18. Arthur Asseraf, *Electric News in Colonial Algeria* (New York: Oxford University Press, 2019), 57–60.

19. Bertrand Taithe, *Citizenship and Wars: France in Turmoil, 1870–1871* (New York: Psychology Press, 2001), 172.

20. Warnier became the prefect of Algiers, Marcel Lucet the prefect of Constantine, and Charles de Bouzet the prefect of Oran. See Pierre Darmon, *Un siècle de passions algériennes: Une histoire de l'Algérie coloniale* (Paris: Fayard, 2009), 259.

21. Marcel Lucet, "Circulaire de le préfet de Constantine aux fonctionnaires placés sous ses ordres," ANOM, F80 1681.

22. A. Lambert, "Aux Algériens," *Le colon*, cited in *L'indépendant de Constantine*, October 6, 1870; John Ruedy, *Modern Algeria: The Origins and Development of a Nation*, 2nd ed. (Bloomington: Indiana University Press, 2005), 76.

23. "République Française: Liberté—Égalité—Fraternité," *Le tell*, October 1, 1870.

24. Ruedy, *Modern Algeria*, 76.

25. Charles-André Julien, *Histoire de l'Algérie contemporaine*, 3rd ed. (Paris: PUF, 1986), 457.

26. "Décret du 24 octobre 1870," in *Bulletin officiel du gouvernement générale d'Algérie* (Algiers: Bouyer, 1871), 331–33.

27. "Nouvelles de la province et de l'étranger," *Le gaulois*, November 3, 1870.

28. "Actes officiels," *Le petit journal*, November 3, 1870. French administrators claimed that citizenship would enable Algerian Jews to assimilate into the French nation just as, they argued, citizenship had led to Jewish assimilation in metropolitan France. At the same time, they claimed that Muslims were incapable of assimilating in the same way. See Joshua Schreier, *Arabs of the Jewish Faith: The Civilizing Mission in Colonial Algeria* (New Brunswick, NJ: Rutgers University Press, 2010), 174, and Naomi Davidson, *Only Muslim: Embodying Islam in Twentieth-Century France* (Ithaca, NY: Cornell University Press, 2012), 26.

29. Juillet St-Lacer, "Les Israélites algériennes et le décret du 24 octobre," *La solidarité d'Alger*, March 11, 1871; Samuel Kalman, *French Colonial Fascism: The Extreme Right in Algeria, 1919–1939* (New York: Palgrave Macmillan, 2013), 4.

30. Romuald Vuillermoz to the minister of the interior in Tours, *Annales de l'Assemblée nationale: Compte-rendu in extenso des séances, annexes; Enquête sur les actes du gouvernement de la défense nationale*, vol. 26 (Paris: Journal-officiel, 1875), 498; Julien, *Histoire de l'Algérie contemporaine*, 458.

31. Vuillermoz was an Algerian lawyer who had been deported from France in 1851 by Napoleon III. See Claude Martin, *La commune d'Alger* (Paris: Éditions Heraklès, 1936), 26, and Perville, *La France en Algérie*, 62.

32. "Conseil municipal à ministre de l'intérieur, Tours," October 31, 1870, in *Actes du gouvernement de la défense nationale*, vol. 3 (Paris: Librairie des publications législatives, 1876), 93.

33. "Maire d'Alger à Gambetta, Tours," November 7, 1870, in *Actes du gouvernement*, 97.

34. They asked the other committees of defense in Algeria to send in telegrams approving the decision. See "Arrête," November 8, 1870, in *Actes du gouvernement*, 97. Algerian newspapers also defended it. See "L'Algérie aux Algériens," *L'avenir algérien*, November 11, 1870.

35. "Arrête," November 11, 1870, in *Actes du Gouvernement*, 101; Darmon, *Un siècle de passions algériennes*, 260.

36. Alexandre Lambert, *Le colon*, reprinted in *Le moniteur de l'Algérie*, November 3, 1870, and *Annales de l'Assemblée nationale*, 505. For more information about Lambert, see Levallois, *Ismaÿl Urbain: Royaume arabe*, 369.

37. "Vaux émis dans une réunion de 600 à 700 personnes à Alger," *L'akhbar*, November 13, 1870.

38. Some colonists disagreed with these actions. The prefect of Constantine, Marcel Lucet, condemned Vuillermoz's appointment and his efforts to reorganize the territory. In telegrams and newspapers, he encouraged the mayors of Constantine's cities to do the same. See "Préfet à maires du département," November 10, 1870, in *Actes du gouvernement*, 103. This statement was later printed in Constantine's newspapers. Several towns sent telegrams to the interim government professing

their loyalty. See "Conseil municipal de Bône à Gouvernement, Tours," November 9, 1870, in *Actes du gouvernement*, 105. Even some settlers who disapproved of the Crémieux decrees condemned the Algiers government. See "Le conflit algérien," *L'indépendant de Constantine*, November 15, 1870.

39. "Gouvernement de Tours à maire d'Alger," November 10, 1870, in *Actes du gouvernement*, 106.

40. Charles-Robert Ageron, *Histoire de l'Algérie contemporaine, 1830–1988* (Paris: PUF, 1990), 38.

41. "Décret," November 18, 1870, in *Actes du gouvernement*, 114.

42. Crémieux, "Bordeaux, 1 janvier 1871," ANOM, F80 1862; Ruedy, *Modern Algeria*, 76; *Actes du gouvernement*, 348.

43. Martin, *La commune d'Alger*, 78; Perville, *La France en Algérie*, 62.

44. *Le colon*, December 8, 1871, reprinted in *Le moniteur de l'Algérie*, December 9, 1871, and *Annales de l'Assemblée nationale*, 422; *L'indépendant de Constantine*, February 9, 1871; Martin, *La commune d'Alger*, 89.

45. Settler associations followed the Commune, partly because Alexandre Lambert, the Algerian deputy to the National Assembly, participated and published articles about Algeria in the Commune's newspaper. See Alexandre Lambert, "M. Lucet," *Le journal officiel de la république française: Commune de Paris*, April 3, 1871, 136.

46. Darmon, *Un siècle de passions algériennes*, 268.

47. Tahar Oussedik, *Mouvement insurrectionnel de 1871* (Alger: Enag éditions, 2005), 15; Ricardo René Laremont, *Islam and the Politics of Resistance in Algeria, 1783–1992* (Trenton, NJ: Africa World Press, 2000), 40.

48. Lorcin, *Imperial Identities*, 174.

49. Ruedy, *Modern Algeria*, 78.

50. Lorcin, *Imperial Identities*, 177; James McDougall, *A History of Algeria* (New York: Cambridge University Press, 2017), 78.

51. Darmon, *Un siècle de passions algériennes*, 268.

52. Vincent Joly, "Les résistances à la conquête," in *Histoire de l'Algérie à la période coloniale*, ed. Abderrahmane Bouchène et al. (Paris: La Découverte, 2012), 94.

53. Mohammed Brahim Salhi, "L'insurrection de 1871," in *Histoire de l'Algérie à la période coloniale*, 107.

54. Kamel Kateb, *Européens, 'indigènes' et juifs en Algérie (1830–1962): Représentations et réalités des populations* (Paris: INED, 2001), 84.

55. Ruedy, *Modern Algeria*, 76; Salhi, "L'insurrection de 1871," 108.

56. Vice-admiral de Gueydon, "9 Avril 1871," ANOM, F80 1862.

57. Perville, *La France en Algérie*, 64.

58. "18 Avril 1871," n. 138, ANOM, F80 1682.

59. Julien, *Histoire de l'Algérie contemporaine*, 472.

60. Even Constantine's municipal council, which had rejected Vuillermoz, protested. See *L'indépendant de Constantine*, April 3, 1871.

61. Rey-Goldzeiguer, *Le royaume arabe*, 688, 689; Perville, *La France en Algérie*, 63; Ruedy, *Modern Algeria*, 76; Abi-Mershed, *Apostles of Modernity*, 201.

62. Claude Collot, *Les institutions de l'Algérie durant la période coloniale, 1830–1962* (Paris: Éditions du CNRS, 1987), 53–54.

63. McDougall, *History of Algeria*, 126.

64. Judith Surkis, *Sex, Law, and Sovereignty in French Algeria, 1830–1930* (Ithaca, NY: Cornell University Press, 2019), 92.

65. Auguste-Hubert Warnier, *L'Algérie et les victimes de la guerre* (Alger: Imprimerie Duclaux, 1871), 11, 57.

66. Rey-Goldzeiguer, *Le royaume arabe*, 688.

67. Saladin, "Lettres algériennes," *Le petit journal*, April 17, 1871; Saladin, "Algérie: Le drame de Palestro," *Le petit journal*, May 7, 1871.

68. Writers on opposite sides of the political spectrum embraced Islam as a key reason behind the revolt. See *L'Algérie devant l'assemblée nationale: Causes des insurrections algériennes* (Versailles: Muzard, 1871), 6; Paul Fawtier, *L'autonomie algérienne et la république fédérale* (Constantine and Paris: Challamel, 1871), v; A. Ducrot, *La vérité sur l'Algérie* (Paris: E. Dentu, 1871), 14; Ferdinand Cambon, *Aux Algériens: Système de colonisation* (Constantine and Paris: L. Marle & Challamel, 1871), 41; "Insurrection de Palestro," *XIX Siècle*, January 3, 1873; *Les Arabes et la colonisation en Algérie* (Paris: A. Pougin, 1873), 54; and Abi-Mershed, *Apostles of Modernity*, 48.

69. Ducrot, *La vérité sur l'Algérie*; Ducos, *L'Algérie: Quelques mots de réponse à la brochure 'La vérité sur l'Algérie' par le général Ducrot* (Paris: Dunod, 1871); "Algérie," *Le salut publique*, May 13, 1871, and *Le pays*, August 5, 1871, excerpts in ANOM, F80 1862.

70. Perville, *La France en Algérie*, 70.

71. See C. Cambier, *République, empire ou royauté* (Paris: Victor Palmé, 1871), 19, 20; Louis Herbette, *Bonapartisme et bonapartistes* (Paris: André Sagnier, 1875), 54; *Le parti bonapartiste et ses hommes par un conservateur* (Paris: Librairie André Sagnier, 1875), 17; *Les doctrines et les faits de l'empire proposés à la méditation des catholiques bonapartistes* (Agen: Imprimerie Demeaux, 1876), 11; *Le dernier empire* (Paris: E. Dentu, 1875), 32; and *Napoléon III et la politique contemporaine* (Espira-de-l'Agly: P. Jammet, 1872), 149.

72. Even in the mid-1870s, commentators continued to draw this connection. See Charles Roussel, "La justice en Algérie: Les tribunaux indigènes," *Le revue des deux mondes*, August 1, 1876.

73. Eugène Beauvois, *En colonne dans la Grande Kabylie: Souvenirs de l'insurrection de 1871* (Paris: Challamel, 1872), 323.

74. Charles Strauss, *L'assimilation et la reconstitution du Ministère de l'Algérie* (Paris: Chez tous les librairies, 1874), 6.

75. Léon de la Sicotière, "Rapport fait au nom de la commission d'enquête chargée d'examiner les actes du Gouvernement de la Défense nationale (Algérie)," in *Annales de l'Assemblée nationale*, vol. 26, 332–970.

76. Some Bonapartists in France invoked Napoleon III's actions in Algeria and his treatment of indigenous peoples to defend him. See Alexandre Bradier, *Les bienfaits d'empire* (Paris: E. Lachaud, 1876), 30, and Fernand Giraudeau, *Vingt ans de la despotisme et quatre ans de liberté*, 3rd ed. (Paris: Lauchaud & Burdin, 1874), 22.

77. Louis Serre, *Les Arabes martyrs: Étude sur l'insurrection de 1871 en Algérie* (Paris: E. Lachaud, 1873), 8.

78. Serre, *Les Arabes martyrs*, 9.

79. See also Ducrot, *La vérité*, 40; François Leblanc de Prébois, *Bilan du régime civil de l'Algérie à la fin de 1871* (Paris: E. Dentu, 1871), 5.

80. Prébois, *Bilan du régime*, 3.

81. Prébois, *Bilan du régime*, 11, 13. This defense of the military regime also extended into literature. See Ernest Feydeau, *Souna: Mœurs Arabes* (Paris: Ancien Maison Michel Lévy Frères, 1876), 19, 182.

82. Creuzat de Salvière, "L'Insurrection de l'Algérie," *Le gaulois*, August 22, 1871.

83. Salvière, "L'Insurrection de l'Algérie," 2.

84. An anonymous former officer offered a similar argument. See *L'Algérie devant l'Assemblée nationale*, 1.

85. Serre, *Les Arabes martyrs*, 12. See also Roger de Versy, "Le 4 septembre et l'insurrection indigène en Algérie," *La revue de France* (January 1875): 989.

86. Prébois, *Bilan du régime civil*, 5. See also Auguste Lenthéric, "La Guerre en Algérie," *La gazette de France*, August 1, 1871, excerpt in ANOM, F80 1862.

87. Jules Quinemant, *Du peuplement et de la vraie colonisation de l'Algérie* (Constantine: L. Arnolet, 1871), 5.

88. Quinemant, *Du peuplement*, 7.

89. Quinemant, *Du peuplement*, 12.

90. For a similar suggestion, see *Colonisation de l'Algérie par le système du Maréchal Bugeaud* (Algiers: Victor Aillaud, 1871); Surkis, *Sex, Law, and Sovereignty*, 154; and Benjamin Brower, *A Desert Named Peace: The Violence of France's Empire in the Algerian Sahara* (New York: Columbia University Press 2009), 65.

91. Prébois, *Bilan du régime civil*, 5; Salvière, "L'insurrection de l'Algérie," 2.

92. Auguste Lenthéric, "La guerre en Algérie," *La gazette de France*, August 1, 1871, excerpt in ANOM, F80 1862; Auguste Lepage, *Les boutiques d'esprit* (Paris: Théodore Olmer, 1879), 30.

93. Auguste Lenthéric, "Les conseils généraux algériens," *La gazette de France*, November 23, 1872; "L'enquête sur l'Algérie," *La gazette de France*, May 23, 1874.

94. "Alger," *L'akhbar*, September 30, 1871, excerpt in ANOM, F80 1862.

95. *L'Alger française*, May 11, 1871, excerpt in ANOM, F80 1862. See also Victor Basset, "L'insurrection arabe, ses causes et les israélites," *La solidarité*, May 2, 1871, excerpt in AN 47 AP 17; Émile Thuillier, *Le royaume arabe devant le jury de Constantine* (Constantine: A. Robert, 1873), 15.

96. Schreier, *Arabs of the Jewish Faith*, 8.

97. Charles Jourdan, *Le siècle*, August 6, 1871, excerpt in ANOM, F80 1862. This claim appeared in other metropolitan newspapers. See *La république française*, March 13, 1873.

98. Jourdan, *Le siècle*, August 6, 1871.

99. See Fawtier, *L'autonomie algérienne*, vi; Hector France, *L'homme qui tue!* (Brussells: H. Kistemaeckers, 1878), 63, 203, 232; "Lettre d'Algérie," *Le sémaphore de Marseille*, May 13, 1873.

100. "Le royaume arabe," *La république française*, January 23, 1872; "Le royaume arabe," *L'union de Sétif*, February 3, 1872. "Théâtre-Valette," *Le petit marseillais*, June 11, 1872; "Le royaume arabe," *Le petit marseillais*, June 13, 1872.

101. Asseraf, *Electric News in Colonial Algeria*, 52.

102. "Le parti militaire," *Le temps*, October 2, 1871; "Algérie," *Le temps*, December 5, 1871; *La république française*, March 13, 1873.

103. Félix Robiou de la Trehonnais, *L'Algérie en 1871* (Paris: Masson et fils, 1871), 19.

104. Trehonnais, *L'Algérie en 1871*, 21. For a similar argument, see Louis Rinn, *L'Algérie assimilée: Étude sur la constitution et la réorganisation de l'Algérie par un chef de bureau arabe* (Constantine and Paris: Challamel, 1871), 7; "Algérie," *Le constitutionnel*, November 20, 1872; A. Villacrose, *Vingt ans en Algérie* (Paris: Challamel Ainé, 1875), 310.

105. Trehonnais, *L'Algérie en 1871*, 27.

106. Trehonnais, *L'Algérie en 1871*, 44.

107. René de Semallé, *Projet d'organisation de l'Algérie* (Versailles: Dufaure, 1871); Strauss, *L'assimilation*.

108. Semallé, *Projet d'organisation de l'Algérie*, 5; Auguste Pomel, *Les races indigènes de l'Algérie: Arabes, Kabyles, Maures et Juifs; Du rôle que leur réservent leurs aptitudes* (Oran: Veuve Dagorn, 1871); Henri de Senhaux, *La France et l'Algérie* (Paris: Challamel Ainé, 1871); *À Monsieur le Vice-Amiral de Gueydon: La pacification de l'Algérie* (Constantine: Louis Marle, 1871).

109. Trehonnais, *L'Algérie en 1871*; Villacrose, *Vingt ans en Algérie*; G. Bézy, *Notes sur l'Algérie* (Oran: Ch. Pothier, 1879).

110. Bézy, *Notes sur l'Algérie*, 21.

111. Fawtier, *L'autonomie algérienne*; T.-E.-A Juillet Saint-Lager, *France et Algérie: Solutions de quelques-unes des questions à l'ordre de jour* (Alger: Imprimerie de Juillet Saint-Lager, 1871).

112. Henri Verne, *De Bône à Hammam-Meskhoutine: Étude sur la question algérienne* (Lyon: H. Storck, 1869); Fawtier, *L'autonomie algérienne*; Herbette, *Bonapartisme et bonapartistes*, 27.

113. Lorcin, *Imperial Identities*.

114. Fawtier devoted less attention to Algeria's indigenous population, but he maintained that it could also assimilate into the settler community. See Fawtier, *L'autonomie algérienne*, 3.

115. Fawtier, *L'autonomie algérienne*, 6, 15.

116. Diana Davis, *Resurrecting the Granary of Rome: Environmental History and French Colonial Expansion in North Africa* (Athens: Ohio University Press, 2007), 61.

117. Henri Verne, *La France en Algérie* (Paris: Challamel aîné, 1869), 107, v, 6. See also Henri Verne, *La France en Algérie: Deuxième partie* (Paris: Challamel aîné, 1873), 56, and Verne, *De Bône à Hammam-Meskhoutine*, vi.

118. Donny Gluckstein, *Paris Commune: A Revolution in Democracy* (Chicago: Haymarket Books, 2006), 40.

119. Käthe Panick, *La Race Latine: Politischer Romanismus im Frankreich des 19. Jahrhunderts* (Bonn: Ludwig Röhrscheid Verlag, 1978), 258.

120. The installation of a military official as Algeria's new civil governor-general consolidated this impression. See Lucet, "18 April 1871," ANOM, F80 1862; "La resolution adoptée par le Conseil general de Constantine," *Le bien public*, December 4, 1871; and "Administration communale," *La république française*, July 27, 1872. Advocates for settler interests most often invoked the connection between the military regime and the insurrection to attack what they described as the remains of the military administration. See A. B., "Lettre d'Algérie," *La sémaphore de Marseille*, November 23, 1872; *La république française*, March 13, 1873; "Le régime militaire en Algérie," *Le phare de la Loire*, September 24, 1873; and "Lettre d'Algérie," *Le sémaphore de Marseille*, May 13, 1873.

121. "Alger," *L'akhbar*, September 30, 1871, excerpt in ANOM, F80 1862.

122. Lucien-Anatole Prévost-Paradol, *La France nouvelle*, 10th ed. (Paris: Michel Lévy frères, 1869), 397.

123. Prévost-Paradol, *La France nouvelle*, 341.

124. Senhaux, *La France et l'Algérie*, 179; *Le pays*, August 7, 1871, ANOM, F80 1682; J. J. Clamageran, *L'Algérie: Impressions de voyage suivie d'une étude sur les institutions kabyles et la colonisation* (Paris: Librairie Germer Ballière, 1874). Prévost-Paradol's ideas about Algeria cast a long shadow. In 1877 a geography textbook aimed at families reminded them that "there exists on the other side of the Mediterranean a vast region that a great writer, Prévost-Paradol, named *France nouvelle*." See Odilon Neil, *Géographie de l'Algérie: Géographie politique et l'itinéraire de l'Algérie* (Paris: Challamel, 1878), 2:xiv. Even in 1879, *Le temps* invoked Prévost-Paradol, noting that he had shown that "the future of French nationality" depended in large part on Algeria. See "Insurrection algérienne," *Le temps*, August 13, 1879.

125. *Le temps*, August 4, 1871, excerpt in ANOM, F80 1862.

126. *Le temps*, August 4, 1871.

127. This book was taken up by the school system for the *cours moyen*, or middle grades. See Wolfgang Schivelbusch, *The Culture of Defeat: On National Trauma, Mourning, and Recovery* (New York: Macmillan, 2003), 166.

128. A few writers invoked Alsace-Lorraine to criticize French policy toward Algerians. See Serre, *Les Arabes martyrs*, 33.

129. Schivelbusch, *Culture of Defeat*, 166.

130. Warnier, *L'Algérie et les victims de la guerre*, 5, 59.

131. Approximately 5 percent of the population of the annexed territories left by 1876. See Dan Silverman, *Reluctant Union: Alsace-Lorraine and Imperial Germany* (Pittsburgh: Pennsylvania State University Press, 1972), 66.

132. Albert Lavigne, *Questions algériennes: Le régime du sabre* (Paris: A. Lacroix, 1871), 43; Schivelbusch, *Culture of Defeat*, 166.

133. French atlases and geography textbooks published in the 1870s included this information in their sections on Alsace-Lorraine. See F. de la Brugère, *Atlas national* (Paris: Arthême Fayard, 1877), 452.

134. "Contribution extraordinaire et séquestre 1872/1873," ANOM, ALG GGA/3E74.

135. "Immigration alsacienne et lorraine," ANOM, ALG GGA/3E73.

136. Guynemer, *Situation des alsaciens-lorrains en Algérie* (Paris: A. Chaix, 1873), 3, 79.

137. Société de Protection des Alsaciens et Lorrains demeurés français, *Explication des ouvrages de peinture exposés au profit de la colonisation de l'Algérie par les alsaciens lorrains demeurés français* (Paris: Imprimerie de Jules Claye, 1874).

138. Of the 125,000 Alsatians and Lorrainers who left, only 5,000 settled in Algeria, most of whom went to major cities. See Ruedy, *Modern Algeria*, 80, and Perville, *La France en Algérie*, 66.

139. Schivelbusch, *Culture of Defeat*, 167.

140. Taithe, *Citizenship and Wars*, 172.

141. This was especially true after the Kabylia uprising when the National Assembly passed the *code de l'indigénat*, which included thirty-three infractions that only applied to native Algerians. See Ruedy, *Modern Algeria*, 89.

4. Expeditions and Expansion between Algeria and Senegal

1. Auguste Warnier to the president of the Algiers Chamber of Commerce, April 25, 1873, AN, F 17/3007B

2. Jacques Valette, "Pénétration française au Sahara et exploration: Le cas de Paul Soleillet," *La revue française d'histoire d'outre-mer* 67 (1980): 257.

3. *Compagnie d'encouragement pour des explorations commerciales dans le Sahara central: Exposé* (1873); Paul Soleillet, *Exploration du Sahara central: Voyage de Paul Soleillet d'Alger à l'oasis d'In-Çalah: Rapport présenté à la Chambre de Commerce d'Alger* (July 1874), 5, ANOM, ALG GGA 4 H.

4. Paul Soleillet to the minister of agriculture and commerce, November 25, 1876, AN F 12/7212; Paul Soleillet to the minister of public instruction, April 15, 1881, AN F 17/3007B; Paul Soleillet, "Mission Paul Soleillet: Note à consulter," May 21, 1881, AN F 17/3007B.

5. Valette, "Pénétration française," 257–59; Algiers Chamber of Commerce, "Rapport: Sahara & Soudan importations et exportations: Première exploration commerciale et scientifique faite par M. Paul Soleillet" (1874), ANOM, ALG GGA/4H7.

6. M. Henri fils to Chanzy, June 23, 1873, ANOM, ALG GGA/4H7.

7. Commanding general of the subdivision of Médéa to the commanding general of the division of Algiers, April 13, 1874, ANOM ALG GGA/4H7.

8. He promised to undertake meteorological observations. H. Valnore to the minister of public instruction, July 31, 1873, AN F 17/3007B. See also Chanzy to the minister of the interior, July 30, 1873; minister of the interior to the governor-general, November 5, 1873; and minister of foreign affairs to Soleillet, November 12, 1873, ANOM, ALG GGA/4H7.

9. Henri Duveyrier, "Instructions pour le voyage à In-Çalah projeté par M. M. Soleillet et Vignaud" (September 1873), BNF, SG, Colis 27, notices 3788; Charles Daney, "De Norbert Dournaux-Dupéré à Fernand Foureau: Le patronage saharien de la Société de Géographie," *Acta geographica* 71 (1987): 21; George Trumbull IV, *Empire of Facts: Colonial Power, Cultural Knowledge, and Islam in Algeria, 1870–1914* (New York: Cambridge University Press, 2009), 62.

10. Florence Deprest, *Géographes en Algérie, 1880–1950: Savoirs universitaires en situation coloniale* (Paris: Belin, 2009), 28–29.

11. Valette, "Pénétration française," 254.

12. Soleillet to the governor-general, October 19, 1873, ANOM, ALG GGA/4H7.

13. Patricia Lorcin, *Imperial Identities: Stereotyping, Prejudice, and Race in Colonial Algeria* (New York: I. B. Tauris, 1995), 105.

14. Soleillet, *Exploration du Sahara central*, 13.

15. Jacques Frémeaux, *Le Sahara et la France* (Paris: Éditions Soteca, 2010), 53.

16. Beau Riffenburgh, *The Myth of the Explorer: The Press, Sensationalism, and Geographical Discovery* (London: Belhaven, 1993); Emmanuelle Sibeud, *Une science impériale pour l'Afrique? La construction des savoirs africanistes en France, 1878–1830* (Paris: Éditions de l'EHESS, 2002); Isabelle Surun, "Les figures de l'explorateur dans la presse du XIXe siècle," *Le temps des médias* 8 (2007): 57–74; Pierre Singaravélou, ed., *L'empire des géographes: Géographie, exploration, et colonisation XIXe-XX siècle* (Paris: Belin, 2008); Edward Berenson, *Heroes of Empire: Five Charismatic Men and the Conquest of Africa* (Berkeley: University of California Press, 2011); Berny Sèbe, *Heroic Imperialists in*

Africa: The Promotion of British and French Colonial Heroes, 1870–1939 (Manchester: Manchester University Press, 2013).

17. Berny Sèbe, "The Making of British and French Legends of Exploration, 1821–1914," in *Reinterpreting Exploration: The West in the World*, ed. Dane Kennedy (New York: Oxford University Press, 2014), 110.

18. Michael J. Heffernan, "The Science of Empire: The French Geographical Movement and the Forms of French Imperialism, 1870–1920," in *Geography and Empire*, ed. Anne Godlewska and Neil Smith (Oxford: Blackwell, 1994), 99.

19. Sèbe, *Heroic Imperialists in Africa*, 2.

20. Berenson, *Heroes of Empire*; Sèbe, *Heroic Imperialists in Africa*.

21. Valette, "Pénétration française," 253.

22. Raoul Girardet, *L'idée coloniale en France de 1871 à 1962* (Paris: La Table ronde, 1972), 41; Wolfgang Schivelbusch, *The Culture of Defeat: On National Trauma, Mourning, and Recovery* (New York: Macmillan, 2003), 162; James Lehning, *To Be a Citizen: The Political Culture of the Early French Third Republic* (Ithaca, NY: Cornell University Press, 2001), 136.

23. Ernest Renan, *La réforme intellectuelle et morale de la France* (Paris: Michel Lévy frères, 1872), 92.

24. Philip Nord, *The Republican Moment: Struggles for Democracy in Nineteenth-Century France* (Cambridge, MA: Harvard University Press, 1995), 3; Roger Price, *The French Second Empire: An Anatomy of Political Power* (New York: Cambridge University Press, 2001), 465.

25. Berenson, *Heroes of Empire*, 5.

26. Clyde Thogmartin, *The National Daily Press of France* (Birmingham, AL: Summa Publications, 1998), 69; Arthur Asseraf, *Electric News in Colonial Algeria* (New York: Oxford University Press, 2019), 52.

27. Christiane Souriau-Hoebrechts, *La presse Maghrébine: Libye-Tunisie-Maroc-Algérie* (Paris: CNRS éditions, 1969), 73.

28. It would later be exported across France's colonies. See Emmanuelle Saada, *Empire's Children: Race, Filiation, and Citizenship in the French Colonies* (Chicago: University of Chicago Press, 2007), 96.

29. Asseraf, *Electric News in Colonial Algeria*, 57–60.

30. Zahir Ihaddaden, *Histoire de la presse indigène en Algérie des origines jusqu'en 1930* (Algiers: ENAL, 1983), 50.

31. A. S. Kanya-Forstner, *The Conquest of the Western Sudan* (Cambridge: Cambridge University Press, 1969), 53.

32. Francine N'Diaye, "La colonie du Sénégal au temps de Brière de l'Isle," *Bulletin de l'insitut fondamental d'Afrique noire: Série B, sciences humaines* 30, no. 2 (1968): 478.

33. Elizabeth Foster, *Faith in Empire: Religion, Politics, and Colonial Rule in French Senegal, 1880–1940* (Stanford, CA: Stanford University Press, 2013), 36.

34. Tamba M'bayo, *Muslim Interpreters in Colonial Senegal, 1850–1920: Mediations of Knowledge and Power in the Lower and Middle Senegal River Valley* (Lanham, MD: Lexington Books, 2016), xiv.

35. Hilary Jones, *The Métis of Senegal: Urban Life and Politics in French West Africa* (Bloomington: Indiana University Press, 2013), 114.

36. M'bayo, *Muslim Interpreters in Colonial Senegal*, 1–2.

37. Lehning, *To Be a Citizen*, 132; David Prochaska, *Making Algeria French: Colonialism in Bône, 1870–1920* (New York: Cambridge University Press, 1990); J. P. Daughton, *An Empire Divided: Religion, Republicanism, and the Making of French Colonialism, 1880–1914* (New York: Oxford University Press, 2006), 10.

38. Jules Duval, *Les colonies et la politique colonial de la France* (Paris: Arthus Bertrand, 1864), xviii.

39. Duval, *Les colonies et la politique colonial*, xx.

40. Duval, *Les colonies et la politique colonial*, 13, 19. 21.

41. Duval, *Les colonies et la politique colonial*, 445.

42. Duval, *Les colonies et la politique colonial*, 467.

43. Leroy-Beaulieu composed the first version for a competition for the Léon Faucher Prize, granted annually by the Academy of Moral and Political Science to the "author of the best essay on a question of political economy." The subject of the 1868 prize was the "colonial system of modern people." In early 1870 the academy pronounced Leroy-Beaulieu the winner. He published the manuscript several years later in 1874. See Dan Warshaw, *Paul Leroy-Beaulieu and Established Liberalism in France* (Dekalb: Northern Illinois University Press, 1991), 84; Pierre Trépanier, 'Du système colonial des peuples modernes: Un inédit de Rameau de Saint-Père," *La revue d'histoire de l'Amérique française* 34, no. 1 (1982), 55–56.

44. Paul Leroy-Beaulieu, *De la colonisation chez les peuples modernes* (Paris: Guillamin, 1874), ii, v, vi.

45. Leroy-Beaulieu, *De la colonisation*, 446, 167, 524, 593, 235, 341.

46. Leroy-Beaulieu, *De la colonisation*, 537.

47. Leroy-Beaulieu, *De la colonisation*, 535, 536.

48. Leroy-Beaulieu, *De la colonisation*, 606.

49. Leroy-Beaulieu, *De la colonisation*, 4, 336.

50. Leroy-Beaulieu, *De la colonisation*, 339, 354, 356.

51. Leroy-Beaulieu, *De la colonisation*, 355.

52. Leroy-Beaulieu, *De la colonisation*, 383, 606, 385.

53. Pierre Raboisson, *Étude sur les colonies et la colonisation au regard de la France* (Paris: Challamel Ainé, 1877), 69.

54. Raboisson, *Étude sur les colonies*, 5, 8.

55. Raboisson, *Étude sur les colonies*, 17, 61.

56. Raboisson, *Étude sur les colonies*, 65.

57. Raboisson, *Étude sur les colonies*, 7.

58. Raboisson, *Étude sur les colonies*, 6, 67, 105–6.

59. Raboisson, *Étude sur les colonies*, 49, 113.

60. Raboisson, *Étude sur les colonies*, 53.

61. *Bulletin de la société des études coloniales et maritimes* 2, no. 1 (January 1878): 31.

62. Warshaw, *Paul Leroy-Beaulieu*, 48.

63. Dominique Lejeune, *Les sociétés de géographie en France et l'expansion coloniale au XIXe siècle* (Paris: Albin Michel, 1993), 76.

64. Pierre Brocheux and Daniel Hémery, *Indochina: An Ambiguous Colonization, 1858–1954* (Berkeley: University of California Press, 2009), 21.

65. Sèbe, "Making of British and French Legends," 119.

66. Dominique Casajus, *Henri Duveyrier: Un Saint-Simonien au désert* (Paris: Ibn Press, 2007), 57, 148, 168.

67. Casajus, *Henri Duveyrier*, 171, 175.

68. Lejeune, *Les sociétés de géographie*, 79.

69. Lejeune, *Les sociétés de géographie*, 91.

70. Heffernan, " Science of Empire," 98; Philippe Boulanger, *La géographie militaire française, 1871–1939* (Paris: Economica, 2002), 35.

71. Sèbe, "Making of British and French Legends," 118.

72. Sibeud, *Un science impériale pour l'Afrique?*, 21.

73. "Dépêche télégraphique," March 22, 1874, ANOM, FR GGA 4H7.

74. Valette, "Pénétration française," 259.

75. Algiers Chamber of Commerce, "Rapport: Sahara & Soudan importations et exportations: Première exploration commerciale et scientifique faite par M. Paul Soleillet" (1874), 9; ANOM, ALG GGA/4H7.

76. Minister of foreign affairs to the governor-general, February 18, 1875; M. Henri to the governor-general, July 1875, ANOM, ALG GGA/4H7; "Note: Demande de secours formé pour M. Paul Soleillet," February 1877, AN, F 12/7212.

77. Daney, "De Norbert Dournaux-Dupéré," 23.

78. E. Vignard, "Monsieur le Directeur," *La vigie algérienne*, September 15, 1874.

79. "Dossier Soleillet: Exploration de 1873–1874, Réclamation pour dettes," ANOM, ALG GGA/4H7.

80. General de Loverdo to the commanding general of the Division of Algiers, June 15, 1877, ANOM, ALG GGA/4H7.

81. "Note: Demande de secours formé pour M. Paul Soleillet," February 1877, AN F 12/7212.

82. Paul Soleillet, *Voyage d'Alger à St. Louis du Sénégal par Tombouctou: Conférence de M. Paul Soleillet* (Avignon: François Seguin Ainé, 1875), 9.

83. "Lettres du ministère de l'intérieur et de celui de la guerre sur la subvention pour un voyage d'Alger au Sénégal par Tombouctou" (August 14 and 16 1872), BNF SG, Colis 4, notices 1682.

84. Paul Soleillet, *Avenir de la France en Afrique* (Paris: Challamel Ainé, 1876), 48–49.

85. Soleillet, *Voyage d'Alger à St. Louis du Sénégal*, 7.

86. Paul Soleillet to the minister of commerce, January 13, 1875, AN F 12/7212.

87. Soleillet, *Avenir de la France*, 2, 3.

88. Soleillet, *Avenir de la France*, 23.

89. Paul Soleillet to the minister of commerce, January 13, 1875, AN F 12/7212.

90. Soleillet, *Avenir de la France*, 63.

91. As the head of the Chamber of Commerce in Avignon pointed out, this was a contradictory position, as the transatlantic slave trade had been based on commerce. Soleillet, *Voyage d'Alger à St. Louis*, 6.

92. Soleillet, *Avenir de la France*, 57–64.

93. Benjamin Brower, *A Desert Named Peace: The Violence of France's Empire in the Algerian Sahara* (New York: Columbia University Press 2009); Julia Clancy-Smith, *Rebel and Saint: Muslim Notables, Populist Protest, Colonial Encounters* (Berkeley: University of California Press, 1997).

94. Emmanuelle Sibeud, *Une science impériale pour l'Afrique? La construction des savoirs africanistes en France, 1878–1930* (Paris: EHESS, 2002), 21; Jennifer Pitts, *A Turn to Empire: The Rise of Imperial Liberalism in Britain and France* (Princeton, NJ: Princeton University Press, 2005), 17.

95. Daney, "De Norbert Dournaux-Dupéré," 21; Frémeaux, *Le Sahara et la France*, 53.

96. "Voyage d'Alger au Sénégal par Tombouctou: Conférence de M. Paul Soleillet," *Le salut public*, February 24, 1875, AN F 17/3007B.

97. Berenson, *Heroes of Empire*, 58.

98. Minister of agriculture and commerce, "Note," May 1879, AN F 12/7212.

99. Valette, "Pénétration française," 262.

100. Martin Ewans, *European Atrocity, African Catastrophe: Leopold II, the Congo Free State and Its Aftermath* (London: Routledge Curzon, 2002), 39.

101. Sanford Bederman, "The 1876 Brussels Geographical Conference and the Charade of European Cooperation in African Exploration," *Terrae Incognitae* 21, no. 1 (1989): 64.

102. "Assemblée générale du 20 décembre 1876," *Le bulletin de la Société de géographie* (1877), 95.

103. Charles Maunoir, "Rapport sur les travaux de la Société de géographie et sur les progrès des sciences géographiques pendant l'année 1876," *Le bulletin de la Société de géographie* (1877).

104. "Cercle Rouennais de la Ligue de l'enseignement: Conférence de M. Paul Soleillet," January 3, 1876, 6, AN F 17/3007B.

105. Minister of public instruction to Soleillet, January, 29, 1877, AN F 17/3007B ; Soleillet to the minister of the navy and colonies, January 28, 1877, ANOM COL 50COL2.

106. "Paul Soleillet," *Le monde illustré*, August 24, 1878, 128.

107. Kanya-Forstner, *Conquest of the Western Sudan*, 67–69.

108. G. Brière de l'Isle, "Arrêté portant ouverture d'un crédit supplémentaire de 5000 francs au budget du service local, exercice 1878," ANOM 50COL2; Isabelle Surun, "French Military Officers and the Mapping of West Africa: The Case of Captain Brosselard-Faidherbe," *Journal of Historical Geography* 37 (2011): 169.

109. Conseil d'administration, "Extrait du registre des délibérations," April 14, 1878, ANOM 50COL2.

110. Brière de l'Isle, "Analyse: Au sujet du retour de M. Paul Soleillet à Saint Louis," March 22, 1879, 50COL2.

111. Soleillet to the minister of public instruction, *Le journal officiel de la République Française*, April 11, 1879, 3237.

112. Soleillet to minister of public instruction, April 11, 1879, 3238.

113. Minister of public instruction to Soleillet, April 12, 1879, AN F 17/3007B.

114. "Petites nouvelles," *Le petit journal*, June 18, 1878; "Nouvelles diverses," *Le journal des débats*, August 29, 1878; "Société de géographie," *Le temps*, May 9, 1879.

115. "Bordeaux, 7 mai," *La presse*, May 9, 1879 ; "M. Paul Soleillet à Marseille," *La presse*, May 24, 1879; "Voyage de M. Soleillet dans le centre d'Afrique," *La presse*, May 28, 1879.

116. Conseil d'administration, "Extrait du registre des délibérations," April 4, 1879, ANOM 50COL2.

117. "Envoi d'un extrait du registre des délibérations du Conseil d'Adou concernant les allocations votées en faveur de M. Soleillet, voyageur français," May 7, 1879, and "Envoi d'un extrait du registre des délibérations du conseil d'Adou concernant les allocations votées en faveur de M. Soleillet, voyageur français," May 24, 1879, ANOM 50COL2; Valette, "Pénétration française," 264.

118. C. W. Newbury and A. S. Kanya-Forstner, "French Policy and the Origins of the Scramble for West Africa," *Journal of African History* 10, no. 2 (1969): 253–76; Marcel Cassou, *Le Transsaharien: L'échec sanglant des missions Flatters, 1881* (Paris: L'Harmattan, 2005); Natalia Starostina, "Ambiguous Modernity: Representations of French Colonial Railways in the Third Republic," *Journal of the Western Society for French History* 38 (2010): 179–99; T. W. Roberts, "Republicanism, Railway Imperialism, and the French Empire in Africa, 1879–1889," *Historical Journal* 52, no. 2 (2011): 401–20.

119. Cassou, *Le Transsaharien*, 21.

120. Roberts, "Republicanism, Railway Imperialism," 406.

121. Adolphe Duponchel, *Le chemin de fer de l'Afrique centrale* (Paris: A. Pougin, 1877),10.

122. Duponchel, *Le chemin de fer*, 21–22, 31.

123. Cassou, *Le Transsaharien*, 26.

124. Paul Leroy-Beaulieu, "Variétés: Le chemin de fer transsaharien," *Le journal des débats politiques et littéraires*, January 26, 1879.

125. Charles Freycinet, "Rapport du ministre des travaux publics au président de la république sur le projet de chemin de fer transsaharien, et décret subséquent du président de la république instituant une commission supérieure pour l'étude des questions relatives à la mise en communication par voie ferrée de l'Algérie et du Sénégal avec l'intérieur du Soudan," July 12, 1879, AN F 14/12437.

126. Cassou, *Le Transsaharien*, 33–46.

127. Commission supérieure pour l'étude des questions relatives à la mise en communication par voie ferrée de l'Algérie et du Sénégal avec l'intérieur du Soudan, "Première session, 1879–1880, première séance," July 21, 1879, 3–4. AN F 14/8594.

128. Commission supérieure pour l'étude des questions relatives à la mise en communication par voie ferrée de l'Algérie et du Sénégal avec l'intérieur du Soudan, "Première session, 1879–1880, troisième séance," October 27, 1879, 51. AN F 14/8594.

129. Commission supérieure, "Première session, 1879–1880, troisième séance," 64.

130. Commission supérieure pour l'étude des questions relatives à la mise en communication par voie ferrée de l'Algérie et du Sénégal avec l'intérieur du Soudan, "1e et 3e Sous-Commissions réunies," July 30, 1879, 6, AN F 14/12437; Commission supérieure pour l'étude des questions relatives à la mise en communication par voie ferrée de l'Algérie et du Sénégal avec l'intérieur du Soudan, "Première session, 1879–1880, deuxième séance," August 1, 1879, 35, AN F 14/8594.

131. Commission supérieure, "Première session, 1879–1880, deuxième séance," 38. See also Commission supérieure pour l'étude des questions relatives à la mise en communication par voie ferrée de l'Algérie et du Sénégal avec l'intérieur du Soudan, "3e et 4e Sous-Commissions réunies," August 13, 1879, 3–4, AN F 14/12437.

132. Commission supérieure, "Première session, 1879–1880, troisième séance," 58.

133. Commission supérieure, "Première session, 1879–1880, deuxième séance," 29.

134. Commission supérieure, "Première session, 1879–1880, troisième séance," 64.

135. They also commissioned two more technical missions in the northern part of the Sahara led by Auguste Choisy and Justin Pouyanne. See Cassou, *Le Transsaharien*, 85.

136. Commission supérieure, "Première session, 1879–1880, troisième séance," 65.

137. A. S. Kanya-Forstner, *The Conquest of the Western Sudan* (Cambridge: Cambridge University Press, 1969), 68.

138. *Le journal des débats politiques et littéraires*, October 29, 1879. See also "Une conférence sur le Sahara," *Le gaulois*, November 26, 1879; Victor Meunier, "Les Mélano-Gétules," *Le rappel*, January 11, 1880 ; "Lettres, Sciences, Arts," *La presse*, December 21, 1879; *Le petit journal*, December 22, 1879; "Journée politique: France," *Le rappel*, January 10, 1880; "L'exploration française dans l'Afrique centrale," *Le journal des débats politiques et littéraires*, February 11, 1880; "Gazette du Jour," *La justice*, February 13, 1880.

139. *Le journal des débats politiques et littéraires*, October 29, 1879.

140. Victor Meunier, "Correspondance," *Le rappel*, April 30, 1880.

141. Paul Soleillet, "Comment j'ai été pillé dans l'Adrar (20 mars 1880)," ANOM 50COL2; David Robinson, *Paths of Accomodation: Muslim Societies and French Colonial Authorities in Senegal and Mauritania, 1880–1920* (Athens: Ohio University Press, 2000), 165.

142. Commission supérieure pour l'étude des questions relatives à la mise en communication par voie ferrée de l'Algérie et du Sénégal avec l'intérieur du Soudan, "Deuxième session, 1880, deuxième séance," June 28, 1880, 5. AN F 14/8594.

143. Commission supérieure, "Deuxième session, 1880, deuxième séance," 2, 8; "La commission supérieur du Transsaharien," *Le temps*, June 30, 1880.

144. La Fare, "Le départ de M. Soleillet," *Le gaulois*, July 19, 1880; "Échos de partout," *Le petit parisien*, July 20, 1880; "Gazette du Jour," *La justice*, July 20, 1880; "Banquet offert à M. Soleillet," *Le temps*, July 20, 1880.

145. "Un Explorateur en Afrique," *Le petit journal*, February 21, 1881.

146. Soleillet to the minister of public works, April 15, 1880, ANOM 50COL2.

147. Monteil to Brière de l'Isle, April 24, 1880, ANOM 50COL2.

148. Robinson, *Paths of Accommodation*, 106.

149. N'Diaye, "La colonie du Sénégal," 482–97.

150. Martin Klein, *Slavery and Colonial Rule in French West Africa* (New York: Cambridge University Press, 1998), 62.

151. Cassou, *Le Transsaharien*, 84, 147.

152. "Soleillet: Pièces à conserver avec grand soin à la direction si ce dossier est demandé," January 23, 1881, ANOM 50COL2.

153. Valette, "Pénétration française," 264; Paul Soleillet, "Mon cher monsieur," *Le rappel*, November 2, 1880.

154. Ministère des travaux publics, "Chemin de l'Algérie et du Sénégal avec le Soudan: Mission Soleillet," June 23, 1881, ANOM 50COL2.

155. Cassou, *Le Transsaharien*, 153.

156. Ministère des travaux publics, "Avant-projets de chemins de fer étudiés en vue de la mise en communication de l'Algérie avec le Soudan," June 10, 1881, 10–11, AN F 14/12437.

157. Valette, *Pénétration française*, 264.

5. New Colonial Vocabularies and Overseas Conquest in Vietnam

1. Émile Lonchampt, *Dupleix et la politique coloniale sous Louis XV* (Reims: Matot-Braine, 1886), 28, 29.

2. Lonchampt, *Dupleix et la politique colonial*, 31.

3. Lonchampt, *Dupleix et la politique colonial*, 32. See also Émile Lonchampt, *Pourquoi l'Amérique du Nord n'est pas française?* (Paris: Challamel Ainé, 1888).

4. Kate Marsh and Nicola Frith, eds., *France's Lost Empires: Fragmentation, Nostalgia, and* la Fracture Coloniale (Lanham, MD: Lexington Books, 2011), 5.

5. William Roger Louis, *Ends of British Imperialism: The Scramble for Empire, Suez, and Decolonization* (New York: I. B. Tauris, 2006), 77; M. E. Chamberlain, *The Scramble for Africa* (New York: Routledge, 2014), 48–53.

6. Chamberlain, *Scramble for Africa*, 3.

7. Gilles Manceron, ed., *1885: Le tournant colonial de la république* (Paris: La Découverte, 2007), 9.

8. Jérôme Grévy, *La république des opportunistes* (Paris: Perrin, 1998), 219; Chamberlain, *Scramble for Africa*, 35, 48; Philip Nord, *The Republican Moment: Struggles for Democracy in Nineteenth-Century France* (Cambridge, MA: Harvard University Press, 1995), 191.

9. Nord, *Republican Moment*, 192.

10. Wolfgang Schivelbusch, *The Culture of Defeat: On National Trauma, Mourning, and Recovery* (New York: Macmillan, 2003), 150, 181.

11. James Lehning, *To Be a Citizen: The Political Culture of the Early French Third Republic* (Ithaca, NY: Cornell University Press, 2001), 136.

12. The term "Indochina" first appeared in orientalist literature in the early 1800s. Until 1887, when the French created the Union indochinoise, the area that it referred to was ambiguous, but it included contemporary Vietnam, Cambodia, and Laos. While "Indochina" was a European construction, it affected colonized peoples because the French restructured political and economic structures around it. See Pierre Brocheux and Daniel Hémery, *Indochina: An Ambiguous Colonization, 1858–1954* (Berkeley: University of California Press, 2009), 3, 46.

13. Clyde Thogmartin, *The National Daily Press of France* (Birmingham, AL: Summa Publications, 1998), 91–93.

14. Christophe Charle, *Le siècle de la presse, 1830–1939* (Paris: Seuil, 2004), 145–47.

15. Milton E. Osborne, *The French Presence in Cochinchina and Cambodia: Rule and Response* (Ithaca, NY: Cornell University Press, 1969), 107.

16. Philippe Peycam, *The Birth of Vietnamese Political Journalism: Saigon, 1916–1930* (New York: Columbia University Press, 2012), 68.

17. Some of these elites published journal articles and geographies and histories about Vietnam. See Tran-Nguyen-Hanh, "La préparation en Cochinchine des fromages de pate de haricot," *Le bulletin de la Société des études indochinoises* (1885), 29–32; Truong-Vinh-Ky, *Petit cours de géographie de la basse-Cochinchine* (Saigon: Imprimerie du gouvernement, 1875); Truong-Vinh-Ky, *Cours d'histoire annamite*, vol. 2 (Saigon: Imprimerie du gouvernement, 1877)

18. David Marr, *Vietnamese Tradition on Trial, 1920–1945* (Berkeley: University of California Press, 1981), 147.

19. Peycam, *Birth of Vietnamese Political Journalism*, 66.

20. Tellingly, when the quoc ngu press emerged in force during the early twentieth century, the colonial administration responded by seeking to police materials printed in languages other than French. See Shawn Frederick McHale, *Print and Power: Confucianism, Communism, and Buddhism in the Making of Modern Vietnam* (Honolulu: University of Hawai'i Press, 2004), 47.

21. Brocheux and Hémery, *Indochina*, 77.

22. Osborne, *French Presence in Cochinchina and Cambodia*, 121.

23. Mark McLeod, *The Vietnamese Response to French Intervention, 1862–1874* (New York: Praeger, 1991) 124.

24. "Création de l'organisation de 4 bataillons de Chausseurs annamites," May 4, 1886, SHD, Vincennes, GR10 H8; Osborne, *French Presence in Cochinchina and Cambodia*, 64.

25. Manceron, *1885*, 14, 17; Jean-Noël Jeanneney, ed., *La politique coloniale: Clemenceau contre Ferry* (Paris: Magellan, 2012), 15; Lehning, *To Be a Citizen*, 139; Charles Ageron, *L'anticolonialisme en France de 1871 à 1914* (Paris: PUF, 1973), 40.

26. Lehning, *To Be a Citizen*, 137; Michel Bodin, *Les français au Tonkin, 1870–1902: Une conquête difficile* (Paris: Éditions Soteca, 2012), 84.

27. Brocheux and Hémery, *Indochina*, 48; Nicola Cooper, *France in Indochina: Colonial Encounters* (New York: Oxford University Press, 2001), 16.

28. Jean-Pierre Pecqueur, *Indochine-France: Conquête et rupture, 1620–1954* (Paris: Alan Sutton, 2009), 41.

29. Brocheux and Hémery, *Indochina*, 24.

30. Arthur Dommen, *The Indochinese Experience of the French and the Americans* (Bloomington: Indiana University Press, 2001), 8.

31. Pierre-Paul de La Grandière, "Considérations générales sur la Cochinchine" (1864), AN 45 AP 17; Brocheux and Hémery, *Indochina*, 21, 23, 26.

32. Justin Corfield, *The History of Cambodia* (Santa Barbara, CA: ABC-Clio, 2009), 23.

33. Cooper, *France in Indochina*, 14.

34. Brocheux and Hémery, *Indochina*, 28–29.

35. Bradley Camp Davis, *Imperial Bandits: Outlaws and Rebels in the China-Vietnam Borderlands* (Seattle: University of Washington Press, 2017), 61–64.

36. "Traité conclu à Saigon, le 5 Mars 1874, entre la France et le royaume d'Annam," *Historique de la conquête du Tonkin par les capitaines Sergent et Margueron avec cartes et annexes*, SHD, Vincennes, GR10 H1.

37. McLeod, *Vietnamese Response to French Intervention*, 123.

38. The army had formed in China in connection to the Kingdom of Yanling, a small rebellion in Guangxi Province that broke out in the early 1860s. The Black Flags fled to northern Vietnam after the rebellion failed. By the late 1870s, this force essentially controlled northern Vietnam, which has led some scholars to argue that this part of Vietnam was on its way to becoming part of China when the French intervened. See Ella Laffey, "French Adventurers and Chinese Bandits in Tonkin: The Garnier Affair and Its Local Context," *Journal of Southeast Asian Studies* 6, no. 1 (1975): 49, Pecquer, *Indo-Chine*, 48; Davis, *Imperial Bandits*, 33.

39. Brocheux and Hémery, *Indochina*, 41.

40. Jean Dupuis and E. Millot, "Rapport sur la question du Tong-Kin," July 8, 1880, Lasserre to Freycinet, June 20, 1880, AMAE PA-AP Freycinet, 4:81–98, 105–17; Bernard Jauréguiberry to Charles Duclerc, March 4, 1882, AMAE CP Indochine,

38:35–38; Jauréguiberry to Duclerc August 22, 1882, Myre de Vilers to Rheinart, July 15, 1882, and Myre de Vilers to Jauréguiberry September 24, 1882, AMAE CP Indochine, 39:10–11, 100–102, 107–13; Manceron, *1885*, 9.

41. Davis, *Imperial Bandits*, 86.

42. Minister of foreign affairs of the Annam court to the governor of Cochinchina, July 5, 1882; minister of foreign affairs of the Annam court to the minister of foreign affairs of the French Republic, AMAE CP Indochine, 39:94–99; 197–200.

43. K. W. Taylor, *A History of the Vietnamese* (Cambridge: Cambridge University Press, 2013), 469.

44. Brocheux and Hémery, *Indochina*, 43.

45. Henry McAleavy, *Black Flags in Vietnam: The Story of a Chinese Intervention* (New York: Macmillan, 1968), 41.

46. Kim Munholland, "Admiral Jauréguiberry and the French Scramble for Tonkin," *French Historical Studies* 11, no. 1 (September 1979): 100–102; Myre de Vilers to Jauréguiberry, September 8, 1882, Myre de Vilers to Jauréguiberry, September 24, 1882, Royal Envoy Trau to the Consulate of Hanoi, September 24, 1882, Jauréguiberry to Charles Duclerc, October 15, 1882, and Jauréguiberry to Charles Duclerc, October 31, 1882, AMAE CP Indochine, 39:221–29, 137–38, 147–49, 187–88, 256–63.

47. Grévy, *La république des opportunistes*, 219.

48. Bodin, *Les français au Tonkin*, 256.

49. Even the left voted for the measure. See Albert Millaud, "Gazette Parlementaire," *Le Figaro*, May 27, 1883.

50. F. Joussenet, *Le journal des débats politiques*, May 27, 1883; "Bulletin du jour," *Le temps*, May 28, 1883; "L'affaire du Tonkin: Mort du commandant Rivière," *Le petit journal*, May 28, 1883; "La mort du commandant Rivière," *Le rappel*, May 28, 1883.

51. Charles Lemire, *L'Indo-Chine: Cochinchine française, royaume de Cambodge, royaume d'Annam, et Tonkin* (Paris: Challamel Ainé, 1884), 13; Henry Thureau, *Notre colonie, le Tong-Kin: Explorations et conquêtes, aperçus géographiques, les produits naturels, les ressources commerciales* (Paris: Dreyfous, 1883), 6; Armand Rivière, *La guerre avec la Chine: La politique coloniale et la question du Tonkin* (Paris: Auguste Giro, 1883), 6; A. S. Doncourt (Antoinette Joséphine Françoise Anne Drohojowska), *Les français dans l'Extrême-Orient: Chine, Japon, Indo-Chine, Annam* (Paris: Librairie de J. Lefort, 1884), vii, 313; Otto Lorenz, *Catalogue générale de la librairie française* (Paris: Lorenz, 1968), 2I:; Paul Deschanel, *La question du Tonkin* (Paris: Berger-Levrault, 1883), 2.

52. "Une leçon sévère," *Le siècle*, May 28, 1883. See also Henry Fouquier, "Chronique," *Le XIXe siècle*, May 28, 1883; Albert Delangle, "Henri Rivière," *Gil Blas*, May 28, 1883; "L'affaire du Tonkin"; "H. de Pène, "Le Drapeau en Péril," *Le gaulois*, May 27, 1883; Jules Richard, "Le Corps Expéditionnaire du Tonkin," *Le Figaro*, May 30, 1883.

53. Henri de Rochefort, "Vengeance!," *L'intransigeant*, May 29, 1883.

54. See "La Guerre au Tonkin: Mort du Commandant Rivière," *Le petit parisien*, May 28, 1883. Journalists writing for *Le petit parisien* consistently criticized the centrist republican government's policies in Tunisia and Tonkin. See "Le Tonkin," *Le petit parisien*, April 7, 1883, and "Le Tonkin," *Le petit parisien*, April 13, 1883.

55. Charles Fourniau, *Annam-Tonkin, 1885–1896: Lettrés et paysans vietnamiens face à la conquête coloniale* (Paris: Éditions l'Harmattan, 1989), 26–27.

56. "Projet de loi ayant pour objet d'autoriser le président de la république à ratifier le traité conclu à Hué, le 6 juin 1884, entre la république française et le royaume d'Annam," 7–11, AN C 15881.

57. "Histoire de négociation relatives au traité de paix avec la Chine," May 31, 1884; "Fournier Memorandum," May 17, 1884, SHD, Vincennes, GR10 H6; "Charles-Théodore Millot to the Minister of War," July 16, 1884, SHD, Vincennes, GR10 H3; Brocheux and Hémery, *Indochina*, 45; Oscar Chapius, *The Last Emperors of Vietnam* (Westport, CT: Greenwood, 2000), 68.

58. Cooper, *France in Indochina*, 16; Bodin, *Les français au Tonkin*, 261.

59. Bodin, *Les français au Tonkin*, 262.

60. Dommen, *Indochinese Experience*, 13.

61. McAleavy, *Black Flags in Vietnam*, 274. The French military commissioned multiple reports on the defeat; see "Rapport du Colonel Giovanninelli," March 1885, "Rapport du Général de Négrier," March 14, 1885, "Rapport du Général Brière de l'Isle," March 18, 1885, and "Rapport du Desbordes," March 18, 1885, SHD, Vincennes, GR10 H3.

62. Lemaire to Freycinet, April 2, 1885, SHD, Vincennes, GR10 H3.

63. Fourniau, *Annam-Tonkin, 1885–1896*, 12, 17.

64. "Démission du ministère," *Le petit journal*, April 1, 1885.

65. "Bulletin du Jour," *Le temps*, April 1, 1885.

66. "Démission du ministère."

67. "La crise ministérielle," *La presse*, March 31, 1885.

68. Brocheux and Hémery, *Indochina*, 47.

69. McAleavy, *Black Flags in Vietnam*, 276.

70. Chapius, *Last Emperors of Vietnam*, 71; "Traité de paix, d'amitié et de commerce conclu entre la France et la Chine le 9 juin 1885, à Tien-Tsin," AN C 15881.

71. Brocheux and Hémery, *Indochina*, 49. Conflicts over French military leaders' attempts to undermine the court and the emperor emerged before the peace treaty with China was signed. These attempts were a source of disagreement between the military leadership (Henri Roussel de Courcy and Louis Brière de l'Isle) and Victor-Gabriel Lemaire, the resident-general at the court. The colonial administration and the ministry of foreign affairs sided with de Courcy's antagonistic approach. See "Lettre du conseil secret relative à l'entrée irrégulière et à la conduit des soldats français dans la citadelle de Hué," April 6, 1885, secret council to Lemaire, April 9, 1885, and "Note au sujet de l'action tentée à Hué par le général de Courcy en juillet 1885," December 1885, SHD, Vincennes, GR10 H3; Perrot to de Courcy, April 4, 1885, and Foreign Affairs to the French consul in Singapore, May 18, 1885, SHD, Vincennes, GR10 H6; De Courcy to the minister of war, July 20, 1885, "Procès-verbal d'une conférence tenue à la légation de France à Hué," July 30, 1885, Palasne Champeaux to de Courcy, August 13, 1885, August 18, 1885, August 20, 1885, September 15, 1885, and De Courcy to the Minister of War, October 7, 1885, SHD, Vincennes, GR10 H21.

72. Hue-Tam Ho Tai, *Radicalism and the Origins of the Vietnamese Revolution* (Cambridge, MA: Harvard University Press, 1992), 16.

73. For accounts of the coronation of the new king, see de Courcy to the minister of war, September 14, 1885, SHD, Vincennes, GR10 H21, and de Courcy to the minister of war, September 21, 1885, SHD, Vincennes, GR10 H6.

74. For examples of these attempts, see Charles-Théodore Millot, "Aux habitants de Tonkin!," February 12, 1884, SHD, Vincennes, GR10 H6, and Charles-Auguste-Louis Warnet, "Mandarins, Notables, et Hommes du peuple du Tonkin!," February 27, 1886, *Historique de la conquête du Tonkin par les capitaines Sergent et Margueron avec cartes et annexes*, SHD, Vincennes, GR10 H2.

75. Charles Meyer, *Les français en Indochine* (Paris: Hachette, 1985), 170; McAleavy, *Black Flags in Vietnam*, 278; Bodin, *Les français au Tonkin*, 268.

76. Brocheux and Hémery, *Indochina*, 47.

77. Jeanneney, *La politique coloniale*, 57.

78. Jeanneney, *La politique coloniale*, 66, 68.

79. Jeanneney, *La politique coloniale*, 60–62.

80. Paul Leroy-Beaulieu, *De la colonisation chez les peuples modernes* (Paris: Guillamin, 1874), 537.

81. Alice Conklin, *In the Museum of Man: Race, Anthropology, and Empire in France, 1850–1950* (Ithaca, NY: Cornell University Press, 2013), 33.

82. Jennifer Michael Hecht, *The End of the Soul: Scientific Modernity, Atheism, and Anthropology in France* (New York: Columbia University Press, 2003), 34.

83. Carole Reynaud-Paligot, *La république raciale, 1860–1930* (Paris: PUF, 2006), 19. See also Claude Blanckaert, *De la race à l'évolution: Paul Broca et l'anthropologie française, 1850–1900* (Paris: Harmattan, 2009), and Richard Fogarty and Michael Osborne, "Constructions and Functions of Race in French Military Medicine, 1830–1920," in *The Color of Liberty: Histories of Race in France*, ed. Sue Peabody and Tyler Stovall (Durham, NC: Duke University Press, 2003), 207.

84. Martin Staum, *Nature and Nurture in French Social Sciences, 1859–1914 and Beyond* (Montreal: McGill-Queen's University Press, 2011), 7.

85. Conklin, *In the Museum of Man*, 34.

86. Reynaud-Paligot, *La république raciale*, 56, 63.

87. Manceron, *1885*, 139, 91, 116, 70, 66, 73, 30.

88. Manceron, *1885*, 30, 40, 61, 79, 80.

89. Brocheux and Hémery, *Indochina*, 41; Claude Liauzu, *Histoire de l'anticolonialisme en France du XVIe siècle au nos jours* (Paris: Armand Colin, 2007), 70.

90. Manceron, *1885*, 70.

91. Manceron, *1885*, 28, 140.

92. Manceron, *1885*, 68.

93. Manceron, *1885*, 81.

94. Manceron, *1885*, 117.

95. *La république française*, March 31, 1885; "Ce qu'il faut faire," *Le siècle*, March 30, 1885; "La démission du cabinet," *Le siècle*, March 31, 1885.

96. "Affaires coloniales: Chine et Indo-Chine," *Le temps*, April 1, 1885; "Événements de Tonkin," *Le temps*, April 1, 1885; "Une Journée perdue," *Le petit journal*, April 1, 1885.

97. Thomas Grimm, "L'invasion des barbares," *Le petit journal*, March 31, 1885; Jules Simon, "Le Tonkin," *Le matin*, April 1, 1885; "L'évacuation de Lang-Son," *Le journal des débats*, March 31, 1885.

98. Simon, "Le Tonkin."

99. Grimm, "L'invasion des barbares."

100. "L'évacuation de Lang-Son," *Le journal des débats*; Auguste Vacquerie, "L'évacuation de Lang-Son," *Le rappel*, March 31, 1885; Grimm, "L'invasion des barbares."

101. René Lavollé, "Le bilan de la politique coloniale," *Le journal des économistes*, March 1887, found in Charles-Robert Ageron, *L'anticolonialisme en France* (Paris: PUF, 1973), 53.

102. Hecht, *End of the Soul*, 137.

103. Yves Guyot, "Lettre LXXV," in *Lettres sur la politique coloniale* (Paris: C. Reinwald, 1885), found in Ageron, *L'anticolonialisme en France*, 47.

104. "La guerre de Chine," *Le petit journal*, March 30, 1885; Henri Rochefort, "Désastre au Tonkin," *L'intransigeant*, March 31, 1885; Stephen Pichon, "Déchéance," *La justice*, March 30, 1885; Camille Pelletan, "Responsabilités," *La justice*, April 4, 1885; Henry Maret, "L'effondrement," *Le radical*, April 1, 1885; "Les événements," *Le petit parisien*, March 31, 1885; "La guerre de Chine," *Le gaulois*, March 30, 1885; F. M., "Échos de Paris: La Politique," *Le Figaro*, March 30, 1885; H. de Pène, "La mise en accusation," *Le gaulois*, March 30, 1885; "La crise," *La presse*, March 31, 1885; Perry, "Un désastre: Prise de Lang-Son par les chinois," *Le Figaro*, March 30, 1885; *Le soleil*, March 31, 1885; "La chute honteuse," *La presse*, March 31, 1885.

105. Albert de Broglie, "Projet de loi pourtant ouverture du crédits s'élevant à la somme de 59,569,368 fr. pour le service du Tonkin, séance du 11 décembre 1884," *Journal officiel* (Paris: Imprimerie de la Société Anonyme de publications périodiques, 1884), 22.

106. Broglie, "Projet de loi, 20.

107. Jean-Baptiste Chaudordy, *La France à la suite de la guerre de 1870–1871* (Paris: Librairie Plon, 1887), 129.

108. Broglie, "Projet de loi," 26.

109. Broglie, "Projet de loi," 19.

110. *La vérité politique* (Paris: E. Dentu, 1885), 18; Chaudordy, *La France à la suite de la guerre de 1870–1871*, 128; Camille Pelletan, "La Situation," *La justice*, March 31, 1885; "Les événements"; Maret, "L'effondrement"; "La chute honteuse"; Pène, "La mise en accusation"; Étienne Vacherot, "Un Revenant," *Le gaulois*, April 6, 1885; Paul de Cassagnac, "Il . . . !," *Le matin*, March 31, 1885.

111. Charles-Ange Laisant, *La politique radicale en 1885* (Paris: Librairie Henri Messager, 1885), 60, 78–80.

112. Louis Guétant, *La politique d'extension coloniale et les principes républicains: Letter d'un travailleur à M. Jules Ferry* (Lyon: Imprimerie nouvelle, 1885), 2.

113. Guétant, *La politique d'extension coloniale*, 9.

114. Guétant, *La politique d'extension coloniale*, 7.

115. Guétant, *La politique d'extension coloniale*, 4, 7, 10.

116. "Les événements."

117. "La chute honteuse."

118. Pichon, "Déchéance." Pichon—like many of Ferry's critics—would change his mind about colonial conquest, becoming the resident-general of Tunisia in 1900. See Liauzu, *Histoire de l'anticolonialisme en France*, 72.

119. Rochefort, "Désastre au Tonkin."

120. Léon Millot, "Chronique: Champs de bataille," *La justice*, April 11, 1885.

121. "Les événements"; "La chute du ministère," *Le radical*, April 1, 1885; Pelletan, "La situation"; Paul de Cassagnac, "Il . . . !"; "Chute du ministère: La mise en accusation," *Le gaulois*, March 31, 1885; Vacherot, "Un revenant."

122. "La guerre de Chine," *Le gaulois*; F. M., "Échos de Paris"; Pène, "La mise en accusation"; "La crise," *La presse*, March 31, 1885.

123. Élémir Bourges, "Le Prestige de l'épée," *Le gaulois*, April 2, 1885; "La crise," *Le gaulois*, April 1, 1885.

124. Philippe de Grandlieu, "Appel au pays," *Le Figaro*, March 31, 1885.

125. Vacherot, "Un revenant."

126. F. M., "Échos de Paris."

127. Pène, "La mise en accusation."

128. Arthur Bordier, *La colonisation scientifique et les colonies françaises* (Paris: C. Reinwald, 1884), xi; Louis Vignon, *Les colonies françaises* (Paris: Guillaumin, 1886), 2; Gabriel Charmes, *Politique extérieure et coloniale* (Paris: Calmann Lévy, 1885), iii.

129. Pierre Singaravélou, *Professer l'empire: Les "sciences coloniales" en France sous la IIIe République* (Paris: Publications de la Sorbonne, 2011), 140.

130. Girardet, *L'idée coloniale en France*, 111–16; L. Abrams and D. J. Miller, "Who Were the French Colonialists? A Reassessment of the Parti Colonial, 1890–1914," *Historical Journal* 19, no. 3 (1976): 685–725.

131. Charles Gide, "À quoi servent les colonies," *La revue de géographie*, January 1886, 36; Charmes, *Politique extérieure et coloniale*, 95; Girardet, *L'idée coloniale en France*, 57.

132. J. L. de Lanessan, *L'expansion coloniale de la France* (Paris: Félix Alcan, 1886), iii.

133. Lanessan, *L'expansion coloniale*, xxiii. See also Barbié du Bocage, *Essai sur la politique coloniale* (Évreux: Charles Hérissey, 1885), 5; Paul Deschanel, *La question du Tonkin* (Paris: Berger-Levrault, 1883), 2.

134. Christian Solar, *Le campagne du Tonkin* (Paris: Imprimerie Dubuisson, 1884), 6; P. Dabry de Thiersant, *La solution du Tonkin au point de vue des intérêts français* (Paris: Librairie Léopold Cerf, 1885), 38; Doncourt, *Les français dans l'Extrême-Orient*, vi; Paul Bonnetain, *Au Tonkin* (Paris: Victor-Havard, 1885), 192.

135. Julie d'Andurain, *Colonialisme ou impérialisme?: Le parti coloniale en pensée et action* (Paris: Zellige, 2017).

136. Alfred Rambaud, ed., *La France coloniale: Histoire, géographie, commerce* (Paris: Armand Colin, 1886), xxxviii.

137. Henri Avenel, *La presse française au vingtième siècle* (Paris: Ernest Flammarion, 1901), 198.

138. Jacquillou, *Lettres d'un paysan: La politique coloniale* (Paris: Édouard Robbe, 1885), 6, 12.

139. Lanessan, *L'expansion coloniale de la France*, xviii. See also Vignon, *Les colonies françaises*, 174; Thiersant, *La solution*, 6; Rivière, *La guerre avec la Chine*, 7; Bonnetain, *Au Tonkin*, 192.

140. Jules Bossière, "Les colonies françaises," *La presse*, April 21, 1885.

141. Rambaud, *La France coloniale*, 687, 695.

142. Vignon, *Les colonies françaises*, 177. See also *Les colonies nécessaires: Tunisie, Tonkin, Madagascar; par un marin* (Paris: Paul Ollendorff, 1885), 17. Vignon served as the undersecretary of state of the navy and colonies and was the son-in-law of Prime Minister Maurice Rouvier. See William Cohen, *Rulers of Empire: The French Colonial Service in Africa* (Stanford, CA: Hoover Institution Press, 1971), 41; Pierre Singaravélou, "Des historiens sans histoire? La construction de l'historiographie coloniale en France sous la Troisième République," *Le seuil* 185, no. 5 (2010): 33.

143. Rambaud, *La France coloniale*, 688, 700.

144. Vignon, *Les colonies françaises*, 174. See also Thiersant, *La solution*, 5; Onésime Reclus, *France, Algérie et colonies* (Paris: Librairie Hachette, 1883), 4.

145. Gide, "À quoi servent les colonies," 47.

146. Gide, "À quoi servent les colonies," 51.

147. Thiersant, *La solution*, 5; Solar, *La campagne*, 4; Rambaud, *La France coloniale*, 688; Édouard Pétit, *Le Tong-Kin* (Paris: H. Lecène & H. Oudin, 1887), 286; A. Bouinais and A. Paulus, *La France en Indochine* (Paris: Challamel Ainé, 1886), xiii.

148. Gide, "A quoi servent les colonies," 111, 114, 115.

149. Bordier, *La colonisation scientifique*, xv.

150. Bordier, *La colonisation scientifique*, xvi.

151. Staum, *Nature and Nurture in the French Social Sciences*, 78.

152. Jacquillou, *Lettres d'un paysan*, 10.

153. Gilbert Chaitin, *The Enemy Within: Culture Wars and Political Identity in the Novels of the French Third Republic* (Columbus: Ohio State University Press, 2008), 41.

154. Liauzu, *Histoire de l'anticolonialisme en France*, 71.

155. Manceron, *1885*, 14.

156. See Jennifer Pitts, *A Turn to Empire: The Rise of Imperial Liberalism in Britain and France* (Princeton, NJ: Princeton University Press, 2005); Jennifer Sessions, *By Sword and Plow: France and the Conquest of Algeria* (Ithaca, NY: Cornell University Press, 2011); Matthew Fitzpatrick, Uday Singh Mehta, and Jennifer Pitts, "Liberalism and Empire Reconsidered: A Dialogue," *Liberal Imperialism in Europe*, ed. Matthew Fitzpatrick (New York: Palgrave Macmillan, 2012), 255; Andrew Fitzmaurice, "Liberalism and Empire in Nineteenth-Century International Law," *American Historical Review* 17, no. 1 (2012): 133–38; and Gilles Manceron, *Marianne et les colonies* (Paris: La découverte, 2005), 106.

6. Defending a "Colonial Empire" in Republican France

1. Jennifer Cole, *Forget Colonialism? Sacrifice and the Art of Memory in Madagascar* (Berkeley: University of California Press, 2001), 40.

2. Margaret Cook Andersen, *Regeneration through Empire: French Pronatalists and Colonial Settlement in the Third Republic* (Lincoln: University of Nebraska Press, 2015), 120.

3. J. P. Daughton, *An Empire Divided: Religion, Republicanism, and the Making of French Colonialism, 1880–1914* (New York: Oxford University Press, 2006), 169; Stephen Ellis, *The Rising of the Red Shawls: A Revolt in Madagascar, 1895–1899* (New York: Cambridge University Press, 1985), 32.

4. Garland Downum, "The Madagascan Mission to the United States in 1883: Diplomacy and Public Relations," *The Historian* 39, no. 3 (1977): 477.

5. Myre de Vilers to Diplomatie Paris, October 29, 1894, AMAE CP Madagascar, 55:7–8; Philip Allen and Maureen Covell, *The Historical Dictionary of Madagascar* (Lanham, MD: Scarecrow Press, 2005), 214.

6. Ernest Boulanger, "Rapport," December 4, 1894, AMAE CPCOM Madagascar, vol. 7; Michael Finch, *A Progressive Occupation? The Gallieni-Lyautey Method and Colonial Pacification in Tonkin and Madagascar, 1885–1900* (New York: Oxford University Press, 2013), 169–72.

7. "A Madagascar," *Le monde illustré*, September 29, 1894, 11.

8. For examples of these protests, see "Rainilaiarivony to Myre de Vilers," November 3, 1894, and Ranavalona III, "Kabary," October 30, 1894, AMAE CP Madagascar, 55, 18–19, 22–24. See also H. L. Wesseling, *Divide and Rule: The Partition of Africa, 1880–1914* (Westport, CT: Praeger, 1996), 163–65.

9. "Conflit ministerial," *Le matin*, September 21, 1895; Eric Jennings, *Perspectives on French Colonial Madagascar* (New York: Palgrave Macmillan, 2017), 45–48.

10. Gwyn Campbell, "The Menalamba Revolt and Brigandry in Imperial Madagascar, 1820–1897," *International Journal of African Historical Studies* 24, no. 2 (1991): 270, 289–90; Ellis, *Rising of the Red Shawls*, 94–100.

11. Finch, *Progressive Occupation*, 173.

12. Robert Aldrich, *Banished Potentiates: Dethroning and Exiling Indigenous Monarchs under British and French Colonial Rule, 1815–1955* (Manchester: Manchester University Press, 2017), 222–25.

13. Charles-Robert Ageron, *France coloniale ou parti coloniale?* (Paris: PUF, 1978), 122–29.

14. Louis Brunet, *L'œuvre de la France à Madagascar* (Paris: Challamel, 1903), 133–35.

15. "Bulletin politique," *La revue hebdomadaire*, September 1895, 636. See also Maurice Talmeyer, "Causerie," *La revue hebdomadaire*, September 1895, 631.

16. "À Madagascar," *Le monde illustré*, September 28, 1895, 195.

17. Camille Pelletan, "Pour l'armée," *Le rappel*, September 22, 1895.

18. "L'expédition de Madagascar," *Le petit parisien*, September 23, 1895.

19. "Responsabilités," *Le gaulois*, September 22, 1895.

20. "À Madagascar," *La justice*, September 22, 1895.

21. Charles Chincholle, "Retour de Madagascar," *Le Figaro*, September 23, 1895.

22. "Reveux des journaux," *Le Figaro*, September 19, 1895; "A Madagascar," *La justice*, September 20, 1895.

23. Camille Pelletan, *L'éclair*, September 25, 1895, as quoted in Brunet, *L'oeuvre de la France à Madagascar*, 137.

24. "Bulletin: Discours présidentiel," *Le journal des débats*, September 20, 1895.

25. Gaston Calmette, "Ce qu'il faut penser de Madagascar," *Le Figaro*, August 6, 1895.

26. *Le temps*, September 18, 1895; *Le journal des débats*, September 19, 1895.

27. Emmanuelle Sibeud, "Une libre pensée impériale? Le comité de protection et de défense des indigènes, 1892–1914," *Mil neuf cent: Revue d'histoire intellectuelle* 27, no. 1 (2009) : 57–74.

28. François Coppée, "Vingt-cinq ans après," *Le journal*, September 26, 1895.

29. "Politique et grandes manœuvres," *La lanterne*, September 21, 1895.

30. Vicomte de Montfort, "Madagascar: La véritable responsabilité," *Le Figaro*, October 2, 1895.

31. Édouard Durranc, "La vie de Patachon," *La lanterne*, September 23, 1895.

32. At the time, Clemenceau was not in office; he temporarily lost much of his popularity because of the Panama Affair, a series of corruption scandals over the government's financing of the Panama Canal. See Robert Lynn Fuller, *The Origins of the French Nationalist Movement* (Jefferson, NC: McFarland, 2012), 53.

33. Georges Clemenceau, "À un interpellateur," *La justice*, September 24, 1895.

34. "Responsabilités," *Le gaulois*, September 22, 1895. The leftist *La lanterne* also reported on the army's success. See "Madagascar," *La lanterne*, September 22, 1895.

35. "La politique: Le 2 octobre à Tananarive," *Le gaulois*, September 27, 1895.

36. A. Maujan, "Une leçon," *La lanterne*, September 29, 1895.

37. "La prix du succès," *Le petit parisien*, September 27, 1895; "Les responsabilités," *La lanterne*, September 28, 1895.

38. There were some exceptions. The nationalist *L'intransigeant* insisted that Madagascar was a foolishly undertaken "awful war." See Ph. Dubois, "Les responsabilités," *L'intransigeant*, September 27, 1895.

39. Wolfgang Schivelbusch, *The Culture of Defeat: On National Trauma, Mourning, and Recovery* (New York: Macmillan, 2003), 213; Emmanuelle Saada, "The Absent Empire: The Colonies in French Constitutions," in *Endless Empire: Spain's Retreat, Europe's Eclipse, America's Decline*, ed. Alfred McCoy, Josep Fradera, and Stephen Jacobson (Madison: University of Wisconsin Press: 2012), 205–15.

40. Pierre Brocheux and Daniel Hémery, *Indochina: An Ambiguous Colonization, 1858–1954* (Berkeley: University of California Press, 2009), 46.

41. Kevin Passmore, *The Right in France from the Third Republic to Vichy* (New York: Oxford University Press, 2013), 46.

42. William Irvine, "Royalists and the Politics of Nationalism," *Nationhood and Nationalism in France: From Boulangism to the Great War*, ed. Robert Tombs (New York: Routledge, 1992), 115.

43. James Lehning, *To Be a Citizen: The Political Culture of the Early French Third Republic* (Ithaca, NY: Cornell University Press, 2001), 160.

44. William Irvine, *The Boulanger Affair Reconsidered: Royalism, Boulangism, and the Origins of the Radical Right in France* (New York: Oxford University Press, 1988), 4, 159.

45. Passmore, *Right in France*, 74.

46. Irvine, *Boulanger Affair Reconsidered*, 162–66.

47. Bernard Ménager, "Nationalists and Bonapartists," in Tombs, *Nationhood and Nationalism in France*, 137.

48. Fuller, *Origins of the French Nationalist Movement*, 47.

49. Lehning, *To Be a Citizen*, 180.

50. Christopher Forth, *The Dreyfus Affair and the Crisis of French Manhood* (Baltimore: Johns Hopkins University Press, 2004), 237; Frederick Brown, *For the Soul of France: Culture Wars in the Age of Dreyfus* (New York: Alfred Knopf, 2010), 2; Passmore,

Right in France, 102; Robert Gildea, *Children of the Revolution: The French, 1799–1914* (New York: Allen Lane, 2008), 273–75.

51. Fuller, *Origins of the French Nationalist Movement*, 82.

52. David Drake, *French Intellectuals and Politics from the Dreyfus Affair to the Occupation* (New York: Palgrave Macmillan, 2005), 34.

53. Martin P. Johnson, *The Dreyfus Affair: Honour and Politics in the* Belle Époque (New York: St. Martin's, 1999), 115.

54. Fuller, *Origins of the French Nationalist Movement*, 108.

55. Drake, *French Intellectuals and Politics*, 36.

56. Passmore, *Right in France*, 127.

57. Sophie Roberts, *Citizenship and Antisemitism in French Colonial Algeria, 1870–1962* (New York: Cambridge University Press, 2017), 93; Steven Uran, "La réception de l'affaire en Algérie," *L'affaire Dreyfus de A à Z*, ed. Michel Drouin, 521–29 (Paris: Flammarion, 1994).

58. David Proschaska, *Making Algeria French: Colonialism in Bône, 1870-1920* (New York: Cambridge University Press, 1990), 202–5.

59. Samuel Kalman, *French Colonial Fascism: The Extreme Right in Algeria, 1919–1939* (New York: Palgrave Macmillan, 2013), 4–5.

60. Patricia Lorcin, "Pax Romana Transposed: Rome as an Exemplar for Western Imperialism," in *The Routledge History of Western Empires*, ed. Robert Aldrich and Kirsten McKenzie (New York: Routledge, 2014), 415; Roberts, *Citizenship and Antisemitism in French Colonial Algeria*, 106.

61. Michelle Mann, "The Young Algerians and the Question of the Muslim Draft, 1900–1914," *Algeria Revisited: History, Culture, and Identity*, ed. Rabah Aissaoui and Claire Eldridge (London: Bloomsbury Academic, 2017), 46; Claude Liauzu, *Histoire de l'anticolonialisme en France du XVIe siècle au nos jours* (Paris: Armand Colin, 2007), 78; Ruedy, *Modern Algeria*, 81.

62. Patrick Weil, *How to Be French: Nationality in the Making since 1789* (Durham, NC: Duke University Press, 2008), 216; Guy Perville, *La France en Algérie, 1830–1954* (Paris: Vendémiaire, 2012), 88; Charles-Robert Ageron, *Modern Algeria* (London: Africa World Press, 1994), 63–64.

63. Roberts, *Citizenship and Antisemitism in French Colonial Algeria*, 108.

64. James P. Daughton, "A Colonial Affair? Dreyfus and the French Empire," *Historical Reflections / Réflexions Historiques* 31, no. 3 (2005): 471, 485.

65. Johnson, *Dreyfus Affair*, 146.

66. Fuller, *Origins of the French Nationalist Movement*, 108; Gildea, *Children of the Revolution*, 422.

67. The Fashoda Incident was the culmination of a conflict between the French and British governments over the control of the Sudan. A French and a British expeditionary force simultaneously sought to claim the area around Fashoda, threatening war between the two countries; the French ultimately backed down. Martin Thomas and Richard Toye, *Arguing about Empire: Imperial Rhetoric in Britain and France, 1882–1956* (Oxford: Oxford University Press, 2017), 70; Dorian Bell, *Globalizing Race: Antisemitism and Empire in French and European Culture* (Evanston, IL: Northwestern University Press, 2018), 133; Edward Berenson, *Heroes of Empire: Five Charismatic Men and the Conquest of Africa* (Berkeley: California Press, 2011), 167.

68. Passmore, *Right in France*, 50; Bell, *Globalizing Race*, 182.

69. Nancy Stepan, *Picturing Tropical Nature* (London: Reaktion Books, 2001), 85.

70. Alice Conklin, *In the Museum of Man: Race, Anthropology, and Empire, 1850–1950* (Ithaca, NY: Cornell University Press, 2013), 46.

71. Robert E. Stebbins, "France," in *The Comparative Reception of Darwinism*, ed. Thomas F. Glick (Chicago: University of Chicago Press, 1988), 117, 120, 125, 155, 162; Rae Beth Gordon, *Dances with Darwin, 1875–1910: Vernacular Modernity in France* (Burlington, VT: Ashgate, 2009), 60–65.

72. Emmanuelle Saada, *Empire's Children: Race, Filiation, and Citizenship in the French Colonies*, trans. Arthur Goldhammer (Chicago: University of Chicago Press, 2012), 16; Yerri Urban, "Les métis franco-indigènes' dans le second empire colonial," *De quelle couleur sont les blancs: Des "petits blancs' des colonies au "racisme anti-blancs,"* ed. Sylvie Laurent and Thierry Leclère (Paris: La Découverte, 2013); Judith Surkis, *Sex, Law, and Sovereignty in French Algeria, 1830–1930* (Ithaca, NY: Cornell University Press, 2019), 4; Todd Shepard, *The Invention of Decolonization: The Algerian War and the Remaking of France* (New York: Cornell University Press, 2008), 14.

73. Linda Clark, *Social Darwinism in France* (Tuscaloosa: University of Alabama Press, 1984), 161; Jennifer Michael Hecht, *The End of the Soul: Scientific Modernity, Atheism, and Anthropology in France* (New York: Columbia University Press, 2003), 260.

74. Rae Beth Gordon, *Dances with Darwin, 1875–1910: Vernacular Modernity in France* (Burlington, VT: Ashgate Publishing, 2009), 81; Passmore, *Right in France*, 50; Martin Thomas, "Mapping the French Colonial Mind," in *The French Colonial Mind: Mental Maps of Empire and Colonial Encounters*, vol. 1, ed. Martin Thomas (Lincoln: University of Nebraska Press, 2011), xv.

75. Conklin, *In the Museum of Man*, 46.

76. Carole Reynaud-Paligot, *La république raciale, 1860–1930* (Paris: PUF, 2006), 105.

77. Claude Blanckaert, *De la race à l'évolution: Paul Broca et l'anthropologie française, 1850–1900* (Paris: Harmattan, 2009), 446.

78. Conklin, *In the Museum of Man*, 49; Hecht, *End of the Soul*, 186.

79. Paligot, *La république raciale*, 89–92.

80. Hecht, *End of the Soul*, 260.

81. Alice Conklin, *A Mission to Civilize: The Republican Idea of Empire in France and West Africa, 1895–1930* (Stanford, CA: Stanford University Press, 1997), 9, 256; Ann Laura Stoler and Frederick Cooper, "Between Metropole and Colony," in *Tensions of Empire: Colonial Cultures in a Bourgeois World*, ed. Frederick Cooper and Ann Laura Stoler (Berkeley: University of California Press, 1997), 3; Martin Staum, *Nature and Nurture in French Social Sciences, 1859–1914 and Beyond* (Montreal: McGill-Queen's University Press, 2011), 73.

82. Shepard, *Invention of Decolonization*, 13.

83. The colonial lobby included members of colonial organizations such as the Comité d'Afrique française and the Union coloniale, along with the *parti colonial*, an unofficial grouping of proimperialist members of parliament. See Stuart Persell, *The French Colonial Lobby, 1889–1938* (Stanford, CA: Hoover Institution Press, 1983), 3; Pascal Blanchard and Sandrine Lemaire, *Culture coloniale en France, 1871–1931* (Paris: Éditions autrement, 2003), 10.

84. Ageron, *France coloniale ou parti coloniale?*; L. Abrams and D. J. Miller, "Who Were the French Colonialists? A Reassessment of the Parti Colonial, 1890–1914," *Historical Journal* 19, no. 3 (1976): 685–725.

85. Eric T. Jennings, "Visions and Representations of French Empire," *Journal of Modern History* 77, no. 3 (2005): 720.

86. Daughton, *Empire Divided*, 10.

87. Jérôme Grévy, *La république des opportunistes* (Paris: Perrin, 1998), 219.

88. Pierre Singaravélou, *Professer l'empire: Les "sciences coloniales" en France sous la IIIe* République (Paris: Publications de la Sorbonne, 2011), 142.

89. William Schneider, *An Empire for the Masses: The French Popular Image of Africa* (London: Greenwood, 1982); Annie E. Coombes, *Reinventing Africa: Museums, Material Culture and Popular Imagination* (New Haven, CT: Yale University Press, 1994); Anne Maxwell, *Colonial Photography and Exhibitions* (London: Leicester University Press, 1999); Jean-Christophe Mabire, ed., *L'exposition universelle de 1900* (Paris: L'Harmattan, 2000); Darcy Grimaldo Grigsby, *Extremities: Painting Empire in Post-Revolutionary France* (New Haven, CT: Yale University Press, 2002); Roger Benjamin, *Orientalist Aesthetics: Art, Colonialism, and French North Africa, 1880–1930* (Berkeley: University of California Press, 2003); Martin Evans, ed., *Empire and Culture: The French Experience, 1830–1940* (New York: Palgrave Macmillan, 2004); Daniel Sherman,"'Peoples Ethnographic': Objects, Museums, and the Colonial Inheritance of French Ethnography," *French Historical Studies* 27, no. 3 (2004): 669–703; Blanchard and Lemaire, *Culture coloniale en France, 1871–1931*.

90. Sibeud, "Une libre pensée impériale?," 57–74.

91. Conklin, *Mission to Civilize*; Cooper and Stoler, *Tensions of Empire*; Frederick Cooper, *Colonialism in Question: History, Theory, Knowledge* (Berkeley: University of California Press, 2005); Gary Wilder, *The French Imperial Nation-State: Négritude and Colonial Humanism between the Two World Wars* (Chicago: Chicago University Press, 2005); Dino Costantino, *Mission civilisatrice: Le rôle de l'histoire coloniale dans la construction de l'identité politique française* (Paris: La Découverte, 2008); Shepard, *Invention of Decolonization*; Pitts, "Political Theory of Empire and Imperialism: An Appendix," *Empire and Modern Political Thought*, ed. Sankar Muthu (New York: Cambridge University Press, 2012), 355–73.

92. Emmanuelle Saada, "Penser le fait colonial à travers le droit en 1900," *Mil neuf cent: Revue d'histoire intellectuelle* 27, no. 1 (2009): 105; Singaravélou, *Professer l'empire*, 70.

93. Constantino, *Mission civilisatrice*, 79.

94. This book was used by colonial administrators and helped define French colonial law. The last edition, published just before Girault's death, was commissioned by the Vichy government. See Samia El Mechat, "Sur les *Principes de colonisation* d'Arthur Girault (1895)," *La revue historique* 657 (January 2011): 119.

95. Arthur Girault, *Principes de la colonisation et de la législation coloniale* (Paris: L. Larose, 1895).

96. El Mechat, "Sur les *Principes de colonisation*," 132.

97. Girault, *Principes de la colonisation*, 12.

98. Girault, *Principes de la colonisation*, 23–24.

99. Girault, *Principes de la colonisation*, 29, 31, 32, 42, 40.

100. Girault's invocation of Darwinian competition was not unusual; many French intellectuals combined it with neo-Lamarckian theory. See Hecht, *End of the Soul*, 260. Social Darwinism especially had become popular thanks to recent translations of Herbert Spencer. See Saada, "Penser le fait colonial," 115.

101. Girault, *Principes de la colonisation*, 46.

102. Girault, *Principes de la colonisation*, 49.

103. He seems to be referring to the abolition of slavery here. Elsewhere, he does not indicate that all peoples should enjoy the same political and legal rights. See Girault, *Principes de la colonisation*, 50.

104. Girault, *Principes de la colonisation*, 53.

105. Girault, *Principes de la colonisation*, 58.

106. El Mechat, "Sur les *Principes de colonisation*," 33.

107. El Mechat, "Sur les *Principes de colonisation*, 38.

108. Girault, *Principes de la colonisation*, 55.

109. Betts, *Assimilation and Association in French Colonial Theory*, 12, 17.

110. Saada, *Empire's Children*, 108; Wilder, *French Imperial Nation-State*, 81.

111. Osama Abi-Mershed, *Apostles of Modernity: Saint-Simonians and the Civilizing Mission in Algeria* (Stanford, CA: Stanford University Press, 2010), 3.

112. Cooper, *Colonialism in Question*, 28.

113. Cooper, *Colonialism in Question*, 46.

114. Ann Laura Stoler and Carole McGranahan, "Introduction: Reconfiguring Imperial Terrains," in *Imperial Formations*, ed. Ann Laura Stoler, Carole McGranahan, and Peter Perdue (Santa Fe, NM: School for Advance Research Press, 2007), 10.

115. Léon Deschamps, *Histoire sommaire de la colonisation française* (Paris: Fernand Nathan, 1894) ; Léon Deschamps, *Histoire de la question coloniale en France* (Paris: E. Plon & Nourri, 1891).

116. Paul Leroy-Beaulieu, *De la colonisation chez les peuples modernes*, 5th ed. (Paris: Guillaumin, 1902), 1:ii.

117. Xavier Daumalin, "Le doctrine coloniale africaine de Paul Leroy-Beaulieu (1870–1916): Essai d'analyse thématique," *Publications de la Société française d'histoire d'outre-mer* 6 (2008): 104.

118. Dan Warshaw, *Paul Leroy-Beaulieu and Established Liberalism in France* (Dekalb: Northern Illinois University Press, 1991), 107.

119. Leroy-Beaulieu, *De la colonisation chez les peuples modernes*, 5th ed., 1:ii.

120. He still insisted that the best part of this colonial empire was located in North Africa. See Leroy-Beaulieu, *De la colonisation chez les peuples modernes*, 5th ed., 1:v.

121. Leroy-Beaulieu, *De la colonisation chez les peuples modernes*, 5th ed., 2:711.

122. Leroy-Beaulieu, *De la colonisation chez les peuples modernes*, 5th ed., 2:504.

123. Warshaw, *Paul Leroy-Beaulieu*, 87.

124. Leroy-Beaulieu, *De la colonisation chez les peuples modernes*, 5th ed., 2:565.

125. The turn from "settlement" was not universal. See Charles Combette, *Guide du voyageur et de l'émigrant: Géographie commerciale des colonies françaises* (Paris: Augustin Challamel, 1890); Louis Vignon, *L'expansion de la France* (Paris: Librairie Guillaumin, 1891); Ernest Allard, *L'immigration française à Madagascar* (Paris: Challamel, 1895); Eugène Poiré, *L'émigration aux colonies* (Paris: Plon, Nourrit, 1897);

Jean-Baptiste Piolet, *La France hors de la France* (Paris: Félix Alcan, 1900); and Paul Bory, *Le colon* (Tours: Maison Alfred Mame, 1904).

126. Warshaw, *Paul Leroy-Beaulieu*, 136–37.

127. Paul Leroy-Beaulieu, *De la colonisation chez les peuples modernes*, 1st ed. (Paris : Guillamin, 1874), 606.

128. Leroy-Beaulieu, *De la colonisation chez les peuples modernes*, 5th ed., 2:709.

129. Leroy-Beaulieu, *De la colonisation chez les peuples modernes*, 5th ed., 2:707.

130. Paligot, *La république raciale*, 245.

131. Singaravélou, *Professer l'empire*, 102, 121.

132. Paligot, *La république raciale*, 36; Clark, *Social Darwinism in France*, 69.

133. Jean Marie Antoine de Lanessan, *Principes de la colonisation* (Paris: Félix Alcan, 1897), 6.

134. Lanessan, *Principes de la colonization*, 24, 25, 22.

135. El Mechat, "Sur les *Principes de colonisation*," 123.

136. Staum, *Nature and Nurture*, 42.

137. Singaravélou, *Professer l'empire*, 135; Stuart Persell, "Joseph Chailley-Bert and the Importance of the Union Coloniale Française," *Historical Journal* 17, no. 1 (1974): 177; Joseph Chailley-Bert, "Un tournant de la politique coloniale," *La quinzaine coloniale*, July 25, 1901, 417.

138. The Union coloniale focused on promoting mise en valeur, so its central role here is unsurprising. See Persell, *French Colonial Lobby*, 26–27. Alice Conklin has described mise en valeur as part of "the official ideology of the Third Republic's vast new empire" by the mid-1890s. See Conklin, *Mission to Civilize*, 23.

139. Joseph Chailley-Bert, *Dix années de politique coloniale* (Paris: Libraire Armand Colin, 1902), 3.

140. Chailley-Bert, "Un tournant de la politique coloniale," 417.

141. Chailley-Bert, *Dix années de politique coloniale*, 45.

142. Chailley-Bert, *Dix années de politique coloniale*, 49, 50.

143. Chailley-Bert, *Dix années de politique coloniale*, 54, 158.

144. Raymond Betts, *Assimilation and Association in French Colonial Theory, 1890–1914* (Lincoln: University of Nebraska Press, 2005), 106; Conklin, *Mission to Civilize*, 6–7; Saada, *Empire's Children*, 109.

145. *La quinzaine coloniale*, Chailley-Bert's journal, later published a defense of Napoleon III's royaume arabe, claiming that the decision to replace that model with assimilation had been mistaken. See "La réparation d'une erreur coloniale," *La quinzaine coloniale*, July 25, 1902, 417.

146. Chailley-Bert structured his thinking about empire around comparisons, making recommendations for métis children in Indochina based on travels in the Dutch East Indies. This impulse toward comparison may have contributed to his interest in Bonapartist policies. See Ann Laura Stoler, *Carnal Knowledge and Imperial Power: Race and the Intimate in Colonial Rule*, 2nd ed. (Berkeley: University of California Press, 2010), 91.

147. Leroy-Beaulieu, *La colonisation chez les peuples modernes*, 5th ed., 2:iv.

148. Paligot, *La république raciale*, 19; Conklin, *In the Museum of Man*, 22–23.

149. These publications were not only authored by republicans. See Les frères des écoles chrétiennes, *Les colonies françaises illustrées*, 2nd ed. (Paris: Ch. Poussielgue, 1892), 5, 8.

150. Maurice Wahl, *La France aux colonies* (Paris: Librairies-Imprimeries Réunies, 1896), 297.

151. Wahl, *La France aux colonies*, 299.

152. François Bernard, "Introduction: De la colonisation," in *Les colonies françaises: Petite encyclopédie coloniale*, ed. Maxime Petit (Paris: Librairie Larousse, 1903), vi.

153. Bernard, "Introduction," xi.

154. Bernard, "Introduction," xv.

155. R. Demogue, "La loi française aux colonies," in Petit, *Les colonies françaises*, 40.

156. Hecht, *End of the Soul*, 259–61.

157. Publications in the 1890s continued to criticize the colonial empire; socialists especially continued to oppose it. See Armand Corre, *Comment se fondent les colonies* (Paris: Éditions de la Société nouvelle, 1894), 347–60; Isidore Chessé, *Vérités coloniales: Le désordre, les abus, le danger* (Paris: Chamuel, 1895); Jean Baptiste Alexandre Damaze de Chaudordy, *Considérations de la politique extérieure de la France* (Paris: Plon, Nourrit, 1897).

Conclusion

1. Benali el Hassar, *Les Jeunes algériens et la mouvance moderniste au début du XXe siècle: Les frères Larbi et Bénali Fekar* (Saint-Denis: Edilivre classique, 2013), 8.

2. Ben Ali Fékar, "La représentation des musulmans algériens," *La revue du monde musulman*, no. 7 (Paris: Ernest Leroux, 1909), 5.

3. Fékar, "La représentation," 11.

4. Fékar, "La représentation," 20.

5. Michelle Mann, "The Young Algerians and the Question of the Muslim Draft, 1900–1914," *Algeria Revisited: History, Culture, and Identity*, ed. Rabah Aissaoui and Claire Eldridge (London: Bloomsbury Academic, 2017), 48.

6. Rabah Aissaoui, "'Between Two Worlds': Emir Khaled and the Young Algerians at the Beginning of the Twentieth Century in Algeria," in Aissaoui and Eldridge, *Algeria Revisited*, 58.

7. Charles-Robert Ageron, *Genèse de l'Algérie algérienne* (Paris : Éditions Bouchène, 2005), 111.

8. Julien Fromage, "L'expérience des 'Jeunes algériens' et l'émergence du militantisme moderne en Algérie," in *Histoire de l'Algérie à la période coloniale*, ed. Abderrahmane Bouchène et al. (Paris: La Découverte, 2012), 241.

9. Peter Dunwoodie, *Francophone Writing in Transition: Algeria 1900–1945* (Bern: Peter Lang, 2005), 25; Medjoub ben Kalafat, "De l'instruction des indigènes," and Mokhtar Hadj Said, "Lettre au rédacteur de la dépêche de Constantine," *Les Jeunes algériens: Correspondances et rapports, 1837–1918*, ed. Mahfound Smati (Algiers: Thala éditions, 2011), 157, 163.

10. Martyn Lyons, *Reading Culture and Writing Practices in Nineteenth-Century France* (Toronto: University of Toronto Press, 2008), 48.

11. Arthur Asseraf, *Electric News in Colonial Algeria* (New York: Oxford University Press, 2019), 57–60.

12. Zessin, "Presse et journalistes 'indigènes' en Algérie coloniale (années 1890–années 1950)," *Le mouvement sociale* 236 (2011): 36.

13. Robert Aldrich, *Banished Potentiates: Dethroning and Exiling Indigenous Monarchs under British and French Colonial Rule, 1815–1955* (Manchester: Manchester University Press, 2017).

14. Philip Nord, *The Republican Moment: Struggles for Democracy in Nineteenth-Century France* (Cambridge, MA: Harvard University Press, 1995), 251.

15. Dunwoodie, *Francophone Writing in Transition*, 52.

16. Mann, "Young Algerians and the Muslim Draft," 46.

17. Mahfoud Kaddache, *Histoire du nationalisme algérien*, book 1, 1919–39 (Algiers: Éditions Paris-Méditerranée, 2003), 72.

18. Patrick Weil, *How to Be French: Nationality in the Making since 1789* (Durham, NC: Duke University Press, 2008), 220.

19. Taïeb Ould Morsly, "Contribution à la question indigène, 1894," in Smati, *Les Jeunes algériens*, 172. See also Sadek Denden, "Notre Action," *L'Islam*, January 7, 1912; Numa-Léal, "Services militaire et naturalisation," *Le Rachidi*, June 28, 1912.

20. Émir Khaled, *Réflexions sur le rapprochement franco-arabe en Algérie* (Alger: Imprimerie Gojosso, 1913), 11.

21. Khaled, *Réflexions sur le rapprochement*, 9.

22. Rabah Aissaouai, "'Between Two Worlds': Emir Khaled and the Young Algerians at the Beginning of the Twentieth Century in Algeria," *Algeria Revisited*, 59.

23. Mann, "Young Algerians and Muslim Draft," 50.

24. Emmanuelle Saada, "The Absent Empire: The Colonies in French Constitutions," in *Endless Empire: Spain's Retreat, Europe's Eclipse, America's Decline*, ed. Alfred McCoy, Josep Fradera, and Stephen Jacobson (Madison: University of Wisconsin Press: 2012), 210.

25. Richard S. Fogarty, "The French Empire," in *Empires at War: 1911–1923*, ed. Robert Gerwarth and Erez Manela (New York: Oxford University Press, 2014), 129; Robert Aldrich, *Greater France: A History of French Overseas Expansion* (New York: Palgrave Macmillan, 1996), 117.

26. From 1944 to 1960, some African leaders proposed to restructure the empire to allow for political and social equality and cultural difference. See Frederick Cooper, "Alternatives to Empire: France and Africa after World War II," in *The State of Sovereignty: Territories, Laws, Populations*, ed. Douglas Howland and Luise White (Bloomington: Indiana University Press, 2009), 94–123.

27. Pascal Blanchard, Sandrine Lemaire, Nicolas Bancel, and Dominic Thomas, "Introduction: The Creation of a Colonial Culture in France, from the Colonial Era to the Memory Wars," in *Colonial Culture in France since the Revolution* (Bloomington: Indiana University Press, 2014), 6; Frederick Cooper, *Citizenship between Empire and Nation: Remaking France and French Africa, 1945–1960* (Princeton, NJ: Princeton University Press, 2014), 10.

INDEX

CPSIA information can be obtained
at www.ICGtesting.com
Printed in the USA
LVHW101633270422
717381LV00017B/449/J

9 781501 763083